AS GOOD AS DEAD

OTHER BOOKS BY STEPHEN L. MOORE

THE BATTLE FOR HELL'S ISLAND:
HOW A SMALL BAND OF CARRIER DIVE-BOMBERS
HELPED SAVE GUADALCANAL

TEXAS RISING:
THE EPIC TRUE STORY OF THE LONE STAR REPUBLIC AND THE RISE OF TEXAS

PACIFIC PAYBACK:
THE CARRIER AVIATORS WHO AVENGED PEARL HARBOR
AT THE BATTLE OF MIDWAY

BATTLE SURFACE!:
LAWSON P. "RED" RAMAGE AND THE WAR PATROLS
OF THE USS *PARCHE*

PRESUMED LOST:
THE INCREDIBLE ORDEAL OF AMERICA'S SUBMARINE
VETERAN POWS OF WORLD WAR II

RELIC QUEST:
A GUIDE TO RESPONSIBLE RELIC RECOVERY TECHNIQUES
WITH METAL DETECTORS

SAVAGE FRONTIER:
RANGERS, RIFLEMEN, AND INDIAN WARS IN TEXAS
VOLUME IV: 1842–1845

LAST STAND OF THE TEXAS CHEROKEES:
CHIEF BOWLES AND THE 1839 CHEROKEE WAR IN TEXAS

WAR OF THE WOLF:
TEXAS'S MEMORIAL SUBMARINE, WORLD WAR II'S FAMOUS USS *SEAWOLF*

SAVAGE FRONTIER:
RANGERS, RIFLEMEN, AND INDIAN WARS IN TEXAS
VOLUME III: 1840–1841

SPADEFISH:
ON PATROL WITH A TOP-SCORING WORLD WAR II SUBMARINE

SAVAGE FRONTIER:
RANGERS, RIFLEMEN, AND INDIAN WARS IN TEXAS
VOLUME II: 1838–1839

EIGHTEEN MINUTES:
THE BATTLE OF SAN JACINTO AND THE TEXAS INDEPENDENCE CAMPAIGN

SAVAGE FRONTIER:
RANGERS, RIFLEMEN, AND INDIAN WARS IN TEXAS
VOLUME I: 1835–1837

TAMING TEXAS:
CAPTAIN WILLIAM T. SADLER'S LONE STAR SERVICE

THE BUZZARD BRIGADE:
TORPEDO SQUADRON TEN AT WAR
(with William J. Shinneman and Robert W. Gruebel)

AS GOOD
AS DEAD

THE DARING ESCAPE OF
AMERICAN POWS
FROM A JAPANESE DEATH CAMP

STEPHEN L. MOORE

CALIBER
NEW YORK

CALIBER
Published by Berkley
An imprint of Penguin Random House LLC
375 Hudson Street, New York, New York 10014

Copyright © 2016 by Stephen L. Moore

Maps by David Lindroth

Library of Congress Cataloging-in-Publication Data
Names: Moore, Stephen L., author.
Title: As good as dead: the daring escape of American POWs from a Japanese Death Camp/Stephen L. Moore.
Description: New York: CALIBER, 2016. | Includes bibliographical references and index.
Identifiers: LCCN 2016029721 (print) | LCCN 2016029942 (ebook) |
ISBN 9780399583551 (hardback) | ISBN 9780399583575 (ebook)
Subjects: LCSH: Prisoner-of-war escapes—Philippines—Palawan Island—History—
20th century. | World War, 1939–1945—Prisoners and prisons, Japanese. | Prisoners of war—
Japan—Biography. | Prisoners of war—United States—Biography. | Palawan Island
(Philippines)—History, Military—20th century.
Classification: LCC D805.P6 M64 2016 (print) | LCC D805.P6 (ebook) |
DDC 940.54/7252095994—dc23
LC record available at https://lccn.loc.gov/2016029721

First Edition: November 2016

Printed in the United States of America
3 5 7 9 10 8 6 4 2

Jacket art: Image of wildfire by David McNew/Staff/Getty Images News;
image of storm clouds by Dave and Les Jacobs/Blend Images/Getty Images;
image of barbed wire by Hidetoshi Tanaka/EyeEm/Getty Images
Jacket design by Michael Nagin
Title page image of barbed wire by Hidetoshi Tanaka/EyeEm/Getty Images
Book design by Tiffany Estreicher

CONTENTS

AS GOOD AS DEAD

PROLOGUE

Doug Bogue wished he could make himself invisible.

Crouching behind large rocks on the beach of Palawan Island, the Marine sergeant watched as Japanese soldiers shot and bayoneted American POWs who were fleeing for their lives along the shore. Sixty feet above, atop the steep bluff overlooking the rocky coastline, black smoke rose into the blue sky, a vivid reminder of the unspeakable horrors he had just escaped, scraping through the barbed wire fencing and tumbling down the cliff toward the Sulu Sea below.

Bogue's body was a mass of injuries. His hands and torso had been slashed as he plunged through the razor wire. His right leg throbbed from a rifle bullet embedded in his thigh, and his bare feet were lacerated and bloody from running along the rough coral beach. As he hid behind the boulders, nearly naked, trying to catch his breath and wondering what to do, two POWs ran past him in an attempt to swim to freedom. Both men were cut down by Japanese riflemen.

It was December 14, 1944. For twenty-eight months, Bogue had slaved as a prisoner of war for the Imperial Japanese Army, working to build the second-largest airfield in the region—one being used to attack Allied forces in the Philippines. He had endured unbearable heat and humidity, illness, physical abuse and torture, and near starvation, and his once-powerful frame had been reduced to skin and bones. That dismal life now seemed merciful in comparison.

All around him, Bogue could hear the screams of other Americans being slaughtered as they tried to escape. If he ran for it, he knew he might be shot down like the rest. If he stayed put . . . Either way, the odds were stacked against him. He had to do something, and quickly.

One thought raced through his mind: *They're going to hunt us down and kill every last one of us.*

PART ONE

BATAAN

THE DEATH MARCH

I T WAS A time when even the most optimistic of souls had little left to believe in. American servicemen, who just a year earlier had relished duty in the Philippines for its enviable life, now questioned their purpose. They were men abandoned by their own government, left to hold out against a fate already cast, and now, late in the afternoon of April 8, 1942, their five-day fight for freedom and survival was nearing its futile end.

Still, Beto Pacheco was not about to surrender. Handsome, athletic, and quick to flash a toothy smile in better times, the private first class now looked like a bum: His once-sharp uniform had been reduced to rags, his shoes were nearly worn through, and even his underwear was in shreds. Weeks of exposure to the brutal tropical sun had burned his skin, but Pacheco's Spanish and Mexican ancestry had at least provided him more natural protection than some of his fair-complected companions.

The air smelled of death, dirt, smoke, and gunpowder. The once-lush green jungles were denuded of vegetation, swept bare by endless weeks of pounding artillery and aerial bombardments from the Imperial Japanese Army. Explosions sent shock waves through the earth around

Pacheco as he and his comrades continued firing back with their few antiaircraft guns that were still marginally operational. Silver-winged Japanese warplanes flashed past, unleashing violent bomb blasts and chattering rounds of machine-gun bullets that shredded the nearby jungle surrounding the last two American airfields on the Bataan Peninsula.

For Pacheco, the last stand at Bataan was a true test of his devout Catholic faith. At one point, as a strong force flung him from his foxhole, he felt as if the hand of God had saved him. A brilliant red-orange blast left him no time to determine whether a nearby artillery round had propelled him. When the acrid black smoke parted, two of his comrades lay dead in the hole from which he had been thrown.

Even surrounded by the din of battle, he could feel the gnawing hunger in his gut. Army rations had been gone for weeks. The American and Filipino troops had exhausted their meager supplies of rice and canned goods, and by now they had even hunted the native wildlife in the vicinity to extinction. Pacheco had learned to eat anything—from the insides of palm trees to iguanas, snakes, crickets, and even worms. He was a slight man, standing five foot nine and weighing only 160 pounds when the war started. His weight had dropped quickly, and by this point he would have killed for a bite of wild boar meat, or even a freshly picked mango. But food was not an option.

Beto Pacheco's U.S. Army regiment, the 200th Coast Artillery, was hanging on by threads along with its sister unit, the 515th Coast Artillery Regiment—the last remnants of resistance facing the Japanese on the tip of a peninsula of Luzon Island in the Philippines. The men were firing back at the surging Japanese forces threatening to overrun the Cabcaben and Bataan airfields. Dirty, dehydrated, and exhausted, Pacheco was nonetheless determined to fight beside his comrades to the very end. And now Army brass was spreading the news that the end had come.

At 0300 on April 9, Captain Albert Fields returned from the I Corps headquarters and told his executive officer, "It's all over." Runners reached Pacheco's artillery unit before dawn with orders that the 200th and 515th were to rendezvous on the road west of Cabcaben by 2200.

But first, they were to destroy their antiaircraft guns and range equipment, leaving them just their rifles. *We're being reduced to infantrymen!* Pacheco thought with disgust.[1]

The disheartened men dutifully sabotaged their weapons and marched out with rifles, canteens, bayonets, and a belt of ammunition each. Men much older than Pacheco trudged along with tears streaming down their dusty, blood-caked faces as they carried out the dreaded orders. The young soldier brushed aside his wavy dark hair—untrimmed for long enough to hang over his sweaty brow—adjusted his gear, and moved forward. He was armed with only a rusting 1903 model .306-caliber Springfield bolt-action rifle, but he still had his pride.

Somehow, some way, he intended to carry on the fight. He was not about to willingly surrender himself to the Japanese.

PACHECO'S 200TH COAST Artillery unit had been the first to fire on the Japanese warplanes that swept over Manila on December 8, 1941. Seven hours earlier—December 7 Hawaii time—Japanese carrier aircraft had unleashed a devastating surprise assault on the United States Pacific Fleet at Pearl Harbor. With the capture of the Philippines critical to Japan's effort to control the Southwest Pacific, their planes attacked within hours the main aviation bases on Manila and the headquarters of the United States Asiatic Fleet at Cavite. In only a single day Japan gained air superiority over the Philippines and forced the surviving ships of the U.S. fleet to withdraw from Cavite.

Tens of thousands of American military personnel were left stranded on the ground in and around Manila, the Philippine capital. Pacheco's 200th Coast Artillery, the only American antiaircraft unit on Luzon, had been assigned to protect nearly three dozen B-17 bombers on Clark Field with their single battery of .50-caliber machine guns, twenty-one 37mm guns, and a dozen three-inch antiaircraft guns. Prior to that day, Pacheco's unit had never actually fired a live round of ammunition in the islands.[2] Yet since firing that first shot at the Japanese on December 8, Pacheco's antiaircraft regiment had expended some forty thousand rounds in the months that followed. They had been credited with destroying eighty-six Japanese aircraft—a proud accomplishment, but not nearly enough to save the Philippines.

The 200th Coast Artillery, formerly the 111th Cavalry of the New Mexico National Guard, had arrived in the Philippines in August 1941. The unit was composed of eighteen hundred artillery specialists, more than half of whom were New Mexicans from Spanish-speaking border and mountain communities that used little English. The New Mexico National Guard, the oldest continuously active militia in the United States, dating to 1598, had participated in the Mexican War, the Civil War, and the frontier Indian wars. New Mexico's militiamen had charged up San Juan Hill with Teddy Roosevelt's Rough Riders, had ridden against Pancho Villa's banditos south of the Rio Grande, and had served in France during World War I.[3]

Now hundreds of these proud men were moving out, overwhelmed, while other antiaircraft batteries continued firing back at the approaching enemy. Its companies were widely scattered, hanging on to what little ground they could still hold. Pacheco, a battlewise veteran after four months of hell on Luzon, knew that the last stand of the 200th would be short-lived.

He had heard others whisper the word *surrender*. The heavily reinforced Japanese forces sweeping down the Bataan Peninsula had pounded the dug-in Americans with blistering air and artillery fire for days. The Japanese had broken through Allied lines on April 7, and the following day, the senior U.S. commander on Bataan, Major General Edward P. King, had seen the futility of further resistance. He began offering plans for capitulation.

As they hustled along, Pacheco tried to offer encouragement to some of the younger men in his Headquarters Battery. Several of his hometown companions from Deming, New Mexico—Angelo Sakelares, Lawrence "Buddy" Byrne, and Jim Huxtable—had been wearing high school graduation caps and gowns just months ago. By August 1941, these fresh-faced boys on the cusp of manhood had been selected for overseas duty in the Philippines by virtue of their reputation as the best antiaircraft regiment in the U.S. Armed Forces. Now they were starving, grimy, and haggard, clothed in tatters, and facing a defeat the likes of which no modern American unit had been forced to reckon with.[4]

In early 1941, the 200th had trained at Fort Bliss, the Army's second-largest installation, headquartered in El Paso, Texas. There, Pacheco had met sixteen-year-old Catalina "Katie" Valles, an attractive girl with green eyes and long dark brown hair. The two were soon an item, and even began dreaming of a future together—against the wishes of her father, because she was so young. Pacheco's plans took a sudden detour with the selection of the 200th for overseas assignment. He promised Katie he would be gone only a year. When he returned, they could get married and start a life together.

If his proud regiment was now truly surrendering to the Japanese, that future with Katie seemed an impossibility.

THE AMERICAN SURRENDER on the Bataan Peninsula had been months in the making.

Pacheco's artillery regiment had started the war based at Fort Stotsenburg, which abutted Clark Field some seventy-five miles north of Manila. The destruction of the B-17s at Clark in December forced the 200th and 515th to withdraw to Bataan by the first days of 1942. There, the artillery regiments had set up their antiaircraft defenses in and around Manila to protect the airstrips at Cabcaben and Bataan, where only seven P-40s were still flying by the first of the year.

By January 9, the strung-out artillery regiments were already living on reduced rations as the drubbing of Japanese artillery signaled the beginning of the Battle of Bataan. Lieutenant General Masaharu Homma, a graduate of the Imperial Japanese Army Academy in 1907, had landed his troops of the Japanese 14th Army at Lingayen Gulf on Luzon and advanced toward Manila. His army found little resistance at first, as General Douglas MacArthur had ordered his own forces to withdraw from the capital city to the Bataan Peninsula. During the early months of the siege, MacArthur was fed false hope by President Franklin Delano Roosevelt, who promised hundreds of planes and thousands of troops. To await his reinforcements, the general took up headquarters more than two miles across the water from Bataan on Corregidor Island, known to most as "the Rock."

MacArthur was unaware that as early as late December 1941, President Roosevelt and War Secretary Henry Stimson had already privately written off the remote outpost of Bataan—a decision they confided to Winston Churchill. In so doing, Washington had also forsaken the Philippines and all of its defenders.

The four-month stand made by General King's men had been doomed from the start. The American troops in Manila were unable to receive supplies and ammunition due to their own crippled Navy and the blockade that the Imperial Japanese Navy had placed on the Philippines. Now, on April 9, King, adorned in his last clean uniform, was prepared to surrender to General Homma some seventy-eight thousand American and Filipino soldiers under his command. By doing so, he hoped to avoid a slaughter.

The Americans had agreed to a cease-fire, but the Japanese ignored the surrender talks and kept right on bombing into the morning of April 9. One artillery officer told Pacheco's gun crew that they could either flee into the hills near Bataan or head across the bay for Corregidor. The officer was going to the island, so Pacheco decided to follow.[5]

They were just two among hundreds of other Americans who headed for the coast several miles away in search of passage to Corregidor, determined to avoid surrender. One of them was Seaman First Class Bruce Gordon Elliott, a dark-haired teenager with bushy eyebrows and a poker face that helped hide that he was just shy of his nineteenth birthday. On the beach at Mariveles, Pacheco, Elliott, and many others found mass confusion—hundreds of frustrated servicemen milling about with no more boats left to transport them across the bay.[6]

As many as two thousand Filipinos and Americans, including nurses at the local hospitals, would manage to escape Bataan during the surrender by taking to boats and barges—or some even by swimming. Yet Pacheco, Elliott, and many other soldiers had emerged from the jungle too late to catch any of the outgoing launches. They found the water dotted with hundreds of swimmers attempting to cross the bay. Some were hanging on to lifeboats or bamboo rafts, or clinging to floating debris.[7]

Though it was two and a half miles across choppy, shark-infested waters swirling with dangerous undercurrents to reach Corregidor, Pacheco and Elliott individually decided to join those swimming for the island rather than surrendering to the Japanese. The tides helped push the men out toward sea, but soon they were exhausted. Bruce Elliott had been swimming for about six hours, feeling that he was about to drown at any minute, when a launch plucked him from the sea in only his skivvies. Pacheco had made it only a third of the way before a small Filipino fishing boat came along and its crew pulled him from the water. He and several others were transferred to a larger Navy launch.

Safely aboard the Navy interisland boat, Pacheco was reunited with other members of his artillery unit. The men lay flat on the steel deck as Japanese planes strafed and bombed the boats bobbing across Manila Bay, headed for the Rock.[8]

He and his companions were able to obtain new clothes after reaching the island. New arrivals were assigned to machine-gun nests at Monkey Point, facing away from the hell they had escaped at Bataan. Pacheco was still a free man on Corregidor, but his future did not look bright.

THOSE REMAINING FACED a perilous path. Even as their countrymen reached the relative safety of the Rock on April 9, tens of thousands of American and Filipino soldiers on Bataan laid down their weapons, and they were soon relieved of their valuables by Japanese soldiers. Months of fighting had come to this. General MacArthur had long since fled to Corregidor, where he stayed until March 11, when, under orders of the U.S. President, a PT boat whisked him away on the first leg of a journey to Australia. Without their commander in chief, the men had sensed that they were expendable. Frank Hewlett, the only U.S. war correspondent left in the Philippines, summed up the feeling of the remaining servicemen in poetry:[9]

We're the battling bastards of Bataan.
No mama, no papa, no Uncle Sam,
No aunts, no uncles, no cousins, no nieces,
No pills, no planes, no artillery pieces,
And nobody gives a damn.

The nearly twelve thousand captured American servicemen, as well as fifty-eight thousand Filipino troops, were now little more than an obstacle to the operational plans of General Homma. His conquest of the Philippines would not be complete until his forces could kill or capture the American troops that remained on Corregidor and the other islands in Manila Bay. To accomplish his goal, his forces needed to move their prisoners of war northward to an area where they could contain them.

The men who surrendered were from all branches of the service: aviators, mechanics, radiomen, artillerymen, infantrymen, all rates and ranks. There were sailors without ships, pilots without planes, and ground crew without squadrons to service. Private First Class Edwin Petry was a twenty-one-year-old airman from San Antonio whose 19th Bomb Group had been stationed at Clark Field. After his aircraft was shot down over Lingayen Gulf on December 16, he had eluded capture and made his way to Bataan to fight with the infantry. Another Texan, Private Thomas Tinsley Daniels, served as a mechanic and carpenter with the Army Air Corps's 28th Material Squadron. At age thirty-eight, Tommie Daniels was one of the oldest privates in his outfit, and many of his fellow soldiers who were young enough to be his sons called him "Pop."[10]

Now they were no longer soldiers, but prisoners of war. On April 10, they were assembled at Mariveles and Saisaih Point on Bataan and ordered to march toward San Fernando, near Clark Field. The Japanese command planned to house the POWs at Camp O'Donnell, located at Capas in North Central Luzon. The seventy-thousand American and

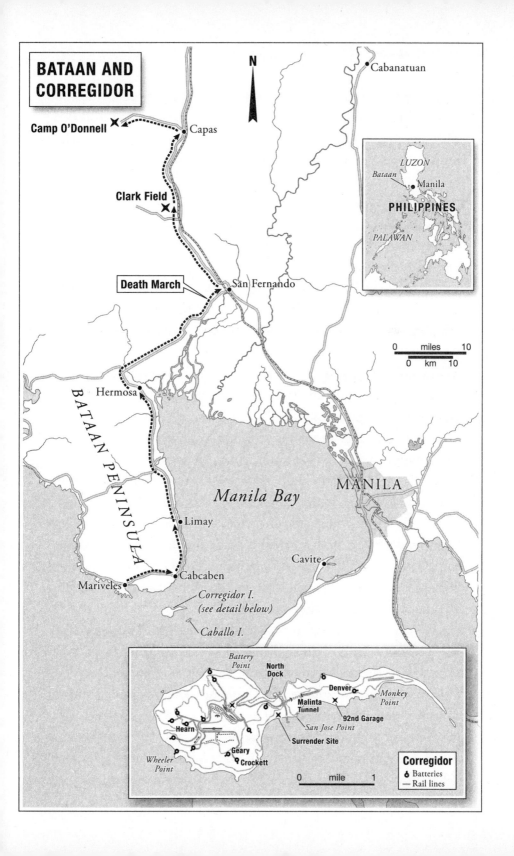

BATAAN AND CORREGIDOR

N

Cabanatuan

Camp O'Donnell ✕
Capas

Clark Field ✕

Death March
San Fernando

PHILIPPINES

LUZON

Bataan • Manila

PALAWAN

miles 10

km 10

Hermosa

BATAAN PENINSULA

Manila Bay

MANILA

Limay

Cavite

Mariveles
Cabcaben

Corregidor I.
(see detail below)

Caballo I.

Battery Point
North Dock
Denver
Monkey Point

Malinta Tunnel
92nd Garage
San Jose Point
Surrender Site

Hearn

Geary
Crockett

Wheeler Point

0 mile 1

Corregidor
♦ Batteries
— Rail lines

Filipino prisoners, Petry and Daniels among them, were divided into groups of several hundred men each and prompted down the road along with small groups of Japanese guards. Ahead of them lay a grueling sixty-mile trek that would come to be known as the Bataan Death March.

Sweat-streaked bodies plodded through heavy clouds of dust kicked up by Japanese trucks, cavalry, and infantrymen who taunted and beat the surrendered men, many bloodied and limping with broken limbs. During one rest period when the prisoners were finally allowed to sleep, Japanese soldiers patrolled the crowd, stepping on men's faces with hobnailed shoes. Ed Petry figured that he could have escaped during the forced march, but too many of his comrades were sick and needed his support. They had simply refused to believe that the Japanese would treat them unmercifully if they remained as prisoners. Now they were finding out otherwise. The Japanese had a cruel trick of marching the men for miles, then forcing them to walk back over the same road they had just traversed. Prisoners were provided with neither food nor water. Petry's only water came from drinking out of ditches littered with dead men and animals. By the third day, those who fell behind or were too injured to walk were beaten, bayoneted, or shot.[11]

The other Americans could do little to help their comrades, although Army medic Philip Brodsky tried his best. The Japanese had failed to confiscate his medical kit, filled with bandages, iodine, morphine, atropine, and a few other supplies. Each time the marching stopped, Brodsky moved about to tend to the wounded.[12]

The Japanese herded their prisoners down the highways under cloudless skies until the dusty road along the edge of sparkling Manila Bay snaked westward for a stretch. Along the way, men were killed for all kinds of reasons. Some were left lying dead along the road with their pants down, slaughtered while simply trying to take care of their most basic bodily functions. Between seven thousand and ten thousand Americans and Filipinos died along the way from beating, execution, exhaustion, or disease. Those who survived had marched distances varying from fifty to sixty-five miles before reaching the staging area at San Fernando, the capital of Pampanga Province. There, the men were crowded into a small area to lie down until they could be moved into proper prison camps. They were given two handfuls of rice and a pinch of salt per man—their first food in five days.

They stayed in San Fernando until the next morning, when they were loaded onto freight trains and transported to Capas, a distance of about thirty miles. The small boxcars were crowded with a hundred men in each, and three men suffocated in the same car with Petry. Three hours later, at Capas, they were unloaded and started on a six-mile march to Camp O'Donnell, an unfinished former Philippine Constabulary facility that the Japanese would use as an internment camp for the POWs. Along the way, the Filipinos warned the Americans that if they had any Japanese money, they should throw it away or they would be shot, as would anyone who fell out of line.

Upon arrival at O'Donnell, the men were lined up and searched. Five men found to have Japanese cash were immediately executed by soldiers who claimed that they must have taken it from a Japanese soldier they had killed. The remaining men were then separated by services: Army, Army Air Force, Navy, and Marines. Conditions were terrible. Only one small water spigot in the yard served thousands of men. With no medical attention, many died, at a rate of about fifty Americans and five hundred Filipinos per day.[13]

Ed Petry, Pop Daniels, and the others who once called themselves "the Battling Bastards of Bataan" had been reduced to masses of desperate souls surviving on mere crumbs. General Homma's forces were now able to concentrate their efforts on seizing control of the remaining American forces holed up on the Rock.

2

PRISONERS OF THE ROCK

ORPORAL RUFUS WILLIAM "Smitty" Smith was a bitter man. While Ed Petry and Pop Daniels were beginning the Bataan Death March a little more than two miles away, Smitty and some twelve thousand other Americans were trapped on tiny Corregidor Island. Facing a Japanese army that had already routed most of the American and Filipino forces on Luzon, he and his fellow marines were left to fight with little more than old bolt-action Springfield rifles, a firearm left over from the Great War, which had ended the year Smitty was born. The government, it seemed, had never given its men a fighting chance.

Just four months earlier, when the Japanese wrecked the Cavite Navy Yard, Smitty had manned a .50-caliber machine gun, a weapon that packed considerably more power than a Springfield. In the aftermath of the attack, the tall, lean Texan had spent several days collecting bodies before his gunnery unit was moved on December 20 through Manila and down the Bataan Peninsula to another position near Mariveles. After only a few days there, Smitty was ordered to cross the bay to Corregidor, where a new machine-gun company was being organized. Disappointed to find that the Army boys on the Rock had but a few .50-calibers, he joined a crew on a three-inch antiaircraft gun.[1]

On the morning of April 9, Smitty watched as thousands of soldiers and even nurses arrived on Corregidor's shore, some via boats, others swimming the wide channel. New personnel were assigned to help man various defensive positions. There were plenty of heavy guns on the island, but Smitty knew the American gun crews had little chance of holding off a large-scale Japanese invasion force when it inevitably came ashore.

General MacArthur had retreated to Australia weeks before, leaving fifty-eight-year-old Lieutenant General Jonathan M. "Skinny" Wainwright as the senior commander of the Manila Bay island fortresses. His headquarters was at Fort Mills, as Corregidor was officially known, but Wainwright also presided over the military personnel on four nearby islands: La Monja Island, Fort Hughes on Caballo Island, Fort Drum on El Fraile Island, and Fort Frank on Carabao Island. Tadpole-shaped and some 1,735 acres in total, Corregidor was the largest of the five islands and lay a little more than two miles from the tip of Bataan and seven miles from Cavite Province. Wainwright's island base divided the mouth of Manila Bay into northern and southern channels. Called an "impregnable fortress," it was known the world over as the "Gibraltar of the East."

Skinny Wainwright was determined not to give up the Rock without a fight. War was in his blood—his father was an officer killed in the Philippines in 1902, and his grandfather died in action during the Civil War. Wainwright's best chance at holding off the Imperial Japanese Army now lay in the thousands of American and Filipino troops manning artillery positions along Corregidor's nearly four-mile length.

Private First Class Gene Nielsen from South Logan, Utah, was one of the servicemen of the 59th Coast Artillery unit operating Corregidor's two main sea-defense batteries. Nielsen and his comrades had been under almost constant assault by Japanese forces since December 29, when they had endured their first two hours of Japanese aerial bombardments.

Private Ernie Koblos from Chicago was stationed a short distance west from Nielsen's Battery B. He was assigned as a gun mechanic on the sixty-man crew of the dual twelve-inch gun Battery C, also known as Wheeler Battery. Koblos had once had visions of remaining in the Philippines for years, but now he was not so sure. Slightly west and north of Koblos was Corporal Elmo Deal's Battery A, also known as Battery Hearn—a single twelve-inch gun located near the two-story stone barracks high atop Malinta Hill, at the base of the island's tadpole head. An expert marksman with both a .30-caliber rifle and a .45-caliber pistol, "Mo" Deal served as an artillery spotter, but in the heat of combat he also helped load and fire the massive gun. Deal's future plans, including a girlfriend back in Yuba City, California, were looking dark at the moment.

Corregidor was split into three elevations, dubbed Topside, Middleside, and Bottomside. The larger cannons mounted on Malinta Hill's Topside area were old by modern standards, originally installed decades before to protect Manila Bay from enemy ships. The island also sported forty-five coastal guns and mortars organized into twenty-three batteries, plus some seventy-two antiaircraft weapons assigned to thirteen batteries, and approximately thirty-five groups of controlled mines to protect the rocky coastline.

Gene Nielsen, Ernie Koblos, and Mo Deal were relative strangers among the 59th Coast Artillery gun crews scattered about on the Rock, but in the weeks and years ahead, the three men would build a bond forged in blood, sacrifice, and survival.

The garrison on Corregidor hung on during April 1942, just as it had since the start of the war. The island was now squarely in the crosshairs of the Japanese military, subject to almost daily aerial, naval, and artillery bombardments. Living conditions became increasingly difficult for the American defenders. Rations were cut to about thirty ounces of food per day, and drinking water was distributed only twice daily as the month wore on. At times, the men were forced to cook the carcasses of cavalry mules killed by the enemy's bombardments just to fill their aching bellies.

Men like Radioman First Class Fern Joseph Barta resorted to extreme measures to sustain themselves. Transferred from Radio Cavite in June 1941, Barta was among those responsible for manning the Monkey Point Navy Communications Center at Fort Mills. His job became increasingly dangerous as the fort experienced frequent and intense enemy bombardment and artillery fire. Monkey Point, located on Corregidor's north beach, was vital to the Navy, as it had become the main communications hub for the 16th Naval District after the war commenced.

Simply to keep the vital station in operation, Barta's radio gang was forced to undertake dangerous trips to fetch food, drinking water, and other supplies. He used a supply truck to make the three-mile run from Monkey Point to Malinta Tunnel, an extensive system drilled through solid rock that ran beneath Malinta Hill. The labyrinth of subcorridors housed Corregidor's thousand-bed underground hospital, ammunition and fuel storage areas, communications facilities, offices, and supply rooms. Twice daily, Barta cheated death numerous times along the journey. On one occasion, a Japanese dive-bomber loaded with incendiary bombs attacked his truck as the men returned from the tunnel with a full load of water. As the aircraft swept in low, Barta ditched the truck, took cover, and braced himself as three bombs landed. One exploded about fifty feet behind the prone radiomen, another ten feet to their side, and another about fifty feet in front of them. The crew and their truck escaped injury, but such runs became more perilous by the day.[2]

On another occasion, Barta was caught high atop his radio station's antenna pole making a repair when antiaircraft guns opened up. As he scurried back down the pole, a plane swooped in low, ready to strike, but it did not open fire before Barta reached the safety of the radio tunnel. His bravery in keeping communications open during six months of Japanese attacks would earn him the Silver Star.

By early May, Barta could see that future supply runs were impossible. The Japanese had launched their final assault on the Rock. There was nowhere to swim and no way to leave now. On the night of May 3, the submarine *Spearfish* met the last evacuees from Corregidor. Eluding a Japanese destroyer and minesweeper, the sub slipped beneath the surface of Manila Bay to the Rock, where General Wainwright saw off those departing at the dock.

The group included Army and Navy officers and nurses, plus one civilian female and two unauthorized stowaways to be transported to Fremantle, Australia. Lieutenant (junior grade) John Ragner Janson Jr. had a final, tearful hug from his wife, Margaret, before putting her on board *Spearfish* and bidding her good-bye. Janson, a reservist, had been living with his wife in Manila in his role as a diesel engineer for an American gold mining company. The two would never see each other again.[3]

During the next day, an estimated sixteen thousand shells rained down on Corregidor. The once-lush green island became a smoky ruin of splintered tree stumps, blackened hunks of granite, and smoldering bomb craters. Gene Nielsen's artillery crew returned fire with a vengeance. Weeks earlier, his twelve-inch cannon had shelled only areas of Bataan where leaders felt it was safe enough to do so without hitting friendly forces. Nobody gave a damn now, as persistent Japanese shelling and bombing assaults had whittled down the defense on the Rock. Battery Geary, once sporting eight twelve-inch mortars, had only one gun left by the night of May 4. Nielsen's crew helped fire that last gun until it became so hot, they could not close its breech.[4]

An initial Japanese landing force of 790 soldiers began slogging ashore during the early morning hours of May 5. The American and Filipino defenders on the Rock offered fierce resistance to the first wave, but a second wave of 785 soldiers soon landed.

Beto Pacheco and Bruce Elliott, who now manned .50-caliber machine guns, were armed with .306-caliber Springfield rifles, hand grenades, and two boxes of ammunition. Elliott waited until the ramps dropped on the landing barges, just twenty yards from his position, before he, Pacheco, and other gunners let loose. Smitty and his 4th Marine Regiment ripped into the khaki-clad Japanese infantrymen with rifle fire, machine guns, and hand grenades until the rocky shores were splattered crimson and littered with twisted and torn bodies.[5]

Such early victories were short-lived. Around 0130 on May 6, more Japanese landing barges began coming ashore. The Japanese landed three light tanks around from Monkey Point, on Corregidor's north beach, and within hours, they had captured Denver Battery. Nielsen and his companions snatched up Springfields, grenades, Browning automatic rifles, three-inch trench mortars, and machine guns as Americans were ordered to help defend the beach. Infantry-trained since boot camp, Nielsen had little concern when asked to abandon his artillery piece in favor of a rifle.[6]

The Marine officer in charge of the Monkey Point station finally decided that it was futile to maintain his radio gang. Around 0300, the lieutenant ordered Joe Barta's team to haul a machine gun down toward the front line at the beach. Barta had never seen the machine gun before and had no training on how to use it, but his group ran ahead through the clatter of gunfire and pounding artillery explosions. By the time they arrived, four of his comrades had disappeared, leaving Barta and the remaining radioman to carry their machine gun from one place to another until a marine asked to take charge of it. Barta made his way over to Battery Keyes, a rapid-fire three-incher pointed toward distant Fort Hughes.[7]

The Americans fought valiantly on the Rock during the early stages of the Japanese landings, inflicting twenty-one hundred enemy casualties on the beaches, including more than nine hundred killed. General Homma grew worried that his whole amphibious force might be wiped out, but by midmorning of May 6, defenders like Nielsen, Pacheco, and Elliott could only do so much with rifles and hand grenades. Nearby, three Japanese tanks were grinding steadily toward the main entrance to Malinta Tunnel, and General Wainwright fretted they might wreak a heavy death toll if their seventy-five-millimeter cannons could be fired within the tunnels.[8]

Shortly after 1000 on May 6, Wainwright told his staff that his troops could not hold out much longer. He sent word to General Mac-Arthur in Australia that he was ordering a cease-fire at noon. He also had his radio operator send out a farewell message to President Roosevelt that he would go "with broken heart and head bowed in sadness" to arrange for a surrender of the fortified islands of Manila Bay. "There is a limit of human endurance, and that point has long been passed," he said.[9]

"With profound regret and continued pride in my gallant troops, I go to meet the Japanese commander," Wainwright detailed in his last transmission. "Good-bye, Mr. President."

JOE BARTA SLIPPED over the back wall of Battery Keyes and made his way toward Malinta Hill. By 1100, he had reached the tunnel, where he found other radiomen—having sent the last messages from Corregidor—in the process of destroying all communications equipment. General Wainwright's surrender message was broadcast three times between 1100 and 1230, during which time the Marine 4th Regiment burned its flag and the national colors to prevent their capture by the enemy.

"Execute Pontiac" was the code phrase issued instructing soldiers to destroy their weapons and surrender. Smitty reluctantly gave up his post at the .50-caliber machine gun. An older marine near him who had fought in the First World War became emotional and teary-eyed as the order to destroy weapons was passed. "I never thought I'd see the day when a bunch of damn marines would throw in the rag and just quit!" he groused.[10]

By 1330 on May 6, Skinny Wainwright had given up the fight. He and five staff officers soon marched before the Japanese command to negotiate terms. He offered to surrender four of the fortified islands in Manila Bay—Corregidor, Fort Drum, Fort Frank, and Fort Hughes. Colonel Motto Nakyama—the same officer who had taken General King's surrender on Bataan a month earlier—insisted that no surrender would be accepted that did not include all U.S. forces in the Philippines.[11]

Wainwright's staff was taken by boat to General Homma's headquarters at Cabcaben on Bataan, where Wainwright was informed that hostilities against American troops would continue unless an unconditional surrender was agreed upon. His troops had little chance of holding out much longer, so Wainwright was forced to do the unthinkable and sign the surrender documents. Tears filled his eyes as he was taken under guard shortly after midnight.[12]

The surrender of so many troops proved to be mass confusion. Japanese soldiers soon made their way into the underground hospital and the jam-packed Malinta Tunnel, where thousands of soldiers had gathered once their guns were wrecked. One Imperial Japanese Army soldier wearing horn-rimmed glasses moved through, demanding that the Americans give up their rings, watches, and other valuables.[13]

Joe Barta's radio gang was marched out of the tunnel that afternoon and put to work carrying artillery, ammunition, and supplies from Japanese landing barges to the beach. Once that task was complete, Barta was moved to Corregidor's own tiny Kindley Field, where he spent his next four days working to get the airfield back into commission so that his captors could use it.[14]

Beginning on the afternoon of May 6, all of Corregidor's defenders—Marine, Army, Navy, Army Air Corps, and Filipino soldiers—were ordered to gather at the 92nd Maintenance Garage near Monkey Point. The small garage included a concrete ramp that extended into the ocean, a landing area for Catalina PBY flying boats. The area was devoid of any shade, far from the most suitable spot for more than eleven thousand defenders to surrender their weapons and be held. Packed in like cattle, the men were soon cooking in the blistering sun.

With no food or water available, the wounded suffered greatly. Able-bodied men constructed crude shelters from battle debris and blankets. During the next few days, several thousand more military personnel were shuttled to the maintenance garage area as they were rounded up from the other surrendered island fortresses in Manila Bay.

HANDSOME AND HOT-TEMPERED, Mac McDole was emotionally and physically spent by the time he was forced to surrender at Fort Hughes on Caballo Island. The twenty-one-year-old marine had been shuffled about since the Japanese initiated their assault on the Philippines. For the last few months, he had helped man a machine-gun nest at Fort Hughes, but now after a seemingly endless standoff against an overpowering enemy, hoping daily for reinforcements that never arrived, he was subjected to the humiliation of destroying his own weapons. His gun crew drained the hydraulic oil from the fourteen-inch rifles, emptied the water from their water-cooled .50-calibers, and fired all of the weapons until their barrels burned out. Mac took one last look at his Marine-issued Springfield Model 1903 rifle. He knew it intimately, including its serial number 24109. Then he tossed it into the bay.[15]

Japanese motor launches reached Fort Hughes that afternoon and began taking American prisoners. Mac and the rest placed their hands on top of their heads, walked to the shoreline, and surrendered. He was herded onto an overcrowded launch and taken on the short ride to Corregidor, where he was shocked at the scene before him. In an area that would scarcely constitute one block in a major American city, some seven thousand Americans and nine thousand Filipinos were separated and kept under guard on the concrete PBY landing ramp.

The Japanese took down name, rank, and serial number from each prisoner. As the information was recorded, a Japanese soldier searched each man. Fearful of losing his high school ring, Mac quickly shoved it into his mouth. He stepped up to the table and offered his basic information to the Japanese guard: "Glenn W. McDole, Corporal, United States Marine Corps, serial number three-oh-one-oh-five-one." Three guards removed his watch and confiscated his wallet.

Angry about losing his family photos, he yelled, "Damn it! Give me that back!" He was struck from behind with a club that dropped him to his knees. He thought briefly of fighting back, until he noticed three more Japanese soldiers with billy clubs smiling at him. Mac stood up, dusted himself off, and walked toward the prisoner-holding area. He felt some relief that his ring was still in his mouth. *These bastards will not take away my pride or my spirit,* he thought.[16]

GENE NIELSEN'S PRIMARY concern was water. Like most of the others, he had been forced to surrender not only his weapons but also his canteens.[17]

Corregidor was close enough to the equator that the heat was relentless—compounded by standing on concrete all day. The weeks of constant shelling had destroyed most of the water lines. At night, there was barely enough room for the now sixteen thousand men to even lie down in their containment area, which measured only about fifteen hundred yards by eight hundred yards. Severe thirst during the day replaced sleep issues at night. Near the 92nd Garage area, a wide bomb crater filled with fresh rainwater. It was difficult to reach at first, but the Americans soon found it to be their only source of drinking water. Nielsen joined the line of men that soon trod a well-worn path to the water hole.

During the next three days, the men were given nothing to eat. The stench of sweat, human excrement, and rotting corpses hung in the air. Straddle ditches were dug to help with sanitation, but the exposed trenches reeked of feces and soon began to spread dysentery to the prisoners. The area where the Americans were held, including the ditches, was marked off by a single boundary wire. Gene Nielsen went right under the wire to defecate one day, forgetting all about the warnings. He had scarcely stepped across the line when a Japanese machine gun opened up from a nearby ridge. The gunfire missed him by only a few yards.[18]

Sergeant Doug Bogue of the 4th Marine Regiment was resolute in his intent to stay alive. After the third day, Colonel Paul D. Bunker attempted to organize the men, and he was permitted to send out details in search of provisions. Bogue was quick to volunteer, and he obtained his first food and water in days while out on a work detail with 150 other men. They were forced to help carry wounded Japanese soldiers as far as two miles from distant beaches into the Malinta Tunnel hospital, and then help bury their dead. The American fatalities, left decomposing on the beach for two days, were denied proper funerals. Some bodies were piled and burned, while others were unceremoniously dumped into shallow trenches. If a hole was just deep enough for one corpse, five would be jammed in. No dog tags were allowed to be removed to later identify the dead.[19]

American soldiers—from officers to the lowest ranking—were viciously abused without bias. The Japanese made it known that the lowest Japanese private was far better than the highest-ranking American officer. Military protocol began to disintegrate. One serviceman told his commander to go to hell. The officer reported the man to the Japanese, who had the serviceman shot to death on the spot.[20]

Corregidor became a special kind of hell for Doug Bogue. He had known since childhood that he wanted to be a U.S. Marine, but this was not at all how he had envisioned the life of the glorious warriors of his dreams. By early May, Bogue was grimy, weary, smelly, and unshaven; though seven years a marine, he was forced to carry out filthy work that the Japanese infantry refused to do. One afternoon, when his work party was approaching McKinley Field, guards pulled ten men from the rear of their detail. The Americans were tied to nearby trees and used for bayonet and sword practice. Bogue and the other men watched as their fellow servicemen were slashed, hacked, and run through with swords.

The long work hours in the tropical sun took their toll on men who suffered from malnutrition and dehydration. The open latrines were overflowing, swarming with flies that spread dysentery to the prisoners. After three days of such conditions, Bogue contracted the disease. There was no chance for him to go to a hospital in spite of his severe illness. A Navy physician advised him to help carry other sick men to the hospital, where he at least would have the chance to contact someone who could treat him. Bogue managed to find a U.S. Army doctor who confirmed that he did have amoebic dysentery, and he was admitted to the Malinta hospital for the next two weeks for treatment.[21]

Mac McDole received his first food—a can of Carnation milk—after three days of wasting away near the maintenance garage. The former 185-pound athlete had been dropping weight fast by the time he shared that meager ration with two other soldiers. His mood took an upturn that day when he spotted two of his closest friends from the base basketball team, Roy Henderson and Willie Smith. Henderson, like Smitty, had been raised in a rural East Texas farming community. Henderson told his friends how troubled he had been to give up the fight—the hardest thing he had done in his life was to lay down his weapon and surrender. The three marines were soon assigned to work details, stacking sun-bloated carcasses and gathering scrap metal that would later be melted down in Japan to help their war effort.

Suffering and death continued on the old seaplane ramp for seventeen days. On May 23, the Japanese passed the word that the prisoners were to move to the dock area at Bottomside for transfer the next day to better facilities in Manila. The starving men could only wonder how much improved the conditions would be.

3

PASSAGE TO PALAWAN

ORPORAL WILLIE BALCHUS was eager for change, even if he knew nothing of what it would be. Seventeen days of cooking in the open sun on the concrete containment area had caused his lean five-foot-eight frame to grow even thinner. He had endured the final weeks of the assault on Corregidor as a member of the 60th Coast Artillery Regiment on I Battery. Now the twenty-year-old Pennsylvanian, his scraggly brown hair well beyond Army regulation, joined thousands of other broken men in a slow shuffle toward the island's south docks.

Only three years before, Army life had seemed a good choice to William Joseph Balchus. He had quit school after the eighth grade to go to work, and by the time he was seventeen, his parents allowed him to join the service in hopes of establishing a career. But now, on May 24, 1942, Balchus was nothing more than a number, a prisoner without rights being pushed and prodded along by shouting Japanese guards.

Ten harbor launches were waiting at Bottomside's south dock to move the American and Filipino prisoners, about a hundred per trip, from the Rock to three Japanese troop transport ships anchored in the south channel of Manila Bay. In the Corregidor hospital, everyone able to walk was ordered to return to the main camp at the maintenance garage. Doug Bogue, still recovering from endless diarrhea and vomiting caused by amoebic dysentery, staggered toward Bottomside in the blistering afternoon heat. Bogue became irritated as he watched Japanese sailors and soldiers strip the prisoners of leftover valuables as they moved them to the ships. Captain John Wright Jr. wrote in his diary of the Japanese crews: "They slapped faces, kicked shins, shoved groups of men until they fell down, then got together and laughed."[1]

Aboard a transport, Bogue saw in the distance that the Japanese Rising Sun flag had replaced Old Glory atop their former hillside base. The thousands of men crammed like cargo onto the ships included Bogue, Balchus, Ernie Koblos, Bruce Elliott, Gene Nielsen, Beto Pacheco, Roy Henderson, Mo Deal, Joe Barta, and Willie Smith. Some were shoved into the holds and left to sweat it out after the hatches were closed, while others were packed topside on decks so crowded men could not even sit down. The following day, May 25, the transports moved across the bay to a point just south of Manila opposite Nichols Field.

There would be no easy debarking by pulling into the Manila docks. Instead, the ships anchored about a half mile offshore, where LST-type landing barges moved the POWs from the vessels to the beach and lowered their ramps for the men to exit. The water was anywhere from waist deep to eight feet, depending on where the ramps were dropped.[2]

Gene Nielsen moved out onto the LST ramp and paused to gauge the water depth. Anyone who hesitated was jabbed with bayonets by Japanese guards, or had his head smashed with a rifle butt. *They're really enjoying this,* Nielsen thought angrily. Mac McDole made it ashore with Smitty and Roy Henderson, where they were greeted by a horde of screaming soldiers.[3]

Their clothes were soaking wet as they were made to march in columns four abreast, either barefoot or in squishing shoes filled with beach sand. The Americans and Filipinos were paraded down Dewey Boulevard, the bayfront main highway named after famous Admiral George Dewey, who sank the Spanish fleet in Manila Bay in 1898. Some Japanese soldiers rode vehicles to help herd their prisoners, while other guards were on horseback as they alternately walked, cantered, trotted, and walked again. The net effect kept Army veteran Francis Galligan off pace all day, forcing him to jog at times to keep from being stepped on by horses.[4]

The men realized they were being marched through the streets of Manila as a propaganda maneuver for the Japanese to show off the crushed Allied military. The Filipino citizens felt pity, but those who rushed out to throw food to the marching prisoners were quickly beaten back by Japanese guards who drew sabers. The midday heat caused some men to fall out from dehydration, previous wounds, or sickness. McDole and Smitty tried to help carry some of the fallen as long as their energy held out, but the six-mile march took hours longer than it should have as the Japanese paraded their human prizes on a circuitous route through Manila. Dewey Boulevard soon ran red with blood as Japanese cavalrymen shot or ran sabers through those who stopped to rest on the curbsides.[5]

Their destination, McDole learned, was the old Bilibid Prison, established in 1865 by the Spanish colonial government as the first national penitentiary of the Philippines. The correctional facility, originally known as Carcel y Presidio, was rumored to be the equivalent of America's Alcatraz. The fact that the Americans and their fellow Filipinos were now being marched into this notorious prison spoke volumes to McDole: The Japanese considered them no better than the worst murderers, rapists, and thieves the jail was built to contain.

THOSE WHO SURVIVED the grueling march entered a seventeen-acre complex surrounded by solid mason walls. A guard tower stood at the center of Bilibid Prison, with cell blocks spreading out from the tower like spokes on a wheel. The sick and wounded were taken into a makeshift hospital area while the rest of Corregidor's survivors were left outside. Water was available in the yard from only two faucets, from which the men had to wait in long lines to drink or fill their canteens.

At least the first meal at Bilibid was an improvement. Each man received a baseball-size rice ball, with no meat or flavoring. During the previous two weeks, most men had survived on only one-third of a can of Carnation milk per day. Stocky Mac McDole had already shed quite a few pounds when he decided in the Bilibid prison yard to make a pact with Roy Henderson and Smitty. "What's mine is yours, and what's yours is mine," they agreed. The marines pledged that they would share any water, food, or other supplies with one another as long as their prisoner of war ordeal should continue.[6]

The Americans had little to do in the Bilibid prison yard but sit together, talking and singing as a cold rain fell that night. The men took cover within four ancient prison buildings, huddling next to those with blankets as rain leaked through the roofs. Their stay at Bilibid was short. On May 27, the Americans were awakened by guards who, screaming in Japanese, herded them into another long column and again hiked them through Manila toward a train depot. More sick and wounded dropped during the long march, but the local people once again lined the streets to pass goods to the prisoners: rice balls, lumps of brown sugar, and *balutes* (partially incubated chicken eggs).[7]

The parade reached a Manila train depot during the late-morning hours and was lined up alongside a freight train. Doug Bogue estimated that each of the fifteen boxcars—only about one-third the size of those in America—could feasibly hold about forty men in close proximity, yet the Japanese brutally forced in a hundred men per steel car. With the prisoners packed so tightly that no man could move or even raise his arms, panicked shouting and screaming commenced as soon as the doors were slammed shut.

McDole was fortunate. He was among the last shoved into his car, leaving him near the door. The heat quickly became suffocating and the screams so deafening that the guard in McDole's car finally cracked the door enough to let some air in as the prisoners cursed him soundly. Smitty, McDole, and Henderson tried to fan air to the others packed farther in the car, but their efforts were in vain. Dozens of men in each boxcar passed out from the heat and soon began dying. Gene

Nielsen—unable to sit or stretch out—felt like he was in an oven as the midday sun baked the train cars.[8]

The train inched its way north from Manila toward the POWs' next destination—Cabanatuan, a newly opened prison camp about sixty miles away on the Pampanga River. The journey took most of the day at slow speed, forcing the sweating men to relieve themselves as they stood shoulder to shoulder. The stench soon became unbearable. Fortunately, kindly Filipinos crowded near the railroad tracks at each village and threw rice balls, cookies, eggs, and bread into the open boxcar doors as the train rumbled slowly past. McDole managed to catch a large block of brown sugar, which he dutifully shared with Henderson and Smitty as part of their survival pact. Smitty in turn caught some rice bread, shared it with his two buddies, and passed the rest to other prisoners.

That evening the train finally came to a jerking halt in Cabanatuan, where Japanese guards appeared, screaming and cursing at the delirious, excrement-covered prisoners. McDole received his first wound when a guard jabbed his bayonet deep into the left side of his back as he tried to exit his boxcar. As blood spurted from the incision below his rib cage, McDole angrily turned to attack the guard who had stabbed him. He was physically restrained by Smitty, who pulled him away.[9]

"Your temper is gonna get you killed, Dole!" he snapped.

McDole reluctantly joined the long march toward his next detainment area. Along the way, another prisoner tried to help by using a block of salt tossed to him by a caring Filipino villager. He lifted Mac's shirt and wiped salt into the open gash to clean out the wound. Despite the pain, McDole was at least more fortunate than the 130 men estimated by Doug Bogue to have suffocated to death during the train ride.[10]

The filthy procession of bloodied, stinking men stumbled northward through Cabanatuan along a nearly fourteen-mile route. They drank no water save what they could sneak from mucky brown ditches along the way. Once again, those who slowed to rest were kicked, beaten, and even murdered. The fifteen hundred men were allowed to sleep that night at an old school yard in which the Japanese placed a huge kettle to boil rations. Those who endured the long chow line each received a meager rice portion as the only meal of the day, although many simply gave up and declined to eat.[11]

A heavy rain fell during the night. The water was a blessing for parched throats, but as the temperatures dropped, Mac McDole had to huddle under a blanket for warmth with Smitty as he nursed his throbbing back wound. Daybreak came with screaming, cursing, kicking guards and more marching. The Japanese rode in trucks while the sick, weary, and wounded POWs shuffled down the dusty road under an increasingly hot sun. Gene Nielsen, suffering greatly from thirst, noted at one point a large artesian well right alongside the road. Water flowed steadily from a ten-inch pipe, but the guards would not allow any Americans to drink from its basin or to fill their canteens. Hundreds of marching feet and overnight rain had turned the road to mud, and Nielsen watched as desperate men bent down and drank from the stagnant puddles.[12]

Outside the city of Cabanatuan, the prisoners finally reached the gates of the newly opened camp, a rotting former Philippine army training camp with dilapidated barracks known as Cabanatuan Camp 3. The long hike had caused some men to fall out, but Nielsen admired the grit of one poor man who seemed determined to endure. Once inside, Gene saw the man lie down under a tree to rest, appearing tremendously relieved. He never awoke again.

Encircled by an eight-foot barbed wire fence, the camp's interior contained numerous rustic *nipa* huts built of palms, bamboo, and thatched roofs. The larger huts, roughly eighteen feet by fifty-five feet, could house between one hundred fifty and two hundred men while the smaller ones—about eighteen feet by forty feet—could hold a hundred each. All around the edges of the camp were guard towers, manned by Japanese soldiers armed with machine guns, rifles, and spotlights to prevent anyone from trying to escape to the distant mountains.

Doug Bogue slept on the bamboo floor without a mat as water dripped from the leaky hut roof. His first meal in the new Cabanatuan prison compound was dirty rice and a thin soup that tasted like nothing but salty water. By morning, Bogue noticed several men in his hut had died from dysentery and malaria. His group was then marched another twelve-plus miles to a prison between Laur and Bongabong Stock Farm, while other work parties were sent out under armed guards to gather wood for the camp's cooking fire. McDole waited in line near the two hefty black pots in order to receive a small portion of rice laced with the extra nutrition of bugs and worms. Bogue considered the daily ration, a weak cup of tea served with two half mess kits of rice per day, to be poor in quality and insufficient in quantity. The prevailing dysentery and malaria caused several deaths each day as work parties unloaded supplies for the Japanese, cleared rocks and debris, or gathered firewood. Those not assigned to work had little to do but sit around the compound, telling stories of their former home life as they sweated in the broiling tropic sun.[13]

By MAY 30, the American and Filipino population at Cabanatuan Camp 3 had swelled to six thousand POWs. Untreated battle wounds festered, became infected by the unsanitary conditions and meager diets, and claimed more lives daily in alarming numbers.

The few camp doctors could offer only the most primitive first aid to those suffering from pellagra, dengue fever, dysentery, malaria, beriberi, and scurvy. Mac McDole, Roy Henderson, and Smitty were fortunate enough to have a bottle of quinine pills Mac had smuggled with him from Corregidor, keeping them in better health than most as others around them succumbed during the first weeks at Cabanatuan. Doug Bogue benefited from medicine obtained at great risk by a daring few who slipped away from the guards to purchase goods from the Filipinos with pooled money.[14]

The camp was the perfect breeding ground for all types of diseases. For toilets, the prisoners had "straddle trenches"—crude latrines dug about fifteen feet long, six feet deep, and several feet wide. A constant line of men waited their turn to squat over the trenches, but many of the sick simply could not make it in time and their bowels let loose. Each rainfall mixed human waste into the mud, further spreading filth and the ever-present humming swarms of green flies into nearby cooking areas.

Joe Barta was put to work in the camp galley for two months. He enjoyed one little luxury of being able to take a bath each night from a five-gallon can of water, maintaining at least some hygiene while his comrades had only a river to bathe in when allowed. Marine Joe Dupont was assigned to a vegetable farm where at harvest time he watched the fruits of his labor go entirely to his Japanese captors.[15]

The camp commandant, Lieutenant Colonel Masao Mori, organized his Cabanatuan prisoners into groups of ten to prevent escape attempts. At any hour, his guards could hold a roll call in which every member of the ten-man groups was required to be present. If anyone was missing, the other nine were subjected to torture or even execution. In one case witnessed by Doug Bogue, the "guilty" were four U.S. soldiers accused of trying to escape while on a work detail on May 30.[16]

The Americans, who claimed they had become lost while foraging for food, were returned to camp, beaten severely, and hog-tied in such a manner that any movements caused near strangulation. They were left squatting in the prison yard for two days under a merciless sun while the Japanese forced local Filipinos who passed by the camp to beat the Americans with clubs and ax handles. The bloodied men begged for water, but no one was allowed to help them. On the third day, the guards ordered the prisoners to dig their own graves up on a small bank, while the rest of the POWs in camp were lined up to watch. After declining blindfolds and final cups of tea, the four accused were shot and crumpled into their shallow, fresh graves. A Japanese officer stepped forward and fired a final bullet into each head.[17]

In mid-July, a prisoner lost his temper and got into a fight with a guard. For punishment, the Japanese cut off the man's ears and nailed his hands to the camp gate. Each time guards passed through the gate, it would swing the poor man into a barbed wire fence, which cut repeatedly into his legs. He was left nailed to the fence for three days without food or water before he was removed and buried in a trench. McDole, Smitty, and Henderson heard from the men assigned to the burial detail that the victim was still breathing as dirt was shoveled on top of him.[18]

The horror of such executions—coupled with sun exposure, thirst, disease, and starvation—caused many men to lose the will to live. The fair-complected suffered the most from excessive sunburn. Joe Dupont's hot, sweaty underarms became covered with pus-filled tropical ulcers the men came to call "Guam blisters." Insufficient food caused bodies to shrivel until some men resembled walking skeletons, their tight skin stretched over protruding bones. McDole could soon look at a man's face and tell whether he would live much longer. Those who had given up hope wore a dim expression about their eyes, and they usually did not survive many days longer. Men with a certain burning glow in their eyes still had the will to live.

Gene Nielsen was most troubled by the lack of sufficient food. He had watched friends die at Cabanatuan, and his gnawing hunger made him consider eating the local vegetation. Having read how cows lived off the many minerals in grass, Nielsen picked the greenest blades near water sources but found they tasted like straw and were impossible to choke down. He next began sampling leaves plucked from a small tree, just small bites at first. *It's not good, but it's not too bad,* he thought. *It has a little bit of a citrus flavor to it.*[19]

He ate tiny bites of a leaf and waited to see whether it had any adverse effects on his body. Within days, he progressed from a quarter leaf to a half leaf and finally an entire leaf. Soon he was picking handfuls of leaves and eating them. The local trees gave him something to add to his meager rice-and-soup diet, but Nielsen was concerned as he watched the growing number of Americans falling deathly ill with malaria, dysentery, and other tropical ailments.

Smitty noticed that Japanese guards periodically entered camp looking for stronger prisoners to assign to special work details. Willing to assume any opportunity that would take him away from the hell of Cabanatuan, he recognized his chance in July when he heard rumors that the Japanese were looking for healthy men for a special project. Smitty quizzed the American officers to see how he could volunteer. When the work detail list was posted, he was pleased to see his name, along with buddies Roy Henderson and Mac McDole. They heard that the assignment involved a three-month project, but they knew little else. It did not matter. Joe Dupont, still suffering from his painful Guam blisters, was happy to make the cut as well.[20]

Hundreds of volunteers were marched out of the front gate on July 24, 1942, with their scant possessions. Ensign Bob Russell was sorry to be leaving his friends, but he was optimistic about becoming part of a small group going somewhere—anywhere—outside of Cabanatuan Camp 3. Many of those selected—including Beto Pacheco, Willie Balchus, Bruce Elliott, Mo Deal, Joe Barta, and Doug Bogue—had all been captured on Corregidor in April. The American prisoners were marched toward town and loaded onto waiting trucks, a merciful change from the previous deadly train ride.[21]

Balchus counted 442 total Americans in the work detail that departed Cabanatuan. After a three-hour truck ride along bumpy roads to Manila, the men were detained briefly at the old Bilibid Prison, where those suffering from malaria or too weak in any way were culled out. By late afternoon, the final group was moved to the Manila Harbor docks. There, Balchus and his comrades were put to work loading two small transport ships with construction supplies: wheelbarrows, shovels, picks, tons of bulk cement, rice, salt, and other food supplies. They were clearly preparing for an extended work project on one of the other Philippine islands.[22]

The final group numbered 340 Army, Navy, and Marine enlisted men, plus 6 officers. The ranking officer was Marine Captain Ted Ernest Pulos. There were two Navy officers: Ensign Bob Russell and Lieutenant (junior grade) John Janson, the man who had sent his wife out on the submarine *Spearfish* just days before the surrender of Corregidor. Filling out the officer ranks were Warrant Officer Glenn Turner and two U.S. Army doctors.

The senior medical officer was Captain Harold Samuel Hickman, a twenty-nine-year-old former medical intern originally from Winnipeg, Canada, who had joined the U.S. Army's Medical Corps in 1941. Hickman, promoted from second lieutenant to captain in February 1942, was a Bataan Death March survivor who had most recently been interned at Camp O'Donnell. The other doctor included in the work program was First Lieutenant Carl Louis Mango. Hickman also selected several junior medics, including Bataan survivor Phil Brodsky and his friend Private First Class Everett Bancroft, to be on the work detail.[23]

The men labored on Pier 7 in Manila Harbor for several days as they loaded the ships, most working with no shoes and little clothing to protect them from the sun. Toiling below decks in intense heat, inhaling cement dust, Mac McDole could scarcely breathe as he worked. On July 29, the men were marched on board the two transport ships, the last "cargo" to be loaded. Most of the prisoners were placed on board the rusting 5,461-ton merchant ship *Sanko Maru*. They huddled together on deck as their vessel sailed out of Manila Harbor, passing within clear view of Corregidor, now blackened and blasted with thousands of bomb and shell craters.[24]

The voyage from Manila was less severe than what other Allied POWs would later endure on so-called hellships used by the Japanese to move prisoners over the ocean. Some were put to work in *Sanko Maru*'s galley, where Smitty was excited by a change of menu: rice, seaweed soup, and mongo beans. He hoped that his prospects were looking brighter. One Japanese guard, who had spent time in the United States and spoke good English, enjoyed American music, so he prompted Joe Dupont and other prisoners to sing popular dance songs such as "Star Dust" as they lay on deck at night.[25]

The POWs were unaware of their destination during the first day at sea. The ranking Japanese officer in charge, Captain Kishimoto, finally pulled two American officers—Captain Pulos and Ensign Russell—aside to tell them via his interpreter that they were bound for the island of Palawan, where they would be consigned to work on a farm. Kishimoto said he realized that his prisoners were unhappy, but that he would like to make their new camp as pleasant as possible under the circumstances.[26]

Around 1000 on July 30, *Sanko Maru* dropped anchor off Culion, a small island of the Philippines chain north of Palawan. Bruce Elliott was ready to make a break for it. He had no intention of living out the war as a POW if he could help it. He had found a twenty-foot length of rope in the hold and coiled it around his body beneath his shirt, hoping to slip over the side and escape to the island during the stopover. A work party was organized from among the American prisoners to load a barge with supplies for the island's inhabitants, all patients of the Culion leper colony. Once Elliott learned the island was inhabited only by lepers, he quietly canceled his escape plans.[27]

McDole, Smitty, and Henderson were among the group that went ashore with the barge. When they reached land, the Japanese guards—fearful of catching leprosy—refused to advance until the American prisoners had sprayed the landing area with a disinfectant. The island's Catholic priest greeted the prisoners, who began unloading the barges while many of the lepers—men, women, and children—came forward with curiosity to watch the newcomers and offer prayers. McDole felt great pity for the people, all covered in oozing sores and some horribly disfigured by their disease.

The prisoners unloaded stores throughout the afternoon and into the next morning before they were herded back onto the barge and returned to the *Sanko Maru*. They waved at the priest and the lepers as they departed, wondering why the Japanese had bothered to help these poor people when they treated the American POWs so terribly. As the ship began to get under way around 1630, the prisoners were told what Captain Pulos and Ensign Russell had already learned: They would be part

of a road-building detail on one of the larger Philippine islands, Palawan. A guard told McDole that the men could expect better treatment
there and American food.[28]

Mac and his friends chatted and smiled at the guards as they phonily
tried to display pleasure at the news. Few believed their treatment would
be any better on Palawan.

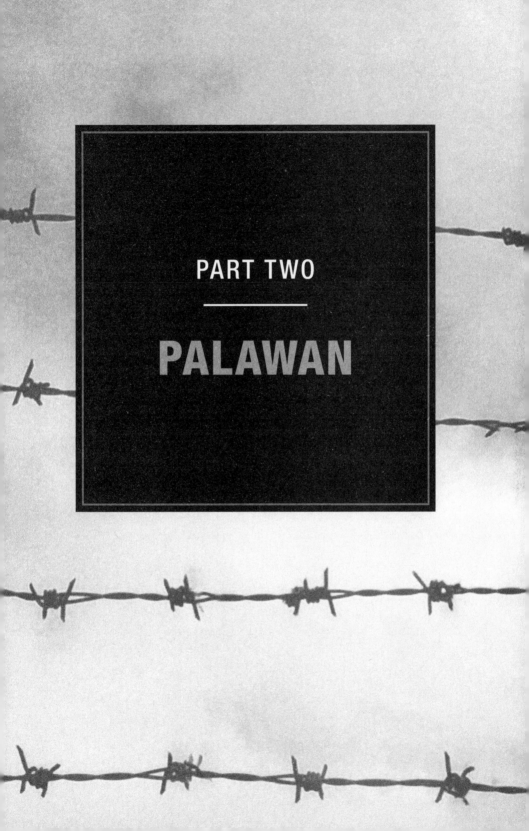

PART TWO

PALAWAN

4

CAMP 10-A

MEDIC PHIL BRODSKY was impressed with what he saw as his prison ship reached the harbor at Palawan. The island was beautiful. Lush and green, it was surrounded by sparkling turquoise waters, and a light, warm breeze wafted the pleasant aroma of tropical flowers. The surrounding coastline appeared clean and even clear of flies and mosquitoes. *This would be an ideal place to vacation if there was not a war going on,* he thought.[1]

Sanko Maru and its companion merchant ship arrived off Palawan Island around noon on August 1, 1942, and anchored in Puerto Princesa Bay by midafternoon, having completed the 334-mile voyage from Manila. The American prisoners of war spent the next day and a half transferring stores from the ships to barges and to the dock. Upon completion on August 3, the men were ushered from the port along a dirt road toward their new camp adjacent to the bay. They were strangers on a strange island, still wondering what destiny awaited them on Palawan.[2]

Sanko Maru had arrived in the harbor of Puerto Princesa, the capital city of Palawan, the fifth largest of the 7,100 islands in the Philippine group. The island stretched two hundred seventy miles north to south, with a mountain range that ran down its center like a spinal cord. It averaged only fifteen miles wide, bordered on the east by the Sulu Sea and by the South China Sea on the west. This time, the ragged POWs were not greeted by cheering Filipinos throwing food as they hiked from the dock area. Most locals had long since disappeared into the mountains to escape the Japanese, leaving behind a town now largely deserted. Palawan had a long history, dating to the original aboriginal tribes such as the Tagbanua and Batak, whose men, who wore nothing more than a loincloth, hunted with bow and arrow and the *cerbatana*, a blowpipe for poisoned darts. Europeans arrived in the seventeenth century, with the Spanish establishing missions before erecting the first military post in 1861. The jungles of Palawan contained numerous animal species found nowhere else in the Philippines: the Malay civet cat (*musang*), porcupines (*durians*), stink badgers, armadillos, and the Palawan bearcat (*binturong*).[3]

Puerto Princesa Bay, situated on the east coast of Palawan, had currents flowing through its deep waters that moved south to north, and its banks were indented by secondary bays into which numerous rivers emptied. The capital city of Puerto Princesa had been established in 1872 in a virgin forest that sheltered the clear blue bay from the eastern winds. From the town, several mountains were visible. Northwest of town, two peaks were prominent: Mount Pulgar at 4,250 feet, and Mount Beaufort, which rose almost as high.[4]

By 1890, the population of Puerto Princesa was about fifteen hundred. Spanish rule over the area persisted for some twenty years, but the province of Puerto Princesa was placed under military government after the cession of the Philippines to the United States on December 10, 1898, when the Treaty of Paris was signed. In 1904, an abandoned Spanish royal farm at Iwahig was founded as the Iwahig Prison and Penal Colony. Originally planned as a prison labor camp to help clear forested areas of Palawan for settlement, the Iwahig colony was redesignated in 1907 as a settlement for the rehabilitation of reformed criminals— prisoners that included soldiers and civilians convicted of crimes and deportees charged with offenses against civil or religious authorities.

Located roughly fourteen miles south of Puerto Princesa City, Iwahig was developed as a sugar estate or plantation where prison labor was used.[5]

The forests of Iwahig—bountiful with birds and wild animals— were composed of camagong, ipil, and other hardwoods prized for shipbuilding and cabinetry. Officers, employees, and ranking inmates supervised the work conducted by those living within the penal colony, which became known as a "prison without bars." Its citizens enjoyed freedoms similar to those experienced outside the colony, with families allowed to live in groups.

Beto Pacheco noticed the absence of civilians as he and the other 345 Americans were marched through Puerto Princesa. They would soon learn that most of the women and children had fled for their own safety after the Japanese military landed on Palawan in early May 1942, when Vicente M. Palanca was still serving his second term as the municipal president of Puerto Princesa. Attorney Iñigo Racela Peña was captured and forced to serve as the governor and later congressman of Palawan. Peña walked a fine line between pleasing the occupying Japanese military and trying to protect his compatriots from cruelty and abuse. By May 18, the Imperial Japanese Army had established a garrison at Puerto Princesa, with more than twelve hundred soldiers billeted in houses within the city. Many Palaweños, subjected to air raids and wide-ranging abuses from the Japanese, fled into the hills to build primitive homes near the native Batak tribesmen.[6]

The newly arrived POWs were marched into an abandoned Philippine Constabulary barracks at Puerto Princesa, through a pair of soaring stone pillars that marked the entrance. About a dozen coconut trees lined a road that began at the front gate and ran through the courtyard of the constabulary. The U-shaped barracks within had metal roofs and wooden floors, an improvement over the huts at Cabanatuan, though they were in some disarray.

Captain Ted Pulos and the small group of officers were assigned to one room in the two-story brick-and-stucco building. The enlisted men were divided into four smaller companies that occupied two large rooms in the old barracks, where they were ordered to bed down for the night. Many opted to sleep on the wooden floor, while others improvised bedding. Ensign Bob Russell built a crude bed with two-by-fours, a half-inch wire mesh screen, and a straw mat. He found it only slightly more comfortable than sleeping on the floor.[7]

CAPTAIN KISHIMOTO, THE senior officer who had accompanied the prisoners from Manila, soon took the opportunity to address his prisoners. He spoke in Japanese, pausing long enough for his interpreter to relay his message. He announced that he was now their camp commandant. "My commander says if you work hard and do as you're told, someday you'll get back home to be with your family," the interpreter related. Those who did not cooperate would be punished and denied food.[8]

Kishimoto was short, about five foot two, with an athletic build and closely cropped hair. He wore an army summer uniform and thick-rimmed glasses. Standing atop a small stepladder so he could look down upon the Americans he was addressing, he said that if they worked hard as ordered, they could have Sundays off and even hold athletic contests during their downtime.[9]

The first order of business for the prisoners was to establish latrines and repair their new base, officially designated as Japanese POW Camp 10-A. They were divided into groups of ten, with one guard assigned to each work group. The old constabulary was located near the shores of Puerto Princesa Bay, perched atop a sixty-foot cliff above a narrow coral rock beach below. The southern boundary of the camp that ran along the bluffs was still exposed, but the men were put to work in the first week erecting an eight-foot double row of barbed wire to discourage any attempts at fleeing to the beach. Another party of Americans began building a proper guard tower that could accommodate two guards and a machine gun.

Bruce Elliott's party was assigned to pull weeds and clear brush around the immediate camp area. Once the men had piles gathered, they loaded them into wheelbarrows and dumped them over the edge of the cliff to the coral rocks below. Elliott, determined to sabotage any effort of the Japanese he could, allowed his wheelbarrow to "slip" from his hands and plummet over the edge. Japanese guards beat the living hell out of him for the stunt, which only fueled Elliott's desire to escape.[10]

Mac McDole, Smitty, and Roy Henderson were sent under armed guard to scavenge the deserted village for tools and building materials. During their first week on Palawan, the Americans improved their barracks by scrubbing the floors, strengthening the sagging veranda, and rebuilding the wood steps. Marine George Burlage, a twenty-four-year-old Californian who had weighed in at one hundred ninety pounds when the war started, had already dropped forty pounds in his first months as a POW. He was quick to scour anything of value when he and other prisoners were allowed into abandoned buildings to secure supplies. He grabbed a stack of books, including a geography text, from an empty schoolhouse and soon had to do some quick explaining to convince the guards he would not be using it to help plan an escape route from the island.[11]

The men dug their latrine a short distance from the veranda of their barracks for easy access. This time, they laid boards across the trenches to form seats and even added a lower board to serve as a toilet footrest to prevent them from slipping into the waste below on rainy days. The prisoner galley consisted of a large black pot resting on a brick base. They had a tea barrel covered with a thatched roof, which provided some shade for those assigned to cook in the hot galley area.

Each man was responsible for his own bunk in the constabulary barracks. Some found old doors to create beds. McDole, Smitty, and Henderson opted to simply sleep on the floor, using their folded blankets as mattresses. The Japanese provided ceiling-to-floor mosquito netting, each section large enough to cover ten men. Each night, they would lower the netting in place and stay in it until morning reveille. Despite this protection, it would be only a matter of time before the men were hit by malaria, as McDole's pilfered quinine pills had long since run out.[12]

McDole was among the men assigned to a ten-man plumbing detail to provide water to the camp. They made their way up the nearby mountainside, dragging twenty-foot sections of three-inch piping, which they connected, one by one, from a mountain stream all the way back to camp. McDole hated the Japanese, with one exception: a short, plump guard in his late thirties who appeared older than most of the young soldiers. His name was Kuta Schugota, but Mac and his plumbing detail came to know him as "Smiley." Schugota allowed the men to take breaks and looked the other way when McDole and his companions ate coconuts, papayas, and bananas they found in the bush.[13]

Smiley was unlike any of the other guards. He did not scream at the Americans and did not strike them, but maintained a pleasant disposition and a ready smile as he escorted POWs to and from their work details. At times, he even encouraged McDole to climb the tall trees and knock down coconuts for the men, as long as they ate the fruit far away from camp where his commandant could not see.

Once they successfully connected the water pipes down to the camp, the men in the plumbing crew placed a large storage barrel over their latrines. With water pressure from the pipes, they could now flush the waste from the latrine pits down toward the ocean and into the camp's garbage pile located on the beach below. They did this flushing every three days to help control the smell and the flies that bred disease. Personal hygiene became a priority among the men who had the strongest desires to live. Some even improvised toilet paper by using pieces of heavy brown paper from cement sacks.[14]

Each workday began the same way. Reveille was at 0600, when Japanese guards entered their building, kicking and screaming at the Americans to get them moving to the parade ground outside. There, the prisoners were ordered to count off in Japanese to make sure that no one had escaped overnight. Then they had to perform several minutes of calisthenics to loosen them up for the workday ahead. Mac McDole was irritated by having to stand at attention each morning while the Japanese flag was raised atop the camp's flagpole. He was more agitated by the guards who performed Bushido rituals each morning, saluting their emperor and engaging in mock swordplay.

The Americans soon created nicknames for each of their Japanese guards, both as a source of amusement and as a way to keep track of the more dangerous ones. Chief Signalman Norval Smith and his buddies began calling Captain Kishimoto "Duck" because of his desire to wear rubber boots on the hottest of days. Smith's name for the tall, heavyset supply sergeant with large gold teeth was "Smiling Jack."[15]

Sergeant Billy Ballou and his friends came up with other names. A thin guard with thick eyeglasses was called "Harry Night School" and "Joe College." Another guard who always whistled and gave a hitchhiking salute when hailing an American was known to Ballou as "Whistling Charlie." The more abusive Japanese soldiers who administered the most frequent beatings were known as the "Bull of the Woods" and "Punchy," the latter name chosen for a guard who had once been a boxer. First Class Private Oguri, a chubby man with glasses, spoke enough English to become Kishimoto's interpreter for the Americans. He claimed to have been raised by missionaries, so the prisoners referred to him as "John the Baptist." As time and abuse wore the men down, Oguri would eventually become known as "John the Bastard."[16]

Morning chow on most days was a mess kit of rice, occasionally mixed with *camote* vines. The guards devoured the local potatoes, leaving only the vines for the Americans to eat. Phil Brodsky and his buddies soon dubbed the thin, watery green soup "whistle weed." Joe Barta could hardly stomach the vine soup, and he believed even the prisoners' daily allotment of rice was the poorest quality possible. Barta was almost amused that such a diet was supplemented by a daily vitamin tablet the Japanese provided to keep the prisoners strong enough to work.[17]

Only the men too ill to walk were allowed to stay behind as the work details set out each morning. Smitty and Roy Henderson soon realized that being sick enough to remain behind also meant that they would receive nothing to eat. Food became more important than debilitating rashes or high fevers.

Mac McDole turned into a pack rat, collecting all the boxes that the prisoners' pills came in. Since he was not a smoker, he traded his weekly ration of ten cigarettes for other items he and his buddies could use for their own survival.

Captain Ted Pulos, as the senior American officer, was allowed by the Japanese to deal with any of his own men who got out of line in terms of minor offenses. The prisoners were largely responsible for taking care of their own needs. Marine Private First Class John Warren became the camp barber. One prisoner found a pair of clippers within an abandoned home in Puerto Princesa, and soon Warren was using these to cut hair. He managed to shape other crude barbering tools, including a razor crafted from the steel insole of an old Army boot. The two Army doctors, Captain Harry Hickman and First Lieutenant Carl Mango, were responsible for treating the sick or injured. Mango determined each day whether any man was too sick to perform work details.[18]

Mango, thirty-five, hailed from Erie, Pennsylvania. Having first attended the University of Pittsburgh on a basketball scholarship, he graduated from the University of West Virginia. In 1936, he received his medical degree from Temple School of Medicine, where he was on the swim team. After three years of internship, Mango opened his medical practice in Erie in mid-1939. As calls for war intensified throughout the United States, he volunteered to join the Army Air Force in the fall of 1941. Lieutenant Carl Mango had arrived in the Philippines in November, and his wife, Mae, gave birth to their daughter, Frances Marie Mango, back Stateside in February 1942—one month before her father was seized in Manila and forced on the Bataan Death March.[19]

By August 8, the American prisoners of Camp 10-A completed the remodeling work on their barracks, but there would be no rest. The next day, after morning roll call and calisthenics, the men were loaded onto captured Filipino trucks and driven out of camp. They bounced along nearly two miles of dusty road until they reached the edge of the jungle, overlooking flat land that stretched for some distance down to Caniga-ran Beach on the Sulu Sea. Captain Kishimoto had the Americans line up before him. Taking a spade in hand, he formally broke ground on what was to be the new "three-month project" for his POWs. In response, the Japanese guards shouted with approval.[20]

Kishimoto addressed the men as Private Oguri—"John the Baptist"—interpreted. The prisoners were to clear the area of all trees and underbrush to make a new road. Many who scanned the rough, relatively flat jungle land near the beach were skeptical about what they were being asked to do. They were disappointed to find almost no modern machinery to work with. Each work group was given one ax, one pick, a wheelbarrow, and other hand tools. Removing the island trees proved to be grueling work. Each had to be dug up by the roots, some requiring eight or more men digging and pulling to get the tree down.[21]

Joe Dupont's work party had to cut down some of the larger trees. One group of men would chop the roots with axes while another party used a winch attached to a Japanese army truck to help tug it out of the earth. The fibrous coconut trees were the worst to pull down. Each had hundreds of tough, fibrous roots running through the dirt that the men had to chop before employing the motorized winch. Once the trees were felled, Dupont and dozens of other men hoisted the heavy logs up and hauled them to a pile some distance away. Then they had to fill in the holes. Some of the larger mahogany trees could only be brought down with the use of dynamite.[22]

Captain Kishimoto often rode along on the truck with the prisoners and remained at the airfield site throughout the day to observe the progress. On occasion, he would even chop down a tree to show his POWs how efficiently they should be working. Those in Francis Galligan's detail were putting forth a feeble effort one day when they learned a secret about their camp commandant. Galligan and four men were down in a large hole, standing among the spaghetti-like mass of small roots that had attached a large coconut tree to the soil. The men groaned and pretended to struggle for some time, pushing the stump from the hole. Angry at their halfhearted efforts, Kishimoto removed his waist belt and saber and handed them to a guard. He jumped into the hole, put his shoulder to the stump, and pushed it over.[23]

He climbed out and barked, "Okay, you guys, cut the horseshit!"

One of Galligan's workmates stammered, "You speak English?"

"Naturally," snapped Kishimoto. "And quite well. I graduated from Stanford University."

Workdays went on with little relief. Joe Dupont felt like he was working in a zoo filled with beautiful parrots in red and blue colors with long tail feathers. His comrades were less amused by the countless monkeys that ran along and chattered at them. Dupont laughed as some men became unnerved by the endless shrieks and resorted to throwing rocks at the monkeys, screaming at them to shut up. Other men suffered painful encounters with large scorpions that left nasty red welts where their venomous tails struck skin.[24]

Each workday consisted of at least ten hours of slave labor, chopping trees and clearing brush for the new "road" bed. The only day off was Sunday, or when the occasional serious rainstorm swept the island. The Americans had arrived at Puerto Princesa during its rainy season, which ran from June through September, when monthly rainfall often averaged more than fifteen inches.

McDole, Smitty, and Henderson soon found new friends in privates first class Evan Bunn and Clarence Clough, fellow marines assigned to their work group who slept near them in the barracks. McDole and his buddies decided that Clough and Bunn were trustworthy enough to invite into their survival group.[25]

Bunn, an amateur boxer, and Clough had become best friends upon joining the same Marine platoon in 1940. The former machine-gun crew, captured on Corregidor, did time in the Cabanatuan camp before volunteering for the Palawan detail. Both men were happy to be part of their new clique. The five would sit on the veranda outside their barracks in the evening to share stories of home. Clough talked about family life back in rural Wisconsin and learned of girlfriends his buddies had dated. Most of their talk ended up revolving around food.[26]

Together, they believed they could survive Palawan by relying upon their shared pilfering. The men returned to their camp compound each evening, exhausted after long hours of toiling in the sun and high humidity. They were making progress on the jungle undergrowth, but few still believed they were clearing the way for a road. Soon they came to realize they were actually preparing for a new airfield for the use of the Japanese air force.

BRUCE ELLIOTT HAD not relinquished his desire to escape. Less than two weeks earlier, the sailor had decided not to jump ship on the island of Culion to join the leper colony. Two days into the jungle airfield construction project, he made up his mind to escape from Palawan. The barbed wire fencing that would encircle the camp had not yet been completed, and Elliott had learned how to scale a stone wall that partially surrounded the compound by leaning a wooden plank against it. He had seen some Filipino detainees who were forced to do labor around the camp scurry up a twelve-foot pole and climb over the wall to spend time with their families during the night.[27]

One evening soon after arriving at the constabulary, Elliott scaled the wall during a heavy rainstorm, entered the local Catholic church, located the priest, and told him that he was escaping. The priest gave Elliott a small map of the Philippines, a compass, and an alarm clock. Elliott climbed back into the barracks and began talking up his getaway plans with other prisoners. Lieutenant Janson dismissed the idea, telling Elliott there was no way they could make it. At first, seven men agreed to do it, but when the time came, only five joined in the escape.

At 2230 on August 10, Bruce Elliott went over the compound wall in the company of two other Navy prisoners and three marines: Seaman First Class Robert Morris "Bobby" Hodges from the USS *Genesee*; Seaman First Class Robert William Kellam, a coxswain from the 16th Naval District; Private First Class George Dorrell Davis from M Company,

3rd Battalion, 4th Marine Regiment; Private Buddy Henderson, a Texan from the 4th Marine Regiment; and Corporal Sidney Thomas Wright from Headquarters Company, 3rd Battalion, 4th Marine Regiment. Wright, a lanky six-foot former machine-gun operator with a heavy Texas drawl, had been among the first to join Elliott's escape team.[28]

Cloud cover and a scant guard detail afforded the men the chance to bound onto a small trail leading down the sixty-foot cliffs on the south side of their camp to the beach below. They scrambled more than a mile along the narrow, rocky beach until they found an abandoned Filipino *banca*, a long, slender outrigger-type canoe. The men grabbed some lumber to use as paddles and pushed out into Puerto Princesa Bay, heading south in the general direction of Australia. Their twelve-foot boat had a large sail and a tattered stabilizing rig beyond its side, but the hull leaked like a sieve, requiring constant bailing. Wright and Elliott took turns with others covering the hole with their feet while using coconut shells as buckets as they paddled and sailed all night. Just outside of Puerto Princesa Bay, they turned into a swamp before dawn, hiding themselves and their *banca* beneath foliage.[29]

The next morning, the six men nervously watched as a Japanese patrol boat searched along the coast. It finally returned to port, but they waited until dark to resume their rowing. The escape party spent the next three days rowing their *banca* along the coast within sight of shore. By dawn of August 14, they had reached the settlement of Brooke's Point, about sixty miles south of Camp 10-A. As they staggered up onto the beach, Wright noticed a cluster of Filipino natives closing in. They quickly showed their friendly intentions, and one of them, Ben Aroose, led the escapees nine miles uphill to the house of Thomas H. "Harry" Edwards, an American who lived in splendid, sultanlike style.

Edwards, a schoolteacher and staunch Christian, had come to the Philippines after the Spanish-American War and was now the largest landowner in Brooke's Point, the second-largest town on Palawan after Puerto Princesa. His wife, Rosario, was a Muslim from Mindanao, and together they had carved out a comfortable lifestyle once he retired from teaching. The Edwardses owned a sprawling coconut plantation between Brooke's Point and the inland mountains, as well as a sawmill, a logging operation, and other businesses. Edwards had grown successful enough to send his oldest children off to college in the United States. Two of his daughters still lived with the family in the settlement of Macagua, located in the foothills eight miles up from the coast.[30]

Harry and Rosario Edwards, sympathetic to the plight of the escapees, welcomed them into their bamboo-and-thatched-roof evacuation home in the mountains. The men were in need of rest, and Bruce Elliott was fighting off a nasty bout of malaria by the time he reached Brooke's Point. He was now bedridden, flat on his back. Edwards gave him yellow Atabrine tablets, bitter-tasting synthetic quinine pills, to quell the malaria, along with ample food and drink. After several months of hard living as POWs, the men had little problem staying with the local family for a few weeks.

An efficient underground guerrilla network operated by Filipino residents received word of their escape. Two civilian brothers, Paul and Alfred Cobb, who operated with the northern guerrillas of Palawan, sent word to the escapees that they should journey north to join their band of rebels. As August slipped into early September, the men prepared themselves for their next move. The locals assured them that the Japanese had so far not ventured this far south. Several of the men began collaborating with the local guerrillas, and even managed to obtain rifles for themselves.[31]

Elliott noted that Bob Kellam minded the idle time the least. He had quickly become smitten with one of Harry Edwards's attractive daughters.

5

PALAWAN'S
"FIGHTING ONE THOUSAND"

T HE MORNING ROLL call on August 11 came up six Americans short. The fact that Captain Kishimoto was so upset helped Ensign Bob Russell to better endure standing at attention all day in camp. The commandant ranted, telling them that "honorable" prisoners would never treat their honorable captors in such a way. George Burlage tried to suppress his pleasure at seeing Kishimoto both hurt by the actions of the escapees and so mad that his shouting at times became incoherent.[1]

Some prisoners heard later from their guards that Kishimoto wired Manila to ask his superiors what actions he should take. The answer was to restrict the POWs to camp and cut their rations by two-thirds, so for the next three days, each prisoner received only one mess kit of rice per day. Armed guards now patrolled both inside and outside of the barbed wire, both day and night. Airfield work ceased, and no one was allowed outside the wire for any reason. As his shriveling stomach churned, Mac McDole spent his time lying about the barracks, dreaming of the pancake breakfasts he and his sisters used to enjoy in civilian life.[2]

The guards remained on edge about the escape, as Yeoman First Class Hubert Dwight Hough found out the hard way on the afternoon of August 11. The twenty-two-year-old Iowa native was passing near the camp's main gate when he failed to notice a guard who expected him to salute. The Japanese soldier attacked with fury and knocked Hough completely out cold. The beating reopened an older wound on the yeoman's head, and he was bleeding heavily as he was assisted to the sick bay within the prisoner barracks so Captain Harry Hickman, the senior Army doctor, could stitch him up. Hough was still out of commission the next day when a Japanese major from Manila paid a visit to the camp. The officer advised Hough not to work in the field while recovering from his wound, but asked him to assist in other ways.[3]

Hough had nearly four years in the Navy when he was taken prisoner at Corregidor. He was an experienced yeoman who knew his way around a typewriter, so the Japanese put him to work as their camp clerk to assist the interpreters, maintain muster rolls of American prisoners, and type out various documents. Hough found it easier to maintain his own secret records in the months ahead with less suspicion. For some time, he had been keeping an abbreviated personal diary in a tiny black leather Japanese journal booklet.

The visiting Japanese officer made it clear that the Americans were to work diligently on the new airfield project. "He told us that anybody that got sick and was not able to work would be sent back to Manila," Hough noted in his diary. "And this airfield was going to be built over our dead bodies."[4]

AFTER THREE DAYS on restrictions, the Americans were lined up on the parade grounds. Captain Kishimoto expressed his ire with the disrespect his escape-minded prisoners were showing him. "I can put you in chains and take you back to the field, and you can work in chains," he scolded. "Or I can order my men to shoot you right here and now, or I can forget about it." The commandant concluded his tirade with the stern warning, "I'm going to give you one more chance."[5]

Airfield work resumed that day—chopping gnarly roots, breaking up rocky soil, shouldering downed tree trunks, all under an unforgiving sky. Chief Machinist's Mate Henry Henderson Jr., who had served on the submarine tender USS *Otus* before his capture, described the jungle-clearing work in his own forbidden diary. "As a result of this hard labor, our hands were bloody pulps from using the *juji* (pick ax) [*sic*] and the *impi* (shovel)," he wrote. "We worked almost naked in this boiling hot sun. We were so weak, it was almost impossible to work."[6]

Puerto Princesa generally received less rain than other regions of the long island, and each day the heat grew intense. In mid-August, the prisoners received precautionary shots against typhoid and cholera, but little to prevent them from contracting malaria. Smitty learned to supplement his intake by stealing the abundant mangoes, papayas, bananas, and coconuts, but doing so carried a severe penalty if he was caught smuggling the fruit back into camp.

Some guards allowed the men to eat what they found at their work site. Everything was fair game, from fruit to island animals such as lizards, snakes, birds, and even monkeys. Some simply could not stomach the sight of a small primate, its skin similar to a human baby, roasting over a fire. Snakes proved to be a big concern, particularly the black cobras occasionally encountered while clearing mahogany trees among the large ant mounds. Marine Bill Kerr was surprised that no American POW was ever bitten by a deadly snake, as any killed by a prisoner had to be delivered to one particular Japanese guard who thrived on eating cobra hearts.[7] On one occasion, Private First Class Heraclio Arispe awoke his barrack mates, screaming like a crazy man. A ten-foot python had slithered in through an opening and slid across Arispe. Several starving prisoners, not about to waste anything, found the python to be quite filling.[8]

THE TEMPTATION TO escape was too strong for some men to resist. Bruce Elliott and his five comrades had disappeared eighteen days earlier, and although little was known of their fate, other prisoners contemplated making their own break. The next two men to do so were Seaman First Class Charles Oscar Watkins and Aviation Ordnanceman Third Class Jopaul "Joe" Little.

Months of scant rations had dropped his body weight to 120 pounds, but five-foot-eight Watkins still maintained a ready smile beneath his shaggy mass of curly black hair. At age twenty, he had witnessed more cruelty at Corregidor and Cabanatuan than others would see in a lifetime. He and Charlie Watkins, friends since serving together prewar in PBY Catalina flying boat squadron VP-102, plotted busting out of the Puerto Princesa camp after Elliott's group did so with success. Their first attempt to slip out at night was foiled by alert guards, and they narrowly made it back to their beds.[9]

Watkins and Little then decided against escaping at night again since the Americans who failed to report them would be held accountable. Little noticed the Japanese counted the POWs at morning roll call, at chow time, and when they climbed off their trucks to begin work at the airfield. The best time to flee would be after the count at the noontime lunch break. After that, the POWs would not be counted again until work ended.[10]

On August 28, the right opportunity arose after lunch, when Little spotted three truckloads of guards leave the airfield to sell rice to the locals. As he and Little chopped jungle growth with machetes, Watkins moved ahead of the cutting crew to look for guards stationed on the perimeter of their work area. He found none. The two men slipped into the dense brush with only their machetes and the clothes on their backs. They moved swiftly through the jungle for hours, not stopping until 1730, when they knew the guards would conduct a prisoner count and find that two men were missing. They eased into a marshy swamp, crawled into a thickly wooded high spot, and remained hidden under a heavy rainstorm for the next ninety minutes. Then they set out hiking through the moonless night, stumbling through underbrush until the moon appeared to illuminate a nearby path.

Watkins and Little followed trails until they encountered a road around 0400 on August 29. Reasoning that they were far enough away from Puerto Princesa that they would not encounter Japanese soldiers, they walked along the road for several miles and at daybreak slipped back into the jungle. Just inside, the escapees stumbled across a Filipino evacuation camp. As one of the locals poked his head out of his hut, Little inquired, "Hey, Joe. How's about some chow? We're hungry."[11]

The Filipino offered to take them to Major Pedro Manigque, the senior commander of all Palawan guerrilla outfits. Watkins and Little were soon introduced to Manigque, a former schoolteacher and a member of the Philippine Constabulary who had not surrendered to the Japanese. He led the Americans deeper into the jungle to a secluded place near a small creek and kept them hidden for the next eleven days, waiting until the search for them cooled down.

Manigque next led them to another local who was to help take them to the northern end of Palawan in a sailboat. They found that the man remained drunk for most of the day, and failed to procure the boat. He did, however, convince Little, who had hoped to move south, that they would be in greater danger there from the Moros, an aggressive tribe of Muslim natives.

Radio communication with other islands was primitive during 1942, and efforts to raise an American base for rescue met with no luck. They soon discovered an old motor launch, but were unable to obtain fuel for the engine or a generator to charge the burned-out battery. They finally acquired a small boat and paddled nearly twenty-five miles during the night until they reached the village of Tanabag, where they lived for a week with five Philippine Constabulary soldiers. The two American escapees were moved from village to village, staying about five weeks at Rizal near Brooke's Point. Their diet consisted mainly of rice, although some of the soldiers were able to kill cattle and other meat—including monkeys on three occasions—with their rifles.[12]

Watkins and Little were soon introduced to brothers Paul and Alfred Cobb, the northern guerrilla leaders who had traveled down to assist them. The two Americans remained free and on the run into late 1942, moving into the northern reaches of the island at the same time that six other Camp 10-A escapees were also on the lam. Their fates were yet to be determined, but the strong resistance network in place on Palawan greatly increased their odds of survival.[13]

FAMILIES BY THE names of Mendoza, Clark, Mayor, Loudon, and Edwards would assist both the prisoners who remained under Japanese captivity and those crafty few who had already busted out.

Dr. Higinio Acosta Mendoza was one of the earliest leaders of the island's guerrilla network. Born in Puerto Princesa in 1898, Mendoza traveled to the United States during the 1920s for his schooling and attended the University of Iowa. He returned to the Philippines with the degree of Doctor of Medicine and ran a successful practice until 1931, when he was persuaded to run for governor of Palawan. After he was reelected in 1934, his governorship was marked by civic improvement projects such as extending roads, installing a water system in Puerto Princesa, planting trees along the roads, and establishing a botanical garden.[14]

Once the Japanese occupied Puerto Princesa, Mendoza moved his wife, Triny, and their four children to a safer area on a mountainside between the towns of Babuyan and Tanabag. As the war progressed, Mendoza wasted little time in establishing a guerrilla movement, with his headquarters located in the coastal town of Tinitian. His family holed up farther inland at a place called Jolo near a local river while his resistance movement grew as the people of Palawan tired of their own mistreatment by the occupying Japanese army.[15]

Law and order in the Philippine Islands had been maintained since 1901 by the Philippine Constabulary, a police force that replaced the former Spanish Guardia Civil. Following the Japanese invasion, regular PC soldiers helped form the nucleus of the guerrilla movement. Mendoza had first organized a guerrilla unit in Puerto Princesa on February 9, 1942—three months before the Japanese even invaded Palawan. Pro-Allied sentiment was strong, and it was later estimated that during the war as many as 1,154 Filipino guerrillas worked against the Japanese on the island. Those in the underground network would proudly refer to themselves as "Palawan's Fighting One Thousand."[16]

Other pioneers in the Palawan guerrilla network were influential businessman Thomas F. Loudon and his extended family. A resident of the island for nearly four decades, Loudon was well-known throughout the area. During the early 1900s, he had owned and managed the Del-awan Bay Company in the settlement of Balabac, where he lived with his family on company property where his corporation operated a store. Tragedy befell the Loudon family on July 18, 1913, when a large group of Moros attacked the family home with lances and *barongs*, Moro fighting knives.[17] Loudon managed to escape to find help, but upon his return, he found his home ransacked and his wife and infant daughter murdered, along with six others. By 1918, he had relocated his business to Bugsuk Island, where his family resided at the beginning of the hostilities with Japan in World War II.[18]

Two of Loudon's daughters had been away in Manila when their mother and sibling were murdered in 1913. The oldest, Mary Loudon, went to the United States for school during the 1920s. There, she met another Filipino native named Nazario Benito Mayor—born in 1901 on Robalon Island off Palawan—who was studying at the University of Kansas. Mary and Nazario were married in 1928 after returning to her father's home on Bugsuk Island, where the Mayors began raising a large family while Nazario worked with his father-in-law in the lumber business. Thomas Loudon happened to be in Manila on business when the Japanese invaded, and he was soon captured. The Japanese suspected him of aiding the new guerrilla movement on the islands, and Loudon would be held under arrest away from his family for the next three years.

Nazario Mayor evaded capture in Manila and made his way back to his family at Bugsuk Island by boat. He had good reason to hate the Japanese for holding his father-in-law prisoner and for the general abuse being rained upon the Filipino people. Nazario thus became involved with the Palawan guerrilla movement early in 1942, leaving Mary with their children. Robert, their oldest son, born in Puerto Princesa in 1930, became the man of the house at age twelve, left to help provide for his siblings.

Mayor's company operated in the Brooke's Point district. Other regional units, inspired by the direction of Dr. Mendoza, were in operation throughout Palawan by the time the first six Americans escaped from the Puerto Princesa camp in August 1942. Those in Mendoza's unit had moved between several villages during the early months of the war, but eventually established themselves at Tinitian, where he set up his permanent headquarters.[19]

The Loudon, Mendoza, and Mayor families sacrificed plenty as the war played out in the Philippines. Their names, in time, would be ones that some Americans held on Palawan would never forget.

"WE GOT THE THIRD AND FOURTH DEGREE"

T HE DISAPPEARANCE OF Charlie Watkins and Joe Little was finally realized shortly after airfield construction work ceased at 1600. Once again, Captain Kishimoto flew into a rage. For the second time in less than three weeks, his reputation was tarnished by POWs escaping under his charge. From the original roster of 346 Camp 10-A prisoners, the number had already dwindled to 338. Eight Americans were simply gone, vanished into the jungles of Palawan.

Kishimoto again held the remaining prisoners in the compound for three days, their rations cut by two-thirds. Now the daily allotment of food was a half small loaf of bread with a half cup of beans for breakfast, and a half ration of rice and a half cup of soup for supper. Over those three days, the prisoners were vaccinated for smallpox as rumors swirled as to what had become of Watkins and Little. Sometime later, after the men were allowed to return to their construction work, a Filipino crept close enough to the airfield site to whisper to some Americans that their two comrades were being led through the jungle with the assistance of a Filipino guide.[1]

For the time being, the Americans could only offer prayers that Watkins and Little would continue to avoid recapture. On August 30,

Kishimoto assembled his prisoners and lectured them on the disloyal tendencies they were displaying to his guards. "I'm left with three ways of treating you men," the commandant barked. "We can continue to let you work as you are. Or you can work with chains on your legs. Or you can stay in your barracks and grow thin."

At length, Kishimoto announced that work would soon recommence under new restrictions: All Americans would form into ten-man groups, each monitored by a Japanese guard. Any man who escaped would bring severe consequences to those he left behind. Never mind that most men were too weak from malnutrition to give serious thought to taking flight.[2]

The following day, the POWs returned to the airfield. September passed as a seemingly endless string of days under a scorching sun, hundreds of bone-thin men laboring with picks, shovels, and axes to clear coconut, mahogany, and kamagong trees that towered above the wicked undergrowth. The Americans were given more inoculations to prevent tropical ailments, but within two weeks, many had fallen seriously ill with various infections.

The absence of the eight escapees stifled the mood in camp as much as the intense heat and the dust. Tensions between the prisoners and their guards reached new heights as the Japanese became even more abusive, lashing out at their captives for the slightest transgression. Mac McDole found it difficult to maintain his short temper—his aggressive nature forbade him from being passive to abuse. On one occasion, he was chopping down a coconut tree when a guard barked orders to him in Japanese. Mac, having no idea what was being said, simply muttered, "Okay."[3] The guard's heavy club struck him squarely in the mouth. Furious, he stumbled back to his feet with a loose tooth and a mouthful of blood, and received a lecture from Smitty about maintaining his calm.

But calm just wasn't a part of Mac's character. He had grown up a child of the Great Depression, an era in which boys learned from an early age that life was tough even under the best of circumstances. His father was a sign painter by trade, forced to shuffle his family from

Nebraska to Texas to California to Colorado, and then back to Nebraska, chasing a paycheck. The McDoles eventually settled for good in
Iowa, where Glenn became a star athlete on both his high school football
and basketball teams. Standing five foot ten and weighing in at 185
pounds when he enlisted in the Corps, Mac was eager to become an
Iowa Highway Safety Patrol officer once he completed his service with
the Marines.[4]

Mac knew he could not strike back at the Japanese, but he could at
least rebel in other ways. He became lazy, picking up half shovels of dirt
and aimlessly scattering them around. Smitty warned him during one
listless routine that an angry guard was approaching, but Mac just
smiled and kept up his slow pace. The guard smashed both their heads
with his club, their skulls spared serious injury only by the pith helmets
they wore. Despite the blow, McDole enjoyed seeing the guard so riled
up, and it was far from the last time he and Smitty would be beaten for
his lackluster efforts.

Determined to maintain progress on the airstrip, Captain Kishimoto
called for additional American prisoners to replace those who had escaped or fallen ill. The first new group of one hundred prisoners arrived
on October 6, 1942, nine weeks after the original POWs had arrived.
The total American population at Camp 10-A now stood at 438, but
injury, illness, and death would ensure that the roster would never sur-
pass this figure.

The new arrivals included ninety-eight enlisted men and two officers,
Captain Fred Tobias Bruni of the U.S. Army and Lieutenant (junior
grade) Francis Xavier Golden. Heavyset, with oval-framed glasses that
sat on his rounded face, Bruni was a reservist from Wisconsin who had
previously been in command of the Headquarters Company of the
192nd Tank Battalion. Frank Golden, a thirty-six-year-old from Rich-
mond, Virginia, had previously worked for the U.S. Alcohol Tax Unit
of the Bureau of Internal Revenue before going into the Navy. Captain
Bruni, a survivor of the Bataan Death March, had been a GM assembly
plant foreman in his previous civilian life. Ensign Bob Russell doubted

Bruni's rough, crude style would mix well with the restrained nature of Captain Ted Pulos, the senior American officer at Puerto Princesa.[5]

Private First Class Ernie Koblos, a new arrival on Palawan, had spent the previous four months suffering in the overcrowded Cabanatuan prison camp on Luzon. The twenty-four-year-old from Chicago had been enamored with the islands upon first arriving in January 1940. "I sure like it here in the Philippines," he wrote to his father. "I want to make it my home."[6] Finding that his monthly pay of twenty-one dollars did not go far, he soon volunteered for higher-paying service aboard the Army mine planter SS *Harrison*, working in the engine room as a second oiler. Eventually he returned to artillery duty at Fort Mills, until the Japanese invasion ruined his stint in paradise.

Herded now into the barracks at Puerto Princesa, he was offered neither bedding nor a change of clothes. No soap was issued to him, and there would be no regular baths. His shoes long since confiscated, he would be forced to work barefoot. In the months ahead, he would sleep on the wooden floor in the same tattered rags he had arrived in.[7]

Still, his desire to exit the hell of Cabanatuan had been intense, a desire shared by Private First Class Gene Nielsen. Nielsen had seen enough death there that the decision to volunteer for other duty was a simple one. In this new Puerto Princesa camp, he was assigned to a ten-man work team, toiling at removing jungle undergrowth one day and bringing down coconut trees the next. The tools were crude and clumsy, the conditions threatening at all times, and he quickly learned which guards were the meanest. If a man was caught resting, a Japanese soldier would swing a wooden club into his kidneys, slam the backs of his legs, or cuff his skull with enough force to drop him to the dirt.[8]

Nielsen had learned survival at an early age. His father passed away when he was twelve, leaving his family to struggle through the hungry years of the Great Depression. Like many young men, he turned to the Civilian Conservation Corps for a paycheck, serving on projects in Utah before joining the Army in January 1941. He chose the Philippines as his assignment, but his hopes of fulfilling his military service amid sea breezes and swaying palms ended at the bloody last stand on Corregidor, where he served as a range setter on Crockett Battery until his capture.

From seasoned Palawan prisoners, he learned that smuggling fruit back into camp was forbidden. He found it easy enough to grab a coconut or banana by asking a guard for a break to go defecate in the jungle, away from the runway work. Still, he could not resist the urge to tuck a few bananas under his shirt one evening to take back to his barracks. Alert guards spotted the unusual bulge and made Nielsen stand with his arms raised over his head while a pair of Japanese soldiers thrashed him with wooden pick handles. He struggled to keep his footing as crushing blows rained down on his buttocks, legs, and lower back. Told he would receive fifty licks, he made it through several dozen before his legs finally buckled. To his chagrin, the guards were not satisfied. They screamed and kicked at him until he struggled back to his feet for the beating to continue.[9]

Nielsen reported to sick bay the next morning with black welts covering his lower body. Doc Mango advised him not to show his injuries to anyone. Not wanting to be seen as sympathetic in the eyes of the Japanese by letting a man stay in with only minor injuries, Mango gave Nielsen only one day off before he sent the bruised and bloodied soldier back to the work zone.

Nielsen's punishment may have seemed minor next to that of Army Private Richard McClellan. Caught smuggling fruit as he returned to camp, he was slapped around by a guard. He assumed the "forbidden fruit" incident was over, but at roll call the next morning, Kishimoto approached the ranking American officer, Captain Pulos, demanding to know McClellan's name. The Japanese insisted on the execution of Private McClellan, but Pulos intervened on his behalf. Instead, the American was tied to a flagpole, his feet lashed to the base and his hands secured behind his back with rope. After he had endured twelve hours on the pole without food or water under the blistering hot sun, McClellan's feet were so swollen that they took two days to return to normal.[10]

Abuse and injuries piled up during October. One Japanese corporal nicknamed "Mushmouth"—a man of small stature with an ugly scar on his temple—delighted in beating prisoners for no reason at all. Mushmouth took his aggressions out late one afternoon with a two-by-four on three Americans who were digging out a tree stump. Sergeant Gerald Skripsky crumpled from a blow to his forehead that left a permanent scar above his right eye. Private First Class Joseph Viterna suffered a broken arm, and Mushmouth rendered Navy prisoner Francis Parrish unconscious with a blow to the head.[11]

By late October, Doc Mango and Captain Hickman had several dozen men on their sick bay list, deemed too ill to work. Many suffered from malaria, convulsing with teeth-chattering chills or sweating profusely from spiking fevers. The dysentery victims hunched over the fly-infested straddle ditches as their bowels expelled any food they ate long before their bodies could process any life-sustaining nutrients. Mango fashioned a sling for Staff Sergeant Raymond Mullins, whose arm had been broken by a Japanese guard he was arguing with about whether American forces in the Pacific were defeated. Mullins struggled to shovel with only one arm the next day, but he refused to back down when the same guard tried provoking him again about America's impending downfall.[12]

On October 26, the Japanese shipped twenty-one of the sickest enlisted men back to Manila on a transport ship while Sergeant Mullins, broken arm and all, stayed with the remaining 417 Americans on Palawan. One of the men returned to Bilibid Prison had fallen under suspicion of his fellow prisoners for being too friendly with some of the guards. They nicknamed him "Boots" because of the black pair he was suspiciously allowed to wear while most others worked barefoot.

McDole and Smitty had become curious when they saw Boots stuff a scribbled note into one of his prized boots. Days later, they confronted him at the airfield site when he trudged into the brush to relieve himself. Mac knocked him to the ground and held him while Smitty retrieved the slip of paper. On it was a message written in Japanese script. In the barracks that night, Mac and Smitty found a prisoner who could decipher the language well enough to determine the note was a declaration that Boots would give up his American citizenship if he could join the Japanese army. Guards had to break up a scuffle in the compound yard after Mac and Smitty confronted the traitor. When Captain Kishimoto learned of the note, he declared his disgust for anyone who turned his back on his own country, and he put Boots on the first outgoing ship to Bilibid.[13]

The unspoken code among prisoners was that collaborating with the enemy was unacceptable. Communication with the Filipinos, though, was a different matter. Mac McDole encountered his first friendly guerrilla while on a jungle bathroom break and was badly startled when a voice called out, "Hey, Joe. Don't look. I leave something for you!"[14] The man was gone before McDole could spot him, but he found a piece of bread placed nearby on a coral rock. Other prisoners had similar initial encounters, and they learned in time that the local guerrilla company had been spying on them from the moment they first arrived. McDole and others who communicated with the underground network picked up scraps of information on the war's progress: In June, the U.S. Navy had won a major victory against the Japanese during the Battle of Midway, and their enemy had been suffering in the Solomon Islands since the 1st Marine Division had landed on Guadalcanal and Tulagi.

The Americans had little understanding of how deeply the Palaweños despised the Japanese soldiers, but the thought of others sneaking about the jungle to deliver food and outside intelligence gave them reason to be optimistic. Gene Nielsen found little else to appreciate. The men were forced to work on Thanksgiving Day, and the food provided left little to be thankful for. Nielsen learned to stomach the moldy, mushy rice and ignore the ever-present worms, which were white with black heads about the size of a kernel of rice.

Two meals stood out from the rest. The first was a creation of Nielsen's group when they managed to scrounge discarded cabbage from the trash to add to their rice. Beto Pacheco felt little better than a slopped hog as he gathered scraps from the dirt, but he did so in order to add calories to his shrinking frame. Gene's second-favorite meal came from the remnants of a caribou slaughtered by the Japanese. Prisoners were allowed to bust up the bones with sledgehammers on a chopping block. The bone fragments contained very little meat, but once they were boiled, and with salt added, the slight flavor they contained seemed to be a delicacy.[15]

MANY PRISONERS FORMED "survival groups" for mutual support, looking out for another member if he became ill and sharing contraband goods. Survival group members also covered for one another when someone slipped up with the guards.

Smitty narrowly escaped severe punishment thanks to his group's quick thinking. The tall, lean Texan, now sporting a long beard after months of neglect, had grown particularly jumpy, and his trouble started when some buddies learned that he could be badly startled if someone "goosed" his rear from behind. Another American somehow managed to convince a young Japanese guard to sneak behind Smitty and grab his rear end. The guard fell for the joke and seized Smitty's hind end when he was looking away. The startled prisoner jumped high in the air, spun around, and instinctively swung a strong punch toward the jokester.[16]

Before he realized what he had done, Smitty's fist connected with the guard's jaw and knocked him cold. Horrified, several prisoners grabbed Smitty, hauled him into the barracks, found camp barber John Warren, and told him that Smitty would probably be killed if they could not disguise him. Warren quickly dry-shaved his beard with his crude razor and prisoners smeared mud on his pale, white face to further mask his looks.

As expected, the humiliated guard soon appeared with other soldiers to find the man who had punched him. Smitty's new face helped him survive the search, but the guard was not through. He waited at the camp gate the next morning and every morning thereafter, looking for Smitty as columns of POWs were marched out to work. Fortunately, camp doctor Carl Mango put him on the sick list for an extended period, keeping him covered with sheets near other critically ill patients until some time had passed. Smitty was fortunate: The "goosing" joke could well have cost him his life. One prisoner, out of fear that everyone else would be punished, threatened to turn him in as the guilty party. These thoughts were quickly dispelled when Navy Chief Petty Officer Theodore McNally pulled a small knife from his mess kit, pressed it to the prisoner's throat, and warned him that if Smitty was ever found out, he would personally kill the snitch.

Doc Mango earned Smitty's top respect with his action in this case. Other prisoners came to admire Mango for a variety of reasons, not just because of his medical training. He was not opposed to physically putting an end to trouble when necessary. One incident witnessed by many happened when a young marine, Private First Class Frederick Lutz, decided he was unable to work. Mango refused to put him on the sick list, and Lutz challenged the Army doctor to a fight. Mango initially declined to fight a fellow American, but Lutz came after him. They squared off, and Mango laid out his opponent in twenty seconds.[17] The marines were stunned to see one of their own decked by a single hard right punch to the head. To his credit, Lutz picked himself up, shook hands, and made peace with the doctor. The two thereafter understood each other well, and no further disagreements arose regarding Mango's authority over the sick list.

Gene Nielsen considered Mango the bravest and most caring man in camp. The doctor became a favorite among the enlisted men because he was willing to stand up to both Japanese officers and prison guards. Nielsen believed even the Japanese respected Mango to a certain degree for his unflinching resolve.

Yet survival groups and Doc Mango could not prevent abuse. Mac McDole continued his slow work routine, tempting his guards to beat him for it. As he was picking up shovels of dirt one afternoon and slowly shaking them back onto the same ground, a Japanese soldier approached, tapping a club in his hand. Mac couldn't have cared less—this had happened before. He continued screwing around until the guard smashed the wooden bat across the top of his pith helmet, sending him to his knees.[18]

"Ya didn't hurt me, you son of a bitch!" Mac growled as he pulled himself up.

Again the guard swung his club, slamming it into the side of Mac's head. This time he fell to the ground, where he lay dazed for a moment. But he brushed himself off, stood to glare at the guard, and said defiantly, "Ya still didn't hurt me, you son of a bitch!"

Smitty was shocked when the guard just shook his head and walked away. He warned his buddy that such actions were going to get him killed, but McDole would continue to draw the ire of his guards in the future by slacking off on the job. On another occasion, he was attacked for accidentally hitting Evan Bunn's hand with a sledgehammer. Bunn was spurting blood from his wound, but he could not control his own laughter as a guard beat McDole for apparently removing Bunn's thumb with the blow. After Bunn explained that his thumb had been lost long ago, the guard became so angry that he refused to let him return to camp for the rest of the day to have his hand treated.[19]

Physical pain was something marines like Mac McDole and Evan Bunn could handle, but what truly hurt McDole was the theft of his high school ring. He lost it for a while in the barracks, then discovered it jammed between two floorboards near his blanket. He was so happy to see this relic from home again that he fell asleep with it on his finger that night and forgot all about it until a Japanese guard spotted it at the airfield the next day. The man demanded the ring, but Mac pretended it was stuck and could not be removed. Only when the guard threatened to slice off the finger with his bayonet did Mac angrily hand it over. He was left feeling bitter with himself. Someone had stolen his small Bible weeks before. Now his last material possession from Iowa was gone too.[20]

Such losses only added to Mac's desire to piss off his guards, and he was not alone. George Burlage did anything he could to slow the progress of Japanese work details. He was not blatantly defiant like McDole but always made sure that the men in his party fell a bit short of their goal. Burlage had long since recognized the reality of the situation: *If we ever make our quota, they're just going to give us a bigger one the next day.*[21]

KEMPEI TAI.

It was the name of a special Japanese military police unit the American prisoners learned to fear. Based in Manila, the Kempei Tai was first assigned to send a small unit of its men to Palawan Island in October 1942. The group had wide authority to handle any problems it encountered—from Filipino guerrilla resistance to American prisoner insubordination—with whatever means necessary.

The small Kempei Tai force arriving at Puerto Princesa in October was commanded by Sublieutenant Tadayoshi Watanabe. He arrived on a transport ship with eight subordinates: sergeant majors Ogura and Shiro Isono; sergeants Susumu Kato, Zentaro Sawada, Munekazu Miyahara, and Tatsuo Nakaya; corporals Yukihiko Kuroiwa and Takeo Kusumoto; interpreter Kintoku Uehara; and a cook, Yoshikatsu Ito.[22]

Sergeant Major Isono was unimpressed by his new assignment. The largely abandoned capital city appeared to be a desolate place lacking all facilities for recreation. His commander, Lieutenant Watanabe, felt the small population at Puerto Princesa was meaningless, but his military police unit nonetheless set up station in an abandoned two-story concrete brig located near the entrance to the American POW compound.[23]

Commandant Kishimoto could now hand over the punishment of his Camp 10-A prisoners to the new military police, and the Americans found the Kempei Tai unit only too happy to oblige. The first challenge for Lieutenant Watanabe's men came soon after their arrival, when Captain Kishimoto learned some of his charges were stealing from the camp kitchen. Camp clerk Hubert Hough noted in his diary that November 8 was the date the "cornbeef deal" started. While the POWs were at work at the airfield, guards conducted a search of their barracks and emerged with cans of purloined corned beef. Hough, Private Bill Bragg, and another prisoner were hauled off to the Kempei Tai brig that evening. They were quizzed in broken English by Senior Private Oguri, the interpreter known to them as "John the Baptist." Watanabe was dissatisfied with their answers. "We got the third and fourth degree," Hough wrote of his beatings.[24]

Hough's trio was determined to be unaware of the identity of the canned goods thieves, and they were released the following morning into the care of Doc Mango for treatment of their fresh interrogation wounds. The investigation was only just beginning. Boatswain's Mate First Class Charlie Weston was also thrown into the brig under suspicion of stealing the corned beef. Weston and marine Carmen Dimeo had been on KP duty during the week of the thefts. Dimeo had actually been caught in the act of stealing by mess sergeant Suzuki, but he was pretty well liked by the Japanese and managed to talk his way out of the tricky situation. Weston had no such luck: He spent three days in the Kempei Tai brig without food, a punishment given in an attempt to make him confess.[25]

During that time, the search for more stolen goods intensified. Guards ransacked the prisoner barracks and soon found a large cache of the canned meat hidden below the floor of Company A. Marine Neal Cleere was angry, pointing out that the food supposedly stolen was actually Red Cross articles sent for the use of American prisoners of war. Nevertheless, Lieutenant Watanabe had the entire company of men stand at attention for hours until someone would admit to the theft. It was 2100 before six men finally stepped forward and accepted the blame to protect their companions.[26]

The rest of Company A was dismissed to the barracks while the guilty were thrown into the brig with Charlie Weston. Those joining him were four sailors and two marines, each fed only one salty rice ball per day, punishment designed to make them even thirstier.

Private First Class Jimmy Barna, a marine from Detroit, was also detained for making contact with Filipino guerrillas while working on the airfield. Captain Kishimoto learned that some of the prisoners had found an abandoned shack in the jungle near their work site and were placing notes and even money in an empty can. A Filipino sneaked into the shack each day to retrieve what the prisoners had hidden; in return, he left food or information. In mid-November, as the Japanese were investigating the stolen-food issue, the Filipino left a note in the shack saying that the Japanese were watching him and that he would no longer be able to help for fear of his family members' lives. Barna, seeking more information, left another note asking for the numbers of Japanese on the island and their locations. Guards found the note on November 18 and informed Kishimoto.[27]

The Palawan camp commandant decided to let the Kempei Tai make an example of these seven Americans. It was Sunday, a day when the other prisoners were off work and could witness the punishments, so Kishimoto had the entire camp lined in formation, and he selected two special guards from his command to administer the justice. The first was Sergeant Kinhichi Tomioka, a noncommissioned officer about thirty years old and known to the POWs as "the Bull." Tomioka, who spoke some English, had a round face, and at five foot eleven and 210 pounds, he was large in comparison to other Japanese. Camp head cook Manichi Nishitani assisted Tomioka. Shorter and huskier in build than Tomoika, Nishitani was nicknamed "Buckteeth" by the prisoners due to his protruding jaw, which made his four large, gold-capped upper teeth prominent.[28]

Seaman Clarence Freeman was the first taken out of the Kempei Tai brig for punishment before the Bull and Buckteeth. His arms were tied around a tall coconut tree in the courtyard of the prisoner barracks, and Tomioka's men began flogging Freeman's bare back with a small whip made of two strands of eighth-inch wire. Charlie Weston, watching through a cell window in the brig, counted about a hundred blows. Suffering with high fever from malaria, Weston was determined to go next to get the punishment over with, so he raced out when the guard opened the door for the next man. Freeman was taken back into the brig as Weston was lashed to a coconut tree, beside which Nishitani was seated with a loaded Luger pistol. He smiled at Weston with his golden buckteeth and said in broken English, "If there is any attempt to resist, I will shoot you very dead." Weston was a bloody pulp by the time the blows ceased.

The third prisoner brought forth was Corporal Jack Taylor, a blond marine of strong build who had maintained his muscular shape by lifting heavy rocks and homemade barbells. Mac McDole, lined up with other prisoners nearby, could see that the Japanese were particularly pleased to torture such a strong American. *They're probably hoping he will make a run for it,* Mac thought.[29]

But Taylor made no effort to flee. Nishitani smiled wickedly while the small wire whip ripped flesh away from the husky marine until his bare backside resembled raw hamburger meat. Charles Norris, a fellow marine, was inspired by Taylor's courage, and Bob Russell was moved by the fact that the man never flinched or cried out.[30]

The beating was so brutal that Weston, still lashed to a neighboring tree, turned his head slightly to look away. This only outraged the Bull. Sergeant Tomioka ordered another of his guards to begin beating Weston with a three-foot club made of Filipino hardwood. The first blow impacted Weston's lower back with such severe force that he cried out, which seemed to please the Bull. Tomioka nodded for his assistant to continue working over Weston until he fell unconscious after fifteen more blows. The guards then resumed their pounding of Taylor's shoulders, back, butt, and skull. Only when the marine was completely collapsed and unconscious did Sergeant Tomioka send for the next victim.

Robert Laidlaw, Jimmy Barna, Delbert Hoefling, Bobby Bacon, and John Yoder endured both the wire whip and the wooden bat. When a guard became too tired to swing any more, the Bull ordered in another Japanese soldier to take over. "Buckteeth" Nishitani even manned the whip and club at times when he was unsatisfied with the work of his subordinates, whom he continually urged to do their utmost to cause pain. At least six other guards participated in the blood sport, most of them largely unknown to the Americans. Neal Cleere knew one of them only by the nickname "Grandma," a name chosen because the soldier was fat and had a squeaky voice that sounded like that of an old woman.

The last six men were each beaten until they passed out. Barna was revived several times by buckets of cold water and was made to stand up again for more punishment. The Japanese guards laughed when the Americans stumbled and fell as flesh was ripped from their backsides. Seaman Yoder, whose arms had not been bound to the coconut tree, also passed out at one point from his beating. When a guard sloshed a bucket of cold water in his face, Yoder leaped up and instinctively assumed a fighting stance. The other POWs yelled at him, telling the disoriented marine he was not in a boxing ring. Yoder's mind quickly cleared, and he allowed his own beating to resume.[31]

The public punishment continued for two hours, although Captain Kishimoto later claimed to have no knowledge that such abuse was going on and that he sent guards to end the torture as soon as it was brought to his attention. The eight bloody Americans were dragged back to the door of the Kempei Tai brig, where Sergeant Tomioka slugged each prisoner in the face until the prisoner collapsed. Charlie Weston, half-conscious, took only one punch to his jaw before he crashed to the floor. The resilient Taylor, however, absorbed several punches before he collapsed.

The victims were heaved into their cells and left to suffer. Jack Taylor could feel the broken, burning skin on his back, and pain racked his body from the backs of his knees on up. Lieutenant Watanabe kept the bloodied prisoners on reduced rations for the next three days, although Chief Torpedoman John Cheek and other prisoners went to great risks to slip rice balls in through the prison cell windows to help feed them.[32]

On November 21, Captain Kishimoto ordered the eight battered men to be shipped back to Manila, along with six other Americans too sick to work—including Lieutenant John Janson, who was suffering from malaria. The thirteen prisoners shipped out of Palawan dropped the camp count to 404 remaining Americans. Those who saw Barna, Freeman, Hoefling, Laidlaw, Taylor, Bacon, Weston, and Yoder as they were led toward their transport ship were shocked and angered. Don Thomas, who had slept next to Laidlaw in the barracks for months, found it hard to even recognize his friend behind the black bruises and swollen face.[33]

Five of the men were returned to Bilibid Prison. Those in the Puerto Princesa camp later heard rumors that Jimmy Barna and Bob Laidlaw were executed shortly after their arrival in Manila, but officially the two men simply disappeared from the record books. At the end of World War II, the status of Laidlaw and Barna was listed as missing in action, and both were later declared dead, bodies not recovered.

ESCAPE AND EVASION

Smitty found Thanksgiving and Christmas a far cry from the happy holidays he had known in East Texas. As he endured the drudgery and boredom of slave labor, his thoughts often turned to the simple cotton farming community where he had attended high school in Naples, Texas, about ten miles north of his family home near Hughes Springs. His classmates called him Willie, and he was much happier with that than his given name of Rufus. After graduating from Naples in 1937, the blue-eyed Texas boy had lived a carefree lifestyle for more than two years as he roamed across his great state and those of New Mexico and Arizona.

When Willie returned to his family farm in December 1939 for Christmas, he had told his parents that he was ready to make a new start with the U.S. Marines. The tall, skinny farm boy soon found himself fresh out of boot camp and aboard the troop ship USS *Henderson*, bound for the beautiful blue waters and sandy beaches of the Philippines. The outbreak of war, capture, and the pitiful life of a prisoner of war had since reduced Willie Smith to longing for simpler holiday seasons back home.[1]

The things Smitty had seen in November 1942 on Palawan made his blood boil. Even the beatings of the eight Americans he had witnessed did not dissuade him and other prisoners from pilfering food, canned or fresh. On November 20, Sergeant Elwin Bigelow, Corporal Robert Farmer, and Corporal John Boswell slipped out from the compound to gather papayas. Mess Sergeant Nishitani happened upon the scene and caught Farmer red-handed up in a tree, tossing fruit down to Boswell. Bigelow avoided detection, but the other two were hauled before Captain Kishimoto, who gave his approval for Nishitani to punish the two guilty men.

The entire camp was again called out from the barracks to witness the barbarity. Nishitani screamed at them and began to beat Farmer and Boswell numerous times across the back and buttocks with a heavy iron rod. Each instinctively raised an arm to help ward off the vicious blows, and both men suffered broken left arms. Once Nishitani was pleased with the beatings he had handed out, he made Boswell and Farmer remain at attention for another fifteen minutes before allowing them to report to sick bay to have their broken limbs splinted.[2]

The only break from construction duty came on the Japanese holiday of the second Harvest Festival on November 23, when Captain Kishimoto announced that no one would work. Two days later, Hubert Hough and several others were sent out to gather fruit for the camp. Hough wrote in his diary that the day marked his first chance encounter with a Filipino guerrilla who slipped him information from the free world. The prisoners continued to toil at their airfield project as poor food and even worse sanitation allowed malaria to dwindle their ranks. The third batch of men to be returned to Manila shipped out on December 22, and the dozen leaving included Boswell and Farmer with their broken arms— reducing the POW camp population to 392 men.[3]

December 23 was a "big day" for Yeoman Hough. He was ordered over to the "Big House" where Captain Kishimoto lived near the compound, a place no American prisoner had yet visited. With the assistance of the camp interpreter, he typed up a speech for Kishimoto to deliver at the Iwahig Penal Colony after lunch. Hough was given a bowl of rice, a new shirt, and trousers for the occasion. At the penal colony, the commandant delivered a speech about not working on the holidays before the trio arrived back at his Big House, where Hough was ordered to return his new clothes. "So, back to my G-string," he wrote.

Kishimoto showed mercy by allowing his prisoners to take three days off for Christmas and the final two days of 1942 for New Year's. Then it was back to airfield work as usual on January 1, 1943. Another supply ship arrived at Puerto Princesa on January 6, bringing with it one new prisoner—Lieutenant Henry Knight, a Navy dentist who would soon work on the teeth of both the Japanese guards and his fellow prisoners.

Days later, Captain Kishimoto ordered the prisoners to get their camp into top shape. The whispered word was that Red Cross officials were coming to make an inspection, requiring the Americans to scrub their barracks and clean the courtyard. Men who had worn only jock straps, homemade shorts, or tattered dungarees were issued blue denim shirts and trousers. The prisoners were even allowed to shower and shave for the inspection. Normally, bathing consisted of swimming in the ocean once a week, at best under armed guard.

Joe Barta was optimistic about change as he stood at attention in the courtyard on January 9. Red Cross officials entered camp, inspected the barracks, and walked up and down the rows of clean, blue-clad prisoners. Barta's optimism fell when the inspectors barely paused to look closely at any man. The POWs were not allowed to speak, and a mere half hour later, the Red Cross men filed out the front stone archway without another word.

As soon as they had departed, camp guards rushed into the barracks and demanded that the prisoners return their borrowed clothing. The POWs quickly realized the whole inspection was a mere matter of official paperwork. Nothing had been done to improve their situation other than the delivery of the prisoners' first Red Cross care packages. Barta and his friend Rob Hubbard were going through their packages when interpreter Oguri approached. "John the Baptist" grabbed a pack of cigarettes from Hubbard's bundle, stuffed them in his pocket, and walked off with only a simple, "Thanks."[4]

The prisoners, bored with their endless airfield labor during the early weeks of 1943, found ways to pass the time. Smitty mentioned to Mac McDole in the barracks one night that he would love to play poker. Mac suddenly remembered all the empty cardboard vitamin boxes he had been hoarding. He decided they could be cut down into small playing cards, so the next morning as they were herded toward their work trucks, Mac signaled the guards that he needed to relieve himself. The column stopped marching, and he ran into an abandoned schoolhouse in Puerto Princesa.[5]

Mac searched frantically through the old building, rummaging through discarded items until he found three old ink pens of different colors, shoved them in his pocket, and raced back out to the prisoner line. That night, he excitedly went to work illustrating his cardboard pillbox scraps into a full deck of poker cards. He carefully drew diamonds, hearts, clubs, and spades and numbered each one. Jokers were drawn to look like Japanese guards, and the kings were each U.S. marines. Poker games began in earnest, with men gambling off rations, cigarettes, or other items. Mac claimed a percentage off the top of the gambling proceeds and kept his buddy Smitty well stocked with cigarettes.

The ten cigarettes each POW earned per week were the highest priority item for trading. The scarcity of tobacco made it worth its weight in gold in terms of swapping for clothes, shoes, blankets, and a surprising variety of equipment. Gambling was an entirely different issue that faced Captain Ted Pulos and Ensign Bob Russell. Gambling led to stealing, and men soon learned to carry anything of value with them at all times. The senior officers, as a last resort, would deprive a fellow prisoner of food or cigarettes to remedy any serious offense of theft.[6]

Some men still quietly contemplated escape attempts. Medic Phil Brodsky was approached by several who came into the dispensary, requesting medications before they made their break. Each time, Brodsky tried to discourage their thoughts. "There is nowhere you're going to go," he lectured. "You're on an island here. The island is occupied by Japanese, and you don't know whether all these Filipinos are friendly."[7]

THE EIGHT AMERICANS who had escaped the Puerto Princesa camp were still on the run.

Navy Yeoman Bruce Elliott and his five comrades—Bob Kellam, Bobby Hodges, Buddy Henderson, George Davis, and Sid Wright—had been the first to break out on August 10, 1942. After making their way to Brooke's Point via a small *banca*, they had thereafter spent several weeks in the company of Harry Edwards's family, hidden in the nearby mountains.

Elliott was still suffering from malaria when two more American escapees reached Brooke's Point around September 5. Lieutenant Damon J. "Rocky" Gause, an Army Air Force pilot, had escaped from Corregidor by boat in April 1942, and months later he made his way to Palawan with Lieutenant William L. Osborne. They stayed at the Edwards home for a week while repairs were made to their leaking escape boat, and they provided some rifles to Edwards and the local guerrillas before they sailed for Australia. Their boat could not hold six more Americans, so marine Sid Wright took the chance to write a long letter to his family. Gause and Osborne, finally reaching Australia on October 11, turned over a number of letters to General MacArthur's staff to have them sent to the families of the six Palawan escapees.[8]

Wright, Elliott, and company armed themselves and moved out from Brooke's Point in a *banca* south down the coast, about seventy miles from Puerto Princesa. They were aided by a local Moro chief, Datu Jolkipli, and narrowly escaped an enemy force that approached the Moro village. Elliott killed a Japanese officer and his comrades subdued a mestizo collaborator, but, their position compromised, it was time to flee once again. Chief Jolkipli sent them on with two of his best warriors as guides.[9]

In early October 1942, the American escapees, their two Moros, and a small group of Filipino guerrillas made a surprise attack on a party of Japanese soldiers stationed at a schoolhouse near the Brooke's Point lighthouse. They killed an estimated twenty enemy combatants and a collaborator, and disabled a motor launch with a hailstorm of bullets. Only about seven Japanese managed to escape the assault in a second motor launch and flee toward Puerto Princesa.

Bruce Elliott's party remained near Brooke's Point for several more weeks, confident that the Japanese would not attack them again. Buddy Henderson decided to go north to the village of Aborlan, where they had landed their boat soon after escaping their prison camp. He was met by a Filipino who claimed to be friendly but who was instead a turncoat collaborating with the Japanese. A few days later, Sid Wright received word that Henderson had been shot and killed by the Filipino. Wright headed north with two cousins of the traitor and, after a seven-day manhunt, eliminated the turncoat who had killed his Marine comrade.[10]

Elliott realized that they were in danger of being discovered and that they must keep moving in order to survive. Bob Kellam, suffering from malaria, remained behind with the Edwards family to recover. Elliott, Wright, Davis, and Hodges moved out, intent on fleeing to Balabac Island in early November with their two Moro guides.

THE FILIPINOS OF Palawan Island who aided such American escapees did so at great personal risk.

Major Pedro Manigque became the undisputed senior commander of all guerrilla outfits on the island, shortly after the Japanese invaded Palawan in the spring of 1942. Manigque learned his enemy had slaughtered dozens of innocent Filipino citizens, so the desire for vengeance was strong. His organized companies spread the latest intelligence and worked hard to disrupt the Japanese military. One guerrilla officer, captured by Japanese soldiers in late 1942, was burned alive. In return, raids made by Palaweño rebels killed more than five dozen Japanese troops, prevented important shipments from arriving, and resulted in the capture of valuable food stores and firearms for future resistance use.[11]

The southern Palawan guerrillas, based out of Brooke's Point, were originally commanded by First Sergeant Emilio Tumbaga. Nazario Mayor was instrumental in recruiting new men in this region during 1942, in training them in jungle warfare, and in gathering food supplies. Datu Jolkipli assisted their unit, providing financial aid and offering some of his followers to join the local guerrillas. Superintendent Pedro Paje, head of the nearby Iwahig Penal Colony, helped supply Mayor and Tumbaga's rebels with food, clothing, medicine, and intelligence gathered from the American POW camp at Puerto Princesa.[12]

The Japanese military put pressure on the acting Palawan government officials to hand over the senior leaders of the island's guerrilla network during the fall of 1942. Dr. Higinio Mendoza, as one of the earliest organizers of the resistance movement, was singled out. A bounty of five thousand dollars was offered for the capture of the former governor, who was now instigating actions against the occupying military, but most Filipinos suffered through abuse and imprisonment to protect their own.[13]

Valentin Macaset, a Palawan resident known to have a close association with Mendoza, was arrested by the Puerto Princesa Kempei Tai on November 22. Lieutenant Watanabe placed Macaset in the brig for interrogation, where he was tortured for information on Mendoza's guerrillas for seventy-two days. Macaset was frequently beaten, abused, and hung from the ceiling by his wrists, which were tied behind him. He was finally released on February 1, 1943.[14]

The Kempei Tai failed in this attempt to bring in Dr. Mendoza. His men, and those under leaders like Emilio Tambaga and Nazario Mayor, were not swayed by threats of capture or even death.

SEVEN OF THE eight Puerto Princesa camp escapees were still seeking freedom in early 1943. Charlie Watkins and Joe Little, from the second escape group, had remained together as they moved across Palawan during late 1942. Along their journey, they were assisted by Paul Cobb's guerrillas and even encountered another American at Danlig on the northern end of Palawan—Corporal Robert T. Johnston Jr.—who had fled from Mindoro when the Japanese invaded the Philippines, and had made his way to Palawan in September 1942.[15]

Little parted company with Watkins in January 1943, as he opted to sail between other islands during the ensuing months. He joined with guerrilla forces on Panay from April to June 1943 before finally making his way to Negros Island in July. Little and twenty-seven others were eventually evacuated from Balatong Point on Negros on February 7, 1944, by the submarine *Narwhal*.[16]

Watkins had many close calls with recapture and received a knife wound in the leg while battling a Japanese sympathizer. He remained on Palawan until June 1943, when he obtained a sailboat and journeyed on toward other islands. Watkins was the sixth American POW from the Japanese camp to leave Palawan Island. Joe Little had preceded him in early 1943, and four members of the original Puerto Princesa escape group had previously departed in November 1942.

Bruce Elliott, Bobby Hodges, George Davis, Sid Wright, and their two Moro guides first sailed to Balabac Island for several weeks. The group conducted a guerrilla raid against Japanese soldiers on Kudat, the northernmost point of Borneo, but returned to Balabac. Bob Kellam, recovered from his malaria, came down from Brooke's Point in a motor launch with an Army captain to join them in early 1943.[17]

The escapees eventually heard word that some Americans were manning a radio outpost on the island of Tawi-Tawi in contact with General MacArthur in Australia. The men set out southeast on a sailboat on August 1, using a small map for guidance and dead reckoning with their compass. Elliott used the alarm clock given to him by the Puerto Princesa priest as a timer for tacking into the wind. Setting the alarm, the crew would sail for a fixed time until the alarm sounded, and then they tacked back an equal time the other direction. During their journey, they made another commando raid against Japanese soldiers stationed at a Moro fishing village on Cagayan Island, killing them before sailing on to Tawi-Tawi.

They arrived on the morning of August 10, 1943—exactly one year after their prison break from Puerto Princesa. Elliott saw that Tawi-Tawi was only nine miles by twenty miles in area—a mere speck in the ocean. He felt that his rudimentary seamanship had been sufficient and just lucky enough. Seven of the eight Camp 10-A escapees had thus made their way from Palawan to other islands of the Philippines chain. Time would tell if any would see their homeland again.

CAPTAIN KISHIMOTO'S POOR attempts at containing his American prisoners continued in early 1943. On the night of February 2—after six months of internment in the Puerto Princesa compound—a third group of prisoners made its break: marine William Dewey Swift, Navy machinist Ray Sherman Pryor, and Army privates Don Thomson Schloat and Richard Charles Hanson.

Bill Swift, who had manned a machine gun on Corregidor with the 4th Marines, was fed up with the abuse he had endured on Palawan. He and a dozen others thus conspired to escape the prison camp, but in the end, everyone backed out except for three men. Swift and Pryor climbed out a window and crawled under the barbed wire fences. Schloat and Hanson eased under the barbed wire in the back of the compound under cover of darkness and descended to the beach front below the cliffs.[18]

Japanese guards became aware of missing prisoners during roll call the following morning, and an intensive manhunt commenced. Soldiers found footprints in the sand that led into a nearby coconut grove, and armed guards tracked the escapees through the jungle on February 3 until they caught up with the group. Swift and Pryor evaded their pursuers and fled deeper into the jungle, but Schloat and Hanson were apprehended and brought back to camp.

The Kempei Tai refused to feed the two, forcing them to stand all night and into the next day. Schloat was beaten and body-slammed onto the concrete floor of the brig when he gave unsatisfactory answers on where the other escapees were located. During another session, he was forced to kneel in front of one of his guards while he was repeatedly punched in the face. Hanson and Schloat were terribly abused for more than a month before the military police moved them out of the brig on March 22 for a return voyage to Bilibid Prison.[19]

The remaining prisoners at Puerto Princesa were kept confined to their barracks for two days following the latest escape. The men fell in and fell out for muster all day on February 4 as the frustrated Japanese continued searching for the two other escapees. Those in the camp picked up only fleeting details of what might have happened to the four from the friendly Filipino guerrilla network. Rumor had it that Schloat and Hanson had been recaptured and sent to Manila. The underground news eventually related that Ray Pryor was later captured and beheaded, his head placed on display in a northern Palawan village. As for the fourth escapee, Bill Swift, the men heard nothing more about him after he faded into the jungle.[20]

Swift and Pryor had been caught in a heavy rainstorm soon after their escape. They became so lost in the downpour and darkness that they moved right through Puerto Princesa and continued north on the morning of February 3. Two days later, they made contact with two natives who gave them food and directed them to the care of Dr. Higinio Mendoza and the local Cobb brothers. Mendoza helped the escapees during the next month as they slowly made their way south toward Brooke's Point.

Swift and Pryor spent time there in the care of Harry Edwards's family, where they encountered Navy escapee Bob Kellam. Pryor and Swift sailed from Palawan without him on April 23, 1943, moving north and east through the Philippines until reaching Tablas Island in June. There, Pryor obtained a thirty-foot Moro *vinta*-type sailboat, and the pair met with other escapees. Senior among them was Captain A. Kenneth Whitehead of the 26th U.S. Cavalry, sent out by the Japanese after the surrender of Panay to deliver orders for other Americans to give up. The captain was determined to sail for Australia with anyone willing to join him in Pryor's *vinta*.

Whitehead set out from Tablas in the sailboat on August 22,

although Pryor and several others—including Aviation Machinist's Mate William F. Young and Private First Class George E. Lear—chose to remain behind. The Tablas group was soon found by Japanese troops and most of them were killed. Bob Johnston, the Mindoro escapee who had moved from Palawan to Coyo Island by this point in 1943, learned that Pryor was beheaded, along with Lear and others.[21]

Palawan escapee Bill Swift sailed with Whitehead and four others: two American servicemen, a Filipino, and guerrilla Alfred Cobb, a thirty-seven-year-old mestizo American rancher with a Palaweña mother and a Texan father. Whitehead's party sailed through the islands near Palawan, narrowly surviving a typhoon. Along their journey, they gathered charts, a compass, and even a barometer that Swift obtained by trading a shotgun. By November 28, 1943, they had reached Batu Batu on Tawi-Tawi Island.[22]

Swift had had enough ocean adventure to last him, so he and Corporal McVea Vigoroux decided to cast their die with the Filipino guerrillas when Whitehead's group sailed once again toward Australia. Nearly three weeks later, on January 6, 1944, a U.S. plane spotted Whitehead's *vinta* as it approached the Australian coast. Their epic voyage came to an end when they were finally greeted by a minesweeper and flown to Brisbane to report to General MacArthur.

Escape from Palawan came with no guarantee of long-term survival. The "Fighting One Thousand" of the island did everything in their power to assist any Americans who busted out of the Puerto Princesa prisoner camp. By late 1943, twelve POWs had gotten away. Of these twelve, Henderson and Pryor had been murdered during their flight. Two others, Schloat and Hanson, had been recaptured, tortured, and returned to Bilibid Prison.

Eight of the dozen were still defying the odds, giving hope to future Palawan escapees that evading recapture by their Japanese oppressors was possible.

CHANGING OF THE GUARD

WITH EACH PRISON break, the Japanese put the remaining Americans on one-third rations and inflicted even more abuse. The reduction of nutrition wreaked severe effects on the men, whose health was already poor. Their thin, sun-bronzed skin tore easily, and any open wound led to infections. Mac McDole developed skin ulcers on his legs and buttocks, which he treated by rubbing salt water into the sores. Others stood in downpours to wash grime and disease from their bodies, scrubbing in the rainfall as if they were in their own bathroom showers back home. Raymond Seagraves, a once-stocky man from Lewisville, Texas, grew so thin from his rice diet that his skin hung from him like a living blanket, allowing him to pull loose flesh away from his belly and knead it like dough. Fellow prisoners nicknamed Seagraves "Rubber," but the guards called him *baka*, or crazy.[1]

The Japanese needed their prisoners alive to build the new airfield, yet they offered few medical supplies for Captain Hickman and Lieutenant Mango to keep their patients healthy. Mango had catgut for sewing wounds, tweezers, forceps, a stethoscope, thermometer, scissors, and a scalpel, but nothing to offer the growing number of men stricken with malaria and other tropical ailments. His only recourse was to place such men on his sick list for transfer back to Manila.

Marine Roy Henderson was among them. Suffering with recurring bouts of malaria that caused him to miss work off and on in early 1943, Henderson grew weak while laid up in the barracks. The spring dry season, also the hottest period for Puerto Princesa, did little to ease his suffering as temperatures climbed into the low nineties. His survival pact buddies convinced him to get up for work each morning, but one day Henderson ended up in a chow-line fight with another prisoner. The stronger man prevailed, inflicting a serious head injury that put Henderson back in the barracks on Mango's sick list.

Henderson's comrades smuggled in bananas and breadfruit to keep him alive until he could be shipped out. Smitty and McDole slipped out of the barracks one night to pilfer some coconuts, Mac keeping watch while slender Smitty shinnied up a tall tree to shake loose some nuts. While he was up there, the sentries went through a changing of the guard, so Mac signaled his buddy to stay put and wait it out. Unfortunately for Smitty, he had disturbed a hornet's nest while ascending and was forced to silently endure stings all over his body as he clung high atop the tree.[2]

Once the guards were clear, he shook down dozens of coconuts, so many that Evan Bunn and Clarence Clough had to help hide them in a homemade locker in the barracks. The coconut milk went a long way to keep Henderson alive until the transport ship arrived. Smitty had grown quite close with his fellow East Texan and was heartbroken to say good-bye to Henderson. Twenty-six prisoners were returned to Bilibid during March and April. Bunn, one of the five clique-mates of Henderson, McDole, Smitty, and Clough, was shipped out with a severe case of malaria that nearly took his life. Clough covered him with blankets to help control his shivering as Bunn's fever reached 108.6 degrees, the highest human temperature ever recorded by the American doctors in the Philippines.[3]

Marine Joe Dupont—stricken with a bad case of beriberi that began to take a toll on his vision—worked as a truck driver until he was shipped back to Manila on April 19. The Japanese would not take Dr. Knight's word that Dupont needed to go, so Captain Hickman created a scheme to get Dupont placed on the next sick ship. Hickman had the prisoner wrap himself in a blanket and warm his face by placing it near the kitchen oven just before the Japanese doctor entered. Dupont's heated skin and Hollywood-class acting job—complete with deep shivering—were enough to convince the Japanese doctor to order him out with the others who were too ill to work.[4]

Captain Kishimoto proved to be the most lenient camp commandant the Palawan prisoners would encounter during the war. Realizing that even his prisoners needed some respite from their slave labor, he declared most Sundays as a day off work, allowing the Americans to wash their clothes and enjoy sports, games, or other forms of entertainment. Some POWs used their wits to create leisure-time musical instruments. Clarence Clough found the remnants of an old piano while foraging through some abandoned buildings, tore out the wires, and created a crude banjo from an old wooden box. He was blessed with a good singing voice, as was Sergeant Doug Bogue, and the two were soon popular entertainers around the barracks at night.[5]

Mac McDole scrounged up old sporting goods equipment on one of his hunts through Puerto Princesa, including a ball, bat, and basketball hoops. The men who were not too fatigued for exercise took up ball games at night. Some of the Japanese guards tried their hand at basketball, but they quickly gave up when able Americans handily defeated them. Kishimoto, who was quite interested in athletics, staged a track meet one day, but when one of the prisoners beat him, he was so infuriated that the men never saw another meet.[6]

After eight months at Palawan, Mac had worn out his dungarees and shoes. His clothing now consisted of a ragged shirt that he rarely wore, a pair of shorts fashioned from an old canvas bag, and a pair of sandals cut from discarded tires. When he awoke on March 17—St. Patrick's Day—something felt wrong. He felt a sharp pain across the lower right side of his body as he reached to put on his rubber sandals and winced as he eased back down onto his blanket. The pain became so severe that beads of perspiration formed on his face and chest.[7]

Smitty had to help Mac to his feet and into his sandals as guards shouted for the prisoners to line up for morning duty. Mac staggered out to the parade ground, suffered through the morning exercises, and choked down his morning ration of rice as the agony increased. He used his shovel as a crutch as guards prodded him to work that day, but by midmorning, the pains in his gut were so intense, he could barely force his shovel into the ground.

One of the guards finally said, "What's wrong with you?"

"I'm sick, you stupid son of a bitch!" Mac snapped.

The guard's club, administered swiftly to Mac's head, dropped him to his knees, but he managed to regain his footing and tried his best to work on past the noon hour. By midafternoon, he collapsed to the ground with his abdomen red and inflamed. Several comrades carried him back to the barracks, where Doc Mango gave him a quick diagnosis.

"I think it's your appendix and it's about to rupture," said Mango. "I'm afraid we're going to have to operate, or you're not going to make it."[8]

Mango explained to the guards that Mac needed immediate surgery. There was no place to do such an operation within the Puerto Princesa compound. Smitty waved good-bye to his best friend as Mac was loaded onto a truck for a rough, hour-long ride around to the Iwahig Penal Colony, located almost directly across Puerto Princesa Bay nearly fourteen miles by white coral gravel road. With Mango at his side, Mac moaned with every jarring bump as three Japanese guards laughed and pointed at the ailing American.

As Mac was carried inside to a makeshift surgical room, Mango could tell that his patient's appendix had likely already ruptured. To complicate matters further, the Japanese informed him that there was no medicine to serve as anesthetic. He told Mac that he would simply have to cut him open without painkillers in order to save his life.

"For Christ's sake, go ahead and get on with it," Mac gasped. "It can't be much more pain than what I'm going through right now!"

Five Japanese guards clustered around the table and held down the marine's arms, legs, and shoulders as Mango made the first incision into Mac's gut. He handled the pain reasonably well until the camp doctor reached his appendix. He screamed as red-hot pains shot through him. When the guards laughed, Mac cursed them as he slipped in and out of consciousness.

The procedure took some three hours for Mango to remove the burst appendix, clean up the area, and suture McDole with catgut from his medical bag. Mac remained in serious condition at the Iwahig facility for two days until the Japanese ordered him to be transported back to Puerto Princesa, where his buddies carried him into the barracks. Seeing that Mac's incision was becoming infected, Mango removed the stitches, poured hot water over the wound, cleaned out the infection, and sewed him up again.[9]

Fortunately for Mac, he was under the care of a doctor who was becoming quite skilled in back-alley surgeries. Private First Class John Oleska underwent the same procedure without anesthetic in a two-and-a-half-hour operation. When Oleska's appendix ruptured and required daily care, Mango improvised with a bamboo shoot and rubber ball from the toilet to clean out the infected area. Mac similarly clung to life in his barracks for the days following his surgery. Smitty snuck in rice rations to feed him, and even managed to kill and boil a chicken with the help of another prisoner. The fresh meat went a long way to help improve Mac's strength, but the infection returned two days later. Mango opened him up again, cleaned the incision, and decided to leave the wound open to prevent further infection.[10]

Mango used boiling water and employed other prisoners as assistants to clean the open area three times a day. Mac could only lie on his back for days until painful bedsores formed on his tailbone. Since he was unable to move, his only hydration came when Smitty braved the guard detail to crawl out into the compound to fetch water with his canteen.

Later that night, something burst within his gut. Thick, odorous pus oozed out of the wound as Mac fell into a deep slumber. Mango cleaned out the area with hot water the next morning and found that the infection had drained itself. Finally, his patient seemed to be improving. Mango continued the cleaning process for another week until he finally decided it was time to close up McDole's gut using the only thing he could find: buttons off Mac's shirt. Using some string, he weaved six buttons along each side of the incision.

Mac's button-weave sutures aroused great interest in the camp. Even Japanese guards entered the barracks in pairs to marvel at the rugged marine. Never one to pass up a chance to barter, Mac insisted that the guards give him several cigarettes before he would expose his incision. He did not smoke, but he offered some of the cigarettes to his buddy Smitty and traded the others for food.[11]

His body was slowly healing. By the time he was well enough to get around, he became aware of a change at Puerto Princesa.

CAPTAIN KISHIMOTO'S LAST day as camp commandant was March 23, 1943. He was assigned to other duties in Manila, quite possibly as punishment for allowing a dozen prisoners to bust out of his camp within nine months.

In some cases, he had shown compassion for his prisoners, even calling out some of his men for delivering unprovoked beatings. Once Kishimoto took a Japanese guard to the side and slapped him in the face—a terrible disgrace to the soldier, to be disciplined in front of an American.[12]

Kishimoto faced his POWs one last time as he took his seat in the rear cockpit of a Japanese dive-bomber—the first aircraft to land on the new airstrip—and encouraged the men to continue working hard so they could one day return home. Then he saluted them before bumping down the dirt runway en route to his next assignment.[13]

Kishimoto's replacement was First Lieutenant Kinoshita, an older man in his late fifties with gray hair and a mustache. He was slight, perhaps 120 pounds, and stood only about five foot six. He was not one for giving long speeches; neither was he seen about camp as often as Kishimoto had been. Kinoshita brought in fresh guards, some of whom soon proved to be even more aggressive than their predecessors, and beatings increased under his regime. Struck by fists and rifle butts on several occasions, Beto Pacheco learned never to look a Japanese guard in the eye, even when spoken to. Work details became harder and longer under Kinoshita, and not a single day passed without Americans being attacked, often with hardwood clubs.

Under Kinoshita's direction, work progressed steadily on the new airfield. Fresh clothing was nonexistent for much of the first year at Palawan, where each man simply maintained what rags he had worn to the island. When the Japanese did finally offer extra apparel, Smitty accepted whatever "new" items were thrown at him, whether the size was appropriate or not. If they fit, he wore them and if they did not, he used the new items as patches to cover up the tattered clothing he had.[14]

By mid-April, Mac McDole was feeling well enough to be given light duty, and he was assigned to work in Kinoshita's office. His job was to keep track of the prisoners each day and record the names of those who were too ill to work. Studying the names and hometowns of his fellow Americans, Mac recited the names in his mind day after day, attempting to memorize the roster in alphabetical order in hope that his memory would be of some future benefit.[15]

By the end of April, the POWs had cleared an airfield space about 690 feet by 7,200 feet—an area roughly a mile and a half in length. The bearded, calloused skeletons had accomplished the work under slavelike conditions using only hand tools. The Japanese were so pleased with the progress that they now initiated the second phase of runway construction. A cargo ship arrived with two motorized cement mixers and a hold full of dry cement for paving the runway.

A crew toiled from early morning until night, unloading the mixers and thousands of bags of cement. The heat in the ship's hold was too extreme for the Japanese, who remained under cover of shade while American prisoners ran the winch to hoist loads to the dock. As George Burlage's team slaved down in the red-hot cargo hold, passing up heavy cement bags, they found several cases of San Miguel beer brewed in

Manila. The Americans quickly arranged half-hour shifts so everyone could enjoy sips of warm beer. After each San Miguel was consumed, the cap was carefully replaced and the bottle repacked into its case. The boxes of empty bottles were later hauled out of the hold and packed onto trucks for the Puerto Princesa guards.[16]

Once the two motorized mixers were hauled to the work site, a yard and a half of cement at a time could be blended while other prisoners hand-mixed more cement in wooden wheelbarrows. They poured the concrete eight inches thick for a length of about forty-six hundred feet—long enough for aircraft landings—as other prisoners cleared more jungle to make room for turntables at each end of the runway and for turnoffs to be used to hide aircraft in the jungle during bombing raids. Francis Galligan helped sabotage the progress by dumping extra barrels of sand into the cement mix when the guards were not paying attention, knowing that the frequent tropical rains would soon turn the freshly poured pads into mush.[17]

Captain Ted Pulos had been shipped out on April 19, leaving Captain Fred Bruni as the senior officer in charge of the American prisoners of war. Bruni, along with Warrant Officer Glen Turner, now had his hands full trying to prevent his men from stirring up the ire of the new commandant. In May, they learned that Lieutenant (junior grade) Frank Golden was conspiring to escape with Private First Class Harding Stutts, Private James Rudd, and Corporal Bill Bragg. Bruni and Turner threatened to turn the men over to Kinoshita if they did not drop their plans, but the threat merely delayed Golden's group for a week before they began new preparations to escape.

A few nights later, the three men were just preparing to slip out of the barracks with their meager belongings when they were discovered by Turner, who argued at some length to prevent their escape. When Turner said he would give them a few minutes' head start before sounding the alarm, Golden's men finally abandoned the plan. The unrest was put to bed when Bruni had Stutts and Golden placed on the sick list. Both men were in good health, but Bruni told the Japanese that Golden was insane, and he was shipped out on June 9 with a group of thirteen men bound for Manila.[18]

As the summer of 1943 crawled by, the Americans did their best to avoid confrontation, but abuse was inevitable. Corporal Walt Ditto was singled out by Private Oguri for spilling gasoline while fueling a work truck. Oguri, now known as "John the Bastard," enlisted another soldier for a quarter hour of kicking and beating Ditto for the offense. One of the few bright spots in June was a change in menu, when a fourteen-foot shark washed up and graced the prisoners' black dinner pot.[19]

Unbeknownst to the Puerto Princesa prisoners, some of their Red Cross letters began arriving in their hometowns during 1943. Most had thought little about the postcards they had been allowed to fill out with brief messages during the first Red Cross visit months before. Mac Mc-Dole's family in Iowa received its first telegram from the War Department on June 16. Ernie Koblos's father had previously received notice in Chicago on February 11 that his son was a prisoner of war of the Japanese government in the Philippines. The families of those notified were provided with a Red Cross mailing address in the event they desired to send any letters or packages to their loved ones.[20]

Palawan's dreaded military police unit, the Kempei Tai, was revamped soon after Kinoshita took command of the Puerto Princesa camp. Around May 23, Watanabe and five of his subordinates were transferred to Manila, although Watanabe would soon return and serve as the senior Kempei Tai officer into early 1944. Arriving in early June was Master Sergeant Taichi Deguchi, who had served with the Manila branch of the Kempei Tai. Deguchi became second in command of the Palawan unit, but he was soon number one on the American prisoners' most-hated list.[21]

Powerfully built and possessing a chilling stare, Deguchi became feared for his irrational and unprovoked outbursts, in which he beat prisoners simply for fun. Deguchi was serving as the acting commander of the Kempei Tai when two more Americans tried to escape from Palawan. His handling of the affair was the most horrific war crime that the POWs had yet experienced.

It was June 23 when the fourth prison break from Puerto Princesa occurred. Marine Private First Class Seldon T. White and Navy Machinist's Mate First Class Earl Vance Wilson slipped into the green vegetation while on airfield work duty. Once the guards discovered their disappearance, the remaining prisoners were marched back to the barracks and made to stand at attention for three hours until Kinoshita decided that the two escapees had acted without assistance.[22]

Kinoshita called in the Philippine Constabulary and ordered them to search the jungle until the Americans were found. The men remained on the loose for five days until their luck ran out. About 1800 on June 28, a guard truck rumbled into camp and unloaded the two escapees. Japanese guards slapped and punched the two men as other prisoners looked on. Wilson, his hands bound, lunged at one of his attackers, but the guards ended the scuffle by using their rifles to prod Wilson and White into the Kempei Tai brig.[23]

When the prisoners returned from airfield duty that evening, they spotted Wilson and White in a stooped position near the guardhouse, their hands tied behind their backs. Most of the Americans who had escaped in the three previous prison breaks had eluded capture—a fact that had not boded well for Kishimoto and Watanabe. As the new compound commander, Kinoshita was not about to make the mistake of leniency, and thus he allowed Sergeant Deguchi free rein in handling these two recaptured POWs.

As the POWs were assembled to watch, Wilson and White, their faces already bloodied and bruised from severe beatings, were lashed to coconut trees. Japanese guards took turns beating the two while others thrust bayonets into their flesh. Some guards stuck hot needles into White's eyes. Kinoshita passed by several times during the session but made no attempt to halt the torture.[24]

When the prisoners were summoned to morning roll call at 0700 the next day, White and Wilson remained slumped against the coconut trees, and their torment continued. When the airfield work party returned that evening, the two prisoners were nowhere to be seen.

Deguchi had had them untied and dragged back into the brig, where they remained for three days without food or water. They were held in company with Corporal George Craft, who had been hauled out of the barracks at 0200 on June 29 and held in the brig for the next week under suspicion of aiding the escapees.

On July 5, Wilson and White were marched from the compound and loaded onto a truck by Deguchi's Kempei Tai guards. Testimony would eventually reveal that Kinoshita accompanied a six-man unit into a coconut grove east of the airfield to dispose of the grievously wounded Americans. Later, he called the other prisoners to attention to inform them that their friends had been put to death for escaping. During the days that followed, further details were leaked to the POWs by both their Filipino contacts and the Japanese guards. One guard said that the two Americans were very brave and had refused blindfolds for their execution.[25]

KINOSHITA INSTITUTED A new policy after the execution of Wilson and White. Retaining his predecessor's ten-man squads, he raised the stakes—if any portion of a squad escaped, the remainder would be executed. The men in Mac McDole's group made a solemn pledge that no one would take flight unless all ten should agree to do so together. Soon after Kinoshita's decree, Corporal Charles Street became lost while returning to the barracks from the airfield. The Japanese assumed that he had tried to escape, so the other nine men of Street's work group were thrown into the brig to await their fate.[26]

Navy prisoner Frank King, one of the nine, was told that his group would be shot at sunrise. When morning came, he was somewhat relieved when his work party was instead taken out for vicious beatings. That night, Sergeant Tomioka, "the Bull," entered the brig, pulled out King, and made him stand at attention while he worked him over first with his fists and then with the riding quirt he always carried. Once satisfied with the number of cuts his whip had cut into King's body, the Bull told his prisoner to return to his cell. "My back is all bloody," King said. "Could I go wash it off first?" Another guard slammed a two-foot chunk of iron pipe against King's skull, knocking him unconscious.[27]

King and his companions endured similar punishment until Street found his bearings and wandered back into camp. Kinoshita did not follow through on his execution threat; instead, he had the Kempei Tai hold the squad for two weeks of punishment, with only one salty rice ball and one cup of water per day. Such severe treatment did not go unnoticed by other prisoners. Mac McDole, upon hearing three men discussing their own plans to escape, became irate. He put an end to their scheme by threatening to kill each of them with his bare hands before he would allow them to put the lives of other prisoners in jeopardy.

In desperation, some men decided their only way out of Palawan was to sustain a work-ending injury. Marine George Burlage was dubbed "the Arm Breaker," as he charged extra food or cigarettes to smash a comrade's dominant arm with a pick handle while the limb was held against a log or between rocks. The men who were able to convince the Japanese that their injury was accidental were shipped out after Doc Mango set their broken limbs and fashioned a sling.[28]

Kinoshita still did nothing to prevent guards like the Bull and Nishitani from abusing the prisoners. During early July, Doug Bogue and several POWs were assigned to boil and carry tea out to those working the airfield. Nishitani asked Navy prisoner Cordell Bingham if he preferred Japanese food or the American goods brought in by the Red Cross, to which he casually replied that fish and rice were not popular items back in America, where his people preferred meat and potatoes. Nishitani exploded in rage, seized a five-gallon can of boiling water, and threw it on Bingham's leg.[29]

Bogue and another prisoner chased him down as he ran away in agony. They removed his shoe and found that his reddened skin was already peeling off. He was taken to Doc Mango, who applied bandages to Bingham's badly burned foot and lower leg, which became so swollen and infected during the next few days that Mango feared he would have to amputate. He eventually won the battle by cutting away large portions of dead skin and draining the large blisters that formed. About a week later, Bingham was forced back to work, hauling more boiling tea while limping along on his lame foot.

PRIVATE FIRST CLASS Ed Petry finally made his way out of Cabanatuan in August 1943.

The Texas-born soldier had endured a full year of hell after surviving the Bataan Death March. During his first three months at Cabanatuan, he had witnessed many severe beatings and even murders of his fellow prisoners. Standing only five foot four, he noted with some selfish relief that the Japanese guards enjoyed tormenting the larger Americans. He learned to wear a shirt when possible to avoid drawing undue enemy attention to the large American eagle and stars tattooed on his upper chest. He was severely stricken by malaria that kept him in the hospital for seven months before he was well enough in January 1943 to return to working on a farm and chopping wood. On August 15, Petry was among the men picked up from their barracks, moved by train to Manila, and shipped out as replacement airfield workers for the ongoing Palawan project. He arrived at Puerto Princesa on August 27 with sixty-nine other men—the last shipment of fresh laborers to be transported to Palawan Island.[30]

Also arriving that day was Private Tommie Daniels, who had survived the Death March only to suffer the next year in Cabanatuan Camp 1. The ruddy, blue-eyed East Texas native looked like the perfect specimen for construction labor. Although he stood only five foot seven, Daniels was 185 pounds and powerfully built, with a bulldog stance and a barrel chest.

The Army Air Corps veteran had turned to the military in 1923 as a way to escape his tough rural upbringing. After three years in the regular Army, Tommie returned home to help his mother—who raised eight children from different fathers—on the family farm. When she passed away in 1929, Tommie reenlisted and spent the next decade working on airfields in Texas and Louisiana, and in the quartermaster corps in Hawaii. Daniels never knew a father figure, and his closest relative, half brother Walter Blalock, was working at the Red River Arsenal as a guard when Tommie headed for the Philippines in June 1941. Raised on the Blalocks' Sugar Hill community farm near Talco, Texas, Daniels had attained only a fourth-grade education, and he could not read or write.

He was approaching his fortieth birthday when he reached Palawan, and his sandy brown hair soon turned gray due to the stress of being a POW. Daniels, one of the oldest privates in the military, had been nick-named "Pop" by fellow soldiers young enough to be his sons. After several older prisoners were returned to Manila, Pop Daniels shared the forty-year-old age bracket with just two other soldiers and two officers, Warrant Officer Glenn Turner and Captain Fred Bruni. He would prove to be more resilient than many men half his age.

Among the newbies were some familiar faces. Mac McDole was reunited with Marine Richard Packer—together the two had gone through boot camp, crossed the Pacific on the USS *Chaumont*, and taken liberty during a brief stopover in Honolulu. Soon after reaching Palawan, Packer became deathly ill with malaria that left him in the barracks, shivering under threadbare blankets. His fever spiked so high that McDole resorted to desperate measures, carrying his friend out to a rainwater vat near their barracks. Mac held him in the cool water for ten minutes, against the protests of Doc Mango. To the doctor's surprise, Packer stopped shaking and his body temperature began to drop. He eventually recovered. It soon became common practice to submerge prisoners with high fevers in the water tank to cool their bodies.[31]

On September 1, 1943, the first accidental POW death occurred. A Japanese dive-bomber was forced to make an emergency landing on one of the adjacent new dirt strips, but the pilot side-slipped his plane off the runway and plowed into a temporary shack. Jack Burton Flynn of Conroe, Texas, resting in the little structure, was unable to evacuate before the aircraft smashed right through, slashing him with its propeller and carrying his body another fifty feet.[32]

Officers Mango, Harry Hickman, Fred Bruni, and Bob Russell were called to be witnesses for the burial held that evening at 1700. Father

Reyes, a priest from the Catholic church at Puerto Princesa, offered a few words in a brief ceremony before Flynn was buried in the town cemetery. Several men used a mess kit to form a simple wooden cross, and they attached an identification tag to it with his name.[33]

MAC McDOLE GOT a brief respite from the cement dust when his ten-man crew was assigned to once again run pipes down from a mountain-side stream to bring in more water, this time for mixing cement at the airfield. Their guard, an older man who spoke little and had a constant tic in a flickering eye, was nicknamed "Blinky."[34]

Blinky was not particularly intelligent. He enjoyed playing a game in which one person guessed how many fingers another was going to use to slap against his opponent's wrist. Marine George Burlage laughed each time Blinky lost and was left with a red wrist when the challenging American fooled him. "Sorry, I was thinking four fingers," said Burlage when Blinky would guess the number three. Some of the men came to regard Blinky—who, they learned, had been injured while serving in tanks during the Lingayen Gulf landings—as something like the prisoners' mascot, as lovable as a dog.[35]

Blinky's ignorance was enough that the Americans began whispering about making an escape as their work truck churned up the mountain-side one day. Camp barber John Warren decided they could easily kill Blinky, steal the truck, and take off. The men thought about it for a moment, and then Smitty grabbed the Japanese guard and put him in a choke hold. The terrified Blinky, his eyes batting rapidly, did not resist. Smitty held him until he realized that Clarence Clough and other members of his work crew were back at camp. Knowing that his friends would be murdered if the men turned up missing, he released his hold on the mild-mannered guard. "You better watch it from now on," Smith said. " 'Cause we can still get to you anytime we want!"

The men completed their work detail without further thoughts of escape. Blinky, apparently happy to be alive, never reported the incident to his camp superiors.

CODE NAME "RED HANKIE"

J OE BARTA LEARNED that even taking a bath could bring on severe punishment.

In the past year, he and the Puerto Princesa prisoners had been allowed to wash themselves once a week in the ocean, but during the fall of 1943, Kinoshita abruptly suspended this privilege. Barta's loose skin began developing sores from the cement dust, island grime, and salt accumulated from perspiration. He was not alone. One night in September, a group of thirty-one prisoners—including Smitty and Mac McDole—decided to slip out of the barracks under cover of darkness for a bath.

The men eased into the barracks' galvanized steel rainwater tank— used for cooking and drinking—and a thin film of residue spread across its surface as they washed away weeks of stench and filth. When Sergeant Nishitani discovered them midway through their cleansing, he angrily ordered the prisoners out of the water tank at rifle point and ushered Barta's large group to the Kempei Tai brig, where a guard detail pounded their backs with a club and a piece of firewood. Two days of confinement in dark cells without food or water was the price for taking a bath.

Some guards employed creative punishment. Corporal Lee Moore's entire work group was beaten across the legs with two-by-fours when one man held up their progress. The group was forced to do push-ups during its morning and afternoon work breaks, with beatings rained down on anyone who became exhausted. One private, unable to maintain position for the full forty-five minutes, was struck so severely by a guard known as "Black Jack" that he suffered a spine fracture. He lay paralyzed in sick bay for two weeks, during which time Black Jack would pay visits to slap him around.[1]

In September, another POW was spotted by Private Oguri as he tried to smuggle bananas back from his work detail. John the Bastard used a chair leg to pummel the prisoner's legs, and within two weeks the resulting cuts became infected ulcers. Doc Mango eventually put him on the transfer list, and he was shipped out on December 15 as part of a sixty-man group that reduced Palawan's Camp 10-A population to 354 Americans. Other men, such as George Burlage, were returned to Luzon in the fall after suffering recurring rounds of malaria.[2]

The most severe punishment during late 1943 occurred in early November after camp guards caught wind of another planned prison break. Marines Walt Ditto and Bob May had hatched up a scheme to escape in a small canoe with the help of three friendly Filipinos. Ditto, severely beaten in June just for spilling gasoline, was more than ready to go. Guards Oguri and Watanabe had taken it out on him again in August when someone in his ten-man group reported late for roll call.[3]

Ditto discussed his escape plans with his buddy May. Ditto was serving as a driver to the military stone quarry at Magaruwa one day when he hailed Vincente Pipori—a seventeen-year-old Filipino engaged in loading stones—to ask for assistance in escaping. Pipori agreed, and thereafter made contact with Ditto during October by leaving messages handwritten on rolled balls of paper in the road. On other occasions, Pipori put a note in an empty cigarette package and dropped it alongside the road, or tossed it out a truck window as he passed Ditto's work group. Pipori met with two other Filipino laborers, who made contact with Ditto on the night of November 7 to share the plans. They told him that on the night of November 15, the Filipinos would tow a *banca* to the rear of the Puerto Princesa camp and escape with the two American prisoners to either northern or southern Palawan.[4]

Within days, the scheme was foiled. Pipori sent another note to Walt Ditto on the afternoon of November 10. "Unfortunately, I can't meet you in the stone quarry," he wrote. "Ordinary citizens aren't allowed to enter the Iwahig Prison Area. If possible, at Magaruwa, if not by letter." Ditto understood that he must meet with his conspirators again to further discuss the plans. That evening around 2155, camp guard Private First Class Kajii observed Ditto quickly slip a note into the bottom of his left shoe. When Kajii asked to see the shoe, Ditto offered only his right foot. Before the guard inspected the left shoe, Ditto managed to hand off the note to Bob May.

Kajii cornered May and quizzed him. When May was ordered to undress, the note was found tucked into his underpants. The two Americans were taken to the brig for examination by Deguchi, who had them strung up by their wrists and severely beaten. The next morning, Deguchi's military police tracked down and arrested the three Filipinos who had conspired to help them escape.[5]

The two marines were beaten in a public demonstration before their fellow prisoners and returned to the Kempei Tai brig, where they would remain for the next ninety-two days. Nearly every day of their internment, they were brought out with their hands tied behind them and lifted over a rafter, their feet dangling helplessly above the floor. Japanese guards took turns pounding them with clubs and lead-filled hoses, kicking them in the stomach and kidneys, spitting on them, and smacking them in the head with sabers. The torture endured by Ditto and May was the longest running of any Palawan prisoners, and May was told on a daily basis that he would be shot or beheaded. Few could understand how they maintained the will to survive on inadequate food and water and the near-daily beatings.[6]

Somehow, they remained there until February 14, 1944, when both men were dragged from the brig and placed on board one of the transport ships. They were sent back to Bilibid Prison, then placed on a hellship to Japan to suffer through the remainder of the war working in coal mines. Ditto had been kicked in the lower intestines to the point that he could not pass urine for days. Afterward, he could only do so from a sitting position for another year.

THE SECOND ACCIDENTAL prisoner death at Palawan occurred on December 10, 1943. Army Private Alton Conrad Burson of Crockett, Texas, fell from a moving truck, struck a post, bounced under the vehicle, and was crushed as the rear wheels passed over his chest. Camp doctors pronounced him dead at 1055, and Burson was buried in another simple ceremony that afternoon by Father Reyes.[7]

Continued abuse from the guards would further dwindle the number of effective workers in the weeks that followed. Supplies for the Palawan camp arrived regularly from Manila on two small interisland steamers, and fights broke out on occasion among American POW stevedores as some were willing to rob their fellow prisoners by pilfering the Red Cross parcels. Most outside stevedores thought of the men held on Palawan as their brothers, and they often smuggled notes of encouragement into the outbound supplies. On some occasions, they even received notes back from the Palawan prisoners, helping the separated Americans keep track of one another.[8]

There was reason to celebrate on Christmas Day 1943 when some Puerto Princesa prisoners received packages from home through the Red Cross. Mac McDole's mother sent him a box containing Colgate toothpaste and new white T-shirts. Knowing the shirts would quickly lose their crisp look if he wore them on the airfield, Mac kept them tucked away at his pallet in the barracks, taking them out only to admire their freshness and remember his home. The men found that their care packs had been rifled through, and some of the contents, including any medicines, had been stolen by the guards. Smitty's Christmas package from East Texas contained only new white bedsheets and a shiny blue pair of swimming trunks. His fellow prisoners howled with laughter as he quipped, "Where in the hell do they think we are, at a Boy Scout camp for a week?"[9]

Barber John Warren's package contained empty shotgun shell boxes packed with chewing tobacco—something he had longed for during his months of imprisonment. Japanese guards watched Warren stuff a considerable chaw in his mouth and became curious to try it, so he gave each a chunk, telling them to chew on it, fill their mouths with juice, and swallow. The guards did as instructed and soon were doubled over, vomiting. Warren escaped a serious beating by pretending to swallow his own juice and telling them it was merely a matter of acquiring a taste for the tobacco.

Other prisoners received basic Red Cross packages that included canned corned beef, liver pâté, Spam, and American cigarettes. The parcels boosted morale considerably and gave the men ample trading opportunities with guards willing to swap twice as many of their own smokes for the American brands. The men were allowed to write return postcards to be sent home to their families, but many, assuming the cards would never be sent, addressed them to Shirley Temple or Mickey Mouse.[10]

Smitty's new bedsheets went to good use. He ripped them apart and used old cable wire to sew four pairs of shorts, two each for himself and his best friend, McDole. Shortly after Christmas, Mac received his first and only letter from home via the Red Cross. His younger sister, Dolores, wrote that she was praying for him and would have pancakes waiting on the griddle when he made it back to Iowa.[11]

THROUGHOUT 1943, THE Palawan guerrilla network kept tabs on the condition of the American prisoners at Puerto Princesa. Nazario Mayor had been promoted to command of the Brooke's Point unit, Company D, when the original commander, Sergeant Tumbaga, drowned while trying to save a comrade.[12]

The reputation of Mayor's company spread quickly, both to the locals and to the Japanese. Bombing raids were made on the town of Caramay on August 29 and September 2, 1943, and in both attacks, the Japanese dropped leaflets asking senior guerrilla leader Major Manigque, Captain Mayor, and all of their men to surrender. Manigque instead moved his men north on Palawan, while Mayor had his company relocate to Tinitian, north of Puerto Princesa, for a while. Another Palawan resistance leader, Dr. Higinio Mendoza, similarly continued in his efforts despite a bounty placed upon his head by the Japanese military.

Such threats did not sway Mayor or Mendoza from continuing to assist the prisoners of war held on their island. The last Americans to escape the Palawan camp successfully had done so on February 2, 1943. By that summer, those still alive had made their way onto other islands. Bruce Elliott and four others from the original August 1942 escape group had reached Tawi-Tawi Island on August 10, 1943. There, they met Captain Jordan A. Hamner, eight or nine Australian officers, and a U.S. Army officer.

Hamner, a mining engineer before the war who escaped to Australia in January 1943, had returned to Tawi-Tawi by submarine in March with a six-man team to establish a coast-watching post to report shipping intelligence by radio back to Australia. Hodges and Davis, deciding to attempt a sailing to Australia, soon departed on their own in a well-stocked boat, never to be seen again. Kellam opted to stay behind when Elliott and Wright left Tawi-Tawi around November 2, 1943, on a boat with several Filipinos and two Australians. They eventually sailed past Jolo Island, and made their way to the western tip of Zamboanga Province.[13]

They were greeted by the local guerrillas, who had electricity and a radio, and received orders to report to Colonel Robert V. Bowler—an American who had not surrendered but stayed on Mindanao. Wright, Elliott, and their Aussie comrades survived a dangerous passage in a double-masted seventy-foot boat, finally reaching the northern coast of Mindanao in January 1944. There, they related their long story of escape and evasion to the local guerrillas—whom Wright and Aussie Rex Blow decided to join. Wright met with the American commander, Colonel

Wendell Fertig, and asked permission to remain in the islands, where he hoped to seek vengeance for slain marine Buddy Henderson. Sid Wright was given a commission as a second lieutenant in the U.S. Army—quite a jump for a private in the Marine Corps—and he would continue fighting with Fertig's guerrillas until his liberation in 1945.[14]

Bruce Elliott remained with several Australians in early 1944, hoping to find rescue. From his Palawan escape group, Bruce was now on his own, holding out for rescue on an American submarine. He could only hope his two-year ordeal would soon end, and that his seemingly endless good luck streak could continue a bit longer.

ON JANUARY 7, 1944, Dr. Higinio Mendoza was sitting down to breakfast with his family in the small settlement of Jolo, located in the jungle about thirty miles north of Puerto Princesa. It was a memorable day, his eleventh wedding anniversary.

Jolo had been relatively peaceful in late 1943. The locals accumulated what rice they could and learned to eat *curot*, a poisonous root that required tedious and careful treatment to remove the toxins before cooking it in coconut milk to produce a local delicacy. Jolo was visited at times during 1943 by men who were fleeing the Japanese military. Among them were Palawan escapees Ray Pryor and Bill Swift, and other men, such as George Marquez and Bob Johnston, who moved through Palawan at various times after their previous escape from other Philippine islands.[15]

Despite the bounty on his head, Mendoza and his guerrilla Company A were instrumental in aiding such escapees. He managed to evade all efforts to seize him during 1943, including one made by his friend Donato Manga, whom the Japanese had sent to convince him to surrender. Mendoza placed Manga under custody of his men and later released him. "I will never surrender to the Japanese," he told Manga.[16]

The good doctor's luck ran out in early 1944. In a firefight at Tarabangan, Japanese troops captured a guerrilla named Namia and brought him to Puerto Princesa for interrogation. They learned the whereabouts of Mendoza and on January 6 sent a force of about sixty armed men to capture him. The troops were moved by a launch towing two barges that landed at Tulariquin, a coastal barrio north of Tinitian, where they seized guards of the local Bolo Battalion, and used members Talim and Namia to guide them toward the Mendoza residence. Another Bolo guard named Dindin escaped and raced ahead to warn the Mendozas of the approaching Japanese.

Trinidad "Triny" Mendoza urged her husband to vacate immediately. He refused, instead inviting Dindin to take shelter in his home for the night. On the morning of January 7, Mendoza went about his usual activities, listening to the radio and jotting down notes regarding the war. He also typed a letter to Lieutenant Felix Rafols to alert him to the presence of Japanese soldiers in the area while Triny spent the early morning hours preparing to celebrate their wedding anniversary. Captain Mendoza was just raising a spoonful of breakfast to his mouth when a single rifle shot shattered the morning silence.[17]

Other shots followed. Mendoza ran to his bedroom to fetch his rifle and his long bolo. His gathered family watched as he cocked the firearm, opened his bedroom door, and was greeted by Japanese soldiers aiming their own rifles at his family. With only two bullets to his name, Mendoza calmly gave himself up in hopes that his family might be spared. As they led him downstairs, his wife, Triny, pleaded, "What shall we do?"

"Sweetheart, be brave," he said. "We can die for our country."

Several soldiers hit Mendoza and used the butts of their rifles against him as they led him away. When Triny rushed forward, she was also struck in the arms with rifle butts and kicked in the abdomen. She and her four children were tied together and separated from Mendoza as the family was marched from Jolo to Tinitian. Mendoza's wife and children were left behind at Tinitian, where they were recovered by guerrillas in pursuit of the retreating Japanese.[18]

Mendoza remained in Tinitian for several days under interrogation before being forced into a motor launch and then beaten during the trip to Puerto Princesa, where he was held in the custody of Watanabe's

Kempei Tai military police. The remaining citizens there were overjoyed to see their beloved captain and even threw a dance in his honor. He was allowed to see other family members in Puerto Princesa, including a brief reunion with his oldest son, John. The last words the elder Mendoza said to his boy were, "Take care of Mama."[19]

As a gimmick to pacify the Palaweños, the Japanese allowed Mendoza to deliver a speech at the public plaza in Puerto Princesa. His sister Agustina and her sons walked nearly forty-five miles from Aborlan just to be near him.

"It is a lucky day, for they came upon me in a house with my family," he told the small crowd. "If I were in camp with my soldiers, there would be much bloodshed, as I will never surrender."

Mendoza held firmly to his beliefs. Japanese command offered him the governorship of Palawan if he would surrender to them, but he refused, saying he could not betray his country. On the morning of January 24, 1944, Lieutenant Shinobu Nakahara appeared at the Kempei Tai headquarters with a telegram. He informed Watanabe and his second in command, Taichi Deguchi, that he had been ordered to execute the guerrilla doctor. Watanabe objected, but Nakahara said that nothing could be done to change a directive from high headquarters.[20]

Nakahara led Mendoza from Puerto Princesa, along with two other Filipinos captured by the Japanese, Renato Marcelo and Bruno Rodriquez. Mendoza's family tried to remain calm while they awaited news. Triny Mendoza confronted Captain Yamagochi, the local Japanese commander, on February 1, demanding to know where her husband was being held. He told her that the doctor had been flown to Fort Santiago in Manila, but she suspected this to be a lie, as not one local had seen her husband taken to any airplane. Six weeks later, Renato Marcelo, released by the Japanese, reappeared in the Jolo settlement bearing cigarettes, candies, and antimalarial pills. Captain Mendoza was still nowhere to be found as his family continued to hear conflicting stories from Japanese officials. Elizabeth Clark Alba, Mendoza's sister-in-law, heard from one Japanese leader that he had been taken to treat sick soldiers near the village of Canigaran, while another said the doctor had been taken to Japan for medical studies.[21]

Evidence would later show that Nakahara had acted upon orders from the 22nd Air Brigade to execute Mendoza for conducting guerrilla activities. A half-dozen soldiers took him by truck to a point near Canigaran Beach and led him into a coconut plantation owned by his in-laws, the Clarks. Several Tagbanua natives, including one named Timod—who happened to be picking shellfish near the beach as the truck approached—crouched in the bushes to watch. Mendoza's hands were untied, and he was made to dig his own grave before he was shot three times by a firing squad. The Japanese removed a woven crocheted belt, adorned with a University of Iowa buckle given to him by his sister-in-law before the war. They left it hanging beside his shallow grave as a crude marker of sorts. The murder of Higinio Mendoza would remain covered up for more than a year.[22]

For the time being, Triny Mendoza and her children were left in despair, ignorant of his fate. Instead of falling into self-pity, Mrs. Mendoza only strengthened her resolve to aid the guerrilla movement and the imprisoned American soldiers near Puerto Princesa.

The disappearance of Captain Mendoza did not sway the efforts of the Filipino guerrillas of Palawan.

Captain Bonife, the senior inspector for the Philippine Constabulary on the island, advocated beating and mistreating the local Palawan people to force cooperation. He took further steps to help eradicate the guerrilla movement by targeting businessman Thomas Loudon, known to oppose the Japanese. Bonife asked the military to force Loudon to go to Balabac and bring back the family of Nazario Mayor, his son-in-law and the leader of the Brooke's Point area guerrillas. The idea was to intern Mayor's wife, Mary, to force him into submission.

Captain Mayor's Company D of the "Palawan Special Battalion" had been raising hell with the Japanese since the guerrilla corps had been more formally organized in October 1943. Mayor's Sector D, by far the largest guerrilla region, included all areas from Puerto Princesa south to

Balabac Island. Although undermanned and ill-equipped, his company was efficient during 1943 and early 1944. His men had killed dozens of Japanese soldiers in several attacks, suffering only one of their own wounded in the process. Mayor's guerrillas had seized weapons and ammunition and had been the first unit to make contact with American submarines supporting the resistance effort.[23]

The Japanese PC thus had good reason to want to dispose of Mayor, as they had done with Mendoza. When they sent Thomas Loudon to Balabac to ask his son-in-law to surrender, Loudon was comforted with prior intel from the guerrilla network that Mary, his daughter, her husband, and Loudon's grandchildren had already vacated Balabac to hide elsewhere. Loudon was thereafter suspected of aiding the Palawan guerrillas and placed under arrest. He was allowed a certain amount of freedom because of his age while he was held for months in Puerto Princesa. Instead of being holed up in a brig, Loudon moved about freely within the largely abandoned capital city and observed the American POWs as they moved to and from their airfield work area. He passed along intelligence to Filipino guerrillas when he could, and he steadfastly refused all further proddings from the Japanese military to help force his son-in-law to surrender.

Loudon quietly planned to make a break from the city when the time was right.

Two former Palawan POWs were making their way to freedom at the time that Thomas Loudon lost his.

Navy Yeoman Bruce Elliott, who had busted out of Puerto Princesa in August 1942, had made his way to northern Mindanao by February 1944. His rescue ship came on March 2 in the form of the submarine USS *Narwhal*, skippered by Commander Frank Latta. He eased his boat near the coast to deliver ammunition and supplies for the guerrillas and took on twenty servicemen and eight civilians, including two women. Among the Americans finally leaving the Philippines were Elliott and two other Navy veterans who had been working on the medical staff at

Colonel Fertig's headquarters. Elliott was taken below to receive his first real American food in two years, and to settle in for the blissful voyage home.[24]

Only two days later, March 5, Latta's *Narwhal* made another stop to deliver additional cargo to the guerrillas on Tawi-Tawi Island. The submarine took on eight passengers, including Captain Jordan Hamner and Palawan escapee Bill Swift. As *Narwhal*'s crew and passengers were unloading ammunition, they had a sudden scare when four Japanese destroyers and two cruisers were spotted bearing down on them. A blaring diving alarm sent everyone scrambling below, including two unintended Filipino guerrillas. *Narwhal* settled on the bottom while depth charges cascaded around it, rocking the boat. Lights and fuses were blown and cork rained down, making Bruce Elliott feel that perhaps his escape via submarine had been a mistake. Latta's boat narrowly escaped tragedy when one of the depth charges landed on its deck but failed to explode.

Two weeks later, *Narwhal*—having attacked several ships with its passengers on board—reached Australia on March 11 and rendezvoused with the Australian fleet tug *Chinampa*. The thirty-eight passengers, including Palawan escapees Elliott and Swift, were transferred over for the trip into Port Darwin. Swift and Elliott were next flown to Brisbane on a C-47 and transferred into Mobile Hospital No. 9. After years on the run from the Japanese, Elliott was unable to sleep in the soft hospital bunk, so he stretched out on the firm floor and drifted right off.

Swift and Elliott made the most of their recovery time in Australia before being flown to Pearl Harbor on a Pan Am China Clipper. Their journey continued to Washington, DC, where they collected back pay, underwent further debriefing, and were finally sent home on leave. The men were treated like heroes, but felt slighted in that they were never given consideration for any medals for all that they had endured. Of some twenty-five thousand POWs held by the Japanese in the Philippines, only a few dozen would ever manage to escape from a prison camp.

Another Palawan prisoner, Joe Little, had already hitched a ride off

Negros Island on the *Narwhal* in early February. His fellow escapee, Charlie Watkins, was still on the run in early 1944, traveling by sailboat on a six-month journey in hopes of finding better luck on other islands. During his first stop on Cuyo Island, he encountered two other American servicemen, George Marquez and William "Red" Wigfield, who had escaped from Bataan in April 1942. Japanese troops became too abundant on Cuyo Island, forcing the Americans to take to the ocean again to travel between other Philippine Islands into the fall of 1943. As fate would have it, their journey brought them back to Brooke's Point on Palawan in December 1943, a rude homecoming of sorts for Charlie. *It feels like I'm just moving around in circles,* he thought.[25]

Watkins spent some of January 1944 fighting off a nasty case of malaria while in the care of the Edwards family, but Captain Mayor's guerrillas helped furnish him with quinine to help shake his ailment. Charlie never gave up, but he was beginning to feel that he would either die on Palawan at some point or get himself killed by the Japanese. As the months ticked away, Watkins could only pray for a miracle rescue like that of Bill Swift and Bruce Elliott.

THE GUERRILLA NETWORK was powerless to prevent the abuse of the American POWs still held on Palawan. Navy prisoner Harold McKee, forced by a Japanese guard to climb a tall coconut tree to shake down the nuts, fell thirty feet, breaking his back and a leg. He lingered for a week before dying on January 2. The number of makeshift crosses created for fallen American POWs in the local Philippine cemetery was becoming alarming.[26]

Prisoners were falling gravely ill from the long months of hard labor and their meager rice diet. Camp barber John Warren began losing his eyesight. His comrades tried to fashion a pair of wire-frame glasses from scrap materials they scavenged. Another prisoner kept his spirits up by sleeping with a smuggled American flag that he kept buried away in his sea bag. He knew that possessing the prized U.S. keepsake could be his own death sentence, so he was careful to show it only to those whom he deeply trusted.[27]

On January 5, the Kempei Tai finally released prisoners Walt Ditto and Bob May from the Puerto Princesa brig, where they had been held since November 10. They were soon transferred back to Bilibid Prison with five other prisoners. One bright spot in February 1944 was a second delivery of Red Cross packages to the prisoners. Marine Corporal Charles Norris was disgusted to see Captain Bruni deliver cigarettes, canned milk, chocolate bars, and corned beef to Kinoshita and his interpreters as a goodwill gesture.[28]

One starving soldier said to Bruni, "What right do you have giving our supplies to the Japs?" Bruni turned the man over to the Japanese, whereupon interpreters Sumita and Oguri beat him with clubs, then forced him to stand at attention all night and work the next day. Norris and many others were left with a bad disposition toward Bruni, and the ill feelings only further splintered the American officer group.

The prisoners worked steadily on extending the concrete runways, enduring their ongoing hell in the Puerto Princesa camp as illness and mistreatment continued to take their toll. On March 21, two POWs were beaten for stealing coconuts in the back of the compound. The Japanese appeared content with the number of prisoners assigned to their project, as no fresh workers were delivered in 1944. Five sick men were shipped out to Manila on May 10, followed by another thirty POWs on June 16. By that point, the prisoner population in the camp had dropped to 309 souls—the lowest roster ever since Camp 10-A had first opened in August 1942 with 346 Americans.[29]

During the summer of 1944, the prisoners became much more actively involved in communicating with the guerrilla resistance network. The three key points of contact became Navy Yeoman Hubert Hough, a Japanese guard, and Triny Mendoza. Assigned to type reports and keep track of prisoner rosters at the camp headquarters, Hough had more liberty than the average American prisoner and came to realize that "Shorty" Sumida—one of the newer guards—held a friendly and sympathetic disposition toward the POWs.

Hough learned to trust Shorty enough that he became the main contact point between the POW camp and the outside world. He found that Sumida would transmit messages from camp to Triny Mendoza, who in turn relayed the intelligence to the Philippine guerrillas. Japanese officers allowed Triny, still unaware of her husband's fate, to stay in town with her children. The officers even offered candies to the youngsters. In the months that followed, the Mendozas and their extended Clark family befriended interpreter Sumida, who said he was particularly close to one prisoner he called "my boy Huff."[30]

Hough soon began receiving care packages from Triny Mendoza through Sumida, each parcel carefully placed where the prisoners would find it, wrapped in Mrs. Mendoza's red bandana. In short order, the thirty-year-old widow's trademark packages earned her the underground nickname "Red Hankie." Hough met with her for the first time on May 29, 1944, to exchange information. During the first of many meetings between the two, he gave her a package containing his collection of Chinese money, personal photos, poems, and short stories he had written while held in various POW camps. He asked her to hang on to his possessions and mail them to his home address in Iowa after the war.[31]

Sergeant Frank Leroy accompanied Hough on one rendezvous with Red Hankie. In company with Sumida, the two slipped out of camp on the night of July 7 and made their way to the nearby Mendoza plantation, located one-third of a mile from the new airfield. Banana plants, coconut trees, and other tempting vegetation were growing on the plantation as far as Hough could see, and Triny was happy to have some of the fruits and vegetables smuggled back for the benefit of the American prisoners.[32]

By the summer of 1944, the "three month" project at Puerto Princesa had stretched into two long years. The American prisoners had made enough progress on the new airfield for the Japanese to begin bringing in small groups of fighter planes and bombers. The POWs had cleared by hand an area 2,400 yards by 225 yards from raw jungle, laid an eight-inch rock base, and poured a runway stretching 1,530 yards by 75 yards wide. They had paved cement turnarounds at the end of the runway and had hacked turnoff lanes for pilots to taxi their aircraft to revetments under the protective cover of the largest trees. Gene Nielsen and others were even used at times to help push airplanes that became stuck in the mud on the unpaved taxi lanes.[33]

Captain Bruni, as senior officer, traded out being in charge of the work details every other day with the senior U.S. Navy officer still in camp, Ensign Bob Russell. Bruni did not get along well with Russell, whose closest officer friend was Army doctor Harry Hickman. By mid-1944, Russell and Bruni rarely spoke to each other. Some enlisted men had lost respect for their captain for his loud language, giving of Red Cross gifts to the Japanese guards, and for allowing other Americans to be reported to the guards for their infractions. On July 11, the tensions boiled over into a heated argument involving Hickman, Russell, and Mango. Russell ended up in a fistfight with Mango that left the doctor with a black eye.[34]

Yeoman Hough continued to have secret meetings with Red Hankie between June and August 1944, often accompanied by Frank Leroy, Churchill Vaughan, or Tom Paddock. During that time, Hough passed along various documents, including names of Americans known to be held by the Japanese. On July 23, Hough became concerned for Triny Mendoza's safety, as he found that there was too much talk going on among the officers and in camp, both about her and the guerrilla force. Hough asked Sumida to meet with her that day, telling him to "notify Mrs. Mendoza to hit the road and leave."[35]

Mendoza did not immediately flee her family plantation. By early August, Shorty Sumida had fallen under the suspicion of Sergeant Deguchi, the acting head of the Palawan Kempei Tai, and his military police unit began investigating Sumida to determine whether he had been double-dealing with the Americans. Sumida was able to sneak out of camp that night after his interrogation to the Mendoza home to warn

Red Hankie on what to say before she was investigated by Deguchi's men. The two somehow were convincing enough in their stories to avoid any direct punishment from the Kempei Tai, but they realized their days were numbered.

By the summer of 1944, the Kempei Tai had moved its main head-quarters north and west of the Puerto Princesa prisoner camp to the colony of Irawan. The senior commander of the unit, Lieutenant Tsuneji Shoji, had arrived in February, but his presence was minimal as he soon fell ill and was rarely seen. His subordinate, Deguchi, would also trans-fer to the Irawan police station in late 1944, leaving Sergeant Susumu Kato as the acting commander of the remaining Kempei Tai force serv-ing at Puerto Princesa.[36]

Hough knew that it was simply too dangerous for the trio to con-tinue meeting, so he sent word to Mrs. Mendoza again, urging her to get out of the area, as her life was now in danger. During her last infor-mation exchange with Sumida and Paddock on August 15, Triny asked Paddock to offer her good-byes to her friends Hough, Leroy, and Vaughan.[37]

She sailed away at dawn four days later. She took her four children, her housekeepers, and her field laborers with her, in a sailboat that docked thirty-one miles from Puerto Princesa. The Japanese officials had granted her only a two-week absence to help harvest rice with her fam-ily, but Mendoza moved all of her possessions with her, with no intention of returning after the two weeks. Her goal was to continue moving north until she could contact the island's guerrilla force. By late August 1944, she was gone from Puerto Princesa, but her involvement in aiding Amer-ican POWs on Palawan was not finished.

10

SUB SURVIVORS AND COASTWATCHERS

PALAWEÑO GUERRILLAS AND informants like Red Hankie were but a part of the underground movement working to support any Americans who might escape the Puerto Princesa POW camp. Also vital were U.S. submarines operating from Australia and the two small teams of coastwatchers they inserted onto Palawan Island during the summer of 1944.

On June 8, the first group of six specialists was landed by Commander Marshall H. "Red" Austin's submarine *Redfin,* nine days after departing from Fremantle, Australia. The commandos disembarked on the eastern side of Ramos Island, a small patch of land that hugged the northern coast of mountainous Balabac Island, off the southern tip of Palawan. Master Sergeant Amando Corpus, Sergeant Carlos A. Placido, and their four comrades paddled provisions and equipment ashore in rubber rafts before *Redfin* disappeared under the inky surface of the Sulu Sea as silently as it had emerged.[1]

Corpus and his team were Americans of Filipino ancestry, part of a covert specialty division, the 978th Signal Corps. They were spies, directed by General MacArthur to send regular radio reports to Australia on the movement of Japanese ships, airplanes, troops, and supplies. By mid-July, the coastwatchers had been convinced by Captain Nazario Mayor to move their operation onto southern Palawan for protection by his guerrillas at Brooke's Point. The Corpus unit set up its radio gear at Macagua, the mountain escape home of American-born Harry Edwards, where they enjoyed the company of three other American soldiers—George Marquez, Red Wigfield, and Puerto Princesa camp escapee Charlie Watkins—who were evading the Japanese.[2]

By July 24, Placido was in radio contact with Australia, sending regular weather and Japanese shipping reports. On August 8, the submarine *Seawolf* landed another team of radio operators on the northern end of Palawan at Pirata Point, near the coastal town of Tinitian. Master Sergeant Eutiquio B. Cabais and five American guerrillas came ashore in rubber boats, set up their radio equipment, and were transmitting effectively by August 27.[3]

The successful landing of the radio teams under Corpus, Cabais, and other coastwatcher units was made possible by the deployment of U.S. submarines operating from Australia. Palawan escapees Bruce Elliott, Bill Swift, and Joe Little had already been whisked away to freedom by the submarine *Narwhal*, and they would not be the last American fugitives to be pulled from Palawan. Such special operations by the "Silent Service" came at high cost in terms of human lives, as evidenced by the number of sailors who perished when two U.S. subs were lost near Palawan during the summer of 1944.

ED PETRY WAS passing near the two-story Kempei Tai brig on August 2 when one of its prisoners caught his attention. A battered arm waved through the black steel bars of a cell window on the concrete-and-brick structure's first floor as a weak voice summoned him.

Petry cautiously approached the window, snatched the folded paper being waved toward him, and slipped away unnoticed. The note listed the names, ranks, home addresses, and serial numbers of four American sailors, all claiming they were being held in the brig for guerrilla activities rather than as POWs. The paper said they were the sole survivors of the submarine USS *Robalo*, which had sunk quickly after an apparent explosion of its after battery. Petry took the note to camp clerk Hubert Hough, who passed the *Robalo* intelligence to Triny Mendoza in one of his final meetings with her. Red Hankie in turn had the new coast-watcher group relay the intelligence and names of the American survivors via radio to General MacArthur and Admiral Ralph Christie in Australia.[4]

Robalo had been lost on the night of July 2, 1944, after striking a mine while transiting Balabac Passage. The violent explosion flung ten officers and men from its conning tower, but seventy-nine others perished as the boat was swallowed up by the Sulu Sea in less than two minutes. Three of the ten drowned quickly, leaving seven survivors to swim toward distant Comiran Island. *Robalo*'s skipper, Lieutenant Commander Manning Kimmel, was the son of Admiral Husband Kimmel and a nephew of Admiral Thomas Kinkaid. Four men floundered onto the beach of Comiran before midday on July 3, but they believed their skipper had drowned.[5]

Ensign Samuel Tucker and three enlisted men—Floyd Laughlin, Wallace Martin, and Mason Poston—drank rainwater and ate coconuts for two days while building a raft. The four *Robalo* castaways sailed for Balabac Island and beached their crude vessel around 0900 on July 7. They were captured the next day by a Japanese patrol tipped off to the presence of American sailors by two Filipinos. Sergeant Taichi Deguchi, Sergeant Takeo Kawamura, and four other noncommissioned officers of Palawan's Kempei Tai went to Balabac by boat to haul the submariners back to Puerto Princesa for interrogation. The *Robalo* survivors were beaten and tortured for two weeks in the Kempei Tai brig, kept from the view of any other American POWs until one of them managed to slip the note of their plight to Petry.[6]

In mid-August, a warrant officer from Luzon arrived with orders for the Palawan military police to ship the *Robalo* men to Manila for further handling. On August 19, Tucker, Martin, Laughlin, and Poston were herded on board Captain Sakutaro Aida's transport ship *Takao Maru*, accompanied by Deguchi and Sergeant Kawamura, the latter going along to draw pay for the Kempei Tai. *Takao Maru* transported the *Robalo* men to the Japanese cruiser *Kinu* on August 22, and *Kinu* reached Manila on August 25. From that point, nothing is known as to the fate of these four American sailors. They simply disappeared after being examined in Manila. It is possible that the four were executed, and also plausible that they did not survive some future voyage to Japan on board a hellship.[7]

After the war was over, American war crimes investigators would follow various leads concerning the fate of the four survivors. "We have heard stories that a public execution was held in Manila in August or September 1944 and that four submarine men were killed," they documented. "We suspect that these were the *Robalo* men."[8]

THE WATERS NEAR Palawan proved particularly deadly for U.S. submariners during the summer of 1944.

On August 13, just five weeks after the loss of the *Robalo*, Commander John Daniel Crowley's USS *Flier* also struck a mine while running surfaced through Balabac Strait, less than fifty miles from where *Robalo* went down. The *Flier* was gone in less than a minute, leaving just fourteen officers and men fighting for survival. Only Crowley and seven others managed to swim some twelve miles in eighteen hours to the nearest land, tiny Byan Island.[9]

Crowley's men constructed a crude raft and sailed from island to island until taking shelter in the abandoned former home of Nazario Mayor on Bugsuk Island. Members of the local Bolo Battalion—coastalwatchers armed only with bolos who had organized in Puerto Princesa in 1942—moved the submariners on August 21 to Buliluyan Point on Palawan's southernmost coast. John Crowley and his men were introduced to Sergeant Pasqual de la Cruz, the commanding officer of the local guerrillas and a member of Captain Mayor's company. De la Cruz informed Crowley that he had recently made a reconnaissance trip to Balabac Island to verify a rumor that some Americans had been captured there. He related that four American submariners had been captured on the beach of Comiran Island. Interestingly, he gave their identities as being Ensign Tucker, Signalman Third Class Wallace Martin, a third sailor whose identity was unknown, and the commanding officer of the submarine. Crowley quickly realized that another U.S. submarine must have been lost shortly before his *Flier*.[10]

Cruz's sources on Balabac told him that the Japanese had shot and killed the submarine skipper and the unknown fourth sailor. Since Tucker, Martin, and two other sailors were taken alive to Puerto Princesa, Cruz's information would indicate that two other *Robalo* survivors were captured separately. It is thus plausible that Kimmel and one other man, either Lieutenant Commander Charlie Fell or radarman Holley Ivey, were shot at some point. Cruz was unable to ascertain whether the two Americans were murdered while attempting to escape or whether they were shot at a later date.

Fortunately, fate and the Palawan guerrilla network proved to be kinder to the eight USS *Flier* survivors. Crowley's *Flier* men remained at Cape Buliluyan overnight before beginning their journey up the Palawan coast in a *kumpit*, a native *banca* about sixteen feet in length with a large sail atop one mast. They arrived at the southern tip of Ipolote Bay on August 23. Captain Mayor greeted them and invited the Navy men to his home several hundred yards deep in the jungle. They also met Harry Edwards, Mary Mayor, and the Mayor children, who would care for the *Flier* survivors for the next few days. Mayor moved the men to the Harry and Rosario Edwards home in Macagua, where Sergeant Amando Corpus was operating his coastwatcher radio unit.[11]

The *Flier* men were welcomed by the Corpus coastwatchers and three other American refugees: Watkins, Marquez, and Wigfield. Radio operator Teodoro "Butch" Rallojay tapped out coded messages to Australia, detailing the loss of the submarine and the names of its survivors. The Australian headquarters staff sent word that they would coordinate a submarine rescue near the beach off Brooke's Point in Ipolote Bay. Admiral Christie sent an Ultra dispatch to Commander Red Austin's submarine *Redfin* on August 23 to proceed immediately to this point off the eastern coast of Palawan.[12]

Sergeant Corpus and his coastwatchers took the loss of *Flier* hard, based on the replies received over the radio from MacArthur's headquarters. "We were reprimanded for not reporting the presence of mines in that area where the unfortunate sub sank," Carlos Placido wrote in his diary. "We felt downhearted. The survivors themselves admitted they knew the place might have been mined, but they had chanced it, nonetheless." Three days later, on August 26, Corpus was so depressed over the *Flier* loss that he shot himself through the heart with a .45.[13]

The submarine detailed to recover the *Flier* men, Red Austin's *Redfin*, was the same boat that had deposited the Corpus coastwatchers on Ramos Island in June 1944. The departure group moved from the mountains on August 30 down to Nazario Mayor's home near the beach to wait for sunset. The seventeen-person party included the eight *Flier* survivors, Palawan escapee Watkins, Bataan escapees Wigfield and Marquez, and six civilians who had been taken in by the guerrilla network.[14]

Sergeant Placido and his radiomen helped direct *Redfin* in to rendezvous with two small boats carrying the seventeen evacuees, and shortly before 0100 on August 31, the pickup was made. Commander Austin sent a hoard of arms and supplies back on the boats for the use of the coastwatchers and Captain Mayor's guerrillas.[15]

The coastwatchers shoved off from the submarine, which got under way and quickly disappeared into the darkness. Austin's *Redfin* sailors took the chance to lob deck gun shells into a Japanese ship anchored off Brooke's Point during their departure. Belowdecks, the escapees were overjoyed to be heading toward safety. Charlie Watkins enjoyed a well-done steak, French fries, corn on the cob, vegetable salad, and pie and ice cream for his first meal.[16]

Redfin reached Darwin, Australia, six days later. Watkins had spent two years and two months on the run since escaping from the Japanese. Joe Little had preceded him in making it back to the States, but Watkins was finally reunited with his mother on October 3. It would be many months later before the U.S. Navy allowed Watkins to tell his incredible story to newspaper journalists.

Following Joe Little, Bruce Elliott, and Bill Swift, Watkins became the fourth American POW from the Japanese compound at Puerto Princesa to make his way back home.

THE WEASEL AND THE BUZZARD

A s Ernie Koblos climbed out of the work truck at the entrance to the Puerto Princesa compound after another grueling day, he noticed an unusual number of guards standing by. At once he knew something was up. Twenty-two months of backbreaking labor had sapped much of his will to live, but even now, his spirits broken and his body battered, any change to his routine put him on high alert. He and his fellow prisoners marched through the tall stone archway and headed for their barracks, but instead of filing inside, they were ordered by Kinoshita to line up in two ranks, ten paces apart, as they were assigned to either Company A or Company B.

Three days earlier, on August 19, the four *Robalo* prisoners had been marched from camp, bringing the camp roster down to 309, of which nine men were currently off work detail due to being on Doc Mango's sick list. Mango had been forced to stand his ground while treating one private for blood in his urine, requiring him to be sent to a Japanese hospital for additional treatment. When the Japanese challenged his call, Mango snapped, "Bring your own damn doctor in!" They did, confirmed the diagnosis, and put the soldier on the sick list.[1]

Now, on August 22, the remaining three hundred men were split into two equal groups. Only a few knew the reason: The Japanese were planning to reduce their work force on Palawan. With the airfield in good order, Kinoshita could get by with half the prisoners to maintain it, while the other "workers" could better serve Japan by being shipped to the homeland. Those assigned to Company A were bound for Bilibid Prison in Manila.

Hubert Hough had helped organize the list of departing men. Captain Harry Hickman, tabbed to depart, selected Phil Brodsky and Russell Lash from his medical unit to go with him, leaving three medics behind: Everett Bancroft, Charles Bartle, and Charles Schubert. With them would remain First Lieutenant Mango for medical needs and Dr. Henry Knight, the dentist.[2] Bob Russell would join Hickman. Hough tried to include Warrant Officer Glenn Turner because he could not see eye to eye with Doc Mango or Captain Bruni, but the Japanese would not allow any more officers to go. Interpreter Shorty Sumida promised to ship Turner out on the next detail. Hough was willing to stay, but something compelled him to add his own name to the list of those departing Palawan.[3]

The newly designated men of Company A were ordered inside the barracks to gather their belongings before being marched to the pier. Mac McDole said good-bye to his Iowa friend, camp cobbler Don Thomas, who found himself on the outbound roster. Francis Galligan, who had been on the island since the beginning in August 1942, wanted to remain with a group of close friends from his home state of Massachusetts, but guards denied the request. Galligan quickly said his good-byes and joined the line of men heading for the water's edge.[4]

The 159 departing prisoners boarded a rusting transport ship, *Maru Hachi*, just arrived with companies of fresh khaki-clad Japanese soldiers. Instead of embarking right away, the Americans were put to work as stevedores, unloading and partially reloading the ship. Twenty trucks were moved into the vessel's forward hold, as well as hundreds of empty metal drums and several hundred twenty-five-foot logs into an afterhold in the rear of the ship's superstructure. *Maru Hachi* remained only half-loaded with cargo, fully capable of carrying another 150 POWs.[5]

For weeks, the outgoing prisoners slept on board the ship at night and worked the docks during the day, wondering if they would ever sail. Meanwhile, Hubert Hough worried about the underground communications system he had run the past two years in conjunction with Filipino guerrillas. He had sent numerous typewritten documents out to be transmitted by radio to the Allies, and as *Maru Hachi* lingered, he fretted that the Japanese would discover his spying. Each arriving boat induced cold chills as he imagined guards coming for him.[6]

When *Maru Hachi* finally sailed on September 22, 1944, the Japanese sailors and prisoner guards, terrified of submarine attacks, never took off their life jackets during the entire voyage to Manila. Despite that risk, Hough could breathe easier only when the green treetops of Palawan faded into the sparkling blue horizon.[7]

Several days later, guards informed the remaining Americans that *Maru Hachi* had been torpedoed and that all men were dead. For several days, a deep gloom set in over the camp before a Filipino informant brought news that it was all a lie: Their comrades had indeed made it safely back to Manila.[8]

SMITTY WAS DISHEARTENED by the half-empty barracks. Of the 150 Americans left behind at Puerto Princesa, only three dozen were fellow marines, including his best friend, Mac McDole, and Doug Bogue. The Navy prisoners now numbered only fifteen, including Smitty's Southern friend C. C. Smith and radioman Joe Barta. The balance of the Palawan camp comprised U.S. Army soldiers and a few Army Air Corps men. The departing close friends and clique-mates left the remaining prisoners feeling as broken as if they had lost family members.

On September 8, while the departing prisoners still lingered in the harbor, the Japanese camp personnel underwent a major change. The III Land Duty Company, which had supervised construction of the

Puerto Princesa airfield, was relieved by the 131st Airfield Battalion, which was under command of the 11th Air Sector of the 4th Air Army.[9]

Incredibly, Palawan's POWs found that each new camp commandant was even crueler and more lethal than his predecessor. After the comparatively lenient Kishimoto was relieved, Kinoshita had taken over; during his sixteen-plus months, three Americans had died from work-related mishaps, and another two had been executed for trying to escape. Unfortunately, Kinoshita's replacement would prove to be the most vicious.

Captain Nagayoshi Kojima, commander of the incoming 131st, took over as the new commandant of Palawan's Camp 10-A. The Americans, always quick with a derogatory nickname for their tormentors, tagged the sly, aggressive Kojima as "the Weasel." Kojima had taught primary school before he first entered infantry service, and as his prisoners would soon discover, he brought a sadistic headmaster's approach to his new job. The Weasel's 342-man company, which had arrived on Palawan in August, ruled over their POWs with an iron fist within weeks.[10]

Second in command of Camp 10-A was "the Buzzard." First Lieutenant Yoshikazu Sato, a short man with beady eyes that seemed to peer right through people, had a thin frame and weighed no more than 120 pounds, but the Buzzard was fierce in his role as base executive officer, in charge of the guard force. Under him, Lieutenant Sho Yoshiwara now commanded the three-platoon garrison company. Lieutenant Ryoji Ozawa became the new officer in charge of supply at Puerto Princesa, while Lieutenant Toru Ogawa's company was tasked with maintaining the vehicle repair shop, the airfield repair work, and the refueling of planes.[11]

While the docile Blinky had departed with Kinoshita, remaining behind were two of the worst guards from the former regime—Master Sergeant Deguchi, in charge of the Kempei Tai, and Manishi "Buckteeth" Nishitani, the mess sergeant who took great pleasure in beating Americans nearly to death. Among the new group of Japanese soldiers, several particularly mean ones stood out. Private Takeo Kawakami was an ex-fighter who enjoyed using his boxing skills to beat prisoners sense-less. A small man named Shubakii carried brass knuckles, which he used to punch men squarely in the mouth.[12]

The Americans could feel change in the air. Through their guerrilla "jungle telegraph," they gradually heard news of the approach of Allied forces. On August 9, U.S. Navy carrier planes had bombed Japanese installations in Davao, and days later, waves of American aircraft attacked the Visayas. On September 11, just after the Weasel and the Buzzard arrived, American planes bombed Japanese vessels in Manila Bay and airstrips around the city. Because of these raids, President José P. Laurel—head of the Japanese puppet state labeled the Second Philippine Republic—proclaimed martial law to protect lives and property, as invasion of the Philippines appeared imminent.[13]

BETO PACHECO COULD feel his body wasting away. After the 159 Americans had set sail on September 22, Captain Kojima cut the remaining prisoners' rations. Work hours stretched from dawn to dusk, seven days a week, without the usual Sundays off, and noon chow on work detail had to be gobbled down in only fifteen to twenty minutes, with no break from the midday sun. Pacheco's already lean frame became dangerously thin. He had shed more than thirty pounds during his two years on Palawan, but he was a survivor by nature, born to rugged parents of mixed Spanish and Mexican heritage. His earliest ancestor in America was Bernardo de Miera y Pacheco, a military engineer and cartographer who created the first maps of the New World area of present New Mexico, where generations of the Pacheco family had lived and ranched since 1734. Beto's upbringing had prepared him for living lean and working hard, but the suffering he endured on Palawan was beyond anything he had experienced during his family's rugged early existence.

Under Captain Kojima's new orders, Pacheco and his comrades received only three-quarters of a mess kit of rice per day and a meager serving of a greenish-colored soup consisting of *camote* vines boiled in salt water. Pacheco's fellow prisoner Gene Nielsen became disgusted with what he called "whistle weed" soup, so watery and bitter that many prisoners ended up with diarrhea. The hollow stalks of the *camote*, a Philippine sweet potato, were more edible when the plants were young. With older plants, the stalks grew larger, forming a hollow middle that earned them their nickname. About once a month, the men would receive the bones of a caribou to boil into a broth, but only after the Japanese guards picked off all the decent meat. The decreasing calories only drove prisoners like Nielsen to take more risks, sneaking into the jungle for papayas and coconuts when the guards weren't looking.[14]

In late September, General Shiyoku Kou, in charge of all POWs in the Philippines, ordered the remaining 150 Americans returned to Manila. Though transportation was available, the order was never carried out. Instead, Captain Kojima's men took up residence in the abandoned homes in Puerto Princesa. As the Allies inched closer to the Philippines, Japanese soldiers began digging revetments for artillery pieces along the shoreline and installing antiaircraft guns around the docks and the airfield.

Mac McDole soon noticed a new Filipino turncoat who seemed far too cozy with the Japanese guards. Pedro Paje, superintendent of the nearby Iwahig Penal Colony, was a small forty-one-year-old whose face sported a large scar that ran from his left cheekbone down to his chin. Nearly every day he brought sake, rice cookies, and other gifts for the Japanese guards, and as he walked the camp, he would cruelly laugh and spit on the Americans.

McDole had no reason to suspect that Paje's actions might actually be part of a larger plan.

ON THE MORNING of October 19, less than a month after half the POWs were sent to Manila, a heavy rain stopped all progress at the airfield, and the prisoners were returned to camp. Smitty and Mac McDole were in their barracks around 1500, awaiting their rice rations, when they heard a strange noise growing louder in the distance.

"That don't sound like a Jap plane," said Smitty.

McDole agreed. As the rumble increased, Smitty looked out toward the bay and spotted a lone four-engine bomber soar out of the clouds, skimming low over the water toward the prison camp. To the two prisoners, it looked to be a foreign warplane, sporting a shiny twin tail and a bulky frame loaded with bombs and machine guns. As it roared low across the Puerto Princesa compound, Smitty and McDole could clearly see blue-and-white U.S. Navy star emblems on the underside of the plane's wings.[15]

Prisoners throughout the camp whooped and hollered, throwing their dented pith helmets into the sky with joy. Some laughed and others broke down in tears as the Army Consolidated B-24 Liberator bomber waggled its wings while passing over at a mere three hundred feet. The Americans watched the pilot climb back to altitude and settle into the business of making an attack.

Commander Justin Albert Miller could not resist signaling a greeting to the POWs below. He was the skipper of Patrol Bombing Squadron 101 (VPB-101), based on Morotai in the Maluku Islands. Earlier that day, he and his crew had taken off in his *Miller's High Life* on a thousand-mile patrol of the South China Sea. During his return to Morotai, Miller diverted his bomber to hit the Japanese seaplane base at Puerto Princesa. He came in low at a hundred feet to attack the dock, where two small interisland ships were moored along with six nestled seaplanes.[16]

Miller dumped ten hundred-pound bombs that destroyed the vessels and set the seaplanes on fire. The POWs could hear the drone of the B-24's four Pratt & Whitney engines as the pilot circled to come in for another run. His *Miller's High Life* roared along the runway, just right of center, so low that Miller's navigator claimed to see mud hit the windshield as they attacked an estimated forty Japanese planes parked on the strip.[17]

Smitty and McDole watched the bombs tumble free from the Liberator and were proud to see the destruction, fires, and chaos created by the American aviators. Many other POWs remained out in the open, exposed to shrapnel, to witness the attack. These included Ed Petry, who enjoyed watching terrified Japanese soldiers dive into shelters for protection.[18]

Miller's crew had less to celebrate. As his Liberator retired low over Puerto Princesa Bay, it was stitched with antiaircraft fire and one engine burst into flames. Miller and his copilot fought their damaged controls for several minutes but lost the battle when their B-24 slammed into the ocean about ten miles off Palawan. Miller was ejected through the windscreen while still strapped into his seat, and three crewmen were killed on impact. The seven survivors of the crash, several seriously injured, clung to a bomb-bay fuel tank until the current carried them to tiny Ramesamey Island, about seven miles from Puerto Princesa. The next day, the crewmen encountered an enemy officer whose own plane had crash-landed. Outnumbered, the Japanese aviator splashed into the ocean, grabbed the Liberator's discarded fuel cell for a flotation device, and paddled away. The Americans feared that they would eventually be discovered on their tiny speck of land, which was only about three thousand yards in circumference.[19]

Many Filipinos, including Triny Mendoza, had witnessed Miller's attack on Puerto Princesa. Now back at her late husband's plantation despite the danger of being apprehended by the Kempei Tai, Mrs. Mendoza felt sure the flaming bomber that she saw crash into the ocean across the bay from her home was American, so she called for two men to sail to Ramesamey Island to look for survivors. They paddled along the coast but returned to Palawan, reporting that they had seen no one. This left the widow to reluctantly write off the hero airmen as lost.[20]

AMERICAN WARPLANES BECAME a regular sight after Miller's attack. From that day forward, the Palawan prisoners saw at least one American bomber almost every day as more B-24s dodged antiaircraft fire to deliver loads of ordnance. One lone Liberator began making regular noontime runs on the Puerto Princesa area, his arrival so routine that the

Americans nicknamed the pilot "Hysterical Harry," in honor of the chaos he created each day as the Japanese sprinted for their air-raid shelters.[21]

The Puerto Princesa prisoners were unaware that American troops began landing on Leyte on October 20 as the retaking of the Philippines commenced. General MacArthur waded ashore that afternoon on Red Beach, just south of Leyte's largest city of Tacloban. Photographers were on hand to capture his triumphant arrival as he sloshed through the waves with staff officers and Philippine president Sergio Osmeña, who had been ruling from exile. By radio, he announced, "People of the Philippines, I have returned."

More island invasions would follow in the weeks and months ahead as ground troops secured the main airfields on Leyte. The Japanese on Palawan, seeing more and more U.S. warplanes passing overhead, realized it was only a matter of time before they might encounter American combat troops on their island. MacArthur warned the Japanese commander in chief in the Philippines, Field Marshal Count Hisaichi Terauchi, that the prisoners should be taken care of or he would be held personally accountable. Leaflets to this effect were dropped by air on enemy positions throughout the Philippines on November 25.[22]

The Palawan airfield, capable of supporting as many as two hundred planes, began slowly emptying as aircraft were moved to safer fields. On October 28, the largest raid yet struck midmorning, when prisoners counted seventeen B-24s glide overhead. Ed Petry was again among many of the prisoners caught in the open, unable to take cover until their Japanese guards fled to their air-raid shelters. With just seconds to spare, Petry and others scrambled to the only nearby protection, a drainage ditch alongside the runway.[23]

The first B-24 bombs exploded a short distance away. One made a direct hit on a four-car garage and lubrication pit, destroying a gasoline truck and the Japanese soldier attempting to start it. Bombs heavily cratered the runway, destroyed dozens of parked planes, and even damaged many of the aircraft tucked away in the jungle revetments. This large raid, as well as smaller ones on subsequent days, disrupted air operations and created plenty of work for the American prisoners to repair with hand tools.

Joe Barta and his friend John Stanley were among the teams charged with refilling the bomb holes one afternoon as black smoke still belched skyward from mangled machines of war. Sergeant Deguchi approached and barked at Stanley to pick up his pace. The prisoner simply replied that there were too many rocks in the way for him to move any faster. Deguchi responded by knocking Stanley to the ground with a blow to the head from a pick handle. His life had been spared only by his hard sun helmet, now smashed flat. Stanley was helped to sick bay with a three-inch gash in his head.[24]

The Japanese guards scampered for cover each day as bombers arrived, but they returned to beat their prisoners with a vengeance once the air raiders departed. McDole took the abuse with some pleasure. To him, the sight of any American bomber raising hell with the Japanese was a thing of great joy, as the end was now in sight. But Captain Kojima cut rations even further, and allowed his soldiers to abuse the POWs at will, even rousing them from their barracks at night for random beatings.[25]

The Americans usually took shelter in the nearby coconut grove when air raids commenced, and they suffered few injuries as a result. One exception occurred during a strafing attack when a bullet ricocheted off a tree and lodged in the right shoulder of marine Earl Joyner. Doc Mango patched him up but did not have proper medical facilities to remove the fragment without seriously endangering his patient.[26]

Such strafing attacks drove many Japanese guards to seek retribution. Private Tomisaburo Sawa, a twenty-one-year-old former fisherman from Hokkaido, grew so fearful of an American landing on Palawan that he took out his frustration on the prisoners, hammering defenseless men with his rifle butt, and at times even his fists. Although married with young children at home, Sawa displayed a frighteningly sadistic temperament, often dropping a POW to his knees and using a bayonet to slice up the soft skin on his face.[27]

American bombers attacked the Palawan airfield with increasing frequency throughout late 1944. POWs working on the field were forced to quickly scramble to whatever cover they could find.

NATIONAL ARCHIVES

After each air strike, prisoners faced the exhausting task of repairing damage to the runway. The white ovals seen dotting the airstrip and jungle floor are bomb craters partially filled with water.   NATIONAL ARCHIVES

Ed Petry did his best to create diversions with the guards to offer some rest to his fellow prisoners. Assigned to drive a gravel truck each day to a nearby settlement, he rode under the eye of a Japanese guard to the gravel pit, where Filipino prisoners from the Iwahig Penal Colony loaded his vehicle before he returned to the airstrip for American POWs to unload.

Petry was supposed to make five trips per day, but he rigged the ignition switch near the accelerator so he could easily turn off the engine with his foot while driving. When the truck rolled to a stop, Petry would jump out and pretend to tinker with the engine for long periods of time. His Japanese guard, ignorant of mechanics, could only watch with frustration as he fumbled with wires and spark plugs. When Petry was ready, he would simply flip on his secret ignition switch and announce that he had cured the problem. The Japanese never caught on to his trick, and Petry was proud to offer the boys at the airfield some much-needed rest until the delivery of the next load of gravel. Petry was surprised the Japanese never realized that his work truck somehow never broke down when he made the noontime chow delivery to his comrades at the airfield.

Hysterical Harry continued to bring mayhem to the Puerto Princesa airfield well into November. The prisoners endured endless beatings from clubs and pick handles each time, and they spent untold hours refilling bomb craters. Captain Bruni requested permission for the POWs to mark the roof of their four-winged barracks as a POW camp for their protection after the first air strikes began on October 19. Captain Kojima angrily refused the request until the large raid made on October 28, after which he allowed them to paint "American Prisoner of War Camp 10-A" on the roof—but only on the wing of the barracks in which the Japanese stored rice and other food.[28]

Rumors of the end of Japan's reign circulated around camp. Mac McDole, who had learned enough Japanese to understand some of what he heard, listened one day to two guards talking about the surrender of Italy and that Germany was about to quit the war. He passed the word, enhancing the tale to help boost morale by adding that Japan would be the next country to surrender.[29]

He was soon hauled to the Kempei Tai brig after the Japanese learned who was spreading the story. Mac believed that Paje, often lurking about with Kojima's guards, was the one who had ratted him out. McDole tried explaining to Deguchi's military police that it was all a joke meant to increase prisoner morale, but the Kempei Tai was not buying it. They quizzed him on how he was getting information from the local guerrillas and threatened to beat him until he confessed. With his hands behind his back, Mac was hoisted from the rafters, and guards took turns beating him like a piñata with a strap and three-foot sticks.

The abuse continued all afternoon and into the night, but the bloodied marine stuck to his story. It was all a joke, he said, and he was not in communication with any outside Filipinos. Deguchi's men finally cut him down and allowed McDole to lie in the dirt for several minutes as he tried to regain his senses. He made it to all fours and was struggling to his feet when a new guard entered the brig. Lieutenant Toru Ogawa was a short, stocky man with a thick neck and gold teeth. *He doesn't appear to have a sense of humor,* thought Mac. *He looks like a sumo wrestler.*

"Huh, some joke!" growled Ogawa.

He lashed out with his fist and caught McDole square in the jaw, knocking him backward over tables and chairs. Mac was out cold. When he regained his senses for the second time that day, he was being dragged back into his barracks. The guards dumped him on the floor and stomped out as Smitty hustled over to help his buddy onto his sleeping mat.

The prisoners could not help but think there might be an ounce of truth to McDole's rumors about Japan's demise.

12

"ANNIHILATE THEM ALL"

TWO DAYS AFTER *Miller's High Life* crashed into the ocean, Ensign Hector McDaniel stood on the beach of tiny Ramesamey Island and decided to swim for Palawan. Of the ten-man crew on board the B-24, only seven had survived, but stuck on this speck of sand with little food or fresh water, their hopes of remaining alive much longer dwindled with each passing hour. Palawan lay only seven miles away, seven miles of seawater and God knew what, but at least there he could scrounge for food and rendezvous with Filipino guerrillas. Splashing through the surf, he threw himself into the water and began swimming. Exhaustion soon overtook him, and he had to turn back.[1]

Undeterred by his crew member's failure, pilot Justin Miller went to work building a crude raft. On October 27, more than a week after his attack on Puerto Princesa, he and McDaniel set out paddling for Palawan, leaving their five comrades behind. Forced to rest on another deserted island for several days en route, the two men finally reached Palawan on November 2. Haggard and sunburned, the Americans encountered a Filipino fisherman on the beach. News of their arrival flashed through the underground network to Triny Mendoza, who had given them up for dead two weeks earlier. To recover the five airmen still stranded on Ramesamey, some too injured to walk, Mendoza organized a crew to paddle dugout canoes to the island that evening.[2]

The wounded men were soon carried ashore at Palawan on bamboo stretchers, and Mendoza hosted the seven aviators for the next four days, treating their wounds before Sergeant Jacinto Cutaran's Filipino fighters moved them north along the coast. By late November, Miller's crew, still awaiting rescue from Palawan, had been joined by four other naval aviators from the carrier *Intrepid* who had been lost in action on September 24.[3]

After an attempt to recover the Americans with an amphibious PBY Catalina was foiled by the Japanese, General MacArthur's staff called upon Admiral Ralph Christie's submarine force to help. Orders were sent on December 1 to Lieutenant Commander Guy E. O'Neill's USS *Gunnel* to attempt the rescue of eleven naval aviators.[4]

By dusk the next day, *Gunnel* was slipping through the waters ten miles off Palawan's Flechas Point. Two guerrilla leaders delivered the American fliers by boat to Cutaran. They boarded the submarine for ice cream, pie, chocolate cake, and other treats they had not enjoyed in years. For their service, Sergeant Cutaran's men were gifted two .50-caliber machine guns along with considerable ammunition, hand grenades, clothing, binoculars, canned food, and medical supplies.

Gunnel skipper O'Neill would receive a Navy Cross for his successful war patrol off Palawan. Justin Miller, Hector McDaniel, and their bow gunner, Lieutenant Bill Read, also received Navy Crosses for their attack on the Puerto Princesa airfield and for the sinking of two ships. No awards were handed out to Palawan's guerrilla network, who had proved essential to safeguarding and coordinating the rescue of eleven Americans.

The remaining Americans imprisoned at Puerto Princesa would not be so fortunate.

AMERICAN WARPLANES CONTINUED to visit the Puerto Princesa airfield with bomb loads throughout November 1944. After each attack, the

POWs were herded onto the runways to fill the craters. Captain Kojima also put his prisoners to work digging proper bomb shelters in the center of the camp compound, reportedly for their own protection against strafing and shrapnel. The three longest trenches were about four feet wide and one hundred fifty feet long. Once the men had dug down to a depth of four feet, they were ordered to construct a roof over each shelter consisting of coconut tree logs and old boards. They then heaped dirt along the entire length of each roof for further protection from flying splinters. The three largest shelters were designated A, B, and C.

Shelter C was located west of the prisoner barracks. The end of the tunnel stopped just near the barbed wire fencing that stood above the cliff's edge, overlooking the rocky coastline below. Shelter B, running parallel to C, hooked toward the bluffs so that one entrance was also near the fencing. Shelter A, on the east side of camp, was slightly larger than the other two and could hold about fifty men. In addition to these three, five smaller holes were dug in areas scattered throughout the compound. Each was little more than a deep foxhole that could hold no more than three to four men in cramped fashion. The Americans tried to convince their guards that a second entrance to each large tunnel was needed in case a direct bomb hit sealed off the main entrance, but their pleas went unheeded. In time, Captain Bruni protested enough that men received permission to dig a secondary entrance to some of the shelters.[5]

McDole, Smitty, and several others took it upon themselves to secretly construct an alternative emergency exit from Shelter C. They began digging into the sidewall of their bunker a few yards from the secondary exit near the barbed wire fence. In the process, they hit a large coral rock, which they had to dig out of the way. They shoveled the excess dirt into a large sandbag as they tunneled toward the edge of the cliff, until just six inches of earth remained. To hide their project, they shoved the sandbag into the hole and forced the sizable coral rock back over the opening, which they camouflaged with limbs and debris. The men knew they could punch through the last bit of earth by removing the rock and the sandbag and make it down the sixty-foot incline to the rocky beach below.

During one November air raid, McDole was filling bomb craters on the airfield when he counted seven waves of seven bombers each flying in low over the ocean. He scrambled into the jungle for cover as the planes tore up the airfield and swung around to attack ships in the harbor. The prisoners had grown used to such attacks and feared little, as their barracks area had never been directly hit. In all of the raids, Private First Class Aubrey Johnson was only the second American to be wounded, hit in the right shoulder by a .50-caliber fragment on October 28.

Two other POWs were injured in the November 29 air strike. Private Robert Stevenson was hit in the left shoulder and suffered a scalp laceration, but Sergeant James Stidham was seriously wounded. A rock blasted from a bomb explosion left him paralyzed with a brain injury. The sergeant was rendered immobilized, only able to lie on a stretcher, staring at the barracks ceiling.[6]

The B-24 Liberators made the most of their regular noontime raids against Puerto Princesa, inflicting much damage and hindering Japanese operations. On less frequent occasions, the bombers would attack around midnight, when they faced no aerial opposition. One afternoon, Mac McDole and Joseph Uballe watched two Zeros land after attacking the American bombers. The two briefly discussed the possibility of stealing one of the Japanese fighters, but they soon dismissed the idea as suicide and returned to their never-ending job of filling in bomb craters.[7]

GENERAL MACARTHUR'S AUDACIOUS return to the Philippines had gotten the attention of the Japanese command. The Americans' landings on Leyte and ever-increasing bomb raids on other islands compelled the Japanese to begin moving their prisoners of war toward their homeland.

During September and October, thousands of American, British, and Australian POWs were herded into transport ships for the voyage out of the Philippines. Locked in cargo holds with little food, water, fresh air, or proper toilet facilities, the men dubbed the vessels "hellships" for the inhumane suffering they endured. Some ships broke down, leaving the POWs stranded for long periods as men agonized within their holds. Other hellships, unmarked as carrying prisoners of war, were torpedoed by American submarines and sunk en route to other bases.

On October 1, more than eleven hundred Americans were moved out of Bilibid Prison on Luzon and shoved into two cargo holds on board the freighter *Hokusen Maru*. Its name was blacked out, leaving many to remember it as only the "Horror Maru." Among the men were some of the former Palawan prisoners who had been returned to Manila the previous week, including camp cobbler Don Thomas and marine George Burlage. The forward hold was packed with coal, and the hot clouds of black dust made it difficult to breathe. Burlage found that the coal was at least useful in soaking up the urine and feces dropped by his fellow captives.[8]

Hokusen Maru joined with eight other hellships and several warships for the long voyage to Japan. On October 6, two prisoner vessels were torpedoed and sunk, and carrier planes and submarines continued to prey on the convoy until only four transport ships remained afloat when they reached Hong Kong on October 11. For five days, the convoy remained anchored off the city's coast, where some prisoners, trapped in the increasingly slimy and odorous holds, lost their sanity. By the time they reached Japan on October 24, dozens of men were dead.

The *Hokusen Maru* survivors were fortunate in comparison to those aboard other hellships. The Japanese were emptying the Philippines of all foreigners, and on October 11, some 1,782 POWs were jammed into the cargo ship *Arisan Maru*. Among them were twenty-seven former Puerto Princesa Camp 10-A prisoners, including Captain Harry Hickman and two of his medics, Phil Brodsky and Russell Lash. *Arisan Maru* departed Manila but was soon forced to take shelter off the coast of Palawan for several days to escape air attacks. The ship returned to Manila, where it spent more days forming up with other vessels until the convoy departed for the large Japanese port of Takao in Taiwan on October 21.[9]

Nine American submarines lay in wait. Their torpedoes slammed into the convoy on the afternoon of October 23, and by early afternoon the next day, seven hellships were sunk, carrying thousands of Allied POWs to their deaths. The remaining ships scattered, leaving the slow-moving *Arisan Maru* on her own, and in the crosshairs of the aptly named USS *Shark*.

Three torpedoes ripped into the transport. As it began slowly sinking, most of the Japanese abandoned ship, but not before cutting the rope ladders into the holds so that the trapped POWs would drown. The men managed to repair the ladders, and many foraged through the doomed ship, helping themselves to supplies. Phil Brodsky thought it was comical to see men smoking two cigarettes at a time, drinking bottles of ketchup, and eating sugar. He sat on deck with hundreds of others who had survived the torpedo explosions, waiting until the passenger ship slowly settled under fifteen-foot waves. Most men drowned, or died of exposure to sun and cold water, during the next few days, but Brodsky managed to climb aboard flotsam that sustained him and another man for days until they were hauled on board a Japanese escort ship. Brodsky was one of only nine POWs to survive the sinking of the *Arisan Maru*. Some 1,770 other Americans—including another two dozen former Palawan POWs—perished.[10]

Brodsky was taken to Takao, interrogated, and placed on board *Hokusan Maru* with other former Palawan prisoners for passage to another Japanese-controlled port on November 8. Many more American POWs would be lost before the war's end. The *Oryoku Maru* departed Manila for Japan on December 13, hauling 1,620 prisoners of war, including a number of former Palawan enlisted prisoners and three officers from the Puerto Princesa camp: Phil Golden, John Janson, and Bob Russell.

As the unmarked *Oryoku Maru* neared the naval base at Olongapo in Subic Bay, the aircraft from the carrier *Hornet* attacked, doing heavy damage. More carrier planes returned on December 15 to finish off the hellship. Nearly two hundred prisoners of war died in the bombing, or were shot in the water by Japanese as they tried to escape. Survivors were held ashore on an open tennis court at Olongapo Naval Base with abysmal sanitary conditions before being moved to another port for further transfer. Fifteen of those too weak or wounded for slave labor were beheaded and dumped into a mass grave.

About one thousand of the original *Oryoku Maru* prisoners were loaded onto two other hellships, *Enoura Maru* and *Brazil Maru*, for passage to Takao Harbor in Taiwan. *Enoura Maru* was bombed on January 9, 1945, causing 350 more POW deaths. Only 403 of the 1,620 original *Oryoku Maru* passengers survived their passage on the hellships and their subsequent prison camps in Japan. Ensign Russell and Private Fred Ludwig survived *Oryoku Maru*, but ten former Palawan prisoners perished.

FOR THE AMERICANS who remained on Palawan, there would be no hellship voyages.

Unbeknownst to the prisoners, the Japanese high command had already given approval for their disposal. In August, the war ministry in Tokyo issued orders to POW camp commandants to kill all American and civilian internees before they could be liberated. Prisoners were to be destroyed individually or in groups—using poisons, decapitations, mass bombings, or whatever the situation might dictate. The directive stated, "It is the aim not to allow the escape of a single one, to annihilate them all, and not to leave any trace."[11]

By the second week of December, the question over the fate of American prisoners on Palawan was coming to a head. Captain Nagayoshi Kojima's 131st Airfield Battalion, in charge of Camp 10-A at Puerto Princesa, fell under the command of Lieutenant General Seiichi Terada, commander of the 2nd Air Division, 4th Air Army. Terada's headquarters was on Negros Island, located southeast of Palawan. On December 9, Terada discussed Palawan and other issues with a senior staff officer of Lieutenant General Kyoji Tominaga, who had been given command of all airfield construction units in the Philippines as of October 20.[12]

The following day, December 10, a Japanese lookout post on Surigao, located on the northern tip of Mindanao, spotted an American convoy of more than three hundred ships heading toward Negros Island. Reconnaissance planes reported a huge trail of American troop transports, battleships, and aircraft carriers steaming west.[13]

Uncertain where the Americans intended to strike, Terada sent out more scouting flights. His aviators returned with reports that the fleet had changed course and was moving northwest into the Sulu Sea. The general, believing the American force was intent on landing at Palawan, sent the following message to all units: "As a result of this morning's reconnaissance, the enemy fleet is sailing northwest on the Sulu Sea. Division will not divert strength from the Leyte area and concentrate on the enemy fleet. Probable landing on Palawan Island expected."

On December 12, the American convoy was just south of the Cuyo Islands when General Terada received a top-secret dispatch from Captain Kojima on Palawan. Terada was then in conference with Major General Masami Kumabe of the 4th Air Army about who held jurisdiction over the Palawan battalion. One message they were studying indicated that the natives in that area held a "hostile attitude" and had made guerrilla attacks on the airfield area in recent weeks.[14]

Terada was faced with a request of how to handle the American POWs if such a landing took place. Regardless of whether he had formal orders on how to act, the general decided to offer his advice, figuring the matter could be sorted out later. After discussions with General Kumabe, Terada sent a dispatch on the evening of December 12 to Tominaga. The general's reply was received that evening, and General Terada sent his own dispatch to Palawan on December 13: "Jurisdiction over your unit is presently being investigated by the Army Chief of Staff and 2nd Air Division. In reference to your wireless request: 1) Pertaining to wiping out the natives, carry on as you see fit. 2) At the time of the enemy landing, if the POWs are harboring an enemy feeling, dispose of them at the appropriate time. The above mentioned lines of action are based on an army order."

Terada had just sent the approval needed to murder every American being held on Palawan.

THE PRISONERS COULD sense that something was wrong. Chatter overheard among the guards indicated that an American fleet had been spotted in their region. Work on the runways continued, the emaciated men toiling with shovels and wheelbarrows to haul dirt to each fresh bomb crater. Some guards, suspecting their time in the camp would soon be ending, sadistically shared the news with the POWs that if the United States invaded Palawan, every single prisoner would be executed.

On December 13, the camp's Japanese cook approached Willie Balchus with a strange question. He was a champion swimmer in Japan, he claimed, and asked Balchus if he thought he could swim across Puerto Princesa Bay, a distance of about four miles. Willie said that he thought he could. The cook asked how long it would take. "About a half hour," Balchus joked. The cook then claimed that if American forces were to land on Palawan, all of the POWs would be killed, and then the Japanese would kill themselves. Balchus, having long since written the man off as crazy, paid little heed to the strange conversation.[15]

That evening, camp commandant Kojima read Terada's dispatch and assembled his senior lieutenants, Ryoji Ozawa, Sho Yoshiwara, Haruo Chino, Yoshiichi Yamamoto, Isao Abe, and Toru Ogawa. He explained that they believed an American invasion force was heading for Palawan and that immediate action was in order. They decided to cover all escape routes and set up fields of fire to prevent any escape. For further protection, Kojima ordered Ogawa to take a gun barge and patrol the waters off the beach of Puerto Princesa, just in case any prisoner slipped through the kill zone and arrived on the beach. All Americans would be exterminated by machine guns, grenades, rifles, clubs, or whatever means were necessary.

More than twenty-seven months had passed since the first American POWs had been moved ashore to Puerto Princesa on August 1, 1942. Since that time, nearly six hundred men had been shuffled in and out of the camp, and many of the remaining one hundred fifty soldiers, sailors, and marines had endured the nightmare on Palawan since the beginning.

Nestled on makeshift pallets on the dirty floors of the Puerto Princesa barracks, Balchus and his 149 comrades settled in for the night, expecting to dodge air raids and repair bomb damage the next day, as usual.

13

THE GAUNTLET

Two HOURS AFTER midnight, Japanese guards burst into the darkened barracks, shouting at the sleeping prisoners to get up and moving. The exhausted men were confused as they pulled on their work rags. They had labored late into the evening, patching holes on the airfield, and now they were being ushered out to work again, long before daylight.

Ed Petry drove a truckload of prisoners to the field, where in darkness they returned to their endless routine of filling craters. When the new day dawned, Petry could finally see in the morning light that more guards than usual were standing by. Stranger still, helmet-clad gun crews were stationed at all the antiaircraft emplacements along the runway. Even McDole and Smitty felt tension in the air. Maybe the Americans were preparing to invade.[1]

Gene Nielsen was accustomed to being hassled while he worked, but today was different. He noticed that one older guard, whose graying hair had earned him the nickname "Silver," remained seated on a small mound, looking forward. Silver never turned his head and spoke to no one. Nielsen had never before seen such pacified guard behavior.[2]

Around 1100, Lieutenant Yoshikazu Sato, "the Buzzard," arrived at the airfield carrying a small box, which he placed on the ground. The guards hustled about, pushing and prodding the prisoners together while Sato whispered to his men. Then he climbed atop the box and addressed the prisoners: "Americans, your working days are over!"[3]

That was it—no lengthy speech, no further details. As the Buzzard stepped off his box, the guards began herding the prisoners toward trucks for the ride back to their camp. Ed Petry climbed into the cab of his vehicle as his comrades clambered aboard. The men were still pondering the strange turn of events as the trucks bumped along the dusty roads that led back to the Puerto Princesa compound.

When they arrived, Nielsen noticed more guards than usual inside the compound, but he figured they had simply beefed up their detail. The prisoners were not allowed to leave the main compound area, so most took seats on the ground near their air-raid shelters to await chow or further orders.

Smitty was starving, so he suggested to McDole that they sneak into their barracks to grab some papayas they had recently stashed. They had just entered the barracks when the clanging of an old Puerto Princesa church bell announced an incoming air raid. The tolling continued as guards shoved the prisoners toward their air-raid shelters. It was just after noon.

Ed Petry had slipped back to his truck with Sammy Glover to retrieve some strips of rubber they had stashed under the driver's seat. The two had sliced the rubber off an airplane tire at the field in hopes of using it to make new sandals. They were just digging under the seat as the alarm resonated through the camp.[4] As the two men raced back into the compound, Deguchi was startled to see them, and he swatted Petry with the flat of his saber as they ran toward their tunnels.

Sergeant Doug Bogue was sitting with a group of friends near his small shelter as the commotion started. Within moments, he heard the drone of aircraft engines and squinted skyward, spotting two P-38 Lightning fighters approaching the island. Urged on by shouting Japanese guards, the men dutifully packed into their tunnels and waited for the all-clear signal.

The P-38s circled high overhead and moved on. About a half hour later, guards rang the church bell to signal the Americans to emerge from their shelters. Petry crawled from Shelter B and took his plane in line for a lunch of rice and whistle weed soup. He was just beginning to eat when the air-raid alarm clanged again, a mere thirty-five minutes after the first alarm had sounded.

Once again, the prisoners were urgently herded into their shelters, but this time, Petry saw only a lone Japanese seaplane buzzing over the compound. They waited until the church bell signaled all clear. Smitty and McDole crawled from Shelter C, hoping to slip back to their barracks for the papayas. But the Buzzard had other ideas. Lieutenant Sato yelled at the POWs, telling them that they were not allowed to return to their barracks.

"You must stay near your shelters!" he ordered.

Nielsen noticed that some sixty armed guards had been distributed throughout the camp. Riflemen and soldiers hoisting machine guns were at spaced intervals outside the double barbed wire enclosure and on the southeast corner of the POW barracks veranda. Other armed men stood between the galley and the barracks, and near shelters A, B, and C. Additional Japanese soldiers gathered along the fencing.[5]

More American bombers were on their way, the prisoners were told. There was nothing to do but settle down on the ground and wait.

AROUND 1400, THE Puerto Princesa church bell rang out for the third time.

Lieutenant Sato and his men began yelling at the Americans to get back in their bomb shelters. Hundreds of American planes were on their way, they said. Some of the prisoners, weary of the air-raid drills, took their time. Dozens of planes, they could believe—but hundreds?

Smitty knew something was wrong. The young marine had loitered during past air raids, once even remaining in the barracks, content to take his chances just to watch the show. Now he had no such option, as angry soldiers prodded him toward his shelter. Others were trying to mill about, wanting to see an airplane before they went underground. The Buzzard, outraged, unsheathed his sword and screamed warnings at the men to get below.[6]

Flustered, some POWs jumped into the wrong shelters. Nielsen had sat out in the open through much of the first air raid, and when the third alarm sounded, he was unable to make it past the sword-wielding guards to his normal dugout. Amid the chaos, he could only reach the closest, Shelter C, which lay nearest to the oceanside bluffs. Nielsen crammed into the entrance near Mac McDole, C. C. Smith, Everett Bancroft, and Willie Smith. Among others he noticed crouched near him were Charles Street, Joe Barta, Doug Burnett, and John Lyons. Nielsen had no idea what to expect next, so he crouched low near the tunnel entrance, his knees pressed close to his face.[7]

Ed Petry remained in the open, avoiding the air-raid shelter, when an angry guard approached, shouting at him to get below. "I would just as soon stay out here," said Petry.[8]

The Japanese soldier slammed his rifle butt into Petry's skull and yelled at him to get in. His head throbbing, Petry duly climbed down into his regular Shelter B, pausing only long enough to take in a disturbing sight: Lieutenant Ogawa was barking at soldiers to load their rifles. There were about forty men packed in. Petry couldn't see them all, as they were jammed throughout the shelter's seventy-five-foot length, but he could smell their sweat as they crammed against one another in the dark. He could just make out Army artillerymen Kenneth Smith, Delbert Thomas, and Sammy Glover; Army infantrymen Johnny Diaz and Robert Anderson; marines Orland Morris and Robert Adkins; and Joseph Uballe from the 28th Material Squadron. Petry also noticed John Harris, a torpedoman who had served on the submarine *Seawolf* before the war. Just outside the entrance, Sergeant James Stidham—paralyzed from the bombing attacks two weeks earlier—was left lying on his stretcher in the open.

THE SENSE OF urgency among the Japanese was simple—the Weasel had passed on the "kill" orders.

Shortly after the first air raid, Kojima had summoned more guards to head to the prisoner camp. Tomisaburo Sawa, known to the Americans as one of the meanest sentries, noticed a sudden commotion, and then all the troops of his Yoshiwara Tai company were called together for an emergency meeting at Canigaran Beach. His 2nd Platoon leader, Warrant Officer Yuichi Yamamoto, came into the barracks shortly after noon on December 14.[9] Yamamoto announced that he had direct orders to kill the POWs, and he ordered his men to bring their rifles, bayonets, and machine guns. At least forty soldiers from the platoon, including Sawa, Yamamoto, and section leader Sergeant Takihiko Shinoda, packed into the back of the transport truck for the bumpy drive to the compound. As he checked his bayonet and the thirty rounds of ammunition he had ready for his rifle, Sawa felt tense during the fifteen-minute ride toward the execution site.[10]

The truck arrived in front of the Puerto Princesa headquarters around 1300. More than sixty soldiers lined up in two ranks facing west as Kojima stepped forward to address them. An American invasion of Palawan was imminent, he claimed. "I am sorry to say," Kojima said, "but it is necessary at this time to kill all of the POWs."

He spoke briefly to company commander Yoshiwara, who then ordered his soldiers to load five rounds of ammunition into each rifle and fix their bayonets. The men were left at attention with loaded weapons, prepared to follow Yoshiwara quickly into the camp when they heard the air-raid alarm.[11]

As the church bell tolled yet again, he led his guards through the main gate and into the middle of camp between the two main buildings. Yoshiwara directed the placement of various men and groups of men. Sawa was assigned a position on the prison camp veranda, on its southeast corner that led down to the latrine. One machine gun had already been set up on the porch, and the guards were ordered to fire at any POW who emerged from the shelters. Sawa noticed other soldiers enter the compound carrying torches and buckets of gasoline obtained from a storage place west of the vehicle repair shop.[12]

It was just past 1400.

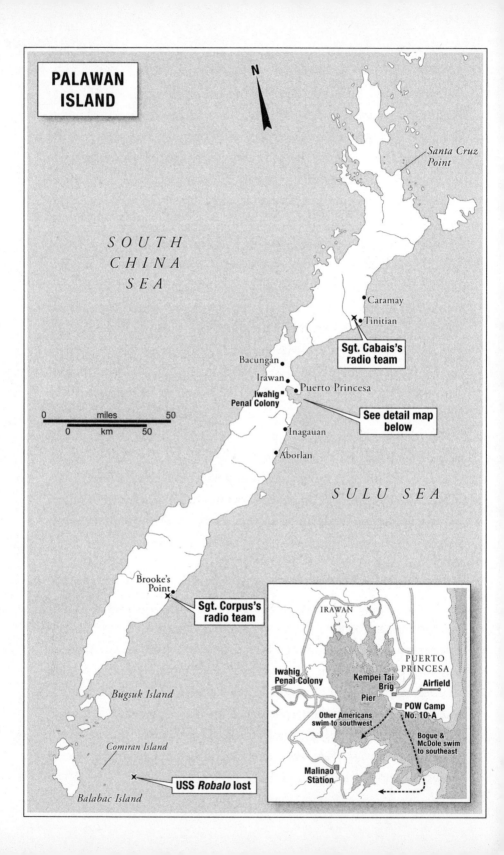

PALAWAN
ISLAND

N

*Santa Cruz
Point*

*S O U T H
C H I N A
S E A*

• Caramay
✕•Tinitian

**Sgt. Cabais's
radio team**

Bacungan •
Irawan •
**Iwahig
Penal Colony** ■ • Puerto Princesa

miles 50
0 km 50

**See detail map
below**

• Inagauan
•Aborlan

S U L U   S E A

Brooke's
Point
✕

**Sgt. Corpus's
radio team**

Bugsuk Island

Comiran Island

✕

USS *Robalo* lost

Balabac Island

IRAWAN

PUERTO
PRINCESA

**Iwahig
Penal Colony** ■

**Kempei Tai
Brig**

Airfield ■

Pier

**POW Camp
No. 10-A** ■

**Other Americans
swim to southwest**

**Bogue &
McDole swim
to southeast**

**Malinao
Station**

* * *

THE THIRD ALARM was ringing, guards were shouting threats, and in the dugout shelters, the American prisoners were puzzled—no one could hear aircraft engines.

Smitty was packed into the entrance to Shelter C near Charles Carlyle Smith Jr., a signalman second class known as C.C. who had once served on the cruiser *Houston*. The unrelated Smith boys were both Southerners, and they had forged a bond during their time together. Smitty could tell that his friend was fed up with staying below ground. C.C. popped up through the shelter opening to see what was going on. Lieutenant Sato swung his sword around above his head and shouted in Japanese, "Get down and don't look out!" Gene Nielsen, squatting near Smitty, watched as Sato then stepped over the opening, raised his sword high, then brought the blade down with full force into C. C. Smith's head, splitting his skull wide open, and sending his body tumbling back into the pit.[13]

Other men peeking from their bunkers witnessed the murder. In Shelter B, a stunned Ed Petry ducked back down. Soon he heard the crack of rifle fire. Doug Bogue, occupying one of the three-man foxholes, had also seen C.C.'s death. As soon as the sword struck, Bogue crouched down and told his two comrades, Gabriel Sierra and Stephen Kozuch.[14]

"Take it easy," one cautioned. "Let's don't get the Japs excited."

Seconds later, men in Shelter C heard a dull, muffled sound, a booming resonation unlike any bomb dropped by an American plane. Smitty would later remember that was the instant when "all hell broke loose." The guards above were still in a screaming frenzy, and Smitty momentarily hoped that the chaos was the result of Filipino guerrillas raiding the camp.[15]

But the screams of American voices and the pungent smell of gasoline drove home the sobering truth: Kojima had ordered the execution of all 150 American prisoners of war. Five soldiers approached Shelter A with buckets of gasoline and dumped the contents onto the roof and into the entrance. Two other soldiers tossed lighted bamboo torches into the front of the trench. The gasoline erupted in a powerful gust, and flames spit from the tunnel's opening.[16]

Packed in like rats in a tube, the men of Shelter A at once began roasting alive. As the fires spread, at least seven Americans charged out from the opening, their clothing aflame as they screamed.

"Shoot them!" shrieked Lieutenant Yoshiwara. "Shoot them!"

A machine gun roared to life, mowing down the suffering Americans who were clawing their way from their underground shelter.

At the entrance to Shelter B, Ed Petry poked his head up again. What he saw was a mass of flames, and burning men staggering out, only to be violently dropped to the dirt. Sergeant Henry Araujo, his clothing and skin ablaze, made it only a short distance before he stumbled, cut down by machine-gun fire from the veranda.[17]

Petry watched in horror as guards fired their rifles into the blazing entrance of Shelter A. Beside him, Delbert Thomas hollered, "They are killing us!" The next instant, a pair of hand grenades sailed into the opening of their own tunnel. Thomas scooped them up and hurled them back out into the open compound. Petry looked out again, saw a guard drawing a bead on his head with his rifle, and ducked down just as bullets peppered the entrance to his dugout.

IN SHELTER C, Smitty squatted beside C.C.'s lifeless body. Despite the risk, he poked his head topside and saw men frantically scrambling from the A trench as their petrol-soaked clothing blazed brightly. Soldiers and sailors twisted and crumpled as machine-gun bullets and rifle slugs ripped into them. Some men, their flesh in flames, begged for mercy, asking to be shot and killed. The guards only laughed or jabbed them with bayonets. Smitty leaned down and shouted a warning to his forty-odd comrades: Japanese were approaching the B trench, and they would be coming to Shelter C in short order.

McDole could not resist stealing a look as well: Japanese soldiers poured more fuel into the air-raid shelters and tossed in burning torches. Men screamed in agony, and any who escaped the shelters were shot down.

"Mac, get your head down!" Smitty shouted. "You'll get it shot off!"

A burst of machine-gun fire sent Mac diving back into the tunnel. He shouted to Smitty, "Pull the sandbag out of the wall!"

Smitty pushed his way back toward the far end of the tunnel, intent on reaching the escape hatch that led to the beach. All he needed to do was to clear away the brush that concealed the passage, remove the coral rock and sandbag, and the men would at least have a chance to avoid being burned alive. When he got to the back, Smitty found no one at work clearing the hatch. His warnings had failed to get his companions moving.[18]

"They're killing everybody out there! Let's go!" Smitty screamed. He slung the debris aside and tugged at the heavy rock, then hoisted out the sandbag. Several other men joined in and began clawing through the last inches of soil. Fingers poked through, followed by fists rammed into the open daylight beyond. The men frantically scooped more soil out of the way, trying to make the exit just wide enough for the malnourished frames of the POWs to wriggle through.

Outside their trench, men were dying by the dozens.

THE GUARDS MOVED from Shelter A to Shelter B, repeating their sadistic process. Petry heard the soldiers approaching as he crouched below the entrance. He could feel a knot on his head where he had been hit with the rifle butt. As the voices grew louder, Petry retreated deeper into the tunnel, the spicy odor of aviation fuel tingling his nostrils. As fuel splashed into the opening, he elbowed his way back toward the other end, which lay closer to the cliffs and the barbed wire fencing.

Japanese guards fired their rifles into the entrance as fuel was poured. The Americans were packed in so tight that Petry knew they could not miss. Flaming torches and rags were tossed into the opening he had just vacated. There was an explosion behind him, and an orange ball of flame swept through Shelter B. Consumed in flames, men near the entrance fell to the ground, writhing in pain. Ernie Koblos, deeper in the tunnel, was uncertain what to do. As the fireball flashed past him, he saw a prisoner dart out of the opening ahead of him. Koblos knew that if he stayed below ground, he would soon be a dead man.

The fire was burning his bottom as he jumped out of the far end of the tunnel and made a dash for the fencing a short distance away. By some miracle, the bullets zinging past his head missed. As he crawled through the barbed wire, Koblos thought briefly about trying to help his comrades escape. Glancing back, he saw men cut down by rifles and machine guns, and he knew he could do nothing. He cleared the barbed wire, jumped over the cliff, and tumbled down the steep embankment toward the rocky shoreline below. He was one of the first to reach the beach, but he had no idea what to do next. He splashed around in the shallow water, looking for someplace to take shelter. He finally spotted a small cove in the edge of the rocks and ran over to hide.[19]

Inside Shelter B, the men bunched near the entrance closest to the veranda had no chance. Five or six charged out in desperation, their clothing and skin ablaze. Yoshiwara ordered the dozen soldiers standing on the veranda to hold their fire since there was danger of hitting their own men. But another noncommissioned officer screamed at them to shoot, and many did. Private Sawa cracked off three shots from his rifle and felt sure that his bullets hit home.[20]

The veranda machine gun, manned by Superior Private Hakaru Yamaguchi and Private First Class Keiichi Ogata, ensured that no one escaped from the main entrances of the first two shelters. Most of the dozen or so Americans who fled from shelters A and B made it only yards before they were cut down. Yoshiwara and a noncommissioned officer tossed two hand grenades inside the blazing shelters to finish the execution.[21]

Other guards resorted to more hands-on methods to murder

prisoners. Superior privates Minoru Onuki and Hiroshi Yamada stood over two Americans who had collapsed with bullet wounds and burns and finished them off with bayonets. Lieutenant Haruo Chino, whom the Americans had nicknamed "Robert Young" after the movie star, seemed greatly aroused by the killing as he shouted encouragement to his men.

Ernie Koblos was already gone by the time Ed Petry reached the end of Shelter B closest to the cliffs. There, Petry encountered several others he knew: Johnny Diaz, Julio Smith, and Beto Pacheco. They quickly discussed their options. They figured more Japanese guards would be dousing their end of the tunnel and torching it within a minute.[22]

"When they set that gas off, they will have to back up," Pacheco said. "We should run and make a break for it then."

As soon as the fuel splashed in, Diaz took off first, racing toward the fence line in hopes of making it to the cliff. Petry was next. As he felt the heat sweeping through the shelter, he leaped from the hole and ran for the double strands of barbed wire. A bullet slammed into his left anklebone and sent him sprawling into the dirt. Other bullets kicked up sand and rocks all around him amid the roar of guns and screams. Pacheco charged past Petry, who jumped up and hobbled to the barbed wire. The sharp prongs sliced his flesh as he tore through it and raced to the edge of the cliff. He tried to slide down but instead plunged over the side.[23]

Pacheco and Petry jumped, crawled, and fell down the sixty-foot incline. Once they reached the beach, they saw several others following them. Japanese guards quickly scrambled to the bluff's edge and opened fire on the escapees. As he and Petry ran, a bullet tore through Pacheco's upper left arm, just inches away from his heart. He was caught on the open beach, lead zipping all around him. He felt a sharp pain as another bullet ripped into his upper left thigh, but he didn't stop. He and the other POWs zigzagged across the beach, frantically searching for cover.

* * *

IN SHELTER C, men huddled around the far end of the dugout, closest to the Japanese guards on the veranda. McDole and Joe Barta each poked their heads up and saw shelters A and B engulfed in flames. Several men were running, their bodies on fire. Mac spotted a fellow marine, Corporal Rob Hubbard, emerge from a nearby bunker, his body in flames. Hubbard made it only a few steps before a machine gun cut him down. Barta had seen enough. It was time to go. He scrambled through the length of the underground bunker toward the rearmost point. Just short of the end, he came upon the men digging out the last inches of soil in the emergency exit.[24]

Mac lingered at the main entrance, transfixed by the slaughter playing out before him. Men charged from various bunkers, each racing toward the cliffside barbed wire. He spotted Doug Bogue, Petry, Pacheco, Don Martyn, Doug Burnett, and Jesse Simpson all making their breaks for freedom. Burning prisoners writhed on the ground as Japanese soldiers murdered them with swords and bayonets.[25]

McDole saw little chance for anyone to make it very far. The prisoners were unarmed, many were injured, and those who did make it from the shelters faced unknown odds of fleeing across an island occupied by the Japanese.

We're as good as dead, he thought.

DOUG BOGUE KNEW he would die if he remained in his small dugout. He was huddled next to Gabriel Sierra and Stephen Kozuch in the shelter they had dug close to the fencing on the edge of the bluff, directly south of the Company B shelter. Their pit was covered, leaving an opening large enough for only one man at a time to enter or exit.

Bogue rose up for quick glances as the first minutes of the massacre unfolded, reporting what he saw to Sierra and Kozuch. A short distance away, he saw James Stidham lying on his stretcher near the entrance to Shelter C. The paralyzed man was helpless to fend off the guards who pierced his body with bayonets before they turned their guns on him.[26]

To the right and farther south of Bogue's shelter was the small bunker reserved for the four remaining American officers, Captain Fred Bruni, First Lieutenant Carl Mango, Lieutenant Henry Knight, and Warrant Officer Glenn Turner. Bogue saw Japanese soldiers soak the shelter in fuel and toss in a torch. Doc Mango charged from the entrance, his clothing ablaze. He raised his arms in the air as he staggered toward the Japanese, begging them to have mercy on the prisoners. A guard riddled his body with bullets from a light machine gun. Other soldiers, including Lieutenant Sato, doused Mango with gasoline and torched him again.

One prisoner charged from his shelter, attacked a Japanese guard, pulled the rifle from his hands, and shot his opponent. The American was quickly taken down by a bayonet plunged into his back. Bogue had seen more than enough. Guards were laying down a steady stream of bullets over the tops of the shelter exits, hoping to keep men below ground until fuel could be dumped into each opening. Bogue ducked as bullets thumped into the wood and soil around his head.[27]

"They're killing everyone!" he shouted to Sierra and Kozuch. "Our only chance is to make a run for it, one at a time. If we can get through the fence, we might have a chance to hide down on the beach!"

Steeling his nerves, Bogue sprang from his cramped shelter. In two quick strides, he reached the six-foot-high rows of barbed wire and plunged through. The spiked prongs tore at his bare hands, flesh, and tattered clothing, but he ripped through the fencing in a flash. He paused at the edge of the bluff to yell back at his two buddies.

"Come on! You can make it now!"

Then he felt a sharp stab of pain as a bullet tore into his right leg. He saw Kozuch charge from the pit with Sierra right on his heels. Both men convulsed as bullets perforated their bodies. Sierra made it through the barbed wire, but Kozuch slumped over the top row of wire, dead.

Sierra disappeared over the bluff as Bogue paused for a last look back. The bullet wound in his leg was throbbing, and other prisoners in the compound were making for the cliff. It was time for him to get moving.

He rolled over the top, jumping, bouncing, and stumbling down the brushy embankment toward the beach below.

A SHORT DISTANCE away, Mo Deal and Willie Balchus were pressed tightly into a five-man foxhole with Leo Lampshire, Erving Evans, and Mike Giuffreda. As gunfire and explosions rang out all around them, a hand grenade plopped into their hole. Balchus quickly flung it back out before it could explode. As he popped up to lob the grenade, he saw Japanese soldiers dumping fuel into another shelter.[28]

"They're trying to kill us off!" he shouted.

Lampshire leaped out of the foxhole and took off toward the barbed wire. Balchus charged out in pursuit, following him toward the nearest large shelter. They had just reached the dugout when a bullet struck the back of Lampshire's head. Balchus pushed him into the opening of Shelter C and jumped in behind him.

Lampshire was dead, so Balchus jumped out of the shelter and scrambled through the barbed wire to the cliff. Behind him, Giuffreda and Evans were following through a barrage of gunfire. Mo Deal remained hidden until guards torched his small shelter. As the pit burst into flames that seared his flesh, he sprang from the bunker and raced under fire toward the barbed wire with Giuffreda and Evans. A bullet slammed into Deal's shoulder, but he kept moving. Each of the three was shot while charging past the Japanese guards, but they plunged over the bluff and tumbled to the beach below.[29]

The group splintered, all in search of cover. Deal and Balchus scurried about for a moment before ducking into a small cave along the coast to hide.

SHELTER C WAS the last tunnel to burn. In its far end nearest the beach, several men had finished punching their way through the secret escape tunnel toward the open air. One man wriggled through and made the short dash to the barbed wire fencing just beyond. Dozens of Japanese soldiers were gathering near the veranda-side entrance as other POWs began crawling out the escape tunnel. Some survived the quick dash to the top of the bluff, but others were shot down as they wriggled through the fence.

Medic Everett Bancroft tried to flee out the main entrance past the Japanese guards. He made it only a few steps before he was doused with gasoline and lit on fire. He jumped back into Shelter C, trying to smother his burning clothes, screaming in pain, and warning everyone that they were about to be murdered.[30]

Joe Barta had seen and heard enough. He had retreated past McDole and Bancroft seconds before as he made his way to the escape exit. Several men squeezed out ahead of him and Barta followed. He forced his way through the hole, with other men right behind him, and scurried under the barbed wire and through an enlarged drain that dumped over the cliff toward the beach below. Once under the fencing, he looked back long enough to see a Japanese soldier throwing buckets of gasoline onto the roof and into the entrance to Shelter C. A second guard tossed a flaming torch into the tunnel opening, and the shelter burst into flames with a roar. Screams filled the air as Barta went over the edge of the cliff toward the beach sixty feet below.[31]

McDole lingered at the Shelter C entrance only a moment longer than Barta. He was pushing his way back toward the beachside exit as the guards approached. One of them tossed in a torch before the gasoline had been poured. Other guards began sloshing buckets of fuel onto the roof of the shelter and into the entrance. Corpsman Bancroft, still smoldering from being lit on fire a moment before, was drenched by the incoming aviation fuel. Some of the fuel splashed onto McDole's backside and shorts as he made his way toward the secret hole. There, he found only two men left near the side exit—Smitty and Pop Daniels.

At that instant, the Japanese heaved torches into the shelter entrance. Fire snaked through the tunnel, engulfing terrified men. Bancroft, covered with fuel, burst into flames and fell to the ground, screaming.

McDole's shorts, soaked in fuel, ignited. He ripped the burning fabric from his body, leaving himself naked.

Gene Nielsen had smelled gasoline as he retreated toward the cliff-side exit. He was ahead of McDole when the fireball swept through. He was not burned, and he charged past Smitty and the other men wriggling through the hole. He paused just beyond them at the far end. Behind him, he heard the blast of two hand grenades tossed into the other entrance.[32]

He couldn't make up his mind what to do. To his left, just a few yards away, was the barbed wire fence. To his right were dozens of Japanese with rifles, killing anybody they encountered. He saw friends burning to death, running for their lives as bullets and bayonets cut them down.

Charles Street acted first. He plowed out past Nielsen and jumped through the barbed wire. Nielsen made a running leap and dived through the opening, landing flat on his stomach in the prison yard. Pulling his hands and feet under his stomach, he sprang like a bullfrog through the nearby barbed wire. He kept low to the ground, crawling through the razor wire to the edge of the cliff. He glanced back and saw two other men—Doug Burnett and the horribly burned Everett Bancroft—escaping with him.[33]

Nielsen's next leap sent him over the bluff toward the rocky shore below. He clawed the air like a falling cat and latched onto a limber tree after plunging several feet. It bent under his weight and helped break his fall enough to prevent any serious injury. He scrambled down to the beach and ran back and forth on the coastline, hesitating.

Back in the tunnel, McDole decided he would rather use the escape exit instead of following Nielsen's group. He and Smitty were about to dive through the opening when he spotted Pop Daniels. The gray-haired airman squatted on the ground, paralyzed with fear.[34]

"Come on, Pop!" Mac yelled.

When Daniels didn't move, he grabbed him and shoved him into the opening. He pushed on Pop's rear, propelling him out the exit hole and sending him tumbling toward the beach below. McDole leaped through the hole right behind him.

That left Smitty. Wearing only a tattered pair of shorts, he squeezed through the opening and plunged down the cliff toward the ocean. He felt certain he was the last man to leave Shelter C, although McDole was equally sure no one followed him. It was a point the two could debate later if they survived.[35]

PART THREE

ESCAPE

14

HUNTED

BELOW THE STEEP bluffs bordering the camp, the green coastline was rocky and narrow, with a thin strip of beach only a few yards wide in places, and heavily sprinkled with jagged black boulders. The turquoise waters had carved deep pockets into the rocky cliffs where they protruded into Puerto Princesa Bay. Ragged undergrowth, small trees, and snaking vines covered the sheer sixty-foot escarpment.

The journey from the precipice to the meager beach below Camp 10-A was perilous. For those few dozen men fortunate enough to make the descent, their odds of survival were even lower. John Stanley and another American made it to the edge of the water before Japanese guards standing along the barbed wire fence far above cut them down. Shot in the back, the men collapsed into the shallow water.[1]

Two others—George Eyre and Waldo Hale—joined Doug Bogue near the water. He told them he planned to follow closely the large rocks southwest along the beach toward the dock area. With luck, Bogue hoped he could slip into the underbrush and circle from there into the jungle. Eyre and Hale disagreed with this plan, figuring they had better odds simply swimming for their lives. Both plunged into the ocean.

Eyre swam only a few yards before guards above laced him with bullets. Hale made it about thirty yards farther, and Bogue watched as lead churned up the water's surface all around the swimmer. He had no chance. "They got me!" Hale cried out, bullets tearing into him. He rolled onto his back and died.

Bogue's right leg ached from a bullet in his thigh, and his bare feet were torn and bleeding from hobbling along the jagged coral. But there was no time to fret over his wounds. He took off like a broken field runner, dodging right and left around the large rocks on the beach.

He headed toward the dock area, but he made it only a hundred feet before stumbling onto three Japanese sailors in their white uniforms with anchor insignias. They were setting up a Lewis gun—a World War I–era light machine gun that fired .30-06-caliber bullets from a top-mounted drum-pan magazine. His path was blocked. If he turned back, they would certainly cut him down in a hail of bullets.

The marine charged headlong into the trio of sailors. The four men slammed into the saltwater shallows, flailing and grasping at one another. Bogue clawed for a grip on their uniforms and tried to hold their faces under the water. Two of the terrified sailors released their grips on him and the Lewis gun and splashed back onto the beach, fearful that the crazed American might drown them.

The third Japanese sailor maintained his grip on the machine gun. The marine tore the weapon free and fell into the shallow water with the sailor still clinging to his back. Bogue struggled up and pulled the actuator, arming the Lewis gun, and began firing. He unloaded the full ninety-seven-round drum, killing the nearest sailor and the two racing ashore. The rapid burst of automatic fire had temporarily saved his life, but the upper drum fell off the weapon, rendering it useless.[2]

Bogue glanced down the beach and spotted more guards setting up another light machine gun. There was no time to lose. He ran back the other way, scanning wildly for a suitable hiding place. Spotting a crevice at the water's edge too small for both him and the gun, Bogue tossed the gun into the salt water, forced his tattered body deep into the jagged hole, and scrunched down as low as he could.

All around him was a deafening din of pleading screams, chattering machine guns, rifle fire, and occasional explosions. The odor of dynamite drifted down to the beach as explosives finished off Americans in the trenches. The smell of burning flesh was almost more than his shriveled stomach could handle. The laughter from some Japanese guards fueled his anger, but Bogue knew there was nothing he could do to help.

The next hour passed slowly as he remained crouched in the rocky crevice. He kept his head down and stared at the blood seeping from his legs and feet. Around 1500—an hour after the massacre had commenced—Bogue heard Japanese guards approaching him. One sloshed so close to his hiding spot that he could smell the man's foul body odor. The canteen on the soldier's belt was close enough to touch, but Bogue remained motionless, his heart pounding, until the rifleman splashed past him.

He could not run yet. There were too many armed soldiers close by. But the prospect of remaining in the rocks was not much better. Bogue shuddered. *They're going to keep probing through these rocks,* he thought. *They're going to hunt us down and kill every last one of us.*

AT LEAST NINE men had escaped from Shelter C's secret exit. Others had scurried through the barbed wire from the main openings of Shelter C, Shelter B, and some of the smaller dugouts. About thirty Americans made it over the bluff and were now running about on the beach. Ed Petry and Beto Pacheco, both wounded by bullets, ran along the rocky coastline until Petry spotted a small cave at the edge of the ocean. He and Pacheco quickly crawled inside and pressed themselves as deep into it as they could. Outside, they heard shouting and screaming and machine-gun fire.

Ernie Koblos had hidden behind a sandbank cove at the water's edge. During the early minutes of mass confusion, Everett Bancroft, Robert Stevenson, and Forest Lindsay pressed into the space near him. Deciding the sandbank offered little protection, he and Lindsay made a break for two nearby large rocks. Koblos made it unscathed, but Lindsay, already badly burned by gasoline before escaping his air-raid shelter, was shot in the arm. Koblos crawled up into the rocks and pressed himself into a small cave opening along with several others. He decided to wait until darkness to move any farther.

Joe Barta half climbed and half fell down the cliff until he reached the beach. He realized he was fortunate to be alive. Orders must have come from Manila to put the Americans to death, he figured. Now, as his comrades were murdered around him, Barta sensed that it was a fouled-up operation. *If they had a well-planned scheme, instead of just having gunners on the beach, they would have hit all three main holes simultaneously instead of one at a time,* he thought. *They had plenty of personnel to do this.*[3]

As he scanned the beach, he saw other Americans crashing down the cliff after plunging through the barbed wire. A minute later, Japanese guards were at the top of the bluff, firing down at the fleeing prisoners. One of their bullets ripped through the left arm of Corporal Dane Hamric as he ran past. Barta stopped him long enough to fix a tourniquet around the shattered limb.

"What a hell of a way to die on my twenty-fourth birthday!" Hamric said as Barta tightened the rag to slow the blood flow.[4]

Hamric dashed off in search of shelter. Barta, unsure of which way to run, soon found himself near two other survivors, Private John Lyons and marine Don Martyn. The trio spotted a potential hiding place and ducked down into an opening in the rocks. The crevice offered enough cover to prevent their heads from being spotted, but it was not enough to prevent any guard who came close from locating them. Barta decided that swimming was not a good option—those who tried were being shot down.

Barta was peering from the rocks when he spotted another man running in their direction. He recognized Private Ken Smith, a prisoner the Japanese had used as a truck driver for the special duty company. Smith was running along the beach until he found a nearby rock to duck behind. One of the roaming guards spotted Smith, aimed his rifle, and shot him dead.[5]

Once the Japanese soldiers moved farther away, Barta, Martyn, and Lyons cautiously eased south along the rocks near the ocean in search of a better hideaway. They happened upon an old sewer outlet used to channel waste products down from the camp above. The smells of the waste mattered little at this point as the three men pressed their bodies deep into the cavernlike opening until they were obscured from view.

GENE NIELSEN HAD reached the beach without serious injury, and along the coast with the others, searched for a good hiding spot. He saw Ernie Koblos and others ducking under rocks as rifle fire rained down from above. Those who ran into the ocean were shot dead before they could begin swimming. Nielsen had never experienced such horror: The sandy shore and the shallow water were both crimson with blood.[6]

By his best count, at least a dozen other surviving prisoners were trying to take cover. Guard patrols were advancing, and their gunfire steadily prevented the escapees from further flight along the coastline. Nielsen had not moved far from the base of the bluff directly below camp. He quickly decided that it was unsafe to take to the water. Glancing up, he noticed the garbage chute above him that extended beyond the barbed wire fencing over the edge of the cliff. Anything not needed in camp—food waste, tree limbs, coconut husks, and other trash—was dumped down the chute to allow the high tide of Puerto Princesa Bay to carry away the refuse.

Nielsen had no desire to join the men hiding among the rocks near the water's edge, so he plunged into the garbage pile, hoping to hide there until he could figure out a better plan. He burrowed his body under the garbage until he was well covered. Less than ten yards away, a dozen POWs remained exposed among the rocks. Once he felt sufficiently hidden, he lay still and listened, waiting to see what would happen as the Japanese guards moved in closer.[7]

*   *   *

SMITTY NOTICED TWO patrol boats roaming the coastline to fire on any prisoners who tried to flee. At the beach, he paused briefly to look over at Mac McDole. The two friends realized they would likely never see each other again. They clasped hands.

"This is it, buddy, isn't it?" McDole said.[8]

Smitty took one last look at his friend. "Yep, Dole. I'll be seein' ya!"

Both men took off running. Smitty's long legs carried him swiftly from the bottom of the bluff to the right, in a westward direction. Japanese soldiers stationed on the beach opened up with automatic rifles, while others fired down from the top of the cliff. Smitty dived into a cluster of coral rocks to hide himself and found several men already there.

"You'd better split up!" he warned. "You ain't gonna be able to hide four or five at a time!"[9]

The others wanted to remain together. Smitty jumped up and sprinted back up the cliff, screening himself behind coral outcroppings as he moved. He crawled to the top. When he stopped, he noticed two Japanese guards no more than thirty feet from him. They couldn't see him under a thick layer of tall grass. He spread out flat on the ground and slowly began wriggling up under the overhanging brush. The weight of the grass and the undergrowth formed a small tunnel of sorts under which he forced himself as deep as he could. It was dark there. He could see out well enough but thought that anyone standing in the bright sunlight would not be able to see in.[10]

Smitty rubbed his arms and face with dirt to further camouflage himself. He felt fortunate so far: He had only a scratch on his right side from running through the coral. His new vantage point allowed him to peek out and see the other men being slaughtered down on the beach. He decided to stay there until darkness.[11]

RIFLE SLUGS RICOCHETED off the coral rocks as Mac McDole sprinted. One bullet sent jagged bits of coral ripping into his right leg. He stopped to take cover and survey his surroundings. Smitty had scampered out of sight, disappearing into a small ravine partway up the cliff.

All around McDole, other Americans who had made it down the bluffs were squatting in holes and outcroppings. He knew their odds of remaining alive were not good. *Where can I go that the Japs won't look?* In an instant, the camp garbage dump came to mind. Mac ran toward the huge pile of refuse that had grown taller and taller during his years of captivity.

The smell was overwhelming, yet he dived in without hesitation and forced his naked body into the slime and filth. The stench made his stomach muscles convulse, and he fought the urge to vomit. He crawled in deeper, pulling the garbage over him, wriggling in as deeply as he could before the weight of the waste pile prevented further penetration. Worms, maggots, and other creatures began creeping across his body.

He had no idea that Gene Nielsen was a short distance away, burrowing under the garbage. Mac lay still, steeling his nerves and trying not to retch. His only hope was to remain there until darkness arrived. Maybe then he could sneak out and run for the ocean.

He had been buried in the dump only a few minutes when he sensed others. Two escapees, Charles Street and Erving Evans, were clawing at the garbage nearby, hoping to dig their own hiding holes in the dump. Mac could hear the shouts and voices of numerous Japanese guards who had reached the beach. He lay still as gunfire crackled in the distance.

Evans dug in right alongside him. "Mac, what are we going to do?"[12]

"Just keep quiet," McDole said. "Maybe they'll pass over us."

Nielsen, burrowed in a short distance away, heard shots and screams from the Americans being tortured and murdered in the compound above. He heard loud banzai cheers as the Japanese guards celebrated, seeming almost as joyful as Americans attending a football game.[13]

The sounds of the torture were almost unbearable. The gunshots and screams finally got the best of Street, who jumped from the trash and ran toward the ocean. He was cut down by rifle fire just short of the water's edge.[14]

Now too frightened to move a muscle, McDole, Evans, and Nielsen froze. Street's flight from the dump brought guards their way, curious to see whether others were hiding there. Nerves seemed to get the best of Erving Evans, who began squirming beneath the trash.

"Quit moving, damn it!" whispered McDole, just a few feet away. "They're going to see us in here!"[15]

Evans suddenly jumped up, refuse falling away from him. "All right, you Jap bastards!" he shouted. "Here I am! And don't miss me, you sons of bitches!"

Rifle shots rang out and Evans jerked, his body landing right on top of the garbage covering McDole. The weight of the corpse pressed Mac down tighter into the refuse until he could barely breathe. He felt the heft of a Japanese soldier as he climbed over the trash above him. Seconds later, he felt Evans's body being pulled away.[16]

Mac could smell the familiar odor of aviation fuel as the corpse was doused and set afire; the stench of burning flesh was almost unbearable. Mac continued to lie perfectly still. Just a few yards away, Nielsen was doing the same.

The guards who killed Evans were soon joined by others, and the ten or so Americans squatting in the nearby rocks did not remain hidden for long. Once the guards moved away from the dump, they spotted the other exposed escapees.

One American grabbed a coral rock, swore at the soldiers, and flung it toward a guard. A quick volley of rifle fire dropped him, and the guards rushed forward. One jabbed an escapee in the groin with his bayonet. The prisoner fell to the sand, screaming as other guards fired their rifles into the bellies of POWs to incapacitate them—there was no desire to kill. The guards howled with laughter as they moved about, thrusting their steel bayonets into the thighs, hips, and bellies of the men who had once been their slave laborers.

Peering through garbage, Nielsen watched it all, furious and terrified. He could do nothing to help as he watched the Japanese soldiers torture his countrymen. Nielsen recognized medic Bancroft and Jose Mascarenas among the men being tortured in the rocky wash near the ocean. *God, why don't they just kill them and spare them the misery?* he thought.[17]

Some men begged for a bullet to put an end to their suffering, but the soldiers just laughed and stabbed them again in their hips and stomachs. The bayonet torture continued for the better part of an hour.

McDole fought the desire to move, especially to swat at the worms and bugs on his flesh. He finally decided it was time to take a chance to peek out, so he cautiously poked a small opening through the waste until a pocket of fresh air entered. Just twenty-five yards away, six Japanese guards had one American soldier surrounded. They were toying with him, jabbing him with bayonets, each thrust opening a new wound in the poor man's lower extremities.

"Please, just shoot me!" he begged.

Mac saw another soldier approach with a bucket of aviation fuel.

"Please don't burn me!" the American cried. "Shoot me! I don't want to burn!"

Several Japanese held the prisoner in place with their bayonets while the bucket man poured gasoline on his foot. Then it was lit with a torch, causing the American to jump about, screaming in pain.

"Shoot me, you bastards!" he yelled. "You stupid sons of bitches, shoot me!"[18]

The Japanese splashed his other foot with gasoline and set it on fire. Then the guards doused the POW's hands and lit them too.

"Oh God! Please! Please!" he screamed as his flesh burned.

Finally, he collapsed. The bucket man stepped forward and dumped fuel over his entire body, which was then torched. Mac could see the man flailing about, screaming as flames consumed his flesh. The guards waited for the fire to subside before dragging the smoldering corpse to a nearby tree, where they lashed the victim up to use for bayonet practice.

McDole closed the peephole in the garbage pile and lay still. An uncontrollable urge to vomit finally took over.

A FEW YARDS away, Gene Nielsen estimated the time to be around 1700.

He had been buried in garbage for hours, and the sounds of torture had long ceased. He peeked out. Most of the prisoners he saw were now dead, and others appeared to be near death, squirming in agony and moaning as several guards were hunkered over, digging a large hole in the sand a short distance away. Once it was large enough, they began kicking bodies into the fresh hole. Some men were still alive as they plopped down on top of one another in the grave. When the hole was adequately filled with dead and dying Americans, the guards shoveled sand over them, determined to hide their massacre.[19]

Once the bodies were covered, a soldier walked over to the dump and began collecting brush, coconut husks, and other refuse to pile atop the grave. As he pulled back an armful of trash, he spotted the bare white legs and lower thighs of an American. Nielsen knew he had been discovered. As he held his breath and remained as still as he could, the guard jabbered to his comrades. Nielsen had learned enough Japanese to make out the man's statement: "His friends have given him a burial!"

They think I'm dead!

The closest soldier stood staring at the American for a moment. *It's hot out here,* Nielsen thought. *He doesn't want to dig another hole just to bury me. I'm sure of that.* The guards appeared to be discussing just what to do with this unexpected victim. The worms and insects crawling on him were maddening, and something was gnawing at a place on his bare back. Once they prodded him and saw signs of life, Nielsen knew it was the end. Perhaps a merciful rifle blast? Or worse, countless bayonet thrusts or the gasoline torture treatment?[20]

From the bluff above came a commotion, and a Japanese voice rang down that it was time to take a break for dinner. The guards dutifully tossed down their shovels, grabbed their rifles, and began climbing the cliffs toward the compound for evening chow. They could take care of the dead American later.

Gene Nielsen knew his good fortune was only a temporary reprieve. As soon as the guards were safely out of sight up the hill, he had to get moving.

In the prison yard, Americans lay in heaps, shot down and bayoneted as they had tried to flee. In the three main shelters and in the smaller ones, bodies smoldered. Some had died while tucked into protective positions. The smoky air was thick with the aroma of cooked flesh and spilled fuel.

Lieutenant Sato's guards moved about, searching for any signs of life. Warrant Officer Yamamoto happened upon one American who was not yet dead, lying facedown but still breathing. Yamamoto unsheathed his sword, raised it high, and swung down, severing the man's head from his body with one slicing blow.[21]

The massacre in the Puerto Princesa prison yard was complete. Within an hour of its beginning, not a single American remained alive inside the camp. Captain Kojima passed orders for his men to make a final count of the bodies. He needed to make sure that every American had been properly disposed of. If the count came up short, he was prepared to continue the manhunt to catch any stragglers remaining on the rocky beach below.

Clothing and hair had been burned away, leaving the POWs' bodies raw and red, their faces monstrously frozen in a wretched, unrecognizable state. Lieutenant Yoshiwara and Warrant Officer Yamamoto ordered the dozen guards standing on the camp veranda to begin filling in the shelters. Many American bodies were piled in heaps, drenched with gasoline, and burned before their charred remains were dumped back into the shelters to be covered over with dirt. Private Tomisaburo Sawa worked on the remnants of Shelter A and one of the smaller individual shelters for the next half hour before he was ordered to move down toward the beach.[22]

It was time to finish off any surviving Americans.

15

FIGHTS AND FLIGHT

SMITTY WAS STILL hiding in the weeds near the top of the cliffs. Now, nearly two hours since his nightmare had started, he kept close watch on a nearby Japanese guard, who was soon joined by two others. One of them slowly made his way up the trail, coming ever closer to Smitty's hiding spot as he lifted up weeds and peered behind each thick clump. He moved within six feet of Smitty's place of concealment, pulled back some of the grass near him, and squinted into the fading light. Seconds passed like hours as Smitty waited for a rifle to explode with the bullet that would take his life. He could smell the man's sweat, even his breath.

Three years of hell, for this! Smitty thought. A steel blade, cold as death, would enter his ribs any second now, and he silently prayed that the soldier would at least do it right the first time to spare him further agony.

But the soldier released the weeds and moved on.

The sun dropped lower in the sky as the manhunt continued. Close to sunset, another group of soldiers approached Smitty's position, walking in a line while jabbing their fixed bayonets into the ground every few feet. One stopped near Smitty and stabbed the sand several times

As Bataan fell, thousands of Americans retreated to Corregidor Island, nicknamed the Rock, where they held out against the Japanese until surrendering on May 6, 1942. For many Palawan prisoners, their POW experience began here.   NATIONAL ARCHIVES

The men left behind on Bataan—some 70,000 Filipino and American troops—were subjected by the Japanese to a brutal march to captivity. Thousands died along the way.

NATIONAL ARCHIVES

New arrivals at Puerto Princesa's Camp 10-A first encountered the imposing twin towers of the facility's entrance. NATIONAL ARCHIVES

Japanese barracks within the compound. NATIONAL ARCHIVES

The headquarters building in the Irawan colony used by Master Sergeant Taichi Deguchi at the time of the massacre.

NATIONAL ARCHIVES

Camp 10-A as seen from above. The large four-building structure in the center is the POW barracks. In the upper-right corner are the Japanese barracks. The white structure in the upper-left corner is the house in which Captain Kojima lived. The air-raid shelters would be dug to the left of the POW barracks, near the edge of the cliff.

NATIONAL ARCHIVES

Above: From August 1942 to December 1944, the American prisoners at Puerto Princesa endured extreme heat and unrelenting sun to carve this airstrip in the Palawan jungle. NATIONAL ARCHIVES

Right: Army Lieutenant Carl Louis Mango, a doctor before the war, helped save many lives at Puerto Princesa. COURTESY OF ALBERT MANGO

1. Marine Corporal Glenn "Mac" McDole
COURTESY OF KATHY McDOLE PARKINS

2. Marine Corporal Rufus "Smitty" Smith
COURTESY OF NITA SMITH ALEXANDER

3. Marine Sergeant Doug Bogue
COURTESY OF KATHY McDOLE PARKINS

4. Army Private First Class Ernie Koblos
COURTESY OF JACK AND FELICE KOBLOS

5. Navy Radioman Joe Barta
COURTESY OF LINDA JO YALE

1. Army Corporal Elmo "Mo" Deal
COURTESY OF SHARON SPEARS

2. Army Corporal William "Willie" Balchus   NATIONAL ARCHIVES

3. Army Private First Class Eugene Nielsen
COURTESY OF LORNA MURRAY

4. Army Corporal Edwin Petry
NATIONAL ARCHIVES

5. Army Private First Class Alberto "Beto" Pacheco
NATIONAL ARCHIVES

1. Navy Yeoman Bruce Elliott—who attempted to swim from Bataan to Corregidor, only to end up as a prisoner of the Japanese—led the first successful escape from Palawan Island in August 1942. COURTESY OF JENNIFER MEIXNER

2. Marine Corporal Sidney Wright joined Elliott's escape. Several months later, when he learned a Filipino collaborating with the Japanese had murdered a fellow escapee, he hunted down the turncoat and killed him. COURTESY OF DAVID WRIGHT

3. Navy Yeoman First Class Hubert Hough, unable to perform airfield construction after a vicious beating at the hands of a Japanese guard, was tasked with keeping clerical records for the POW camp.
COURTESY OF LYNHON STOUT AND MINHON RIDENOUR, DAUGHTERS OF HUBERT HOUGH

4. Marine Corporal George Burlage was nicknamed "the Arm Breaker" for his willingness to bash a comrade's dominant limb with a pick handle to get the man excused from airfield duty. For his service, he charged extra food or cigarettes. COURTESY OF GEORGIANNE BURLAGE

1. Captain Fred Bruni, as the senior Army officer at the camp, was in the precarious position of maintaining discipline among the prisoners while placating their Japanese captors.

U.S. ARMY

2. Ensign Bob Russell, the senior Navy officer, often clashed with Bruni and engaged in a fistfight with Doc Mango.

U.S. NAVY

3. Marine Private First Class Don Martyn attempted to swim across Puerto Princesa Bay on the night of December 14, 1944. He never reached the other side.

COURTESY OF LYNHON STOUT

4. Marine Private First Class Roy Henderson made a survival pact with a clique of fellow prisoners. When he contracted malaria, his friends smuggled pilfered fruit to help keep him alive.

COURTESY OF ETTA HENDERSON HOOKER

1. The "torture trees," where prisoners were lashed and beaten mercilessly by Japanese guards.

NATIONAL ARCHIVES

2. Master Sergeant Taichi Deguchi was the acting commander of the brutal Kempei Tai military police unit at Puerto Princesa in mid-1944. NATIONAL ARCHIVES

3. First Lieutenant Yoshikazu Sato, known to the POWs as the Buzzard, was second in command of Camp 10-A in December 1944 and led the massacre at Puerto Princesa.

NATIONAL ARCHIVES

4. Lieutenant Toru Ogawa was in charge of the vehicle repair shop and airfield repair. During the massacre, he commanded a gun barge whose crew shot Americans attempting to swim across the bay. NATIONAL ARCHIVES

Prisoners fleeing the massacre plunged down this steep bluff at the edge of camp to the narrow, rocky beach below.   NATIONAL ARCHIVES

A view from the water's edge below the camp. Note the small cavern entrance, one of the spots where escapees hid, below the little canvas tent.   NATIONAL ARCHIVES

Another view of the bluff and rocky beach below the camp. Many prisoners attempting to escape the massacre made easy targets as they fled along the beach or into the sea.

Overlooking the bluff below the Shelter C exit from which McDole, Smitty, Daniels, and others escaped to the rocky coastline below.

The view from the bluff, looking across Puerto Princesa Bay.

After swimming throughout the night, Joe Barta landed here on the other side of the bay. The *banca* at the water's edge is the style of outrigger boat used by six American escapees as they sailed along the Palawan coastline.

Above left: The Americans who escaped Camp 10-A looked like walking skeletons after more than two years of malnutrition and slave labor. These five prisoners are seen after their liberation from the Santa Tomás camp on Luzon, a rescue accelerated by testimony from the Palawan massacre survivors. NATIONAL ARCHIVES

Above right: Pedro Paje at his desk in the Iwahig Penal Colony. Though some prisoners suspected him of being a Japanese collaborator, Paje covertly served as the organizer of the Palawan Underground Forces, a guerrilla unit, during the war. NATIONAL ARCHIVES

Some American massacre survivors stumbled upon these Filipino dwellings within the Iwahig Penal Colony, where they found willing support. NATIONAL ARCHIVES

Lieutenant Celerino Poyatos helped guide nine Palawan survivors to safety.

NATIONAL ARCHIVES

Jose Miranda rescued Ed Petry and Beto Pacheco. NATIONAL ARCHIVES

Above: Miranda points out the hut where Petry, Pacheco, and Gene Nielsen hid after swimming from Puerto Princesa.

NATIONAL ARCHIVES

Above left: Thomas Loudon spent three years as a prisoner of the Japanese until his rescue, along with six massacre survivors, from the island in January 1945. COURTESY OF MARY ANNE (MAYOR) ANCHETA

Colonel Nazario Mayor commanded the guerrilla division in the Puerto Princesa region. Following the massacre, his family graciously welcomed survivors into their home. (*Front row, left to right*): Thomas, Lorraine, Mary (holding Lorraine), Nazario, Cornelia, and Mary Anne. (*Back row*): Frank, Robert, and Nellie.

COURTESY OF MARY ANNE
(MAYOR) ANCHETA

Left: Dr. Higinio Acosta Mendoza, captain of Company A of the Palawan Special Battalion. Mendoza was executed by the Japanese on January 24, 1944, for taking part in guerrilla activities.

COURTESY OF HIGINIO "BUDDY"
MENDOZA AND BART DUFF

Trinidad "Triny" Clark Mendoza. After the murder of her husband, Mrs. Mendoza gave assistance to the American POWs at Camp 10-A and was known by the code name Red Hankie.

COURTESY OF LYNHON STOUT AND
MINHON RIDENOUR, DAUGHTERS OF HUBERT HOUGH

A soldier examines the trench from which McDole, Smitty, Pop Daniels, and others escaped. Note at the edge of the cliff the barbed wire fence through which some men struggled as they attempted to escape toward the beach below. NATIONAL ARCHIVES

Soldiers excavate the charred remains of Americans burned to death by the Japanese.
NATIONAL ARCHIVES

Bones of murdered prisoners still lay in an excavated air-raid trench, March 1945.
NATIONAL ARCHIVES

Japanese guards
from Camp 10-A
stand trial for war
crimes in 1948.

NATIONAL ARCHIVES

Edwin Petry was among the
Palawan survivors who gave
testimony at the trials in Japan.

NATIONAL ARCHIVES

Survivors Joe Barta,
Mac McDole, and
Doug Bogue indicate
Palawan on a map to
an intelligence officer
after their return to
the United States in
1945.

COURTESY OF KATHY
McDOLE PARKINS

within inches of him. The next soldier stepped right onto Smitty's weed patch, and he stiffened.[1]

A heavy boot came down on his right shoulder, and a Japanese soldier staggered. He caught himself, but in the twilight, he failed to realize what had caused him to stumble. Smitty held his breath until the guard slowly made his way across the rocky bluff without further investigation. He lay there for hours, unsure what to do next. He could hear the idle chatter of excited guards moving about. He understood just enough Japanese to make out some of their talk. One of them mentioned that 149 Americans had been killed.

Am I the only survivor? he wondered. *Surely they won't stop until they can count the bodies of all one hundred fifty men.*

The guards continued patrolling the rocky beachside crevices and the underbrush along the downslope of the cliff below the charred bomb shelters. At one point, two Japanese walked perilously close to Smitty's hiding spot before plopping down on the rocks to take a breather within ten feet of his position. He fought every urge to stretch, cough, or make any type of noise. After a while, Smitty heard something scuffling down the cliff, shuffling through the foliage toward him, and the scaly face of a large monitor lizard appeared under the brush.[2]

The reptile approached, likely assuming he was a corpse, and moved its mouth closer to his left hand. Fearful of crying out if bitten, Smitty waved a finger. The animal took off through the brush, its long tail swinging about and making awful crashing noises as it lumbered downhill right toward the nearby guards. The frightened Japanese jumped aside to let the creature run past, forgetting in their excitement to consider investigating the source of what had startled the beast.

Three times now I've nearly been discovered, Smitty thought. *How much longer can my luck possibly hold out?*

As the sun began to set, other thoughts entered his mind. *What if they start burning all this underbrush?*

The thought seemed reasonable. The Japanese might just use their fuel to light up all the bushes, debris, and weeds along the steep banks to smoke out any survivors. *Maybe they think it's too green to burn,* Smitty thought. *Or maybe it's too much trouble for finding just one more American.*[3]

He felt certain that no one above him was still living. Throughout the afternoon, he had heard occasional rifle shots echo from the compound as the Japanese apparently finished off prisoners. He later heard explosions, and he figured the guards were using dynamite to make it look like the Americans had been killed by friendly bomb loads. He could not see what was happening on the beach, but he could hear pitiful screams as victims were executed.[4]

Below him was a large rock in the edge of the water with Americans hiding behind it. He watched as a Japanese patrol boat approached from offshore. One man's leg was sticking out far enough to be spotted, and Smitty saw the barge gunners open fire. Apparently hoping to spare his comrades, the wounded man staggered out from his hiding spot and was riddled with gunfire. The gunboat crew moved on in search of other targets, oblivious to the remaining POWs.

That man is a true hero, thought Smitty.

GENE NIELSEN LAY still in the garbage dump, his bare legs exposed, only long enough for the guard detail to retreat up the hill. His life had been spared, if only momentarily. There was no time to lose now. He cautiously crawled from the dump, squinting in the late-afternoon sunlight as he shook off the last of the coconut husks that had partially concealed him. He looked toward the guards moving over the bluff, then ran along the beach.

He shuffled back and forth, searching for shelter. The guards would be back soon, and he knew how he could expect to be treated. He didn't think much better of his chances in the water, though. The Japanese gunboat was still roaming the coastline as its riflemen shot at any prisoners they could see. Nielsen ran along the edge of the water, trying to keep himself concealed from their view. A short distance away, he found a tiny shallow-water cave just on the edge of the beach.[5]

When he began to clamber into the hole, he found other American escapees—Mo Deal, Ernie Koblos, Pop Daniels, Gabriel Sierra, Bill Williams, Willie Balchus, and John Warren—already squeezed into the space. The eight men tried to stay concealed completely behind the coral, but a short time later, they heard the barge returning down the beach on another pass near their position. Each man crouched in the crevice as low as possible.[6]

Nielsen tried to move behind a bush. The men urged one another to keep quiet as the gunboat's engine rattled closer, but Sierra was in agony. His entire body was burned, his hair was singed, and his flesh was rubbing off against any coral surface he brushed against. Sierra muttered continually from the pain. As the barge approached, Nielsen noticed that Warren, closest to the water, was crouching behind the coral rocks only enough to hide his upper torso, leaving his legs exposed.[7]

Lieutenant Toru Ogawa's soldiers spotted one of Warren's legs sticking out from under the rocky overhang and opened up. Bursts of automatic fire peppered the entrance to the cavern, ricocheting lead in all directions. Warren cried out as a bullet struck him squarely in the ankle and left his foot nearly severed, dangling by tendons and bone fragments. He staggered forth from behind the rock, fully exposing himself, and was immediately riddled with gunfire.[8]

As the gunboat chugged on past in search of more survivors, Nielsen stole the chance to shuffle along the edge of the water in search of a better hiding place. Sunset was approaching, but it could not come soon enough. Along the shore and higher up on the bluffs, he could see Japanese ground patrols closing in on the scene of the latest gunfire. About fifty yards from his original hiding spot, he found a small ledge of coral jutting out into the water, and he lay down in the water below it.

Ernie Koblos and several others moved through the underbrush toward a point of land that jutted into the bay. Koblos decided to climb back to the top of the cliff through the underbrush. When he got there, he could see the gunboat moving back along the coast, as well as more guards moving down from the camp. Finding his chances slim on the high ground, he made his way back down to the beach, slipped into a tight cave filled with water, and submerged himself up to his neck, waiting until dark.[9]

When soldiers splashed past Nielsen's hideout, he determined that his small coral overhang was not nearly enough to protect him. He spotted a large coconut floating nearby and grabbed it. He ducked under the water and started swimming, holding the coconut above him with one hand. He had made it only a short distance from shore when he heard shouts. Guards had spotted movement in the water and then the bobbing coconut. Rifle rounds zipped through the sea around him. He glanced back, took a deep breath, and plunged under the surface, stroking hard toward deeper water.[10]

As a kid, he and his friends would ride their bicycles several miles from home to a large community pool in Logan, Utah, where he had trained himself to swim its length underwater with a single breath. His life now depended upon how long he could stay under. His lungs were bursting when he popped up for a quick gulp of air. Then he plunged back under, pulling himself hard away from the beach. Each time his head broke the surface, he heard shouts and the cracking of gunfire. When he was under, he could hear bullets slicing through the water all around him.[11]

Willie Smith, still concealed on the bluff high above, watched at least ten guards firing away with their rifles, trying to hit Nielsen each time he reappeared for a breath. Smitty saw each soldier empty his magazine, reload, and resume firing.

When Nielsen was about seventy-five yards offshore, the first bullet struck him in the armpit. The water slowed the velocity enough that the round did not break his skin, but it still hurt like hell. When he came up again, another bullet grazed the right side of his forehead, knocking him senseless. He nearly drowned before he came to, gasping for air and flailing about.

Before he could swim any farther, a third shot slammed into Gene's left leg just above his knee. It failed to hit bone, but the bullet traveled under his flesh and lodged up near his hip, about a foot from its point of impact. Nielsen's leg went numb, and he found that he could poke his entire thumb into the bullet hole.

Somehow, he found the strength to keep swimming in the eighty-degree water until he felt he was out of range. He knew he could not return now, so he began swimming parallel to the shore. He heard the soldiers' voices drifting across the water and watched them follow along on the beach as they tracked his progress.[12]

SOON AFTER DUCKING inside their crevice, Ed Petry and Beto Pacheco decided they should block off the entrance to prevent the guards from finding them. They stacked coral chunks at the main entrance until the only clear exit to their watery cave was the side jutting out into the open ocean, and the only way in was to wade in from the oceanside.

For hours, the two men listened in agony as murders took place outside their position, and they wondered how long it would be before the Japanese guards found their hideaway. Then they were startled to hear someone moving toward the entrance to the cave. They crouched low, trying to remain unseen. Someone fumbled with the rocks blocking the beachside entrance and began forcing his way inside.

It was another American.

Petry recognized Corporal Dane Hamric as he struggled into their cave, gingerly cradling his bloodied arm. He was in bad shape. A gunshot had nearly severed the limb, and he seemed half-crazed, moaning loudly with pain. Pacheco and Petry slapped him around a bit, urging him to keep quiet before he caused them all to be found by the Japanese guards moving about overhead, looking for openings in the coral.[13]

The three remained hidden until about 1630, when they heard the scuffling sounds of someone approaching. The tide had receded, and the once-submerged oceanside entrance to their cave was exposed. They heard several men splashing toward them.

*　*　*

DOUG BOGUE HAD spent the afternoon hiding in a hole at the base of the cliffs just yards away from the ocean. From his vantage point, he could see well enough to know that it was unsafe to try to move on. Occasionally, he heard excited shouts and gunfire as guards scouring the rocks found Americans hiding. The sight of his comrades being tortured or murdered sickened him, but he opted to stay down and wait it out all afternoon. As the hours passed, he felt a sense of relief that he was still alive.

At about 1700, Bogue finally decided it was time to take his chances. The sun was dropping lower on the horizon, and some of the Japanese soldiers were walking back up the bluffs. The tide was beginning to creep in, washing up into the rocks where he was crouching ankle-deep in the froth. It was time to move. His body stiff from hours in the cramped, rocky crevice, he eased out of his hole and began crawling among the rocks at the ocean's edge, when he encountered another survivor.

Bogue recognized Navy radioman Joe Barta. Two more men appeared beyond him—privates Don Martyn and John Lyons. The trio had emerged from the old sewer outlet, where they had hidden until the tide started rising. Fearful of drowning in the shallow sewer pit, Barta and his companions had scurried out toward the nearby bay. Joining with Bogue, they moved silently along the shoreline until they located a small cluster of caves. Lyons splashed through the shallow water into the opening, followed by Martyn, Bogue, and Barta.[14]

Inside, they were surprised and relieved to find Ed Petry, Beto Pacheco, and Dane Hamric. The seven men huddled together, whispering about what they should do next. Bogue told them that the search along the beach had intensified, and that a barge with armed guards was moving about just offshore, shooting any prisoners the guards encountered. The group decided there was nothing to do but await nightfall. They realized things might change hours later at high tide if rising water should force them from their cave.

Barta, crouching in deep water beside Martyn, grew anxious as he heard voices approach a crack in the coral directly above. A Japanese officer shined his light down into the opening and swept it about as he peered into the space below. As the beam swerved toward them, Martyn and Barta ducked under the water. Barta pinched his nose and remained submerged until his lungs burned. Only when the light disappeared did he resurface.[15]

The danger, however, had not yet passed. Lyons was ill, struggling with an incessant cough, and his hacking soon caught the attention of the guards. His comrades did their best to help stifle the noise as guards gathered topside, but the Japanese chattered away, believing they had heard something. They probed and prodded, but no one came down to the waterside to find the cavern opening. They spotted the barrier erected earlier by Pacheco, decided there was no way into the rocks, and finally moved on down the beach.[16]

The seven Americans breathed easier for the moment. They had nearly been found, but there was still too much daylight to leave their hiding spot. Pacheco, Petry, Lyons, and Hamric were squeezed into a small crevice that was farthest from the ocean while Bogue, Martyn, and Barta remained in a somewhat larger, adjacent cave closer to the water. Once it became completely dark, Pacheco and Petry decided to take their chances and investigate the situation outside. Lyons stayed behind to look after the wounded Hamric.

"The tide is coming in," Petry said. "We have to get out. Me and Pacheco will search around up there. If it's all right, we'll come back down here and get you two."

Petry and Pacheco had to duck underwater to swim into the adjoining larger cavern. There, they conferred with Bogue, Barta, and Martyn. Before they could slip outside, the men heard the sounds of Japanese guards overhead once again. They lay still for about a half hour, not daring to talk as excited voices and footsteps resonated above. There was no chance to slip out of the oceanside exit now without being shot.

The five men glanced nervously at one another. High tide was inching in, and the water inside the larger cavern was already up to their chests.

SMITTY HAD BEEN so frightened all day that as the sun disappeared over the horizon, he felt numb to emotion. Wearily, he crawled from his hideout and eased back down the cliff toward the coral rocks where he had first taken shelter. The path he had traversed earlier made for an easy return. The guards who had sat near him for so long were long gone, and he could not see anyone else.[17]

As he approached the ocean, he spotted a soldier standing on a tall hump of coral. Smitty hunched down perfectly still, waiting until the man turned his back to the bay to look up toward the cliff, then eased down into the water, where the tide would wash away his bloody footprints. He waded silently into the warm sea, ducked his entire body under, and stroked hard, away from the island.

He had contemplated swimming for freedom in the past. In just the past week, he had overheard Army brothers Hugh and Rob Hubbard discuss making a break for it by swimming the bay. Smitty had stepped in, telling them, "You're going to wind up getting all of us killed." He told them that he was in better physical shape than they were, and he did not believe he could swim the bay and survive the currents. He had convinced them to give up their idea. Now he was faced with making the dreaded swim on his own.[18]

Smitty had never been a particularly good swimmer. His only previous experience had come back home in Texas, helping to maneuver hundred-foot fishing seines through deep creeks, and he spent most of his time just trying to stay afloat. During Marine survival course training, he had done well enough to pass the swimming test.

He popped up for air and ducked under again. Once he had moved a fair distance from the shoreline, he looked back. The guard had not noticed his escape, so he began swimming harder on the calm surface. From what he knew, the nearest beach was five miles across the bay. He was wearing only his loose tattered shorts, which created extra drag as he swam. Somewhere along the way, they slipped off, leaving him completely naked. Now the swimming was at least a little easier, and during the next hour, he alternately stroked and paused to rest. Gradually, the Palawan camp and its bluffs receded. He hoped to remain within sight of the shoreline, but the tide pushed him farther into Puerto Princesa Bay than he wanted to go. He became frightened when he could not see the shore, but he pushed on.[19]

About halfway across, large groups of fish gleamed in the phosphorescence of the warm aquamarine water. He kept swimming, trying to remain calm. A dark fin knifed through the water near the fish, cutting a purposeful wake right toward him like a torpedo. He had almost no time to react. He estimated the sand shark that plowed into him was about six feet long. Powerful jaws clamped down on his right forearm like a vise. He flailed at the shark with his left arm, kicking and splashing frantically as sharp teeth tore through his flesh. He thrashed about, trying to fling the shark loose, and finally it jerked back. Blood poured from nasty gashes in his right forearm, but he continued to beat the water to scare it away.

It worked. The shark moved on, but the school of fish remained with him. He struck out swimming again, his arm throbbing. His movements stirred up the phosphorescent waters like a neon light, enabling him to see clearly the school of fish hovering below. He swam for short bursts, then rolled over onto his back to take brief rests. Each time he did, he glanced around anxiously for the shark.[20]

His fish escort stayed with him during the next half hour. Large creatures with black fins broke the surface nearby, and his heart raced each time as he prepared for another shark attack. His apprehensions eased when he realized they were not sharks but curious porpoises following his progress. They seemed to form a protective shield around him and gave him hope they might keep away any more sharks.

In the distance, he could make out the highest point of a mountain near the penal colony's shore, and high above it, the North Star. He lined up his heading on that point and pushed on. En route, he swam head-on into an old floating fish trap, unseen until it bumped his head. Exhausted and bleeding, he clutched the bamboo cage and let his body go limp.

The penal colony's shore was still a long distance away, and he was nearly spent. Smitty clung to the trap until his heavy breathing subsided. He needed to conserve his energy. Daylight was many hours away, and he still had a long distance to swim.

WILLIE BALCHUS AND Mo Deal, hidden in a cave at the edge of the beach, were now the only two men left of those who had escaped earlier from their five-man shelter. In the past hour, they had seen John Warren shot and killed by the Japanese gunboat, while Gene Nielsen had slipped away to pursue his own escape effort, followed by Ernie Koblos and several others who had gone in different directions to hide among the rocky crevices.

Suffering from burns and a bullet wound in his shoulder, Deal reflected on his own life after having watched others lose theirs. He was a lanky six footer who had grown up in a farming family in rural Cloud County, Kansas. His father had moved his clan about in search of work, from Kansas to Nebraska, then to Sutter County, California. Deal had been a hell-raiser as a teenager, frequently landing himself in trouble—though none of that trouble could compare to what he found himself in now. Before enlisting in the Army in 1940, he spent four months doing body and fender repair work in an automotive shop in Modesto.[21]

Now, after years of slave labor in the merciless Pacific sun, after watching friends waste away or be murdered, he would have given anything to be back there in California, toiling in that Modesto garage. As the sun lowered over Palawan Island, death and its prospects were everywhere around him. Now Deal and Balchus decided it was time they made their own escape attempt.

Five Japanese guards still combed the beach a short distance away. All was quiet, and Balchus knew that a run through the jungle would make too much noise and lead to their discovery. The bay looked too wide to swim. The two men discussed options. "If we can kill a couple of the Japanese and get their rifles, we've got a better chance," Willie said.

Deal agreed. They both knew that Filipino guerrillas operated nearby, and if they could arm themselves, they just might make it north into friendly hands. Deal and Balchus started slowly climbing out of their small cave. They were still crawling forward when they spotted a group of soldiers combing the beach in a line. The Japanese moved to within easy earshot of the two hidden Americans and then suddenly froze. Balchus, with his limited Japanese, heard them talking excitedly about a coconut. He was still trying to figure out what that meant when two of the soldiers came to a halt right where he and Deal were crouching in thick brush.[22]

The Japanese opened fire on an American swimming out to sea. The nearest guards were standing no more than twelve inches away from the heads of Deal and Balchus. The two men lay still, counting the barks of about twenty rounds before the guards moved on to join the others who were following the escapee's parallel swim along the coast. While the guards were preoccupied, Deal and Balchus slipped back down to the beach.

Sometime after 2000, they happened across two other Americans, Bill Williams and Pop Daniels. Both men had escaped their shelter, plunged down the cliffs, and hid near the beach throughout the afternoon. The quartet took cover and discussed their options.

Those in the group soon found they had differences of opinion on how best to make their escape. Deal and Balchus still had the idea of overpowering a Japanese guard and fighting their way through the jungle. Williams and Daniels preferred to remain near the ocean, so around 0200 on December 15, the four men decided to split up. Under the moonlight, Deal and Balchus headed for the base of the cliff, hoping to catch a Japanese soldier standing guard alone. They took cover, then began to holler to attract attention. The first guard to appear was a Japanese navy sentry, who shouted for backup. Four other sailors joined him.[23]

Things were not going as planned. Instead of the chance of two unarmed men overpowering a lone guard, Deal and Balchus now faced five armed men heading toward their position. Two of the Japanese were higher up on the bluff, while three others were hurrying down, torches in hand. The two Americans decided to shift uphill quickly in order to escape the trio of guards in the lead. They ducked behind a large coral rock and tried to hide their bodies from the glare of the torches.

The first two guards walked right past the boulder. The third was rushing by when the light of his torch illuminated the two Americans. As he opened his mouth to shout, Balchus sprang, a large chunk of coral in his hand. He slammed it against the guard's head and the man fell. As another guard doubled back, Balchus was ready, knocking him out cold as well. Neither Japanese had a chance to raise his rifle.

With a hunk of jagged coral in hand, Deal lunged at the third guard. In the darkness, Balchus grabbed up a dropped rifle and called out to Deal three times with no reply. He could hear the other two guards closing in, swearing and shouting. He had no idea what was happening with his comrade, but he was in no position to find out. Balchus sprinted down the bluff, rifle in hand. He never saw Mo Deal again.

DEAL HAD SURVIVED his struggle with the guard, but with a bullet in his shoulder, he had no intention of swimming out into the bay. He hoped to sneak over the bluff and disappear into the nearby jungle, but he didn't make it far. In the wake of the scuffle, the other guards opened fire as he fled, and he was quickly cornered near the top of the cliff.

He found himself with another gunshot wound, but the guards decided against killing him outright, resorting instead to the same blood sport used against other captured Americans. He pleaded and cried out in pain as they stabbed him with bayonets, deep puncture wounds lacerating his legs, hips, and torso in more than twenty places. He tried to fend off his assailants' blows and suffered a terrible wound to his right arm in the process.

In seconds, Deal was in severe shape, disoriented from the swiftness of the attacks and loss of blood. From below, several sudden bursts of rifle fire distracted the guards. Deciding the American was nearly dead, one soldier gave a final bayonet thrust into Deal's body and shoved him off the cliff. He tumbled into the brush far below as the Japanese rushed downhill.[24]

Balchus had scrambled down the steep hill, right out to the water's edge, before he dared to look back. Up on the bluff, the other two guards were easy to spot with their torches glaring in the darkness. Balchus aimed his captured rifle and fired. To his disgust, he found there were only three bullets in the rifle, and worse, the flames that spewed from the barrel had clearly given away his position.

He had no choice now—he had to swim. He smashed the rifle against the coral rock and splashed out into the bay. As he moved from shore, he spotted the wreckage of a Japanese seaplane destroyed during the October 19 bombing attack. He reached the partially submerged plane about a hundred yards offshore and grabbed onto its side. Japanese guards were now moving about on the beach, shouting to Lieutenant Ogawa's guards on the barge that was sweeping along the beach from offshore. The gunboat approached the wreckage, making a wide circle around it. Balchus eased around the broken fuselage, keeping himself out of view.

Eventually, the gunboat moved on. Gunfire erupted from the beach, but he knew the bullets were not aimed at him. The guards must have located Mo Deal, Pop Daniels, or Bill Williams. He could only hope for the best for them. The commotion made for a good distraction, so he pushed away from the seaplane wreckage, setting his sights on the far shore of Puerto Princesa Bay. After nearly three years as a prisoner of war, Willie Balchus was finally beginning his swim to freedom.

Gene Nielsen was in excruciating pain. Bullets had struck his temple and armpit, though thankfully failed to penetrate. Another round had torn into his left leg, leaving a gaping hole. As the sun lowered behind Palawan Island, Nielsen slowly swam parallel to the coast, eyeing the Japanese soldiers who continued to follow him down the narrow beach, snapping off occasional shots until complete darkness set in. Reaching a point on the Puerto Princesa shoreline where the land cut back to the northeast, he felt he had no choice but to swim the bay under cover of darkness. He splashed about to make the Japanese guards think he was heading toward shore, then turned and began swimming as silently as possible toward Iwahig on the far shore.[25]

Stars and constellations stood out above him in bright contrast against the black of night. Selecting a large bright star to guide his progress, he continued across the bay. His swimming was labored due to the pain in his leg, but he made steady progress, imagining fresh drinking water from the Iwahig River on the far shore.

He had been swimming for quite some time when he paused to rest for a moment. A large sea creature was moving near him in a counter-clockwise fashion, coming close enough that Nielsen could have reached out and touched it. Fearful at first that a shark was stalking him, he soon noted a round, bulbous nose occasionally breaking the surface, and realized it was a manatee, what the natives called a sea cow. The mana-tee seemed curious and remained close by, swimming around him in slow circles through the night.[26]

Nielsen continued, navigating by the bright star, which he assumed to be the North Star. He had been swimming for hours when he noticed that his guiding star had changed positions. It couldn't be the North Star—his beacon now seemed to be guiding him out toward the open Sulu Sea. He trod water for a few moments and surveyed his horizons. In the distance, he could make out a faint outline of mountains on the far shore above Iwahig. He had been swimming the wrong way for some time. Adjusting his bearings, he used the faint ridges above the Iwahig Penal Colony as his new goal.[27]

His wounded body ached, but he kept a slow, steady course toward the far shore.

WE'RE GOING TO *drown in this cave.* The water had risen almost to Ed Petry's mouth, pulled by the tide into the seaside cavern where he remained huddled with four other escapees—Bogue, Pacheco, Martyn, and Barta. Two additional survivors, Hamric and Lyons, were hidden in a smaller adjacent cave, now unreachable from the main cavity.

Crabs nipped at the men's bare skin. As the water level continued to rise, lifting the men up, Pacheco spotted an opening through the coral at the top of their cavern. Pulling himself up, he wriggled out to the rocks above and lay silent, scanning the beach for Japanese guards. Long moments passed, and down below in the flooding coral cave, Petry became anxious. The crabs pinching his arms and chest seemed to be having a feast, and he had heard nothing from Pacheco. Now he too squeezed up through the tight opening in the rock, but to his dismay, he couldn't see Pacheco anywhere.[28]

Minutes later, Pacheco scurried out of the darkness to where Petry was waiting. "They're gone!" he said. "I went back in the other cave again, and I couldn't find them anyplace."[29] Lyons and Hamric had apparently moved out to seek other shelter. For the five who remained, there was now no other option than to take their chances in the ocean. If they could swim Puerto Princesa Bay, they could seek help from prisoners of the Iwahig Penal Colony. They could hear the engines of the Japanese landing barge approaching as its guards scanned the beach for escaped Americans. The quintet waited nervously until the engines chugged on down the coast before they moved out.[30]

Bogue eased out of the cave into the open water, followed by Martyn, Pacheco, and Petry. Barta was the last to leave. The group hoped to swim across together, but their plan fell apart quickly. Petry was only a short distance off shore when he found that Bogue, hampered by the gunshot wound in his leg, was struggling.[31]

"I can't make it, fellas!" Bogue called. "I'm going back."

Petry, his left ankle shattered by a bullet, was having his own doubts about swimming such a distance, but he was not about to give up. The other four men continued, the distance widening between them as they swam. Barta, a poor swimmer, was struggling mightily. "I can't make it!" he shouted angrily. "I thought you guys were going to help me!"

Dispirited, Barta followed Bogue back toward the shore, and Martyn turned back as well. Pacheco, still bleeding from bullet wounds in his left leg and arm, kept swimming alongside Petry. The two wounded men continued doggedly ahead, determined to stay alive. Petry knew Japanese guards were still patrolling the waterline, ready to kill any American they found, and he did not intend to turn back. The other three would have to find their own way to safety.

Bogue had second thoughts as he paddled back to shore. He caught hold of a floating log, hoping it would help keep him afloat, and kicked himself back toward the open water. With a few words in the darkness, he convinced Barta and Martyn to join him. Martyn was tall, strong, and a good swimmer, but in his weakened condition, he struggled to keep up. Barta managed to keep going. When they were a mile or more offshore, Martyn was falling behind as Bogue made slow progress, clinging to his log with one arm and stroking with the other. Barta soon fell behind as well, and Bogue found himself alone in the water. Shark fins cut the surface of the bay, and Bogue wondered how long he could avoid attack.

NINE AMERICANS WHO had so far survived the Palawan Massacre were now swimming in darkness across Puerto Princesa Bay.

Nielsen, Balchus, and Smith had set out on solo attempts. Bogue, Pacheco, Martyn, Petry, and Barta had started out together, but they were now mostly separated. The ninth man was Ernie Koblos.

Koblos had earlier survived the gun barge attack that killed John Warren. His attempts to navigate back over the cliffs had been fruitless, so he had squeezed himself into an oceanside cavern to await darkness. His body temperature dropped as he rested for hours in salt water up to his neck. Soon he realized that he had to move in order to survive.

To hell with this, Ernie thought. *Enough is enough.*

He slipped from the cavern and decided to warm himself before attempting to swim across the bay. He walked east along the dark beach for two to three miles, along the way picking up a bamboo pole that he figured might offer some support during his swim. He was still dragging the pole behind him when shots rang out a short distance away, followed by the appearance of Japanese guards searching with torches. Koblos quickly slithered into the ocean with his bamboo pole and began stroking away from the narrow beach.[32]

He swam for hours, heading for the far shore, southeast of the Iwahig Penal Colony. His years of swimming in high school and his love for the water as a Chicago youth came in handy. During those early morning hours, he covered miles of ocean, but eventually the strain of his poor diet and trauma-shocked nerves overcame him, and his weakened body finally gave out. He could not swim any farther. He was all alone, and as far as he knew, he was the only survivor to make it that far. But he was beat.

I'm finished, he thought.

16

SWIMMERS AND SURVIVORS

SIX HOURS HAD passed since Beto Pacheco and Ed Petry had taken to the ocean, and twelve hours since the Japanese had sparked the Palawan Massacre with blazing torches and buckets of aviation fuel. Now, in the early hours of December 15, the two Americans were still alive, despite their bullet wounds, but they couldn't say the same for the other three Americans who had started out with them.

Bogue, Martyn, and Barta had long since fallen behind, out of eyeshot. Of the three, Joe Barta may have been by far the worst swimmer, but he was not a quitter. Hard times had defined his young life, and Barta had always found a way to get through them. When he was only three years old, his father had died in the flu epidemic of 1918. His mother had moved her sons from Utah to Nebraska, where she worked while the boys attended a boarding school. Two years later, she died from illness. Joe's last memory of his mother was her sitting at the foot of his bed, telling him, "Joe, you're going to make it."

Joe and his brother were shipped to an uncle and aunt, who were unable to keep them long. The boys were then sent to live in Father Edward Flanagan's orphanage, called Boys Town, near Omaha, Nebraska. Joe was a jokester and often found himself in trouble for the pranks he pulled on the Catholic sisters who ran Boys Town. As punishment, the sisters put him outside one night in the middle of winter. Found the next morning, he was hospitalized with frostbite so serious that the doctors considered amputating his feet. It was little wonder that Barta ran away from Boys Town when he was fifteen.

He picked up odd jobs as he moved about, and by age seventeen, he was working in a chicken slaughterhouse in San Diego, where a foster family took him in. His brother had joined the Navy and was serving as a flight engineer. Barta decided to do the same, thinking the Navy offered him the chance to finally "be someone," and he followed in his brother's footsteps by enlisting in the fall of 1934.

Now, exactly ten years, one month, and two days to the date since he signed those enlistment papers, Joe Barta was alone in the ocean, and he was ready to die. Halfway across the bay, he passed out from exhaustion. Somehow he had the good fortune to remain floating on his back just enough to avoid drowning. As he bobbed along in a delirious state, he had visions of his mother, and remembered how she had promised him that he was going to make it. He swore he could hear his mother's voice again, this time saying, "Swim, Joe. Swim!"

He drifted, semiconscious, for some time. When he finally regained his senses, he found that he was floating on his back out of the mouth of the bay into the Sulu Sea. The edge of the beach was only about fifty yards away, so he pulled himself toward it with renewed hope and made it to dry land just before dawn broke over the Pacific.[1]

He dragged himself up onto the shoreline and lay there, completely spent. He had no idea what to do next. For the moment, he was thankful simply to be alive.

Ernie Koblos had given up on his bamboo pole, and after hours of swimming, his arms now felt like lead weights. He couldn't keep going—he had nothing left. He stopped swimming and decided just to sink. At least it was better to drown here, in the depths of the sea, than to be tortured to death back in Camp 10-A. His kicking ceased, and he allowed his legs to sink down under him. He was shocked when his feet hit solid ground. He had made it!

He staggered forward on rubbery legs through the shallow water to the shoreline and collapsed. It was dawn, and examining the jagged, jungle-cloaked coast that stretched away and the soft curves of mountains in the distance, he estimated his position to be about ten miles southeast of Iwahig.

Despite the bullet he carried in his leg, Doug Bogue had completed his swim sometime before dawn, landing not far from where Koblos would soon touch shore. Lying naked in the surf, having long since lost his tattered shorts, he was so exhausted that he could not pull himself out of the shallow water for another hour. He guessed that he had covered about five miles across the bay. Once sufficiently rested, he plunged into a mangrove swamp—with no food, no water, no clothing, and no idea where he was heading.

With bullet wounds in his arm and leg causing unbearable pain, Beto Pacheco swam near Ed Petry for hours until his body felt ready to give out. Close to three years ago, he had attempted to swim all the way to Corregidor to escape falling prisoner to the Japanese on Bataan. That night, a Navy whaleboat had picked him up and taken him the rest of the way to the Rock. Now, however, no American sailors would come to his rescue.

But unknown to Pacheco, comrades in arms were indeed looking for him. Filipino residents of the Iwahig Penal Colony were on the alert, aware of the events that had taken place before dark across the bay. Rufino G. Bondad, the executive officer of the penal colony and the Palawan Underground Forces, had ordered a number of his men out in their *bancas* to monitor the bay for escapees. During the predawn hours on December 15, a *banca* manned by three Iwahig colonists—Sayadi Moro, Salip Hatai Moro, and Salimada Moro—spotted swimmers in the water. They approached, and from a safe distance determined that the men were Americans making their way onto the beach.[2]

As Pecheco and Petry reached the shoreline near the Iwahig Penal

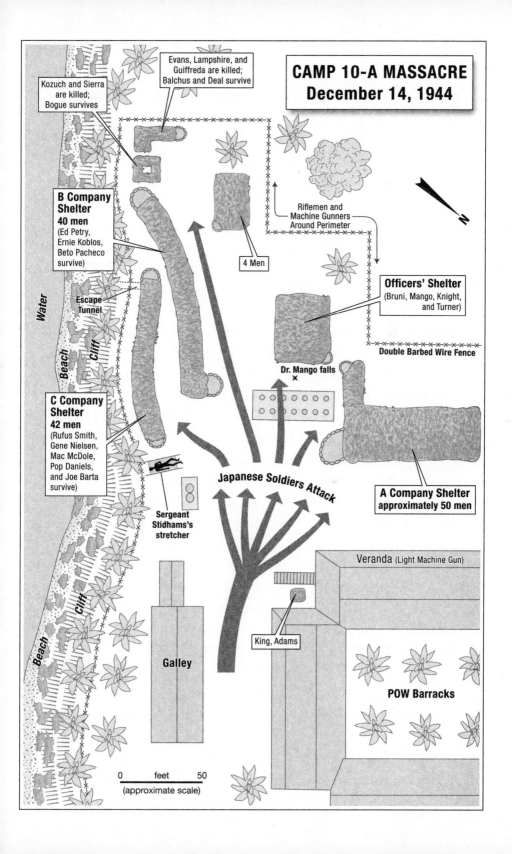

CAMP 10-A MASSACRE
December 14, 1944

Kozuch and Sierra are killed; Bogue survives

Evans, Lampshire, and Guiffreda are killed; Balchus and Deal survive

B Company Shelter
40 men
(Ed Petry, Ernie Koblos, Beto Pacheco survive)

4 Men

Riflemen and Machine Gunners Around Perimeter

Officers' Shelter
(Bruni, Mango, Knight, and Turner)

Double Barbed Wire Fence

Escape Tunnel

Water

Beach

Cliff

Dr. Mango falls
×

C Company Shelter
42 men
(Rufus Smith, Gene Nielsen, Mac McDole, Pop Daniels, and Joe Barta survive)

Japanese Soldiers Attack

A Company Shelter
approximately 50 men

Sergeant Stidhams's stretcher

Beach

Cliff

Veranda (Light Machine Gun)

King, Adams

Galley

POW Barracks

0   feet   50
(approximate scale)

N

Colony sometime before 0400, still under the cover of darkness, they had been in the water for nearly seven hours. Both were naked, having kicked off any remaining clothing long ago. When Pacheco, his energy spent, felt his feet touch bottom, he said to Petry, "Stand up and see how you feel." Petry tried but collapsed from the pain of his shattered ankle. Both men finally floundered up onto the shore and collapsed in sheer exhaustion, unable to move.[3]

Eventually, they headed north through waist-high cogongrass in search of help. Still in darkness, they came upon a house and startled the family's dog. When a man stepped out and spoke to the dog in Tagalog, the escapees scrambled to his door to explain their plight. The man spoke no English and seemed frightened that the two naked men—both darkly tanned and of average height—might be Japanese. His calls for help were answered by six other Filipinos, who approached with deadly bolo knives in hand.

Taken aback, Petry pointed to the large American eagle head and stars tattooed on his upper chest. Pacheco spoke in a mix of Spanish and English until he was finally able to convey their friendly intentions. He related the horrific details of the previous afternoon's slaughter at Puerto Princesa and described how they had remained hidden until darkness. The colonists fed them, provided them with fresh clothing, and in short order moved them to a thatched palm hut in the forest about one and a quarter miles away, where they were allowed to rest for a few hours.

Before the two escapees drifted off to sleep, Iwahig colonist Jose Miranda tended to their various wounds. He even managed to dig out the bullet embedded in Beto's leg. Shortly after daybreak, they were told they must wake up and begin moving, as it was not safe to remain long with Japanese guards hunting them. They were warned that they would not be safe until they could reach the guerrilla outpost near Brooke's Point, so Miranda was detailed to remain with them to serve as their guide.[4]

Petry and Pacheco were a long way from true freedom, but for the moment, at least they were out of the hands of the Japanese.

* * *

OUT IN THE waters of Puerto Princesa Bay, Smitty had rested awhile, clinging to the old fish trap, before he set out again, his curious porpoise friends still following along. Sometime later, he spotted Japanese patrol boats cruising the bay, no doubt looking for survivors. One boat turned and headed right toward him, with its yellow light waving directly over his position, no more than fifty yards away. He inhaled, went deep, and remained down as long as he could. When he resurfaced, the boat was slowly rumbling on past. He waited until it was well away before he resumed swimming in the eerily phosphorescent water, trailed by the school of porpoises.[5]

Smitty swam for what seemed an eternity. When he finally turned over on his back to rest and survey the horizon, he made out trees on a distant mountain ahead of him. With renewed hope, he rolled back over and began swimming again. When he felt he could not swim another stroke, he decided to see how deep it was. He held his nose and drove himself down feet first. He struck bottom immediately. The water was only up to his armpits.

The porpoises that had saved him from the shark and followed him for hours now headed back out to sea. Smitty attempted to walk, but his legs buckled and he fell forward into the ocean, accidentally swallowing a large gulp of muddy salt water as he struggled. Retching and convulsing, he struggled to his feet, stumbled awkwardly forward, then crawled the rest of the way up onto the shore. His muscles ached and his back would not allow him to sit up, so he flopped onto the shore in the darkness and closed his eyes, too exhausted to even swat at the black clouds of hungry mosquitoes that assailed his body.

THERE WERE NO direct Filipino witnesses to the massacre. From the Iwahig Penal Colony, Jose Miranda had heard machine-gun bursts and had seen the fires blazing in Puerto Princesa from a distance, but Pedro Paje, the assistant director of prisons at Iwahig, soon learned of how the Japanese had celebrated following the disposal of their prisoners.[6]

The air reeking of smoke and death within the compound, Captain Kojima gathered his men and commended them on their work. The air-raid trenches had been filled in with soil to cover the mass graves. In the morning, Kojima's men would continue to hunt down survivors, but for now they would celebrate their success.

On the evening of December 14, Paje conducted an inspection of the Inagawan Penal Colony, located about twenty-five miles from the Kempei Tai's new Irawan headquarters. Long believed by the American POWs to be a Japanese sympathizer, Paje was in fact part of Palawan's secret underground and was a key communications link to the island's vast guerrilla network. He had lived more than a dozen years within the Iwahig colony, which housed approximately seventeen hundred prisoners at the start of the war with forty-five supervising guards and employees. When the Japanese occupied the Philippines, President Manuel Quezon had granted Paje special authority to use his inmates to act on sabotage and intelligence.[7]

Paje had started organizing his Palawan Underground Force in 1942 and further refined it into special units in late 1943. He and other officer employees of the Iwahig colony who were reserve officers of the Filipino army took charge of a combat company, an intelligence corps, a quartermaster unit, a transportation corps, and a bolo battalion—the men of each selected from the most loyal, trusted prisoners of his penal colony. About two hundred of Paje's prisoners were Bataan veterans shipped to his colony in late 1943 due to overcrowded conditions at the central prison of Muntinlupa, Rizal.

Paje had managed to keep arms and ammunition for his prison—and, covertly, his Palawan Underground Force—only by maintaining peaceful relations with the Kempei Tai at Puerto Princesa. His spies had monitored the construction of the dual airstrips, noting when the first fighter and bomber planes landed in late 1943, and kept a close watch on the seaplane base that operated near the POW camp. Paje personally visited the new airfield in 1944, counting fighters on the ground and other warplanes hidden under camouflage in the nearby jungle, and recorded the maximum strength of the seaplane base to be eight aircraft.

Paje felt a personal connection to the American prisoners massacred at Camp 10-A. He had met Doc Mango in 1943, when the Japanese had allowed the appendectomy of Mac McDole to take place in the Iwahig hospital unit, and had witnessed the man's devotion to his patients first-hand. Beginning in September 1944, American bombers had dropped leaflets over Paje's colony bearing warnings concerning the treatment of American prisoners of war. Paje had dutifully delivered the leaflets to the Kempei Tai headquarters to show his allegiance, but meanwhile his underground force planted spies in the prison camp, one serving as an interpreter and another as a driver.[8]

When he departed the Inagawan colony on the morning of December 15 to return to his office at Iwahig, Paje did not yet know what had transpired at Camp 10-A, or that some survivors had taken to the bay in hopes of reaching his penal colony. Nor did he know that four Americans were still hiding beneath the bluff at the Puerto Princesa compound, tucked away in the rocks and undergrowth.

MO DEAL, SHOT twice, bayoneted numerous times, and thrown off the cliff when his assailants considered him dead, was still alive. He had tumbled down into the heavy brush, where he lay throughout the night, fading in and out of consciousness. His right arm was nearly useless, slashed through by a bayonet, and the rest of his body was a mass of open wounds, but despite the pain and blood loss, he gradually collected his senses as dawn approached.

Dehydrated, starving, and bleeding heavily, he slowly pulled himself up and began to crawl. He carefully inched through the brush and up over the top of the bluff, determined to work his way past the compound and into the town of Puerto Princesa. A merciful hard rain set in, helping to mask any noises he made as he crept along. At one point, he spotted a guard patrol continuing its sweep for survivors, and he concealed himself in the brush and lay still. The Japanese passed within a hundred feet of him, but they failed to notice the wounded American in the pounding storm.[9]

After hundreds of agonizing yards, he reached the local Roman Catholic church. Still crawling, he found a priestly robe inside to help cover and protect his numerous lacerations. He was careful not to linger too long in the church. The rainstorm made for a perfect diversion, so he continued crawling his way out of the town and into the edge of the jungle. There, he pulled himself painfully to his feet, staggered into the lush, green canopy, and began wandering away from Puerto Princesa.[10]

Pop Daniels awoke before dawn, thirsty, hungry, and in great pain. Hours before, he and Bill Williams had encountered Deal and Balchus on the shoreline, but the four had gone their separate ways. Daniels and Williams opted to move along the beach, where they ran afoul of Japanese guards and a heavy shootout ensued. Both men were wounded, Pop in the legs. He stumbled into the brush and concealed himself as the guards continued after Williams. He never saw the marine again.

His survival instincts told him to keep moving, so as rain poured down, he slowly inched his way from the coastline back into the jungles north of the Puerto Princesa camp. He was alone, facing an uncertain future, as he crawled into the rough terrain of Palawan and its four thousand square miles of jungles and mountains.

GENE NIELSEN HAD been swimming for more than nine hours when he finally kicked sand. Though shot three times, he had survived. In the darkness, he soon realized he had not actually reached the main shore, but had instead bumped up on a small island in the bay that sat about a hundred yards offshore from the Iwahig colony. He tried to stand to walk the rest of the way, but his body was simply too weak. His speck of land was tiny enough that it was likely submerged at high tide, but for now it offered him a place to rest.[11]

He crawled forward on his hands and knees into the thick brush covering the sandbar and collapsed. Curled up in the undergrowth, he drifted off to sleep. Sometime later, a strange humming, slowly growing louder, awoke him. It was still dark, but peeking through the brush, Nielsen spotted a Japanese patrol barge easing through the bay a short distance away. Soldiers were scanning the water, apparently looking for any American escapees. Nielsen lay still as the barge moved past his islet less than two hundred yards away. Once it had moved on, he decided it was time to find safer ground, and he eased off the sandbar and struggled to shore.[12]

He entered a mangrove and stumbled through it in search of the river he had seen during previous visits to Iwahig. Hordes of mosquitoes beset his naked body as he staggered barefoot through the smelly water, but he was too exhausted to even brush them away. Desperate for rest, he crawled under a mass of mangrove roots and tucked his arms into the tangle to support himself. He napped there, his body submerged, with only his nose sticking out above the swamp water, allowing his skin a brief respite from the malicious insects.[13]

Nielsen encountered many strange animals during the night. Starlight created a fluorescent effect on their eyes, similar to a hunter shining a spotlight across the water at night. He could not tell what they were, but merely saw their eyes shining at times—some red, some green, some yellow. Each pair of glowing eyes was only a quarter inch apart, but a larger pair, set about six inches apart, eased up from the swampy waters without a sound. Nielsen reached out with both hands and slapped the water as hard as he could in an attempt to scare the creature. It smacked the water with its thick tail and disappeared, leaving him fearful that it had been a crocodile.

He was hungry and worn out, but he pushed on in search of fresh water. He spotted a Filipino fisherman at one point, but he remained hidden, uncertain how the locals would handle him. He splashed through the swamp until morning light, when he found a house with roosters crowing. Nielsen emerged from the swamp and eased into a field that stretched about three hundred yards wide by six hundred yards long with coconut trees along the edge of the clearing. He attempted to climb up one to reach a coconut, but his wounded left leg was too numb. Instead, he found an older nut on the ground, and used a broken stick to pound off the husk. When the coconut finally burst open, he devoured the rich white pulp inside, his first nourishment in almost twenty-four hours.

He stumbled along, but soon found himself delirious and suffering hallucinations. He could see Japanese lying in the shade, and he moved around them to get away, terrified. Soon he realized the guards were illusions, but other visions tormented his weary brain. He thought he saw Mo Deal at one point. Nielsen knew the man was not really there, but he kept appearing in the undergrowth. He tried to shake off the sight by pushing forward through a field of jungle grass that stood about five feet tall, the sharp blades of grass nicking and slicing his skin.[14]

Then he spotted a young Filipino walking down a trail through the field. As Nielsen hid and watched, the youth passed on through. Nielsen moved closer to the trail and soon saw the man returning. The Filipino sported a large bolo knife hanging from his side, and Nielsen decided he would jump him as he approached, grab the knife, and interrogate him. He crouched down beside the trail under thick grass and waited, but changed his mind. As the Filipino passed, Nielsen called out, "Hey, Joe! Come here! I would like to talk to you."[15]

The man stopped, afraid to move. Nielsen remained hidden, equally afraid to make the first move, but he tried to convince the man to come closer. "Don't worry," Nielsen said. "It's all right. We're friends. I'm not going to hurt you."

The man finally spoke, and Nielsen was relieved to hear English. The Filipino explained that he was an inmate of the Philippine government at the Iwahig colony. His name was Sayadi Moro.

"Can you get me a drink of water?" Nielsen asked.

"Yeah!" Sayadi motioned for the naked American to follow him. At a spring a short distance up the trail, Nielsen received his first clean water since the massacre. He asked for food, and Sayadi ran off, quickly returning with two small roots about three-quarters of an inch in diameter and four inches in length. Gene noted the local vegetable tasted much like sweet potato as he wolfed down the roots.[16]

As Nielsen finished chewing, the young man suddenly announced, "You have friends."

Nielsen did not understand. He asked Sayadi if he could find a pencil and paper so he could compose a statement. The man nodded and told him to remain near the path while he trotted off again. When he returned, Nielsen asked him to take down a letter to be handed over to the American military, including his name, rank, and serial number. He detailed how the American POWs had been slaughtered and explained that he believed he was the only survivor—and that he was sick and wounded and felt he had little chance of escaping the Japanese patrols. He told Sayadi that he wanted somebody besides the government—his family or even other Americans—to understand what had taken place.[17]

Nielsen felt some relief after dictating his letter. He doubted he would live much longer, but he desperately desired some evidence to remain for the United States military as to what had happened to 150 American prisoners of war. As the men started down the trail again, Sayadi repeated, "You have friends."

"What do you mean?" Nielsen asked.

"You have friends."

Nielsen was bewildered. Perhaps the man meant Filipino guerrillas who were waiting for them somewhere ahead in another village. He asked again, "What do you mean?"

Sayadi pointed and said, "Off this trail, you have some friends."

He led Nielsen down a side path through the jungle until they entered an open area where three men waited. Two of them were Americans, lying on grass mats near a Filipino man. He recognized them as Ed Petry and Alberto Pacheco.[18]

For a moment, he thought he was still hallucinating. He moved closer, refusing to believe his own eyes until Petry and Pacheco sat up and greeted him. Nielsen was overjoyed. The two Americans explained that they were taking a rest, waiting for darkness to settle over the jungle before Jose Miranda, their Filipino friend, would lead them far-ther away once it was safe enough to continue. Nielsen learned that Sayadi had been sent to fetch bedding for Petry and Pacheco after they had been found near Iwahig. He had left them in the forest with Mi-randa and was heading back to his dormitory at Kamagong Station when he passed near Nielsen.[19]

Relieved at his incredible luck, Nielsen dropped onto a straw mat alongside Petry and Pacheco and fell fast asleep.

THE SUN WAS just peeking over the Sulu Sea when Joe Barta wearily labored to his feet. He had hoped to reach the Iwahig Penal Colony, but after losing consciousness during the night, he had drifted far off course, and now he had no idea where exactly he was. He did not feel safe re-maining on the shoreline where Japanese patrols would certainly finish off any American they encountered.

Stark naked, he reluctantly advanced into the jungle thicket. He had no real sense of direction, but the heavy growth at least afforded him some sense of protection. He walked for the next two hours until he sensed that he was not alone, and he stopped. Through an opening ahead, he could see six armed, khaki-clad Japanese soldiers on patrol. He crouched low in the underbrush, noticing a nearby gun emplacement.[20]

The soldiers gave no indication they had seen him, so Barta crawled away silently. He slowly scaled a small hill. At the top, he froze when he spotted another soldier moving through the forest below. Once again, he slipped away and made his way over another hill.

Barta had just cleared the hilltop when he found himself face-to-face with another guard, a sight that shocked both men equally. Barta sprinted away before the soldier could react. He dashed through the thick green jungle like a wild man, ignoring the briars that ripped at his skin and the sharp pains as his bare feet were pierced. The pursuing soldier shouted for one of his comrades, apparently the lone soldier that Barta had narrowly avoided moments before.

He ran through the jungle for as long as his body could go before ducking down low to hide and listen. He heard the crashing of the two soldiers in hot pursuit close behind him. Barta jumped to his feet and took off. Each time he stopped, it was the same—he was still being chased. His desperate flight continued well into the afternoon, but his pursuers did not give up.

By late afternoon, his skin was a mass of cuts and bruises, and his strength was fading quickly. He spotted a nasty thicket of dense bamboo and rattan just ahead, and wriggled his way in. The soldiers ran past. He continued to work his way in as deep as he could, then lay still for the next few hours, content to let his body recover.

As evening approached, he realized he was helplessly lost in the bamboo and rattan thicket. Each direction he tried seemed to lead nowhere. He finally decided that he would try to climb up high enough to spot a suitable way into more open jungle. He made his way up a small tree and stood on one of its upper branches. He began to look around, when the branch snapped and he fell to the ground.

Barta had no clothing to protect his skin from the abrasive trunk, or the jagged splinter of a branch that gave way beneath him. The broken stub tore through his crotch, ripping open his scrotum and exposing his testicles. Blood gushed from the open wound as he writhed in agony.

WILLIE SMITH AWOKE on a narrow beach and rubbed the sand from his face and eyes, squinting in the predawn light as daybreak approached. He figured he had slept for a couple of hours. The rest was a godsend, but the sun would be up soon, and he needed to get himself into cover, rather than lying exposed on the open beach. He was so sore that he could barely pull himself to his feet, but he knew he had to keep moving. Mosquitoes were now feasting on his body, so he crawled to the edge of a mangrove swamp and coated himself, face and all, with thick mud.

He rested a bit longer before he tried to walk, but instead found himself stumbling like a drunk. He fell several times against the jagged coral rocks, scraping away chunks of skin. He picked himself up and kept going. As he moved farther into the swamp, his feet sank deeper into the black mud with each step. His shark-bitten arm still throbbed, and thoughts of crocodiles brought new fears. He pulled himself up into a tree to rest until daylight.

Under way again, he wobbled through the jungle for hours, hoping to hit the southern boundary of the Iwahig Penal Colony, where Filipino prisoners would surely take him in. Occasionally, the muck was so thick, he had to pull himself out of it with the endless ropes of vines that snaked down. Some were covered with hard, sharp spines that cut at his hands and wrists like barbed wire. Finally, he came upon a crude wooden shack—a Filipino *nipa* hut—on the outskirts of the penal colony, still quite a distance away up on the side of the mountain he had used for a reference point during his swim. He staggered up the hillside toward the hut, but when he finally reached it, there were no people. From his high vantage point he could see a half-dozen men at work down in the valley. Smitty had stumbled upon Binuan Station, located in the Iwahig Penal Colony Reservation, and spotted seven colonists planting root crops.[21]

The Filipinos' dogs spotted him and began barking. Smitty tried to quiet the animals, but they attracted the attention of the workers far below, and one man started up the trail toward the mountaintop shack. Smitty concealed himself alongside the trail and watched as the Filipino, clad in an orange jumpsuit, moved up the hill. He waited until the man had passed, and then lunged from the brush, grabbing him and his bolo knife before the Filipino had time to react. He whispered that he was an escaped American prisoner and added, "One false move out of you and you're gone! I'll kill you!"[22]

The young marine carefully explained to the farmer about the massacre on Palawan and how he had escaped by swimming the bay.

"Okay, Joe," the man said. "We'll take you in. We're your friends."

The man escorted Smitty into the modest shack, where he prepared food for the bone-thin escapee. He expressed concern about the American's obvious injuries. "I need to get the doctor down here to help you," he said.

"Well, you get anybody you want to," Smitty said. "But if they come in here and make one false move, I'll kill you first."[23]

The man signaled to his coworkers to come join them. As they appeared at the shack, Smitty suspected the worst. The group of farmers included Isidro Dakany, who was in charge of Binuan Station. The men talked for a moment until Dakany spotted several men on horseback in the distance. Shouting and waving to get their attention, he stepped out of the hut, giving Smitty even more reason to worry.[24]

Dakany caught the attention of the three riders, who wheeled their mounts and rode toward the hut. Smitty's heart sank when the three men entered. He knew one of them in an instant. It was Pedro Paje, the turncoat.

Smitty had seen Paje previously in Camp 10-A, where he had witnessed the man laughing with the Japanese guards and at times even spitting on Americans. Now the traitor displayed a .45-caliber pistol on his hip. As he approached him, Smitty lunged for the weapon. Surprisingly, Paje pulled the .45 and tossed it over to him.[25]

"I know what you think," he said. "But I wasn't working for the Japanese. I was gathering intelligence for the guerrillas."[26]

Smitty relaxed. When the food was ready—the best he had tasted in ages—he ate and listened intently as Paje explained his situation. He had long assisted the Palawan guerrillas, he told Smitty, and he was in charge of the underground resistance movement at Iwahig's colony. When Dakany had called out to him, he had been en route to Inagawen with his intelligence officer, Lieutenant Celerino Poyatos, and another man named Dr. Simon.[27]

Runners were sent to fetch additional help for Smitty, and a short time later, the Iwahig medical officer, Dr. Zoilo Bunye, arrived to assist with his injuries. Smitty was covered with thin scratches from jungle vines, his feet were a bloody mess from running on sharp coral, and his left forearm had deep lacerations from his encounter with the shark. Dr. Bunye and Poyatos patted his wounds with the only medicine at their disposal, a bottle of iodine, and helped him into fresh hospital pajamas.

Smitty tried to rest as they waited out the afternoon. When another runner arrived later, his heart raced with the news he heard: Another American escapee had been picked up a number of miles away. Bunye was sent with the messenger to determine his condition.[28]

Smitty remained indoors until after sunset on December 15, as it was far too dangerous for an Anglo man to be moving in broad daylight. In the dark of night, he left with Poyatos and Sergeant Modesto Padilla, who used a large machete to chop through the jungle growth. They explained to Smitty that they had to travel twenty-five miles that night to get beyond the last Japanese outpost. The Filipinos were eager to get the American escapee out of their area, for Japanese soldiers had already been through the penal colony, interrogating the inmates. Some of the locals had been arrested under suspicion of harboring runaway Americans.

They covered several miles in quick fashion. With no time to rest, weary and suffering on rough terrain with bare feet, Smitty did his best to keep pace with the Filipinos. During the early morning hours of December 16, they neared their destination. Smitty brought up the rear, trying to remain optimistic but still fearful his Filipino friends could be leading him right to a waiting Japanese patrol.

PEDRO PAJE COULD well understand the American survivor's belief that he was a turncoat, a fact that only reinforced how well he had maintained the cover of his Palawan Underground Force. But he was furious, trying to comprehend why the Japanese had decided to kill off the helpless prisoners of war. Upon departing Binuan Station, he rode to the Kempei Tai headquarters at Irawan to voice his disapproval.[29]

He tried to maintain his composure as he talked with Sergeant Deguchi. He shared the findings of his latest inspection of the Inagawan colony, then inquired about the increasing number of air raids made by U.S. warplanes. He asked what the military police planned to do with the American POWs, since their camp and its adjacent airfield were a prime target of the bombing attacks. Deguchi casually informed him that there was no further worry—the Americans had been taken away to a more secure location.

Paje knew the truth, but he could do nothing to tip his hand. He could only politely excuse himself and return to his own business. The true nature of that business was now an intense desire on his part to do anything in his power to have his underground network offer aid and escape to any American who might remain alive.

WILLIE BALCHUS FINALLY reached solid ground during the early morning hours of December 15. He rested, then ambled through the mangroves until he could move no farther. Around 1000, he was still resting when he spotted two men moving through the swamp. He was terrified that he was about to be recaptured, but he was too weak to resist. As the strangers moved closer, one called out to him in English. *Filipinos!*

The men introduced themselves as Juan de Gracia and Apolonio de las Alas, members of the Iwahig Penal Colony whose underground leader, Captain Paje, had detailed them to be on the lookout for American survivors of the Palawan atrocity. Gracia and Alas helped Balchus through the rough terrain toward their camp, where he was cared for during the afternoon by their in-charge official, Mazimino Liwag. Then a small group of guides led him to Malinao Station, where he was finally provided with food, medical attention, and clothing.[30]

The Filipinos told Balchus that he must keep moving to reach the safety of the guerrilla zone. He was escorted out that evening to rendezvous with Poyatos and Padilla, two men who were in the midst of a hectic night in the jungle locating American escapees. Balchus was introduced to the two during the early morning hours of December 16, before they summoned a third member of their party forward. Out from the darkness appeared another tall, thin American.

Smitty greeted Balchus like a long-lost brother. The two escapees had scarcely been reunited when the underground members began chattering about another American who had been found nearby. Poyatos had the group stay put while runners were dispatched into the jungle to confirm the intelligence.

LIKE GENE NIELSEN, Ernie Koblos, beset by fever, dehydration, and malnutrition, soon found himself in a haze of hallucinations: A rooster crowed, and two beautiful Filipino girls appeared out of the jungle. He beckoned to them, then lurched after them as they disappeared back into the rain forest. Soon he began to see Japanese soldiers.[31]

I'm losing my mind! he thought. *This isn't real.*

Managing to clear his head, Koblos retraced his steps back to the beach where he had washed ashore. He spent the remainder of the day walking the waterline, trying to find food and fresh water. When darkness fell, he climbed up into a tree to avoid both jungle creatures and enemy patrols. The next day, he wandered aimlessly until he reentered the swamp and found a spot to sleep. When he awoke, he found that his fever had returned, so he went back to the beach and headed for a coconut grove to rest again. He knew he needed to make his way toward the Iwahig Penal Colony, but the mangrove swamps looked too foreboding to penetrate. He finally decided it would be easier to swim around to a point near the colony, and then search for an easier entry point through the jungle.

Koblos was resting in a tree near the edge of the swamp when the sound of splashing water startled him. A native *banca* was easing across the bog toward him. He slid out of the tree and prepared to flee, but as it moved closer, he was relieved to see four Filipino faces on board. The men shouted to him in English, saying they were friends, colonists of the penal colony, and explained that they had been ordered to patrol the shorelines in search of any Americans who had escaped the Palawan Massacre.[32]

The Filipinos helped Koblos to their local camp, treated his wounds, and allowed him to rest throughout the dangerous daylight hours. Once nightfall set in, he was put on the move with two guides, Paterno Gomez and Olimpio Valenzuela. They were detailed to guide him through the jungle to Malinao Station, where other Americans were waiting. There, Koblos was reunited with Smitty and Balchus. The trio had little time to celebrate their reunion before they noticed their guides conversing with another runner who had just reached them. He had traveled a great distance to inform them that three more Americans had been picked up farther away.

Pedro Paje sent word that Koblos, Smitty, and Balchus were to continue moving south and rendezvous with the other three survivors. They traveled with Sergeant Catalino Santos, who would lead them through the jungle to the Inawagan Penal Colony until they were able to rejoin the Iwahig underground movement intelligence officer, Lieutenant Poyatos. The latter had moved out ahead to verify the intelligence of the other Americans who had been found.

They were not yet completely in the clear. To reach Inawagan, they had to first slip past a Japanese guard post, and do it at night.

BETO PACHECO AWOKE to a gentle shake and a whisper. Jose Miranda stood over him. Nearby, Petry and Nielsen were waking from several hours of rest on the jungle floor near the Iwahig Penal Colony. They were informed that Miranda had sent for further instructions from his boss, Captain Paje, who sent back word that two of his men, Sayadi Moro and Jalaidi Moro, were to take the three Americans on to Malinao Station that evening to be received by the underground's intelligence officer.[33]

The bullet wound in his leg still burning with pain, Nielsen asked if the Filipinos had any kind of medicine to treat the injury. One of them left and soon returned with a fifth of rice whiskey, and used it to wash out the gunshot wound, which was steadily looking worse.[34]

Under cover of darkness, the Americans moved through the jungle with Sayadi and Jalaidi. Nielsen struggled with his lame left leg, finding that he had to keep it straight or else it would give way. But doing so meant that each step forced him to come down heavily on the heel of his other foot. Walking barefoot on rough gravel brought fresh pain with each step. Nielsen tried stepping on the smoothest rocks, but each stride left behind a bloody footprint, a crimson splotch that he realized was leaving a dangerous trail.

His comrades were in equally poor shape. Petry and Pacheco were also leaving faint blood trails from their bullet wounds and shredded feet for any potential trackers to follow. The men suffered in silence, limping along the jungle trail through the night. Their guides allowed brief breaks but kept them on the move. They made steady progress until their trail opened up into the village of Malinao Station. There, Lieutenant Poyatos greeted them, assuring the Americans that they were in good hands and that his people were more than willing to continue guiding them toward the main guerrilla headquarters at Brooke's Point.

The Americans were provided with proper civilian clothing, as well as much-appreciated food and water. Dr. Bunye, sent from the Iwahig colony to tend to them, treated their wounds. They were still resting at Malinao Station when they received the news that three other Americans had been found a short distance away. The other group had just been preparing to move out again when Petry, Pacheco, and Nielsen arrived in the village. Smitty, Koblos, and Balchus stepped forward with wide smiles and hearty handshakes to welcome three more of their own.

Poyatos was eager to get his men going again, but he reluctantly allowed the newly arrived Americans a brief rest. Soon he told them that they must keep moving to stay ahead of the searching Japanese. He and Sergeant Modesto Padilla would escort them on to what he called the "guerrilla zone," located outside the area occupied by the Japanese. All six Americans now had decent civilian clothing, they had been fed, and their wounds had received medical attention. Staying put to rest and relax might mean recapture and certain death. They had to press on.

17

MAC'S ODYSSEY

MAC McDOLE AWOKE to the vile odors of the camp dump. He had only been drifting, unable to truly sleep due to fear, pain, and the wretched filth in which he had taken shelter the previous afternoon. Sleep had largely eluded him during the long hours of darkness, as unseen worms and insects had mentally tortured him with their endless slithering, crawling, and nipping. His naked body was covered with mounds of rotting food, coconut husks, and camp refuse of all descriptions in various stages of decomposition.

Sunrise on December 15 brought fresh apprehensions. Mac was alone but alive, and his head was swimming with indecision. He knew that he could not remain buried in the waste pile forever, but if he climbed out in the daylight, he would be quickly killed. As dawn slowly illuminated the coastline below the Puerto Princesa camp, McDole scratched open a peephole. Japanese guards moved along the beach as their manhunt continued. Mac knew at least one man was still unaccounted for.

One of the Japanese turned toward the trash dump. He shuffled through, kicking at the garbage and peering into cracks. Within seconds, he was standing directly above McDole and seemed to be staring him right in the face, so close that Mac could smell his foul body odor, even amid the garbage. He closed his eyes, expecting the worst.[1]

Mac silently prayed, as he had done on other occasions since becoming a prisoner of war, asking for guidance and protection. All the while he expected a cold steel bayonet to be thrust into his chest. When he finally reopened his eyes and peered through the small hole, the Japanese soldier was gone. Then he heard a gunshot ring out down the beach, and the guard joined others running from the dump area toward the sound of the shooting.[2]

Mac jumped to his feet for the first time since he had scurried down the cliff the previous day. He ran along the shore, away from the sounds of the shooting, ignoring the pain as rough coral sliced into his feet. The bloated bodies of his comrades bobbed along the shoreline. Mac noticed he was leaving a blood trail, so he moved into the water and ran through the shallows until he tripped and fell face-first. As he lay panting, he spotted what looked like a small tunnel leading into the edge of the coral rocks. He ducked underwater and came up inside a tiny cave.[3]

There was room inside for only two men to sit on a ledge with their feet in the water. He realized that it was a sewer outlet, into which a small stream of water trickled down on him each time a wave crashed into the rocky shoreline. It was dark inside, but at least he felt safe for the time being. Small crabs scurrying about on the rocks soon began crawling on him, but he would rather tolerate the crustaceans than take his chances topside.

Mac spent the remaining daylight hours hiding in the cave, reliving all the shocking tragedy he had witnessed in the past twenty-four hours. His solitude allowed him to nurse his lacerations and burns, and try to ignore his parched throat and shriveled belly.

As he thought of the horrific deaths he had seen, a wave of nausea swept over him, but his guts had nothing to heave up. He fell back against the rocky wall of his hideaway.

* * *

THANKFUL TO BE alive, he stayed put until the sun began to set. All he needed was a fair chance to get away, and that opportunity finally presented itself when he noticed the guards drifting away from the beach back toward camp as darkness settled over the island.

He exited the sewer outlet, waded into the ocean, and began swimming. As far as he could tell, he was the lone American survivor from the Palawan POW camp. He knew it was miles across Puerto Princesa Bay, but he would feel better about his survival chances if he could reach the penal colony there.

McDole did not make it far before he changed his mind. A storm erupted with a hard downpour and high winds that whipped the waves into a pounding white froth. He would drown if he continued swimming. He cursed his luck and swam back toward the shore he had just departed. He crawled back into the sewer outlet to wait for calmer weather.

He had just curled up to take a nap when a thrashing sound startled him. Someone was splashing up toward the opening of the waste tunnel. When he looked out of the opening in the rocks, he saw a pair of battered, bruised legs that could only belong to one nationality on this island.

"Hey, American!" Mac whispered.

The man bent down and peered into the shadowy rocks. "Where in hell are ya?" he asked.

McDole poked his head up from the hole and recognized Corporal Dane Hamric, whose left arm was nearly severed from a gunshot wound. Hamric explained that he was too badly wounded to swim when five of his companions had abandoned their cave the previous evening. He had reluctantly remained behind and had stayed hidden from the enemy patrols through the day.[4]

Mac could see that Hamric had lost a considerable amount of blood. As he inspected the man's wound, he could see that gangrene had already set in. He knew the man would not live long without proper medical attention. McDole washed the arm with salt water while Hamric struggled through the pain by continuing to relate his ordeal. He rattled off the names of those he recalled who had swum away. Mac hoped to hear the name of his buddy Smitty, but Hamric had not seen him. Mac feared that his friend was dead, but he tried to remain optimistic. He now had companionship, and the comforting knowledge that at least some other Americans had started for the far shore. Maybe there were others out there.

They remained in the cramped outlet through the night, swatting away pinching crabs. Hamric seemed to grow weaker with each passing hour. For the time being, Mac could only pray for calmer seas as they huddled in the darkness.

MAC'S CRACKED LIPS and raw throat were teased by the warm waters swirling around his ankles, but he knew the dangers of drinking salt water. The smell of human waste only added to his misery as the tide slowly carried the camp filth out into the sea. As the sun rose on December 16 and the morning hours slowly passed, he and Hamric starved through another day. Outside their hideaway, Japanese guards were again prowling the beach to explore the rocks, making any hopes of dashing for the jungle or the adjacent bay pointless.[5]

Hamric's strength seemed to fade through the day, his attempts to communicate feeble as he endured unspeakable pain from his wounded arm. Early in the afternoon, Mac heard the welcome sound of American bombers overhead. *Hysterical Harry is at it again,* he thought. He did not dare look, but the number of bomb explosions he heard told him that Harry was not alone this time. Some of the blasts seemed to be closer to the prison camp than before, and one of them was tremendous.[6]

When the sun set that evening, Mac was more than ready to make another attempt to swim the bay. He saw it as his best escape option, compared to the dangers lurking in the unknown Palawan jungles farther away. Hamric was weak, but Mac planned to help him across.

Though barely strong enough to support his own body, he was not about to leave a comrade to die.

Once they entered the ocean, Hamric became resistant. He was barely coherent, and his shredded arm kept him from being of any use in swimming. Mac struggled to keep him afloat and found that Hamric was fighting him—thrashing about in the water, shunning McDole's efforts to keep him afloat. At length, Mac gave up, but Hamric was still fighting him and endangering them both. Mac finally punched him hard enough to render him unconscious and dragged Hamric back into the sewer outlet cave.

Mac knew he was strong enough to make the swim, but his training had taught him never to leave a fellow marine behind to die. *Am I really just going to stay here and die with him?* he thought.

He collapsed back against the cavern wall to suffer through his third night near the bay. Once again, he carefully washed out Hamric's shredded arm with salt water, and noticed additional bleeding from the bullet wound. The gangrene appeared to have spread, making Hamric much weaker by the time Mac drifted off to sleep.

THE NEXT MORNING, ocean water lapping at McDole's feet roused him from his slumber.

His body was terribly weak. Hunger and dehydration were draining his spirits and his strength. The only liquid to sip was the foul water dripping from the roof of their cavern. It had been more than sixty-five hours since he had tasted his last bit of rice between the air-raid alarms. One look at Hamric drove home the brutal truth: His badly wounded friend had no chance of making any swim to freedom.[7]

Still, he offered encouragement, telling him they must try again. Hamric shot McDole a pitiful look and moaned. "I can't make it, Mac. You go on. Get the hell out of here and let me die!"

Mac did not have the heart to do so. He tried consoling Hamric, begging him to just hang on a little longer, since he could not bear to go on with the ordeal alone. Hamric worsened during the afternoon, becoming less responsive as blood loss and spreading infection overcame his body. The small talk began to fade. Mac knew Hamric was dying. He huddled close, whispering encouragement until Hamric lost consciousness. Mac took him in his arms and cradled him, rocking him gently, as tears poured down his own cheeks, not just for Dane Hamric but for all of the friends he had seen die. A short while later, Hamric expired as Mac continued rocking him in his arms. Once he recovered sufficiently from his own grief, McDole eased Hamric's body from the rocky cavern to bury him as the late-afternoon sun set. He found a small depression in the coral beach, laid the body in it, and covered it with coconut husks, leaves, and other debris. He crafted a crude marker near the makeshift grave and crawled back to his sewer cave to await complete darkness.

Once the stars came out, McDole eased out into the ocean. His two previous attempts to swim across the bay had ended in failure, and he knew this was likely his final chance. He had no idea how much longer he could hold out without food or decent water, so he stroked steadily away from Camp 10-A.

He scanned the heavens above for a guide as he moved into deeper water. He picked out the brightest star—which he believed to be the Southern Cross—for a navigational bearing and hoped that the Iwahig Penal Colony, miles away, would afford him some faint hope of salvation.

McDole was the last American survivor of the Palawan Massacre to attempt to swim across the bay.

18

ELEVEN AGAINST THE ELEMENTS

E D Petry plodded forward with mechanical efficiency, mindless of
the warm evening air or the sweat streaming down his face as he
stumbled through thorny vines that snagged his already abused
flesh. Each stream, gorge, and hilltop they crossed came with slips, falls,
and further abuse to their bare feet as the six American escapees and
their two Filipino guides made their way through the rough terrain of
Palawan Island during the predawn hours of December 17.

Petry, Willie Smith, Beto Pacheco, Gene Nielsen, Willie Balchus,
and Ernie Koblos had survived three nights since escaping from Camp
10-A. Lieutenant Poyatos and Sergeant Padilla prodded their charges
forward like shepherds herding a flock as they eased south of Puerto
Princesa toward the relative safety of the guerrilla zone. They reinforced
the urgency of adding distance while darkness afforded them some protection from the roving Japanese patrols. Poyatos and Padilla lifted the
wounded when they collapsed from exhaustion and reminded them that
everyone's life was at stake.

To reach safety, the group still had to slip past one last Japanese
outpost at the village of Inagawan before daylight. Inagawan, a tiny
settlement at the edge of the jungle just hundreds of yards from the sea,

lay immediately off the trail leading south from Malinao Station. Smitty was certain that the Japanese guards had figured out by now that there were not 150 American bodies lying about the compound and the beach area. Patrols were undoubtedly scouring the area near Puerto Princesa for the survivors, and he knew it was only a matter of time before the sweeps expanded farther. Their guerrilla guides had good reason to keep them moving.

The first rays of daybreak were peeking through the lush green vegetation on December 17 as they approached the Japanese outpost. Smitty saw that the guarded post was little more than an old abandoned schoolhouse. Guerrilla intelligence reported that anywhere from twenty-seven to thirty-two Japanese soldiers normally manned the post. As they neared, the Filipinos urged the six Americans to crawl silently through the jungle canopy while they slipped closer to the schoolhouse. The Filipinos kept the Japanese guards in sight, ready to create a distraction if necessary.[1]

Smitty, Nielsen, Petry, Pacheco, Balchus, and Koblos crawled through the brush past the school yard. Once they were safely beyond the Japanese post, their Filipino guides rejoined them. The eight men stayed on the main trail only a short distance before they veered off to the west into the thickets. The main trail leading north toward Puerto Princesa was no place to be caught in the daylight hours.

Poyatos and his comrades traversed only a small portion of the jungle before they rendezvoused with a group of Captain Nazario Mayor's guerrillas who had been awaiting the arrival of the six Americans. Gene Nielsen felt that he could not last much longer. He was stumbling from tree to tree, grabbing branches to help support each painful step as he tried to avoid falling. The rest of his group was making better progress, leaving him farther and farther behind.

"This is as far as I can go," he finally said. "You go ahead. I'm going to have to rest and try to recover a little bit."[2]

His Filipino guides decided the Americans had had enough. "Go ahead and rest now," said Poyatos. "We'll take care of you."

The men flopped down on straw mats on the jungle floor to catch their breath while one of their guides trotted off in search of food. When he returned a short while later with tiny chicken eggs, Nielsen stared in bewilderment, unsure how to go about eating them. One of the Filipinos took one in his hand, showing the Americans how to poke a small hole through the shell and suck down the insides. The others followed suit, gulping down the fresh protein.[3]

Each man collapsed and slept soundly until early afternoon, when they were told it was time to get moving again. Nielsen and Pacheco, both suffering from gunshot wounds, could not move fast enough to keep pace with the pack. Poyatos sent out Padilla to find a better means of transportation, and he returned with a pair of carabao for the former POWs to use. The efficient Palawan guerrilla communications network amazed Smitty. *I don't know how they do it,* he thought. *They know where everybody is, how many of us there are, and what we need.*[4]

Poyatos and Padilla headed back toward Iwahig and reported on the progress of the Americans at this point. One of Captain Mayor's guerrillas, Corporal Pablo Quiliop, who knew the trail that led south to Company D's headquarters, would escort the Palawan survivors for the remainder of their trip to Brooke's Point. Nielsen, with his numbed leg, was the obvious choice to ride one of the carabao most of the way. Pacheco, suffering from two gunshot wounds, rode the other most of the way, although he allowed other weary men to take turns on the beasts. Nielsen found that he had to pound hard on the water buffalo's hump to keep it going. Anytime he stopped pounding, the water buffalo stopped moving. The ride was uncomfortable on his torn-up leg, but it was better than walking.[5]

Late in the afternoon, the seven men approached a river crossing in the jungle, where Quiliop helped four of the Americans across on foot. Nielsen and Koblos were riding the carabao at the time, but as the beasts lumbered across the slippery rocks, Koblos was suddenly pitched off his mount. He came down hard on the shallow rocks, snapping a bone in his arm in the process—one that had been broken before in the Puerto Princesa camp while he was on a work detail.

The group halted as Koblos rolled about in pain. Quiliop looked around for a makeshift splint to help keep the arm set until they could reach better care. He found some small boards and collected strips of bamboo while Koblos's comrades helped reset the bone in his arm. The Filipino used banana leaves for bandages and pressed them down around the nasty break area. After the arm was reset, he carefully placed the boards along Koblos's forearm and secured them in place by weaving the bamboo strips around the crude splint. Finally, small strips of wire were used to tie the whole compound together.

It was far from proper medical care, but Koblos had no options. He and the others needed to keep making time before dark. Quiliop's flock was quite the sight with one man sporting a broken arm, one with an arm ravaged by a shark, and three others suffering from bullet wounds. But he got the group moving again, two men once more riding the large carabao along the shoreline as evening approached. Nielsen found at one point that his water buffalo was intent on drinking water, as his beast suddenly turned and plowed right into the ocean while he pounded on it, trying to turn it. The animal stopped and drank for a while, then continued deeper. Soon it was out far enough that only its nose was above water. Nielsen became so frustrated that he slid off and swam back up to the beach.[6]

With night approaching, the Filipino guide moved the six exhausted Americans a short distance farther to a suitable spot in the jungle to rest.

THE FOUR-MILE SWIM across Puerto Princesa Bay took Mac McDole most of the night of December 17. His arms and legs became numb after several hours, but he stayed with it. When he felt he could go no farther, he would stop to float, and then he would push on again. It was shortly before daybreak when his feet hit sand. As he collapsed on the beach, unable to move for some time, he found that he was only a little off his original mark.

He finally summoned some energy when a coconut washed up beside him. With considerable effort, he managed to beat the nut against a rock and drink its sweet milk, but his lips and hands were so swollen from exposure to salt water and wind that he could not eat the meat.[7]

He lay back on the sand for a while after the drink, trying to gather the strength to keep moving. When he finally rose, Mac made an awkward attempt to run along the edge of the beach, fearful that Japanese soldiers might happen upon him at any moment. He pushed into the jungle foliage, where the leaves and vines scraped his naked flesh. He sank in mud up to his knees in places and finally, when he could go no farther, took a rest near a large tree. He decided that he was the lone survivor of the Palawan Massacre, and if he should be captured, there would be no evidence as to what had happened. He prayed silently again. Finally, he decided that he simply could not make it through the jungle. *I had better go back to that inlet,* he thought.[8]

He plodded forward until he emerged near a mountain range on an inlet perhaps a half mile across. He could see a village in the distance and assumed it had to be part of the Iwahig Penal Colony. Mac decided another short swim across the inlet was better than tearing up his body any further in the jungle, so he took to the water again and made it about halfway across before his strength played out. He was about to give up when he spotted a bamboo Filipino fish trap bobbing nearby. Mac pulled himself up onto the middle of it and passed out.

DOUG BOGUE HAD swum across Puerto Princesa Bay during the night of December 14 and reached the far shore early the next day. Naked, exhausted, hungry, and dehydrated, he was also tormented by his bare feet, shredded from running on the coral, and by his right leg, raw and sore from a bullet wound. After resting for an hour, he had plunged into the harsh mangrove swamps in search of help.

He spent the next two days stumbling through the rough terrain, hoping to make his way to the Iwahig Penal Colony. His only subsistence was rainwater collected in shallow hollows and mud snails he found on the beach. Jungle vines tore at his already battered skin, and a swarm of honeybees forced him to run into the nearby bay, where the salt water helped draw out the poison from dozens of painful stings. After several days, his wounds festered, and maggots began digging into his flesh.[9]

By the morning of December 17, his feet had swollen like water balloons, to the point that the tips of his toes could not even make contact with the ground. He was about to lie down and give up when he came upon the Filipino penal colony, and spotted a man working along the beach. He didn't care what nationality the stranger was. *I don't give a damn if he is Japanese or not,* he thought.

As the man approached, Bogue shouted out to him. The Filipino cautiously approached the naked American. Bogue told him of the massacre that had taken place and how he had survived by making his long swim days before. The Filipino assured him that he was in good hands and would be well taken care of in the village. He led Bogue down a path through the jungle until they emerged near a cluster of native huts. A few men helped find him some clothes to wear and inspected his wounds.[10]

Bogue told them that he had escaped with other POWs. He had lost track of them during his swim, but he held out hope that others might be found. The men left the gaunt American with other Filipinos and headed back to the bay to scour the waters with their canoes while another man was sent to deliver the news of the American to Pedro Paje. Given some water and food, Bogue finally drifted off to sleep in one of the huts.

MAC MCDOLE SLEPT through the night, bobbing up and down atop the Filipino fishing trap as waves rippled steadily toward shore. He awoke on December 18 to the sounds of a village. In the distance, he could see lights coming on in huts near the bay, and the tempting smell of breakfast soon wafted across the water. He heard men talking on the beach and watched as they climbed into their *barcos* to check their traps.

He lay still and quiet, watching. They seemed to be pointing his way. The boats paddled in his direction and then stopped. They appeared to be pulling something from the water, perhaps another American. The Filipinos paddled back to shore and disappeared in the direction of their village. McDole simply lay there, too tired to swim any farther.[11]

The Filipinos returned to their *barcos* and resumed checking their fish traps. Mac was half-submerged on the box, but he raised himself enough that he was soon spotted by the fishermen, who quickly paddled toward him.

"Hey, Joe, you a prisoner?" one of them called.[12]

Mac managed a grin. "I was, but no longer!"

The fishermen, the same group that had rescued Bogue, helped him into their boat and paddled back to shore. They carried him to a bamboo hut, bathed him, and cleaned his sores before giving him a pair of trousers to wear. Then they fed him the most wonderful rice, bread, and papayas he had ever tasted.[13]

Mac lay down in the hut to rest. Sometime later, one of the Filipinos entered his hut and asked him if he knew an American named Sergeant Douglas Bogue. Rising from his cot, McDole said, "I sure do!"[14]

"He's in the hut right next to yours," said the fisherman. "But he's hurt pretty bad."

Mac was helped to the next hut, where he had a joyous reunion with Bogue. The two men were too weak to do anything but talk, and Bogue was unable to get up from his cot. The Filipinos summoned Dr. Zoilo Bunye, who had been a busy man, having already treated first Willie Smith and then the others who joined Smitty's escape party. Zoilo arrived in short order and set to work checking over McDole and Bogue. He was unable to find the bullet in Bogue's leg but cleaned and dressed the wound. The doctor helped hold him down while he allowed McDole to painfully cut out the maggots that had embedded themselves in his shredded feet. Zoilo washed and bandaged Bogue's feet before allowing the men to rest again.

The two survivors spent a good deal of time talking about the massacre and how they had made their escapes. Bogue described his time hiding in the seaside cavern and how he had set out swimming that night with four other prisoners, Martyn, Barta, Petry, and Pacheco. Bogue mentioned others he had seen, but Mac was saddened that Smitty wasn't one of them.

They talked until McDole slipped into a deep slumber, his first night of sleep in friendly hands in three years. It was still fitful, and he awoke several times, screaming.

KOBLOS, NIELSEN, SMITTY, Balchus, Petry, and Pacheco were well south of Puerto Princesa, making their way slowly toward the relatively safe haven of Captain Mayor's guerrilla headquarters at Brooke's Point. Koblos was still nursing his freshly broken arm while the carabao seemed to be content to lounge about, delaying any real progress. Pablo Quiliop sent runners ahead to fetch a new means of transportation to get down the Palawan coast, and in short order, his party was greeted by other Filipinos who arrived at the beach with their *bancas*.

They set out paddling down the coastline. While they were en route, a Japanese observation plane passed overhead. The Filipinos ordered the Americans to keep their heads down and lie in the bottom of the *bancas* on straw mats while the locals waved and hollered greetings to the low-flying aviators. The aircraft continued on its way without harassing them.[15]

Late on the afternoon of December 18, the Filipinos pointed their *bancas* toward the beach, at a heavily timbered location. The guides paddled up to the timber and proceeded up a river a short distance until they disembarked at a small settlement, where a Chinese family lived. The family members had hot food waiting and allowed the escapees to sleep for the night in their home.

The long process of rowing down the coast of Palawan Island toward Brooke's Point resumed early the next morning. At one point, the winds kicked up and the waters became quite choppy. When two of the youngest Filipino guides became seasick, the former POWs took over the oars. They rowed the *bancas* ashore, thanked their young guides, and dismissed them. With Quiliop as their only guide, they pointed the bows of their primitive canoes back into the surf and resumed paddling south.[16]

The seven men covered several miles until a strong breeze blowing down the coast began to impede their progress. Quiliop finally beached the *bancas* and went ashore into the jungle to look for something that could serve as a sail. He scrounged up a large blanket, which the men fashioned into a makeshift sail attached to poles in the bottom of their leading boat. The wind caught the blanket and swiftly pushed the wooden vessels, tied together, steadily along toward Brooke's Point.

THAT SAME DAY, three other American survivors were independently rambling through the jungles of Palawan in search of help.

Despite the terrible wounds he had suffered in both legs, Pop Daniels had maintained a slow but steady crawl through the night. He laboriously made his way through the jungle beyond Puerto Princesa and continued, wandering lost in the jungle for three full days with little to eat. Finally, he had happened upon the home of Emilio Natalico and Dodong Fuertes, who took him in, fed him, and helped tend to his wounds.

Daniels would remain with his new friends for weeks until he was strong enough to begin walking. He was evacuated north of Puerto Princesa to the town of Bacungan, where a guerrilla unit was stationed. There, he received more medical attention and was kept hidden away from Japanese patrols while the guerrillas tried to determine how to move him from Palawan.[17]

Mo Deal, his body ravaged with sores that were now infected, was struggling just to keep moving. It was a miracle that he was alive at all. He had been shot once while escaping from the compound and again the following morning when he tried to fight his way past a Japanese guard patrol. They had bayoneted him repeatedly, then thrown him over the cliff, presumably to his death, in order to pursue other POWs.

Since that time, Mo had crawled through Puerto Princesa during a convenient rainstorm. He moved at a snail's pace but willed himself to keep going, successfully dodging Japanese soldiers who passed close by. After he had left the Catholic church building and slipped into the jungle, his time had become a blur. He had slept mainly during the daylight hours when he had the greatest risk of being spotted. At night, he wandered in a daze through the Palawan wilderness, barefoot and bloody. He stumbled and fell many times, cutting and bruising himself further. After three days and nights straggling through the thickets, he was delirious from blood loss. His infected wounds were now crawling with maggots, but he sustained himself by eating coconuts and jungle fruits.[18]

By the night of December 18, he was ready to die. Delirious, he spotted a light in the distance. He cared little whether it came from Filipinos or Japanese. He staggered toward the house. Soon he heard people inside speaking in Filipino dialects. The family members came out, found him, and helped him into their home, where they attempted to treat his wounds. He remained with the family for days, while word of his discovery spread through the guerrilla network.[19]

On December 26, word of Deal's survival reached Triny Mendoza. She heard that an escaped American POW needed assistance and clothing. After helping Justin Miller's downed B-24 crew escape capture in late October, she had remained on her family plantation throughout November 1944, against the advice of friends who warned her that the Japanese might have learned of her deed. Red Hankie was still just a short distance from the Palawan airfield until December 16, two days after the massacre. She moved a few miles to the north when Japanese patrols began sweeping the area for any surviving Americans.[20]

When she received news of a survivor, she fetched one of her late husband's suits and went with Captain Mayor's guerrillas to see him for herself. She was shocked on first seeing the emaciated young man, all skin and bones and covered with countless bloody wounds. She and her sister, Elizabeth Clark, found the soldier to be at first so confused and shell-shocked that he could scarcely talk. Deal was finally able to provide her with the details of the massacre and his escape. She asked him about her four American friends who had slipped intelligence to her from camp months earlier. He told her that Churchill Vaughan, Tom Paddock, Hubert Hough, and Frank Leroy had all been shipped out in September before the massacre.[21]

Deal was moved to the village of Mentes, where a guerrilla doctor soon arrived to help treat his wounds and burns. Deal now had a fighting chance to make it out alive, but his journey was far from over.[22]

Joe Barta was also still alive but in bad shape. After falling from the tree in the bamboo forest on the evening of December 15, he lay suffering until late that night. His scrotum was torn open, and blood loss made him weak. But he knew he must force himself to find food and water, so he worked his way out of the bamboo thicket and edged his way through the jungle. His only source of water came from dirty water holes used by wild animals. During the next three days, he managed to pick two dozen jungle berries off the trees.[23]

Barta spent another two days wandering lost in the jungle. He nearly ran afoul of Japanese soldiers again at one point, but he had the good fortune to spot one of the guards a short distance away just as he was pushing aside some branches. He slipped away unnoticed, and by the afternoon of December 20, he had made his way back to the edge of the Sulu Sea. Barta's groin area was so swollen that he could barely walk, so he decided to stick to the coastline and work his way back around to the Iwahig Penal Colony. He found it easier to rely on his arms to pull himself through the water. The salt water stung his open wound, but he hoped at least that it might help clean out the infection setting in. He spent the next few days swimming along the coast from point to point, sparing his bare feet from the sharp coral and jungle thorns.

On the night of December 23, he came upon a coconut grove. He climbed one of the trees and secured three coconuts to eat. He slept in the grove overnight and returned to swimming in Puerto Princesa Bay before daybreak, feeling that he was finally on track to reaching Iwahig. He was struggling along around 0700 when he spotted movement on the water. A small boat was paddling his way. Barta was much relieved to see that the vessel was filled with Filipinos, who helped him on board with smiling faces. Sent out to scour the bay for any other possible American survivors, they had encountered Barta just south of the main Iwahig Penal Colony, near a subcolony known as Santa Lucia where the more seriously ill inmates—many of whom had contracted tuberculosis— were kept isolated from the healthy farmworkers. Barta's rescuers helped him into the Santa Lucia colony and sent a runner to inform Pedro Paje at Iwahig.

They were fearful of Japanese patrols making the rounds through the colonies, so they decided it was best for Barta to hide in an abandoned water well. They fed him and provided him with clothing before helping him to crawl into the dark pit for most of the day—Christmas Eve. Around 1600, guerrillas moved Barta from the well and guided him to Malinao Station, where Bogue and McDole had recently been cared for. There, he was joined by Lieutenant Poyatos, who was concerned that the radioman's wounds were too severe for safe movement. Barta insisted that he was feeling well enough to keep traveling, so Poyatos secured a horse to prevent any further injuries from walking. Barta's ruptured scrotum made the ride particularly painful, and even clothing proved to be uncomfortable, so he rode with just a blanket wrapped around his body. Poyatos guided the survivor to the village of Inagawan, where they arrived on Christmas morning.[24]

The prisoners and managers of Inagawan hid Barta during the day. Late in the afternoon, he wrapped himself once again in his blanket, mounted the horse, and allowed Poyatos to guide him toward the next settlement on their route, Aborlan. Each hour on the horse brought agonizing pain, but Barta was thankful to be alive.

19

EXODUS FROM BROOKE'S POINT

WHEN PEDRO PAJE appeared in the doorway of Mac McDole's thatched-roof hut on December 20, the weary American shook his head in disgust and resignation. Here was the traitor who had once turned him in to the Japanese for spreading rumors about the end of the war, the same man who had caused him such abuse from the Kempei Tai. After a day of freedom with his new Filipino friends, Mac assumed that Paje would now be handing him and Bogue over to the Japanese.[1]

"Well, I guess this is the end of it," McDole said, and sighed.[2]

"What do you mean?" asked Paje.

Mac demanded to know how long it would be before Japanese soldiers came to take him away again. Paje laughed and promised McDole that he was friendly. He explained that he had been playing a role in the American POW camp to gain the trust of the guards and that he had been gathering intelligence for Palawan's guerrillas to spread to U.S. forces. He had counted Japanese planes, made notes of ammunition dumps on the island, and had sent the data back to Iwahig to be radioed to American forces. Mac was surprised to learn that Paje was the assistant director of the Iwahig Penal Colony and in charge of local underground activities against the Japanese.

Paje had remained in contact with the two Palawan Kempei Tai substations before and after the prisoner massacre on December 14. A short time after the gruesome act, he attended a wedding party held at the Irawan station. Once the Japanese were well into their drinks, Paje casually asked whether the military police believed that any of the Americans could have escaped the massacre. One drunken soldier gleefully demonstrated, with a slash of fingers to his throat, that there were no survivors. The Kempei Tai was certain the U.S. POWs had all been disposed of. Paje was pleased that the work of his men in aiding the survivors had thus far remained covert.

Paje and Lieutenant Poyatos, who had arrived with him at Malinao Station, both assured the Americans they were in good hands. They explained that it was time to get moving, as Japanese soldiers were en route to the Iwahig village to look for American escapees. Paje had already sent word to Australia of two Americans in the colony who had survived the massacre. He offered fresh clothing to Bogue and McDole and told them to move out immediately with Poyatos and three Filipino scouts who could not speak English. He warned the two escapees to keep quiet as they moved, as they would be passing near Japanese outposts.[3]

Due to his leg wound, Bogue was helped onto a horse to ease his suffering, while Mac was given an ornery water buffalo. As the group set out, Poyatos walked, leading Bogue's horse to keep it from throwing him. This made their progress slow as they rode from the Puerto Princesa region deeper into the jungle. During the night, they passed dangerously close to Japanese patrols, at times within three hundred yards, but the Filipinos slipped them past each danger area without contact.

It was Christmas Eve when the group rode over the top of a hill and approached a Filipino village close to sundown. Mac watched his guides stop for a moment, and was amazed to hear them sing "God Bless America" in almost perfect English. He learned the ceremony marked their official crossing of some invisible line into the region the locals called the guerrilla zone.

"My friends," Poyatos announced, "you are now in the free Philippines!"

Mac was unashamed of the tears that ran down his cheeks. A quick glance at Bogue showed him to be in the same emotional condition.

The Americans were greeted in the village that night by Manuel Palanca, the mayor of the Aborlan district they were entering. Palanca in turn introduced McDole and Bogue to Valentin F. Bacosa, an engineer of the Davao Penal Colony. Poyatos immediately headed back north to report to Paje that he had delivered the escapees to Bacosa, who would move them farther south through the Aborlan district toward Brooke's Point. Their journey would continue again the next day after food and rest in the village.[4]

Although unknown to the two survivors at the time, their Filipino friends had discovered another of the escapees. Around 1730 on December 18, one of the patrols headed by Sentinani Moro had been out combing Puerto Princesa Bay. His men were disguised as fishermen, but their orders were to help any other Americans encountered. They came upon the floating corpse of an American, who had no form of identification on his body. Most likely they had discovered Don Martyn, who had not survived his escape swim with Bogue and company.[5]

Sentinani and his men hauled the body ashore to Camagong in the Iwahig Penal Colony, where Paje came to view it. He saw that the American escapee had been hit by machine-gun bullets in the chest and that he also had two bayonet wounds on both sides of his upper chest. Having duly informed the Kempei Tai of his find, Paje was notified several hours later that he could bury the American body. Paje ordered his men to give the fallen POW a proper burial in his colony's cemetery.[6]

THE NAME NAZARIO Mayor carried considerable weight within Palawan's guerilla network, and the six Americans guided to his home were undoubtedly impressed when the captain greeted them warmly in perfect English. Mayor was a muscular man who stood about five foot nine, with high, wide cheekbones, a broad forehead, and thick black hair, which he brushed back and parted down the middle.

Corporal Pablo Quiliop had been under orders to continue sailing the escapees farther south along the Palawan coast until they reached Mayor's guerrilla headquarters at Brooke's Point. Well ahead of McDole and Bogue's party, Willie Smith, Gene Nielsen, Ernie Koblos, Ed Petry, Beto Pacheco, and Willie Balchus finally reached their destination on the afternoon of December 22. They concluded a full week on the run as they beached their crafts at Brooke's Point and hiked several hundred yards inland to Mayor's jungle dwelling.

Mayor's family had long since abandoned its formal homes and had taken up residence in an abandoned, open-air house in the hills. The soldiers of fortune were armed with rifles and hand grenades, and possessed two-way radios for communicating with the U.S. Army headquarters at Morotai, located hundreds of miles away at Celebes.

Mayor's children were amazed by the sight of the raggedy Americans. His seven-year-old daughter, Mary Anne, would never forget how the men looked. They were darkly tanned with many blisters on their skin from years of sun exposure, their hair was long, their beards were untrimmed, and they wore only hand-me-down, ill-fitting clothing provided by other Filipinos. Mary Anne thought of Americans as powerful, husky men, but these poor wrecks were walking skeletons, some barely weighing a hundred pounds.

Mayor's wife, Mary, had no formal medical training, but she tended to the six as best she could, cleaning and wrapping their wounds. Robert Mayor, the oldest son at age fourteen, was particularly intrigued by how tall Willie Smith was compared to the average Filipino. Despite his injuries and condition, Smitty maintained a humorous demeanor, and he went out of his way to impress the children with his Texas twang. Mary Anne grew fond of Smitty because of the time he spent paying attention to the kids despite all of his personal hardships.

Their makeshift home at the temporary Mayor residence was no four-star hotel, but it was a far cry from the life the POWs had become accustomed to. They were tended to and fed, and allowed to finally catch up on their rest. The Americans were also pleased to be introduced to a man familiar to them, Thomas Loudon. The elder Spanish-American war veteran had arrived on foot at his son-in-law's home at Brooke's Point shortly ahead of the six escapees.

They learned that Loudon had made his own escape from Puerto Princesa with a walking cane one night in December shortly before the massacre. He slipped out from under the watchful eyes of the Japanese guards and silently moved out of town. Despite being seventy-three years old, he made his way alone across the rugged Palawan landscape, over the mountains, and to the west coast residence of Dr. Flores at Caruray. Captain Mayor soon received intelligence of Loudon's escape and journeyed to Caruray to take charge of his father-in-law and lead him back to the family he had not seen during his long detainment by the Japanese.[7]

Smitty was familiar with Loudon. He had seen the older gentleman standing on the streets of Puerto Princesa when the POWs filed out to work at the airfields, and when they were escorted back at night. Loudon had never shown any emotion when the Americans strolled past him, but Smitty felt that the silver-haired gentleman looked more American than most of the locals.[8]

Mayor's guerrillas sent word that two other Americans had been rescued and were making their way south toward his company's camp. He had his men send communications via radio to General MacArthur in Australia, then waited to hear news of what he was to do with the escapees.

PEDRO PAJE SIMPLY had to lie.

Sergeant Deguchi's Kempei Tai unit was scouring the Puerto Princesa region for answers regarding rumors of escaped Americans. He had received intelligence that the assistant director of the Iwahig Penal Colony and his men had found POWs who escaped the massacre. Paje was ordered to report to the Japanese military police substation at Irawan, where Deguchi and an interpreter interrogated him.[9]

Paje insisted he knew of no such reports; his men had found no living Americans since December 14. Deguchi continued to press him. The Palawan Underground Force had moved nine escapees in the past ten days from the Puerto Princesa area toward Brooke's Point, making it difficult for Paje to deny everything. He suddenly remembered the body his scouts had turned up near the Iwahig shore.

"We did find one American," he said, "but he was dead." He related how his men had carried the body ashore to Camagong, and how he had properly reported the discovery to the Kempei Tai. "This must be the report you received about us finding an American in our colony."

Deguchi acknowledged that the colonists had indeed offered up the escapee's body after it was found. He allowed Paje to depart their headquarters and return to Iwahig.

Paje knew that he had just barely escaped Deguchi's office with his life.

It was Christmas night 1944 when McDole and Bogue finally saw Joe Barta again. He rode up to their huts on horseback, a blanket draped over his rail-thin body. As he was helped down, he moaned to Mac, "I'm hurt real bad."

That afternoon, McDole and Bogue had reached the village of Aborlan, where another guerrilla team was waiting to continue guiding them along their journey. They bedded down in huts to rest and were disturbed at one point by the engine drone of a low-flying aircraft. Mac figured it was likely a Japanese plane scouring the coastline for any signs of Palawan camp escapees.[10]

That night around 2000, McDole heard a sudden commotion and excited voices. He slipped out of his hut to investigate. Barta had been brought into Aborlan by the busy Lieutenant Poyatos, who had hurried back to fetch him from Malinao Station. Barta's ruptured scrotum had caused him considerable pain throughout the horseback ride. Mac lifted the blanket and saw that the flesh had been ripped open, his testicles exposed and maggots squirming in the raw, bloody wound. Barta explained that he'd lost sight of Bogue and the other swimmers during the night of December 14, and how he had eluded Japanese patrols until falling from the tree and severely injuring himself. His body showed the effects of the ten days he had since spent wandering the jungle until he had been discovered.[11]

The guerrilla scouts helped carry Barta into one of the huts, where McDole soaked the nasty wound in a purple medicine solution offered by the Filipinos. He cleaned out the infected area with soap and extracted the maggots, counting fifty-two by the time he had finished. Then he tried to remove the remaining dirt and grime and covered Barta's wound with dried brown leaves—another trick the Filipinos had taught him.[12]

As McDole was finishing his work on Barta, one of the scouts entered the hut and announced that other Palawan Massacre survivors had passed through the village just days before. Bogue and McDole asked if they remembered any of the names, in response to which the scout produced a scrap of paper. He read the names of Edwin Petry, William Balchus, Ernest Koblos, Eugene Nielsen, Alberto Pacheco, and Willie Smith.

Mac smiled broadly. "My God, Smitty made it!"

NAZARIO MAYOR TREATED his new American friends to several celebrations during their convalescence at Brooke's Point. The local families prepared great meals for the holidays, which helped the men regain some of their lost weight. On Christmas Eve, Sergeant Placido made doughnuts, and the entire group enjoyed midnight services conducted by the priest. On December 29, they enjoyed a Catholic wedding ceremony, after which a bull was butchered and alcohol flowed freely. Smitty enjoyed the good food but found that his weakened stomach could not handle the booze.[13]

The food and festivities helped lighten the serious danger that the Americans still faced from Japanese soldiers patrolling Palawan. Mayor and Placido continued their communications with MacArthur's Australian headquarters, and by January 1, 1945, they had received encouraging word that efforts were under way to evacuate the first party of American survivors.

The guerrillas received instructions to build large bonfires on the beach the next night to help guide in a Catalina PBY flying boat. If the crew spotted the signal fires at the proper distance, they would land before dawn and pick up the survivors. Spirits soared among the Americans. They waited eagerly at the edge of the jungle the next night as Mayor's men built the fires. They soon heard the drone of engines, and aircraft slowly buzzed about the point, circling to inspect the area in the darkness.

A short while later, the PBY and its escorts moved on. During the next two days, the men experienced both excitement and despair as other American aircraft probed about their area night and day. The signal fires blazed as instructed each evening, leaving the men to wonder what was wrong. Had they spotted Japanese forces close by, or were the sea conditions judged too rough for safe landing?[14]

Carlos Placido's radio crackled to life on January 5 with another update from Australia. The men were to be ready the following day, when another flying boat would be sent in around noon to attempt a daylight pickup. The guerrillas were to set their signal fires on the beach and be prepared to move their evacuees to the aircraft if the wind and sea conditions permitted.

The men were waiting once again after daybreak on January 6, 1945, three weeks since the Palawan Massacre. Koblos, Petry, Nielsen, Balchus, Pacheco, and Smith listened with tempered optimism as the morning hours ticked by. Waiting with them was the elderly Thomas Loudon, as Mayor had decided to send his father-in-law out in company with the Americans to offer intelligence on the guerrilla network on Palawan. Loudon would be killed if the Japanese caught him now.

It was long after the noon hour before the men heard the familiar rumbling of engines approaching. It was a massive PBY from the 18th Army Air Force, piloted by Captain Clarence L. "Solie" Solander. His *Playmate 42* had departed Morotai Island at 0505, rendezvoused at 1110 over the Sulu Islands with an escorting B-24, and set course for Brooke's Point. At 1250, Solander sighted seven men signaling from the beach. The plane landed minutes later and taxied close to shore. One of the crew crawled out onto its wings and began shouting. The man's words faded away with the engine noise, so Nielsen and Pacheco swam out to the flying boat. Solander asked how rocky the bottom was near shore before he chanced bringing his plane into the shallows. The men shouted back that it was just sand, so *Playmate 42* pulled close in.[15]

Eager airmen helped the six escapees and Thomas Loudon into the PBY. Solander remained at the shore's edge long enough to obtain intelligence from Mayor's guerrillas about the disposition of Japanese troops on Palawan and also learn that three other rescued Americans were a short distance away. The captain promised that he would help make arrangements for them to be rescued soon. His escorting B-24 still maintained a vigil overhead.

The plane took off at 1335 and searched the coast for three more escaped prisoners reported to be in the vicinity. But the search was negative, so they departed for Morotai, arriving at 2005. En route, Nielsen was handed a pair of size-twelve shoes—the first proper covering on his feet in three years.[16]

When they arrived over Morotai, they gazed down at hundreds of bombers and fighters that dotted the vast air base. The escapees compared it to their small but heroic air force in the days of Bataan and Corregidor. In the many months since the Japanese had taken the men captive in 1942, America's ramshackle military had morphed into the most powerful fighting force in the world. Morotai, they learned, was but one of many new airfields established across the Pacific as America's efforts to retake the Philippines had progressed.

Helped ashore and moved to the 155th General Hospital for

evaluation and treatment, they were swarmed over by Army physicians. After years of being surrounded by Filipinos and Japanese of smaller build, Smitty was in awe of the countless tall, husky Americans working the base. He and his companions were kept in one end of the ward, away from other patients, for security measures.[17]

Doctors treated the gunshot wounds of Nielsen and Pacheco, and tended to the badly broken left arm of Ernie Koblos. In the next few days, they would perform surgery on it to wire the bones together. Koblos was disappointed that the wounds and surgery had ruined the dragon tattoo on his arm, but he was pleased that the doctor was at least able to pull the dragon back together.

The morning after they arrived, Smitty wandered the U.S. base. He found two Japanese prisoners of war being held in a stockade, with a tent for their home. He was disturbed to see the conditions they were allowed to live in, complete with radios and good food—in sharp contrast to his treatment as a prisoner. He wanted to approach the prisoners to talk to them, but he was cut off by two armed soldiers who informed him that contact with the POWs was prohibited.

Senior army officers arrived that afternoon to begin the process of interrogating the seven Palawan escapees. A general promised the Americans that they would be well taken care of and that he would provide anything they needed. As each man told his story, intelligence officers from the Army's G-2 branch took careful notes on what had happened at the Puerto Princesa camp. The news was disturbing. Since the Japanese had ordered a complete annihilation of the U.S. prisoners held there, the same treatment could likely be expected for thousands more POWs being held throughout the Philippines.

The intelligence was flashed to General MacArthur, who was preparing another strike in his campaign to retake the Philippines. Two days later, on January 9, 1945, the invasion of Luzon commenced in Lingayen Gulf. It involved 164 ships, 3,000 landing craft, and some 280,000 American troops who swarmed ashore with relative ease only a hundred miles north of Manila. Just as he had on Leyte months earlier,

MacArthur—clad in a khaki uniform and wearing his signature Ray-Ban sunglasses—made a well-photographed return as he splashed ashore.[18]

MacArthur's forces, armed with the intelligence from the Palawan escapees, would soon put plans in motion to reach other POW camps near Manila before the Japanese could kill the men held in them. The first raid took place on January 30, sixty miles northeast of Manila at Cabanatuan, where U.S. Army Rangers, Alamo Scouts, and Filipino guerrillas liberated 513 American and Allied prisoners. MacArthur sent the 6th Army's 1st Cavalry Division—seven hundred men with a tank company and a battalion of 105mm howitzers—to smash through the gates of the Santo Tomás prison camp after sunset on February 3 to effect the release of two hundred more hostages. The following day, the 1st Cavalry freed another eight hundred military prisoners being held ten blocks away at Bilibid Prison.[19]

Encouraged by these successes, MacArthur's forces began planning a raid to liberate another two thousand POWs being held at the Luzon prison camp of Los Baños, located forty miles farther south of Bilibid and deep within Japanese-held territory. Conducted on February 23 by a joint U.S. Army Airborne and Filipino guerrilla task force, the raid involved recon teams, paratroopers, and amtracs that crashed through the main gate. Considered one of the most successful rescue operations in modern military history, the Great Raid on the Los Baños camp resulted in the liberation of 2,147 Allied and civilian internees.

The first six men out of the Palawan camp had helped save more than thirty-six hundred other POW lives. But five of their fellow Puerto Princesa survivors were still praying for their own rescues.

THE JOURNEY OF Mac McDole, Joe Barta, and Doug Bogue through the Aborlan region encountered lengthy delays. Barta's wounds slowed their progress, and during that time, McDole was seized with another attack of malaria. A high fever consumed his body, sapping his ability to handle much food. His skinny frame shed another two pounds until he had dwindled to a 118-pound walking skeleton. The Filipinos moved the three escapees south until they finally reached Captain Mayor's guerrilla camp at Brooke's Point on January 7, 1945—just one day after the successful pickup of the first Palawan Massacre survivors.

Bogue, Barta, and McDole were introduced to Mayor and his family as they were taken into the open-air mountainside home for treatment. McDole, still suffering from malaria, would never forget young Mary Anne Mayor, who seemed so genuinely concerned with his health. One day, as he lay in a bamboo hut with a burning fever, he looked up to see the girl staring at him.[20]

"You want drink?" she said.

"Yes," he croaked.

She would bring him water and stare at the skinny man whose skin was curiously white in places not bronzed by the sun. Her mother eased the suffering of those fighting malaria, and she helped Joe Barta remove worms from his wound. As the days passed at Brooke's Point, the three Americans began regaining their strength, shaking their ailments, and putting on pounds as they took in more solid foods.

McDole was soon energetic enough to announce to Captain Mayor that he was not content to ride out the war while awaiting rescue. He shared a plan of sailing by boat to Balabac Island, located about nineteen miles southwest of the southern tip of Palawan. Mac believed they could sail on to Borneo, which lay about thirty-eight miles north of Balabac, then proceed to Australia. But his plans were cut short when Mayor announced that a radio message had been received from MacArthur's forces in Australia. The Americans were to stay put until a rescue team could be sent for them.

A few days later, a revitalized McDole helped carry crates of .30-caliber ammunition delivered by submarine for the use of the guerrillas' M-1 carbines. He became choked up when he set down one of the wooden boxes and noticed, stamped on its side, DES MOINES, IOWA, ORDNANCE PLANT. The plant was only eight miles from his hometown in Urbandale. Mac would later learn that his mother had been working at the facility since early in the war.[21]

Bogue, McDole, and Barta would spend three weeks in the hills above Brooke's Point. As with the previous group of survivors, it took time to coordinate a rescue plane with Australia. Sergeant Placido and his coastwatchers continued to work out the details until they received word that a PBY flying boat would be sent in the next day, January 21, 1945.

The trio made its way to the beach area the next morning—five long weeks since the massacre at Puerto Princesa. Mayor's men set the signal fires and waited. Around 0900, when they heard the engines of a Catalina PBY-5 approaching the coast, several Filipinos scrambled up on coconut trees to signal an all clear to the pilot by lighting smudge pots. Lieutenant Kenneth Felix Brissette, a Navy pilot of Patrol Bombing Squadron 54, came skimming in over the waves. White spray splashed skyward as the plane settled on the water near Brooke's Point on January 21, while a dozen Navy fighters circled overhead.[22]

Bogue, Barta, and McDole were greeted by smiling airmen who handed them their first sodas and candy bars in three years as the PBY lifted into the air. Lieutenant Brissette landed briefly at Mindanao for refueling before he continued to the U.S. base at Tacloban on Leyte Island, where the three Americans were taken on board the hospital ship USS *Tangier* for evaluation and treatment. They noted the curious stares of many *Tangier* sailors as they stepped onto the deck and were helped to bunks below. The American servicemen had not seen the horrors of abused and starved POWs.

HALF A WORLD away, news of the recovery of nine survivors from the Palawan Massacre was being shared with some of their families.

Dessa McDole answered a knock on her front door in Urbandale, Iowa, on January 19, 1944. She was greeted by a Western Union telegram messenger, a sight that would send terror into any mother's heart. As she began reading the brief telegram, her fears melted away. The McDoles were informed that although it was still confidential, their son, Glenn W. McDole, U.S. Marine Corps, "has escaped from the Japanese prison camp in which he was interned. He is in friendly hands, but may be unable to communicate with his family."[23]

Dessa quickly sent word to her family and had the younger children escorted home from school to share the good news. She explained that Glenn had escaped from the Japanese, was still in the process of completing his passage to freedom, and that the family must keep the information completely secret. In the weeks to come, she would receive further news in the form of a letter from Mac that he had been returned into American hands and would be home fairly soon.

THE LONG ROAD HOME

S MITTY WAS GRATEFUL to be alive, but he soon found freedom to be a difficult adjustment. He grew irritated with the life on Morotai and was eager to be on his way back home. There was plenty of food available at the base, and even an occasional beer, but his nerves were still on edge, as evidenced one day as he moved through the chow line. Spotting a pie, he grabbed it and greedily began devouring the dessert with a fork. Another soldier loudly griped that certain people were hogging all the pie. Smitty listened to the man until his temper boiled over.[1]

"Do you want this damned pie?" he snapped.

The man growled, "Yeah, I want some of that!"

"Well, I'll tell you what," Smitty shot back. "I'm going to give you all of it!"

With that, he stood and slammed the pie right into the soldier's face. A scrap broke out until sentries pulled the men apart. In response, Army brass put an end to the frazzled former POWs' lining up in the enlisted men's mess hall and ordered them to use the officers' chow line.

Still, Smitty's group of survivors was being treated well enough at the 155th General Hospital. The men put on weight, and the nourishment quickly dissipated most of the sores and rashes that had once covered their bodies. They endured endless hours of recounting all aspects of the massacre and their escape to the G-2 intelligence officers. They also sat for the making of a 35mm film to discuss their ordeals on Corregidor and Palawan, intended to document the atrocities and serve as a historical documentary.[2]

Smitty, Ernie Koblos, Gene Nielsen, Ed Petry, Willie Balchus, and Beto Pacheco remained on Morotai for thirteen days before they were finally flown on January 19 to Hollandia, New Guinea. The commander of the 51st General Hospital at Hollandia offered them hope that they would be heading home soon, but they were instead subjected to more rounds of interrogation about the names of the massacre victims. The escapees were slowly split up into separate wards. Petry was moved first due to a tropical ulcer on his bullet-smashed ankle, and then Smitty was relocated when he broke out with malaria. Nielsen was shifted to another ward for an operation on the gunshot wound in his leg, and Pacheco was then split from Koblos when Koblos was treated for his broken arm.[3]

Paperwork and more delays ensued. On March 2, the survivors finally boarded a battle-gray troop transport ship, the USS *General A. E. Anderson*. It was packed with thousands of servicemen on rotation furlough. In addition, 272 recently liberated Cabanatuan POWs would journey home alongside the six Palawan Massacre survivors who had triggered their rescue mission. Tokyo Rose, the female voice of Japan's propaganda radio broadcasts, unnerved the passengers with continual announcements during the ensuing days in which she promised that the *Anderson* would be sunk by waiting Japanese submarines.[4]

The delays and enemy threats only added to Smitty's stress. He felt that their years as POWs, followed by their narrow escapes from certain death, should have earned his group quick returns to their families. Instead, they had been shuffled between bases for two months and were

An intelligence officer (*far left*) interviews the first six Palawan Massacre survivors on Morotai Island. (*From second on left*): Gene Nielsen, Ed Petry, Beto Pacheco, Ernie Koblos, Willie Balchus, and Willie "Smitty" Smith.

NATIONAL ARCHIVES

resigned to riding out a long Pacific voyage on an overcrowded troop ship blacked out to prevent air attacks. Smitty's only satisfaction was that each mile between his ship and the Philippines brought him one step closer to his East Texas home.

MAC MCDOLE, JOE Barta, and Doug Bogue had spent two days resting on board the *Tangier* when they were notified on January 23 that Vice Admiral Daniel Edward Barbey wished to see them. They were taken to the Commander, 7th Fleet's headquarters at Tolosa on Leyte, to be interviewed. Though the former POWs had put on some weight after several days of good Navy chow, their emaciated frames were still shocking enough that at first glance the surprised admiral said, "You guys look like you've been through hell."[5]

Barbey handed each man a beer, told them to relax, and asked them to explain what they had been through. They spent the next hour relating the details of their captures in early 1942, their slave labor on Palawan Island, and the final massacre from which they had escaped. The admiral was clearly moved by their stories. Bogue, in a statement to intelligence officers on Leyte, summarized their entire ordeal: "The word for war is hell, but there is no word for being a prisoner of war of the Japs."

Barbey promised to have them on their way to Washington, DC, the following morning. McDole, Barta, and Bogue were given top priority on January 24 to head back for further interrogation as others were bumped off flights to make room. They left with orders to tell no one about what they had survived, as the Navy feared word of their ordeal and escape could endanger the lives of other POWs still held in the Philippines.

The trio was first flown to Hawaii, where the men underwent another round of debriefing while they waited for their next flight. As their plane was being refueled, an Army major boarded, took a seat next to the Palawan survivors, and soon struck up a conversation. McDole found the major to be almost unpleasant as he talked incessantly, peppering them with questions. At one point, he said, "I heard there are some escaped POWs on board."[6]

Bogue said, "Yeah, we heard the same thing."

The major kept it up, wondering aloud where the POWs were sitting. McDole said his guess was they were among the stretcher-bound men in the back of the aircraft. The major continued his questioning until the plane touched down in San Diego hours later, where he finally confessed he had been sent along to test the survivors' ability to keep their secrets confidential. He admitted that they had passed with flying colors and were trusted enough to continue their journey to DC solo.

As they disembarked the aircraft, McDole kissed the ground. He swore he would never leave the United States again. *Free at last!* he thought. He, Barta, and Bogue boarded another plane for Washington, stopping for fuel in Omaha before being forced to land in Chicago due to bad weather. They finished their trip to Washington by train, where they spent the next week with intelligence officers, who compiled their collective story as Evasion and Escape (E&E) Report No. 23, filed on February 23, 1945.

The three continued to eat well and put on weight each day before boarding a train for a cross-country passage. Traveling with his two Palawan companions, McDole was first to arrive home when the train rolled into the town of Ames, Iowa. It was February 6, Mac's twenty-fourth birthday. He hoped to walk into his house in nearby Urbandale and surprise his family, but word had leaked out that he was homeward bound. As the train pulled into the station at Ames, Barta hollered out, "Mac, by the way you've described your family, I swear to God that's them looking in the window right now!"[7]

Mac glanced out and spotted his sisters. He jumped from his seat and raced down the steps from the train. There before him were his mother, Dessa, as well as siblings Colleen, Margaret, Max, and baby brother, Joe. LeRoy Sexton, Mac's old boxing buddy from high school, was also there as a family member—his brother-in-law since marrying Colleen. There were plenty of hugs and tears, and Mac could not contain his own waterworks. In the car riding back to Urbandale, Mac learned that his father, David McDole, had died on December 14, 1943—exactly one year before the Palawan Massacre.

From Iowa, Bogue and Barta continued on to California. Weeks later, on March 4, Doug Bogue was finally reunited with his parents in Los Angeles. He would enjoy many personal home-cooked favorites in the days ahead, but his first request was for his mother's French toast. The following day, he granted an exclusive interview to the *Los Angeles Examiner*, in which he related the massacre and some details of his escape with the help of local Filipinos. One week later, Bogue married his girlfriend, Betty Wearing, who had waited for him throughout the war.

The wedding was followed by a honeymoon in Salt Lake City as he tried to put his prisoner of war experience behind him.

When Joe Barta arrived in California, his aunt Minnie took him in to recover. He had weighed only ninety-eight pounds when he escaped from Palawan, but he soon managed to regain twenty-two pounds, after returning to a stable diet.

As THE FIRST three survivors were settling back into life in the United States, two others were still hiding amid the jungles of Palawan, evading Japanese soldiers.

Pop Daniels had been laid up for weeks in the home of Emilio Natalico and Dodong Fuertes. The locals took good care of the Army Air Force survivor until the wounds in his legs healed enough to allow him to begin walking. During the next week, Filipino guerrillas slowly moved Daniels northward to their stronghold at Bacungan, where he was again allowed to rest and recover.[8]

Mo Deal was also convalescing from his many bayonet and gunshot wounds, thanks to the care afforded him by Triny Mendoza. Captain Mayor's guerrillas had carried him northward to receive attention from a local doctor before he was relocated during January from Babuyan toward the far northern end of Palawan. By February 8, he had reached the barangay of Bantulan, located in the municipality of Taytay. Deal was introduced to Master Sergeant Eutiquio Cabais, whose coastwatcher unit had been landed with its communication equipment by the submarine USS *Seawolf* in August 1944. Cabais sent word via radio to Australia that day, informing the Allies of the safe arrival of an American soldier who had escaped the massacre. He would remain in their safekeeping until details for his rescue could be worked out.

During that time, American forces were preparing to make a full invasion of Palawan Island. Two days after Deal reached Bantulan, the first American invaders arrived on February 10 at Babuyan, where Deal had recently stayed. Two U.S. Navy PT boats brought seven soldiers to coordinate with local guerrillas on laying the groundwork for American troop landings. The advance group was greeted with thunderous applause from the refugee Filipino families as they met with Major Pablo Muyco and others of the Palawan guerrilla network.[9]

Muyco offered intelligence on enemy positions and strength around Puerto Princesa, where he estimated 1,285 Japanese soldiers were stationed. The PT boats returned to base at Mindoro with several men from Captain Mayor's company to help guide the American liberation force of the 41st Division of the 8th Army. Sergeant Placido's coastwatchers stayed very busy during the next two weeks, communicating with the 8th Army Headquarters and the Palawan Task Force stations.[10]

Sergeant Cabais radioed MacArthur's headquarters in Australia on February 13 to advise that Corporal Deal was still "here at our control station at Bantulan." Cabais recommended a suitable location for rescue plane contact to be the northwest cove of Icadambanuan Island, about three miles due northeast of Bantulan and due east of Santa Cruz Point. MacArthur's headquarters radioed that a PBY would be sent the following day to the recommended position, where the guerrillas were to have three signal fires burning fifty yards apart on the beach.

Word came back that the rendezvous would be rescheduled to February 15, but the rescue plane that arrived that day merely circled the location twice and flew away. Cabais radioed MacArthur's headquarters to request another attempt to pick up Mo Deal, and followed with another dispatch on February 17, saying that his guerrillas had boats standing by to help with the supplies. Cabais was becoming frustrated by February 18; his men and their boats had been tied up for three days waiting for a rescue plane.

MacArthur's headquarters replied that an attempt to pick up Deal had been canceled due to rough waters. "Another attempt will be made on 20 February at about 1130," they advised. This time, everything worked as planned. The Luzon-based rescue aircraft was piloted by Lieutenant G. D. Mulford of Patrol Bombing Squadron 17, tasked with flights for photo reconnaissance, transporting supplies to guerrilla forces, and evacuating downed airmen, guerrillas, and battle casualties.[11]

Mulford landed his PBY on February 20 near Bantulan and brought fifteen hundred pounds of supplies to the Palawan guerrillas. In return, his crew evacuated Mo Deal, who spent time in the Philippines recovering before being moved to New Guinea in early March for treatment. His parents in Yuba City, California, finally received word from the military that he was one of only a handful of Americans to escape the POW camp massacre.

Mrs. Pearl Deal had not heard from her son Elmo since July 1944, when a postcard arrived from his camp. In his classic wise-guy nature, her son had tried to keep his sense of humor in the fifty-word Red Cross message. "Celebrate the holidays for me also," Deal wrote on one card. "Am exercising vigorously and eating heartily." In another, he told his parents, "Would appreciate a carton of Dukes and a pair of Levi's."

Now she was handed an official Western Union telegram informing her that her son had been rescued by American forces "and is now safe." Mo's brothers, Floyd Deal, a corporal in the Army stationed in North Carolina, and Navy seaman Gerald Deal, had also survived the war. Mrs. Deal celebrated the news with her daughter, Darlene Deal Bishop, as local newspapermen recorded their jubilant reactions. A statement from Elmo Deal was released on March 3 via the AP news wire in which he briefly recounted how the Japanese had slaughtered American prisoners with machine guns and gasoline.

On March 22, he underwent a five-hour operation on his right arm to mend some of the bayonet damage. Three days later, he felt well enough to write to his family. Struggling to print using his left hand, he explained he was "just beginning to feel myself again. This old Army chow sure tastes good after three years on rice and soup. Finally got a partial pay of $30, first money since December 1941. Of course, the money is different over here. It is in Australian pounds."[12]

Pearl Deal received another Western Union telegram on April 29, stating that her son would soon be returned to the United States. On the first of May, Mo Deal, the tenth survivor of the Palawan Massacre to be liberated, was flown back to San Francisco, where he was held for further treatment.

ON FEBRUARY 28, 1945, an American liberation force more than eight thousand strong began its landing on Palawan. The 186th Regimental Combat Team, U.S. 41st Division of the 8th Army Task Force, commanded by General Harold H. Haney, moved ashore without opposition at Canigaran Beach—within sight of the airfield that the American POWs had built near Puerto Princesa.

Palawan's occupiers of the last three years had long since withdrawn from the vicinity following two days of heavy aerial bombings that preceded the American landings. The remaining Japanese troops of Lieutenant General Sosaku Suzuki's 35th Army had fled into the hills to the northwest, and Puerto Princesa was transformed overnight into a huge U.S. military camp. The town was in ruins from air raids, first from the Japanese, and now from the Americans.

As U.S. troops moved inland, the eleventh and final survivor of the Palawan Massacre was liberated. Pop Daniels, who had been in the care of the guerrilla network for forty-seven days, was on hand when American soldiers liberated Puerto Princesa. He was moved to the Fourth Replacement Depot and was interviewed by the 41st Combat Information Center on Mindoro on March 6. The following day, a telegram was sent to his half brother, Henry Blalock, in Texas to report he had been recovered and was being treated. Daniels received a joyful message from Henry on March 22: "Dear Tom, we are so glad to hear that you are in good health. Hope to see you soon." Daniels received a double promotion from private to corporal, and began his voyage back to the United States on May 14.[13]

Two divisions of Japanese troops put up stiff resistance in the hills of Palawan, and more than nine hundred were killed. Many of the survivors began to surrender, including Private Tomisaburo Sawa, who had served as a rifleman during the Palawan Massacre. One week after his unit retreated into the mountains, he and a friend were in search of food when they were taken into custody by eight American soldiers. Sawa, who had taken pleasure in beating Americans and slicing them with his bayonet, now faced life as a POW. He was interrogated for a week and then moved to Leyte.[14]

Mopping-up actions would continue on Palawan for weeks. Coast-watcher Carlos Placido and his five-man unit received orders on April 7 to return to Australia. Before they departed via PT boat on April 19, the Brooke's Point Filipinos threw a party in their honor. They had communicated Japanese troop and shipping movements, had coordinated the rescue of the submarine *Flier* survivors, had helped get others off the island (including Palawan escapee Charlie Watkins), and had coordinated the escape of nine Palawan Massacre survivors. "We all hoped that whatever little we accomplished had somehow contributed to the success of the Philippine Campaign," wrote Placido. "We had tried our best with what equipment [was] furnished us."[15]

Triny Mendoza struggled emotionally and physically during the liberation of Palawan. She had lost more than her husband. During the war that raged on the island, the Japanese had taken most of her prized possessions, including baby books, photos, and diaries that her husband had been compiling for twenty-seven years. She found that her banana plantation had been leveled to make a landing field. She, her mother, sister, and brother had to fight for enough space just to set up family tents on their own property. Ten months after the American landings on Palawan, the Mendoza family was without a home and without income, and Triny's house had become a makeshift high school for Filipino students.

Following the U.S. landings, a search of the POW enclosure was made between March 15 and 23, 1945. Soldiers recovered fragmentary records concerning U.S. military personnel, and the remains of seventy-nine POW victims were exhumed in the camp area. The body of another American POW, likely Don Martyn, was recovered from the grounds of the Iwahig Penal Colony.

Twenty-six skeletons were piled four and five high in one excavation in the Puerto Princesa compound, their skulls each showing bullet holes, or having been crushed by some blunt instrument. The soldiers found nine total dugouts, two of which were interconnected and ran alongside the bluff. Inside the smallest was a bench built along one of its sides, where searchers found several personal items, including the papers of Captain Fred Bruni. In the larger dugouts, most bodies were found huddled together far from the entrance.

The soldiers unearthed various personal items, such as identification tags, canteens etched with their owners' names, and various ration cans belonging to American POWs. Among the Japanese personal effects recovered was a diary belonging to an officer of the 131st Airfield Battalion. The entry for December 15, the day after the massacre, read as follows: "Although they were prisoners of war, they truly died a pitiful death. The prisoners of war who worked in the repair shop really worked hard. From today on, I will not hear the familiar greeting, 'Good morning, Sergeant Major.'"[16]

General MacArthur announced news of the Palawan Massacre on March 3, 1945, in a special press release that related how American prisoners were doused with gasoline, set afire, then shot and bayoneted as they tried to escape. The scene was described as one of "wholesale slaughter."[17]

THE JAPANESE NEVER made good on their promise to sink the USS *Anderson*. The transport ship finally docked in San Francisco on March 22, 1945, two and a half months after the the rescue of the vessel's six Palawan passengers. The *Anderson* tied up at Fort Mason, and the escapees were soon transferred by boat to Fort McDowell. Western Union telegrams informed their families they were alive.

One night, the Palawan survivors were treated to a steak dinner in their honor in San Francisco. The group was amused when the band asked for requests. "'Don't Fence Me In,'" quipped Ernie Koblos. His comrades chuckled even harder as they ate their meals, which included paper-wrapped baked potatoes. Koblos, who had not seen a baked potato in years, eagerly devoured his, skin and all. Afterward, he complained that he could not stomach the taste and texture of the potato skin. His companions howled with laughter; Koblos had actually eaten paper and all in his haste.

Soon Koblos returned to his native Chicago, where he was checked in to Gardiner General Hospital on April 15 for further treatment. In San Francisco, Nielsen, Petry, Smitty, Pacheco, and Balchus were given freshly tailored uniforms before they were flown to Washington, DC, where they enjoyed first-rate hotel rooms, fancy dinners, and personal sightseeing tours around the capital in a station wagon.[18]

The five survivors were also introduced to General George C. Marshall, the U.S. Army Chief of Staff, at the Pentagon. He showed them maps of the current war effort, apologized that the Philippines could not have been liberated sooner, and asked them to relate their ordeal. Then General Marshall pinned Bronze Star Medals on the former prisoners of war.

BETO PACHECO REACHED El Paso on Friday, April 5, fresh from debriefings in Washington. He was informed that Palawan had been invaded since his recovery and that any talking he did about his escape could be detrimental to the war effort.[19]

He cared little about talking about his hardships; his heart was being pulled elsewhere. He had spent four years thinking of the lovely Katie Valles, whom he had dated while serving at Fort Bliss before shipping out to the Philippines. In spite of her father's objections, Beto had promised Katie he would return to her in a year when his tour of duty was completed. Neither could predict his capture and years of captivity in the Pacific.

Pacheco had no idea what had become of Katie, whether she still lived in El Paso, or even if she was still unmarried. Yet he held on to a glimmer of hope. He had two letters from her, both written long before.

He hurried to the address where Katie had lived during the two months before he shipped off to the Philippines. His heart sank when a stranger answered the door. Pacheco quickly quizzed the neighbors as to the family's whereabouts.

"Try this one," they said. "They moved to nine-one-one East Overland."

Pacheco made his way to the Overland home and anxiously rapped on the door, where another stranger greeted him. He explained who he was and that he was looking for Katie Valles.

"Just a moment," he was told.

Seconds seemed like years, and then she appeared. Katie, the girl he had fallen in love with in early 1941, was standing before him. Instead of giving him a warm smile, she stared at him in a dazed stupor. "She just looked at me like I was a dead person walking," he recalled.

Katie's mind finally processed the unbelievable.

"Alberto!" she shouted with joy. Years of anguish melted away as she clutched him tight.

Katie had wondered if she would ever see Alberto again, having never received a single letter from him. Yet each Wednesday for years she had devoutly offered novenas, special prayers on his behalf, with a feeling in her heart that Beto was still alive. He had no intention of letting her get away. He asked her to be his wife, she accepted, and they were filling out a marriage license application the next morning.

Beto returned home to Deming, New Mexico, to visit his parents and share with them his exciting news. Two weeks later, on April 22, Katie and Alberto Pacheco were married. They honeymooned in Los Angeles while he was still on a ninety-day furlough from the Army. Back pay to the tune of four thousand dollars helped the couple start their new life with some cushion.

Willie Smith spent weeks recovering in hospitals. In between straightening out his military records and collecting back pay, he had a joyous reunion with his family and friends in Hughes Springs, Texas. He was informed he could pick any post he desired to complete his military service, but instead he asked to be discharged from the Marines.

"You can't do that," said his commanding officer. "But you can go anywhere in the United States you want to go."

"Well, if you ain't going to discharge me, then send me back to the Philippines," Smitty demanded.

He was told this was also not an option, so he finally settled on the base at Eagle Mountain Lake, just outside of Fort Worth, Texas. He served light duty until being discharged on September 29, 1945, shortly after the war ended. He returned to his rural home, where he would spend three years fighting bouts of malarial fever.[20]

He started dating Sarah Bess Ross, who had lived with his sister in Texarkana, where the two worked at the Red River Arsenal during the war. Smitty and Bess were married on December 1, 1945. For their honeymoon, the couple went to Gaston, Alabama, where Smitty wanted to visit the family of his friend C. C. "Greasy" Smith. C.C.'s father had contacted Smitty soon after his return, asking for information on his son's fate. In Gaston, Smitty explained the sad news that C.C. had

Smitty *(left)* shares his story of captivity and survival with a re-
porter in 1945.   **COURTESY OF NETA SMITH ALEXANDER**

been cut down with a saber during the early moments of the Palawan
Massacre. The two Smith families would remain in contact for many
years.

THE LAST PUERTO Princesa prisoner to return to America was Second
Lieutenant Sid Wright. He was a Marine private when he and five others escaped Camp 10-A in August 1942, but during 1944, he had accepted
a commission to serve as an American guerrilla with Colonel Fertig's
forces in the Philippines. After the American invasion of Leyte, Wright
was evacuated to Mindanao, where he recovered from double pneumo-
nia before being flown back to San Francisco in July 1945. Wright married Charlotte Motherwell three months later and enjoyed a long career
in the U.S. Army before retiring to El Paso.

    Most of the Palawan survivors were offered commissions to remain
in military service, but few other than Bogue accepted. Willie Balchus

was content to move on with life. He returned to live in Shenandoah, Pennsylvania, married Helen M. Wisniewski, and talked little about his Palawan years. Mo Deal returned to California and was married to Alta June Hammons, a hometown friend he had known before the war. Alta was working as a soda jerk when he returned, and she broke her engagement with another man when she learned that Mo had survived the war. Deal retired from the Army as a sergeant on April 8, 1946, having been awarded two Bronze Stars and the Purple Heart, among other service medals.

Ed Petry, who had dropped to seventy-two pounds before his rescue, quickly put on weight after his return to California, where he married a widow named Priscilla Jane Spurgeon Linder, who had three older children and one young son. Gene Nielsen went home to South Logan, Utah, and met his future wife, Gwynne Allen, the day he returned. The couple was married in the Logan LDS Temple on March 7, 1946, and would begin raising a family of four children.

Pop Daniels retired as a maintenance sergeant from the 1040th Army Air Force Base Unit on February 28, 1947, and returned to Texas. Years later, evidently reflecting on how Mac McDole had helped him make it out of the Shelter C escape tunnel during the Palawan Massacre, Daniels mailed a postcard to his fellow survivor. The message was brief: "Thanks for the shove. Pop."

Mac McDole was released from active duty with the Marine Corps on November 25, 1945, two months after the formal Japanese surrender. He joined the Reserves and settled in Urbandale to begin taking classes at the American Institute of Business. Thoughts of Palawan never left him. It was not long before he contacted a fellow survivor, Walt Ditto, who lived in Des Moines. Ditto and Bob May had been badly beaten for planning an escape from Palawan, and the two had been returned to Manila after surviving the lengthiest torture ever handed out at their camp.[21]

McDole and Ditto grew close. They were out for beers one night when one of Ditto's neighbors asked if he and his sister could catch a ride back home with the two. Ditto was happy to offer a ride to Johnny

Moody and his eighteen-year-old sister, Betty. McDole thought Betty was the most beautiful woman he had ever seen, and they soon began dating. They were married on August 10, 1946, in a simple ceremony in Adel, Iowa. The next major event of Mac's postwar life came a year later when his childhood dream of becoming an Iowa Highway Safety Patrol officer was realized; he was accepted and began training. He was first stationed at Creston, where he was working when he received a letter from the War Crimes Branch in Washington.

Asked if he could be available to testify at the Palawan war crimes trial to be held in Japan, he received permission to take a leave of absence. The next few months would be a new challenge for McDole, but it would offer him and many others a chance to gain some resolution to the Palawan Massacre.

21

TRIALS AND TRIBUTES

THE FIRST JAPANESE soldier arrested for his part in the Palawan
Massacre was Kiyomasa Okamoto. Tracked down at his home in
Japan by U.S. investigators, he was brought in for interrogation
on June 11, 1947, and was questioned for eight hours before being released.

He would never live to see a tribunal.

Okamoto had served in the 3rd Platoon of Lieutenant Sho Yoshiwara's 131st Airfield Battalion company, the unit that carried out the
murders of scores of Puerto Princesa prisoners. After his lengthy interview about the events of December 14, 1944, Okamoto wrote out a
polite note later found on his body, thanking his interrogators for their
kind treatment and adding, "I was not able to give a truthful answer.
Please pity my faintheartedness." That evening, Okamoto committed
suicide by jumping in front of a moving train.[1]

Soon after World War II had ended, America and its Allies convened
the International Military Tribunal of the Far East. Military investigators spent more than two years tracking down and interviewing former
American prisoners of war. Their affidavits would be key evidence in

future war crimes trials for Japanese defendants accused of abusing and murdering thousands of POWs held in the Philippines and Japanese mainland camps.

Yet the effort to round up the Japanese who had participated in the Palawan Massacre proved to be difficult. Some of the murderers had been killed in action when American forces seized the island in early March 1945. Many of the survivors were never located, as countless Japanese records were destroyed or burned when American troops swept into Japan to free the prisoner of war camps.

Okamoto's eight hours of testimony led to the apprehension of a second Palawan Massacre participant, Private First Class Shoniro Nagano of the Yoshiwara Tai. Nagano claimed to have been assigned to other duties away from the Puerto Princesa compound on the day of the mass killings. Others subsequently rounded up and questioned about their role would make the same claim. But a third suspect, Tomisaburo Sawa, taken into custody on June 30, 1947, admitted to his part in the massacre. Two and a half years after the ghastly murders, war crimes investigators finally had good information with which to bring the perpetrators to justice.[2]

The Japanese government claimed that only two members of the 131st Airfield Battalion had been repatriated in 1945; all others were missing or killed in action. The U.S. Investigation Division was dogged in its work and soon found evidence that ex-Japanese army officials were interfering with their investigation and were failing to produce all known evidence. Lieutenant Colonel Richard E. Rudisill, the chief investigator, assigned two lieutenants to conduct a thorough search for other battalion survivors.[3]

They determined that a good number of the 131st Airfield Battalion soldiers had indeed been killed in fighting on Palawan after the Allied landings, and that other Japanese survivors had hidden themselves on Palawan and in the mountains of Borneo after the war. They found that only six known members of the unit had been repatriated to Japan.

They also attempted to track down the senior officers who held command over the Puerto Princesa camp for various lengths of time. Captain Kishimoto, the original commander from August 1942 to March 1943, could not be located. First Lieutenant Kinoshita, who commanded the Palawan compound from March 1943 to July 1944, had been killed in action on Luzon in 1945. Captain Kojima, the commander of Palawan who carried out the massacre, was declared missing by the investigators. Manichi Nishitani, the brutal camp cook, was found living in the Hiroshima area and suffering from illness. Kinhichi Tomioka, "the Bull," was captured in Manila and held for a time, but he managed to escape.[4]

The next step in the prosecution's process involved the proper identification of Japanese defendants by some of their victims. In 1948, Mac McDole flew to Yokosuka, Japan, where he met up with Doug Bogue. The Marines had promoted Bogue to master sergeant and assigned him to duty with the forces occupying conquered Japan. He was currently serving as provost marshal at Yokosuka Naval Base pending duty as a material witness to the Palawan Massacre.

Bogue and McDole were called to identify suspects being held in Tokyo's Sugamo Prison, located six miles from the Imperial Palace in Tokyo. Mac found it difficult to relate once again the story of the massacre to officials, and even harder to control his emotions in a place filled with men who had caused him and his friends such suffering.

One day, he and Bogue were seated in the Dai-Ichi building in Tokyo, which had survived the devastating late-war B-29 fire bombings well enough for Doug MacArthur to have converted it to his postwar acting headquarters. Japanese suspects were brought before their two former POWs and ordered to face left and front so they could be identified as they stepped off the elevator.[5]

The first man off was Manichi Nishitani, the Palawan camp cook who had delivered so much abuse to the American prisoners. Upon sight of the man's face, Mac felt his pulse race; he was sweating and trembling with anger as he helped question the prisoner. Nishitani denied every-thing. When the guards started to take the cook back to his prison cell, Bogue moved in quickly and punched Nishitani in the face before the guards pulled him away.

When asked why he had struck the prisoner, Bogue said, "For the same reason you're going to hang him!"

Presented next was Master Sergeant Taichi Deguchi. Again, Mac tried to control his rage in the presence of the man who had viciously taunted and tortured American POWs. Deguchi stared straight ahead through the questioning. With an expressionless face, he answered, "No!" to each question.[6]

As other Japanese were brought forth, they continued to deny their guilt. The only one to show any emotion was Kuta Schugota—known at Palawan as "Smiley." When he spotted Mac, Smiley bowed his head. When he was brought closer, he dropped to his knees and crawled across the floor to Mac. "Oh, Macky Dole, I thought you had been killed," Smiley said, sobbing.

Interrogators began questioning the former guard, but he refused to cooperate and denied it all. Furious, Mac screamed at him, reminding him of how he had been the most lenient guard, allowing prisoners to sneak food. "I never saw you raise your hand to hit one of us, but if you don't tell us what you know, I'll tell them you were the meanest son of a bitch there was!" said McDole. "Understand?"[7]

Regardless, Smiley stuck with his denial until he was led back to Sugamo Prison. One day weeks later, Mac was eating lunch in the Dai-Ichi building's cafeteria when an MP told him an inmate in Sugamo wanted to speak to him. When he entered the prisoner's cell, he found Smiley to be haggard and sick, unable to eat due to the guilt that had consumed him. He agreed to tell the truth, and Mac summoned the guards. Smiley was escorted back to the Dai-Ichi building, where he told the prosecutors everything: the beatings, the denial of food, the torture. He gave names and dates before he was returned to his cell.

Interrogations stretched on for weeks, and Mac was to depart before the trials commenced in Yokohama and Tokyo. Before he left, he requested that the military prosecutors show leniency to Kuta Schugota for providing key evidence. They agreed to set him free and allowed Mac to personally share the news with the kindliest of the former Palawan guards. Smiley looked even more run-down this time, but the news that he was free to return to his family touched his heart. He clasped Mac's hand through the cell bars and cried like a child. He explained that he had a wife and two daughters whom he supported by painting signs. "When I go home," he said, "I tell my daughters, Macky Dole, an American prisoner of war, saved my life. Thank you so much!"[8]

Pedro Paje, the suspected turncoat who was actually running an underground resistance operation from the Iwahig Penal Colony, was charged with treason by the Philippine government. Falsely named as a Japanese collaborator by one of his own employees whom he had arrested for dealing black market American goods, Paje was detained and held in a concentration camp on Leyte for about eight months, until he was freed on November 5, 1946. During his trial, depositions from both Mac McDole and Smitty helped clear Paje of the false charges made against him. Mac departed Tokyo with high hopes that his three months of testimony would help convict the thirty-three officers and men facing charges and put them to death.[9]

The trials began on August 2, 1948, in Yokohama, and would stretch on for many weeks. Doug Bogue, Joe Barta, and Edwin Petry made appearances to give their testimony concerning their experiences on Palawan and their final escapes. Prosecutors introduced written orders sent to all camp commanders in May 1944, which stated that if Allied landings threatened any branch camp where the American POWs might be retaken, decisive actions must be taken to prevent any prisoners from being saved. But only sixteen of the thirty-three Japanese suspects were actually put to trial, and the end results could not have been more lenient.

Lieutenant General Seiichi Terada's trial began in Tokyo. He had been the commanding general of the 2nd Air Division on Negros Island, but he claimed that he was never provided written orders placing him in control of the Palawan battalion. He believed that control remained with the 4th Air Division headquarters in Manila. Terada denied giving direct orders on December 13, 1944, to have the POWs massacred. Thirteen charges were eventually levied against him, and the court found him guilty of all but four. On November 8, 1948, General Terada was sentenced to a life term in Tokyo's Sugamo Prison.[10]

One who did not escape the death sentence was Lieutenant General Homma, commanding general of the Japanese 14th Army, which had invaded the Philippines. Charged with being responsible for the Bataan Death March and other atrocities, Homma was executed by a firing squad on April 3, 1946, in the city of Los Baños. Lieutenant General Tomoyuki Yamashita, charged with numerous war crimes in the Philippines, and in the Thai and Malay peninsulas, was hanged to death in Manila on February 23, 1946.

Of the Palawan Massacre suspects, Master Sergeant Deguchi was charged with six items. Among the charges against him were beating and killing POWs Seldon White and Earl Vance Wilson; beating, abusing, and holding Walt Ditto and Robert May in the brig for three months; giving orders for his men to beat two other POWs to death; and his involvement in the December 14 massacre. Deguchi pleaded not guilty to all counts, but the evidence against him was overwhelming. On November 8, he was sentenced to be hanged to death, with the final execution order to be confirmed by General MacArthur.

Superior Private Tomisaburo Sawa was more cooperative. During his stay in the Sugamo Prison, he gave written confessions to all sorts of atrocities carried out on Palawan, including personally killing at least three of the one hundred thirty-nine victims on December 14. He received a five-year prison term, but it was reduced to three and a half years for time already served.

Manichi Nishitani, the head cook at the Palawan barracks, was sentenced to five years in prison for the beatings he had administered. Lieutenant General Kizo Mikama, commanding general of the 4th Air Division, 4th Air Army, received a twelve-year prison term for his part in the massacre. Lieutenant Colonel Mamoru Fushimi, who headed the 11th Air Sector Unit of the 4th Air Army, was given ten years in prison. Four others were given prison terms ranging from two to five years, but six of the sixteen charged in the Palawan Massacre were acquitted.

Shortly after Deguchi's death verdict was pronounced, General MacArthur signed an order commuting his sentence to thirty years in prison. Neither Deguchi nor Terada would serve the full term. In 1958, a general amnesty was granted to all Japanese war crimes prisoners, and they were allowed to walk free from Tokyo's Sugamo Prison.

THE ELEVEN PALAWAN Massacre survivors could do nothing to change the outcome of the Japanese war crimes trials. Like many veterans of their generation, they simply moved on with their lives.

Master Sergeant Doug Bogue tried to leave the memories of Palawan in his past. He simply did not wish to talk about his time of captivity, even with his wife and children, though in his later years he was open to reminiscing about his service during the Korean War. Bogue had been awarded the Legion of Merit for his escape from Camp 10-A, during which he killed three Japanese guards. Following the war crimes trials in Japan in 1948, he served with the 6th Marine Division in Tientsin, China, until being evacuated in 1949 when the Communists under Mao Zedung defeated Chiang Kaishek's Chinese Nationalist forces. Bogue was assigned to Korea with the 11th Marines, 1st Marine Division in 1951, where he received a battlefield commission of captain. He participated in such actions as the seizure of Inchon, the securing of Seoul, and the Chosin Campaign. He later served in Japan and was well respected for his leadership abilities. He retired as a major in 1959.

Bogue and his wife, Betty, moved to San Diego, where he worked for the next twenty years for the San Diego and Arizona Eastern Railway. After retirement, he settled in Lompoc, California, where he became a civilian pilot and certified flight instructor. Doug Bogue passed away on March 7, 2004, at his home at the age of eighty-five. He was survived by his wife of fifty-nine years and their three daughters. According to his final wishes, a memorial service was held at Moffett Field by his Marine comrades, and his ashes were scattered at sea.[11]

Edwin Petry lived in Santa Monica, California, after his honorable discharge from the military on August 30, 1946, with the rank of staff sergeant. He became a stepfather to his wife Priscilla's children from a previous marriage, and the couple added two more of their own, Robert and Darlene. Ed was first employed as a truck driver, then spent his final eighteen years of work with the U.S. Postal Service in Reseda as a maintenance man. Petry passed away at the age of sixty-six on May 7, 1987, and was buried in the Los Angeles National Cemetery.

Alberto Pacheco and his wife, Katie, drove their rumble seat sport coupe to California after the war and settled in Monterey Park. Soft-spoken and kind-natured, Pacheco worked hard to overcome the abuse he had suffered. Even looking someone in the eyes took time to relearn, since direct eye contact between Pacheco and a Japanese guard had resulted in a rifle butt or fist to his face. As he and Katie raised five daughters, Pacheco worked a variety of jobs, including stints with the Alameda Pottery Company and Western Lighting in California. He still suffered sporadic attacks of malaria but enjoyed hunting, picnics at the beach, and playing baseball with community leagues in his free time. Beto was not one to linger on the terrible experiences of Palawan, but he did keep in touch with Joe Barta, with whom he exchanged annual holiday greetings. Beto's family learned the value of deep patriotism from a father who was not ashamed to bow his head with misty eyes each time he stood for the National Anthem at a Dodgers ball game. Beto Pacheco passed away in 1997 and was buried in the Desert View Memorial Park Cemetery in Victorville, in San Bernardino County.

Ernie Koblos with his wife, Irene, and son, Jack, about 1948.

COURTESY OF JACK AND FELICE KOBLOS

Ernie Koblos—married to Irene Blanche Auld on August 3, 1945—moved from Chicago to the San Francisco area in the early 1950s. They settled in Tracy, California, and later retired in Klamath Falls, Oregon. Their sons, Jack and William, would provide the Koblos family with seven grandchildren and nine great-grandchildren. Koblos retired from the Alameda Naval Air Station in 1972 and also worked for National Ignition and United Airlines. He died in 1992 after complications from surgery.

Joe Barta was married to Jean Vaughn Koopman on September 25, 1945. He met her in San Diego, where she was working for the Navy, sending teletypes when the scraggly former POW was brought in. Barta was soon assigned to Fort Ward, near Bainbridge Island, Washington, where the two resided until he retired from the Navy. In civilian life, Barta worked for the U.S. Postal Service while attending Seattle Community College to study carpentry. His children found him to be a kind, gentle

Joe Barta with his wife, Jean.

COURTESY OF LINDA JO YALE

man who did not dwell on the morbid details of the horrors he had endured as a prisoner. He remained in contact with Doug Bogue, with whom he swam from Puerto Princesa toward safety in 1944. Joe Barta passed away at the age of eighty-eight on September 27,

2003, and was buried in the West Tennessee Veterans Cemetery in Memphis.

His grandson, Joseph P. Barta, later became engaged to a girl of Filipino birth named Christina Firme. He was shocked to find that his future wife's parents and grandparents lived on Palawan Island and had met his grandfather Joe in the wake of the Palawan Massacre when he was attempting to escape from the Japanese.

Elmo "Mo" Deal and his wife, Alta, settled in Oakland, California, where he began attending watchmaker's school. The nerves in his right hand were so damaged that he had no feeling in it, so he taught himself how to assemble the tiny inner workings of the watches with his left hand. Deal worked for a time in a North Sacramento jewelry store before opening his own business. Mo and Alta raised three daughters—Janet, Sharon, and Denise—and enjoyed traveling in their motor home in later

Elmo "Mo" Deal with his wife, Alta, and daughter Sharon in 1947.

COURTESY OF
SHARON (DEAL) SPEARS

years. Mo Deal, awarded two Bronze Stars and the Purple Heart for his World War II service, passed away on February 10, 2004, in Sacramento.

Tommie "Pop" Daniels returned home to rural Titus County, Texas, after he retired from the service in February 1947. Mac McDole tried to maintain contact with Daniels, but he found that his friend was more content to live the life of a hermit, chasing people from his property at gunpoint. He never worked again, never married, and left no children to carry on his name.[12]

Daniels lived in a modest one-room house with an attached kitchen near the community of Sugar Hill, less than thirty miles away as the crow flies from Smitty's home in Hughes Springs. He assumed the last name Zent in his later years, attributed to his biological father, but he was not the same man he had been before the war. He did not sleep well in his shack, preferring to sleep on a cot in the woods in warmer weather. He built a chain-link fence around his home to keep neighbors away, and when he died of a heart attack on about January 20, 1963, at age fifty-nine, it was days before his body was found sitting in a chair, a rifle across his lap. He was buried in the DeShields Cemetery under a simple granite marker that listed his service as "Cpl 1040 Base Unit AAF World War II."

Gene Nielsen settled in South Logan, Utah, where he and his wife, Gwynne, raised four children, Sharlene, Bruce, Janet, and Lorna. He graduated from Utah State University in 1950 with a degree in business management and economics, worked for the U.S. Postal Service, and later spent the majority of his career at Hill Air Force Base in materials management. He retired in 1978 and enjoyed fishing, boating, camping, hunting, and traveling every chance he had.

Some thirty-five years after Gene left the service, doctors found what appeared to be a blood clot in his leg. The surgeon who opened him up instead discovered a calcium-encrusted .26-caliber Japanese rifle bullet that the Filipinos who had treated him after his escape had missed. Nielsen remained active with World War II reunion groups and shared his story with various historians. He died on February 3, 2011, at age ninety-five.[13]

Glenn "Mac" McDole served twenty-nine years as an Iowa highway patrol officer, his service broken only by a recall to duty in 1950 during the Korean War. The Marines put him to work handling classified reports at Camp Pendleton, California, where he and his wife, Betty, lived until he was discharged back to civilian life the following year. Promoted to lieutenant in December 1960, McDole was assigned to head up a patrol office at Storm Lake, Iowa, where he would complete his service while he and Betty raised their daughters, Glenda and Kathy. McDole

A Palawan "survival pact" reunion in the 1970s (*left to right*): Mac McDole, Roy Henderson, Smitty, Clarence Clough, and Evan Bunn.

COURTESY OF KATHY MCDOLE PARKINS

retired from the Iowa Highway Safety Patrol in 1976 but went on to serve another twelve years with the Polk County Sheriff's Office.[14]

In 1985, McDole was finally awarded the Bronze Star Medal with Valor he had earned during World War II. He was called to the Iowa statehouse, where Governor Terry Branstad pinned the medal on him for his service on Corregidor and his ordeal at Palawan. McDole continued to lead an active life, involved in his church and various veterans and civic organizations. He traveled to the annual reunions of the 4th Marine Regiment of World War II and gave speeches to numerous veterans organizations, schools, churches, and civic groups. He enjoyed fishing and hunting and never failed to fly the American flag each day in front of his home in Ankeny, Iowa. He spoke freely of his experiences on Palawan, but for years was troubled with recurring nightmares of what he had endured.

Willie Smith and his wife, Bess, settled on family land near Hughes Springs, Texas, after he completed his military service. Smitty's

Friends Mac and Smitty
enjoying time together
after retirement.
COURTESY OF KATHY
MCDOLE PARKINS

disability pension amounted to only $157 per month, forcing him to
survive on a number of odd jobs he was able to maintain during his
recurring bouts of sickness. The Smiths raised four children, Glenn,
Don, Nita, and Kathy, and later welcomed ten grandchildren. Smitty
was able to secure a job as a safety inspector at a new U.S. Steel mill that
opened near his farm, and he worked there until 1972, when his health
worsened and he was forced to go on full disability.[15]

Smitty attended several reunions of Philippine POWs, and he particularly enjoyed the time he spent with Mac McDole. He was proud to
return to the Philippines in April 1965 along with Roy Henderson and
other former POWs to visit with the Filipino people who had helped
them survive. Like McDole and Nielsen, Smitty made himself available
to historians and others interested in the Palawan Massacre. He lived
out his final years in East Texas, maintaining a few head of cattle on his
farm until he passed away on April 14, 1994.

Willie Balchus returned to live in Shenandoah, Pennsylvania, where
he talked little about Palawan, content to put his ordeal behind him. He
married Helen M. Wisniewski, and had a son and daughter, six grandchildren, and seven great-grandchildren. Balchus loved fishing and being outdoors in Pennsylvania and California. During his career, he drove
trucks at the coal mines in Pennsylvania, and later operated heavy

construction equipment until his retirement. He died on December 11, 2013, in Yuba City, California, at age ninety-two. He had been living with his son, Joe Balchus, for the previous eight years.

Willie was the last of the eleven Palawan Massacre survivors to pass away, and he had lived his last years just thirty-five miles away from Mo Deal's family without knowing it.

THE AMERICANS IMPRISONED in Puerto Princesa Camp 10-A during World War II never forgot the Filipino people who came to their aid.

For some of the Palaweños, their efforts in the guerrilla movement came at great personal cost. **Triny Mendoza**—known to the prisoners as "Red Hankie"—did not learn of the murder of her husband, Higinio, until February 1945, shortly after the American invasion of Palawan. Only then did a captured Japanese soldier confess that the guerrilla leader had been executed a year prior.

In 1947, Esperanza Clark Marcelo, Triny Mendoza's sister, spotted a woven crocheted belt with a University of Iowa buckle being worn by a man working for a family relative. Esperanza had given the buckle to Dr. Mendoza as a gift before World War II. When questioned, the man, named Timod, related the story of how he and several others had witnessed the execution in January 1944 near Canigaran Beach. Afterward, Timod had retrieved the belt the Japanese left as a marker and kept it.[16]

In August 1947, Timod helped lead a search effort to find the grave of Dr. Mendoza. He was assisted by Triny's cousin, several workers, and three of Governor Mendoza's sons—John, Higinio Jr., and David Mendoza. After two days of intensive scouring, they found the remains, exhumed his body, and buried it again on the family coconut plantation. Higinio Mendoza was laid to rest near the graves of his father-in-law, John T. Clark, and a brother-in-law, Alfred Palanca Clark, who died during World War II.

Several years later, Governor Alfredo M. Abueg Sr. proposed to Triny Mendoza that her late husband be transferred to a more prominent site. After allowing his remains to lie in state for one day at the provincial capital, the people buried former governor Mendoza once again on July 27, 1950—alongside Rizal Avenue in a place now known as Mendoza Park.[17]

Following the liberation of the Philippines, his widow remarried, to an American serviceman, and became Trinidad Hartman. She was on hand at the thirty-fifth anniversary of the fall of Bataan and Corregidor, held in Manila in April 1977. Former prisoner **Hubert Hough** and his wife took time to visit Palawan that month. Hough had married Verla Pauline Scott on October 7, 1945, retired from the Navy as a lieutenant in 1949, and then worked for Iowa Power and later in heavy construction until his retirement. Hough was able to visit the old prisoner camp and to reunite with Mrs. Hartman and other Filipino friends.[18]

Years later, Mac McDole was blessed with a similar happy reunion. **Mary Anne Mayor**, the youngest daughter of **Captain Nazario Mayor**, had helped tend to the young marine and his fellow survivors of the Palawan Massacre in late December 1944 and early 1945. Mary Anne later married Dr. Valentino Ancheta, moved to America in 1960, and settled in Algoma, Wisconsin, where she worked as a nurse. She had not seen or heard from any of the Palawan escapees since the war had ended.

On December 15, 1988, Mary Anne came across a newspaper article about a Washington, DC, memorial service for the men massacred in the Puerto Princesa camp. Reading that Glenn McDole was living in Des Moines, she soon located his home number. She left a message on the family's answering machine, but the device ran out of tape. Mac heard only enough to learn that the caller was a woman named Mary Anne who lived in Wisconsin, so he put out a public appeal for Mary Anne to contact him, and she soon reached him on the phone again.

The story of a young woman who had helped eleven Americans survive a brutal massacre quickly caught the media's attention. A reunion between the Anchetas and the McDoles was arranged to take place on January 9, 1989, in the New York City studio of ABC's *Good Morning America*. Before millions of viewers, Mac and Mary Anne told the story of the Palawan Massacre to the nation.

Mac McDole enjoying a reunion with the Mayors in Mary Anne's home in Algoma, Wisconsin. (*Seated, left to right*): Val Ancheta, Mary Anne Ancheta, Captain Nazario Mayor, McDole, Betty McDole, and Robert Mayor. (*Standing, left to right*): Kathy McDole, friend Heather Sanderson, and Glenda McDole.

COURTESY OF KATHY MCDOLE PARKINS

Immediately after the show, the two telephoned her eighty-eight-year-old father, Nazario Mayor, in Manila to share the exciting news. The next few years would bring more meetings between the families, with Nazario later moving from Palawan to live with his daughter in Wisconsin, and her oldest brother, **Robert Mayor**, later settling in the Chicago area. Nazario Mayor passed away in 1993 at the age of ninety-three while visiting his sister in Manila.

TODAY, THE PALAWAN Massacre is remembered in the Philippines and America thanks to the efforts of several individuals.

Palawan POW Don Schloat, greatly abused for attempting to escape from Puerto Princesa, was returned to Bilibid Prison. He spent the rest of the war there, racked with scurvy, beriberi, dysentery, and pellagra, until his liberation in 1945. Schloat later became a commercial artist who took it upon himself to make sure that the massacre victims were re-membered. In 1989, he completed a series of seventy-seven paintings that depicted the slaughter in abstract and impressionistic forms. His artwork was exhibited in San Diego, and most of the paintings were put on permanent display later in Santa Fe.[19]

Schloat returned to visit Palawan a number of times and became the driving force behind a memorial at the site of the killings. The munici-pal government of Puerto Princesa City erected a permanent monument in the Plaza Cuartel city park—just beside the Immaculate Conception Cathedral—in September 1999. Schloat funded the architect who drew up the design. The Palawan Massacre Monument had a small plaque displaying the names of the few survivors (Schloat's name included by mistake), but his new bronze statue now sits atop the memorial. It de-picts a thin male figure writhing in pain as flames rise from his feet. Efforts are currently under way to construct an updated memorial for the Palawan Massacre in the Puerto Princesa park that is home to the original statue.

Visitors to Puerto Princesa can also tour the Palawan Special Battal-ion WWII Memorial Museum, opened in December 2011 to honor the seventieth anniversary of the bombing of Pearl Harbor and the invasion of the Philippines. It was created through the labors of Higinio C. "Buddy" Mendoza, son of guerrilla leader Dr. Mendoza. The museum, housing memorabilia collected by Mendoza, chronicles the fates of the Palawan Massacre men in addition to paying tribute to the members of the "Palawan Fighting One Thousand" guerrilla unit of World War II.

The remains of 123 of the 139 POWs massacred at the Puerto Prin-cesa camp were removed from Palawan to be buried on February 14, 1952, in a common grave in Section 85 at the Jefferson Barracks National Cemetery near St. Louis, Missouri. The remains of sixteen other victims could not be located. A new marker was dedicated on October 4, 2003, in the St. Louis cemetery, with Palawan POW camp veterans present, including Glenn McDole, Gene Nielsen, Dan Crowley, and Joe "Frenchy" Dupont.

Nielsen and McDole discussed their former camp and the massacre before a crowd of about a hundred people that included veterans, friends, and relatives. The two survivors placed a wreath at the site to dedicate the new plaque before the list of the Palawan victims was read aloud.

The following year, 2004, an account of McDole's wartime experiences, *Last Man Out* by Bob Wilbanks, was published. His story and that of the Palawan Massacre were also told on Oliver North's *War Stories* TV documentary series. He passed away on September 3, 2009, in Alleman, Iowa. Only a week after McDole's death, First Lieutenant Carl Mango—the Army doctor who had saved his life on Palawan—was finally honored with a posthumous Silver Star Medal. Mac McDole had donated much of his time in later years to talking about Palawan in hopes that the men who died there would not be forgotten.

They are remembered, American heroes all.

ν

ACKNOWLEDGMENTS

My interest in Palawan originated years ago while writing another POW story, *Presumed Lost*, but uncovering fresh material on this story proved to be a true collaborative effort. I am indebted to many people who helped me unearth some of the lesser-known events from this dark chapter of World War II history.

I first must offer thanks to the families of the men interned in Puerto Princesa Camp 10-A who allowed me to understand more about who their fathers, brothers, and uncles were by sharing stories, letters, diaries, photos, and newspaper clippings. This group includes Nita Smith Alexander, Kathy McDole Parkins, Glenda McDole Johnson, Kathy Pacheco Martinez, David Martinez, Lorna Nielsen Murray, Florentino Pacheco, Juanita Pacheco, Joe Balchus, Maureen Barta, Joseph P. Barta, Jack and Felice Koblos, Janet Cevering, Janet Dorman, Jacqueline Elliott, Linda Yale, David Wright, Sharon Spears, Lynhon Stout, Etta Hooker, Georgianne Burlage, Jennifer Meixner, Milton Bell, Raymond Stillwell, and Albert Mango.

Mary Anne Mayor Ancheta, Robert Mayor, Joanne Rae Ramirez, Jennifer Ancheta, Higinio "Buddy" Mendoza, and Bart Duff helped me understand the crucial role played by the Filipinos of Palawan in aiding the American POWs who escaped before and during the massacre.

Many of the details of Palawan Camp 10-A came from the war crimes trials documents, eyewitness depositions, and military documentation compiled to help prosecute those who carried out the massacre. Friend and fellow author James Scott, with whom I've exchanged military research for years, shared a number of Palawan files he had previously gathered. Independent researcher Susan Strange was invaluable in tracking down numerous other requested National Archives documents and proved to possess an uncanny ability to snoop out long-forgotten files in non-indexed boxes. Some of the more valuable documents accessed for this project simply would not have been unearthed without her assistance.

I must thank researcher Jaclyn Ostrowski for her perseverance in navigating unforeseen challenges at the National Personnel Records Center in St. Louis until the military papers of survivor Tommie Daniels—damaged by the 1973 fire that destroyed more than sixteen million military files—were finally procured. Further information on Daniels's postwar life came from Jeanette Johnson-McCoy and sources provided by Pam Hill of the Titus County, Texas Historical Preservation Society. Thanks also to Washington researcher Tim Frank; Megan Harris of the Veterans History Project, Library of Congress, who went above and beyond to assist with Palawan-related memoirs; Leslie Ann Murray of the American Chamber of Commerce of the Philippines; Jim Morriss for his tireless genealogical sleuthing, which helped put me in contact with many of the Palawan Massacre survivors' families; Colonel Don Patton of the WWII History Round Table; and James Zobel at the MacArthur Memorial for his assistance in tracking down E&E reports and other documents related to the Palawan survivors.

I truly appreciate the support of my wife and kids during my many long nights spent poring through documents. My agent, Jim Donovan, was crucial in offering editorial assistance and critical advice on this project, helping to trim the story into a narrative with pace and purpose.

My editor at Caliber, Brent Howard, believed from the start that this story needed to be told, and was equally effective in suggesting ways to keep the manuscript on target.

Finally, I wish to remember all the American and Filipino service personnel who endured the Second World War in POW camps throughout the Philippines. Many never came home, and those who did often returned with emotional scars that would not completely heal. No one in this country should forget the sacrifices made by so many, including those who were not fortunate enough to escape from the Palawan Massacre in December 1944. To these veterans, this book is dedicated.

APPENDIX A

VICTIMS OF THE PALAWAN MASSACRE,
DECEMBER 14, 1944

BRANCH	NAME	RANK	HOMETOWN/NEXT OF KIN HOME
USMC	Adams, Jewett Franklin	T/Sgt	San Diego, CA
USMC	Adkins, Robert Arthur	Corp	Portland, OR
Army	Anderson, Robert Sterling	Pvt	Harper, WA
Army	Araujo, Henry Hernandez	Sgt	Denver, CO
Army	Arispe, Heraclio Solie	Pfc	Corpus Christi, TX
USMC	Arnoldy, Arthur Anton	Corp	Tipton, KS
Army	Bailey, Homer Ray	Pfc	Ardmore, OK
Army	Baker, Herbert	Pvt	Roxbury, MA
Army	Bancroft, Everett Richard Jr.	Pfc	Canon City, CO
Navy	Barnes, Carl Ellis	WT2c	Bakersfield, CA
Navy	Barnes, Darrell Leroy	AOM3c	Bayonne, NJ
Army	Bartle, Charles Warren	Sgt	Evansville, IN
Army	Beason, Benjamin Franklin	T/Sgt	Canyon, TX
Navy	Blackburn, Wilbur Burdett	TM2c	Wichita, KS
Army	Bouchey, Mason "J"	Pfc	Saginaw, MI
Army	Brown, William Theodore	Pfc	Antioch, CA
Army	Bruni, Fred Tobias	Capt	Janesville, WI
Navy	Buchanan, Vernon Edward	F1c	Turner, KS
Army	Burnett, Douglas	Cpl	La Grande, OR
USMC	Caldwell, Sammy Lee	Pfc	San Angelo, TX
Army	Carter, Casey	Pvt	Paris, TX
Army	Childers, Roy Raymond	Pvt	Loami, IL
Army	Choate, James Louis	Pvt	Madisonville, KY
Navy	Cook, Harry W.	Aerog1c	San Roque, Cavite, PI
Army	Crandell, Earl Jesse	Pvt	Holdenville, OK
Army	Cravens, William Thomas	Pvt	Port Royal, KY
Army	Cullins, Franklin Ashley	Pvt	Monette, AR
Army	Czajkowski, John	Pvt	Nichols, WI
Army	Diaz, John Francisco	Pfc	Osage, IA
Army	Dutton, Glen Albert	Cpl	Clovis, NM

BRANCH	NAME	RANK	HOMETOWN/NEXT OF KIN HOME
Army	Elix, Clayton Emmett	Pfc	Pueblo, CO
Army	Evans, Erving August	Cpl	Huron, SD
Army	Eyre, George Robert	Pfc	Marion, OH
Army	Fletcher, Houston Everett	Pfc	Oklahoma City, OK
USMC	Fryar, William Ferson	Pfc	Apollo, PA
Army	Gee, Jessie Roy	Cpl	Yuba City, CA
Navy	Gillespie, Bill Edward	S1c	Dallas, TX
Army	Giuffreda, Mike Paul	Pvt	San Jose, CA
USMC	Glacken, Joe Charles Jr.	Pfc	St. Louis, MO
Army	Glover, Sammy	Pfc	Daisetta, TX
Army	Goodykoontz, Richard Eugene	Pvt	Marion, IN
USMC	Grahnert, James Dewey	Cpl	Vancouver, WA
Navy	Hale, Waldo Stedem	S1c	Saybrook, IL
USMC	Hammock, William Lester	Sgt	Dermott, AK
Army	Hamric, Dane Hampton	Cpl	Widen, WV
USMC	Hansen, Kenneth Russell	Pfc	San Luis Obispo, CA
Army	Harbin, Lenton Roger	S/Sgt	Shreveport, LA
Navy	Harris, John Soloman	TM2c	Monticello, GA
Army	Hawkins, Douglas Forrest	Pvt	Coeburn, VA
USMC	Henderson, Clifford Marlin	Pfc	Levi, WV
Army	Henderson, Joseph Patrick	Pvt	Los Angeles, CA
Army	Hicks, Roy Joseph	Pfc	Rantoul, IL
Army	Hinkle, Miner Columbus	Pvt	Ada, OK
Army	Hubbard, Hugh Boyd	Pvt	Yarnell, AZ
Army	Hubbard, Robert Lee	Cpl	Yarnell, AZ
USMC	Hughes, John "F" Jr.	P/Sgt	Gate City, VA
Army	Huston, Thomas Virgle	Pvt	Modesto, CA
Army	Hutchinson, Fred Wallace	Pfc	Los Angeles, CA
Army	Jacobson, Charles Donald	Pfc	Denver, CO
USMC	Johnson, Aubrey Peyton	Pfc	West Monroe, LA
USMC	Joyner, Earl Ezell	Pfc	Goshen Springs, MS
Army	Kazlauskas, Joseph Richard	Pvt	Lowell, MA
USMC	Kernes, Richard Wilfred	Pfc	Madrid, IA
Army	King, Harold Wayne	Pvt	Topeka, KS
Navy	Knight, Henry Carlisle	Lt Cdr	Long Beach, CA
Army	Koerner, Richard Aloysius	S/Sgt	Ellis, KS
USMC	Kozuch, Stephen Thaddeus	Pfc	Chicago, IL
Navy	La Mountain, Arthur Lawrence	S1c	Millers Falls, MA
Army	Lampshire, Leo Nick	Sgt	Lansdowne, PA
Army	Lewis, Kenneth Leaman	Pfc	Taunton, MA
Army	Lindsay, Forest Edison	Pfc	Vale, NC
USMC	Lindsey, Kenneth Clyde	Pfc	Gillette, WY
Army	Lyons, John Aloysius	Pvt	Staples, MN

BRANCH	NAME	RANK	HOMETOWN/NEXT OF KIN HOME
Army	Mango, Carl Louis	1Lt	Erie, PA
Army	Manzi, George Vicente	S/Sgt	Bridgeport, CT
USMC	Martyn, Donald Joseph	Pfc	North Hollywood, CA
Army	Mascarenas, Jose Thomas	Pvt	Penasco, NM
Army	McAnany, Richard Emmett	Tec4	Ecorse, MI
Army	McElveen, William Muton	Pvt	New Orleans, LA
Navy	McNally, Theodore	CMM	Kansas City, MO
Army	Million, Joe Baxter	S/Sgt	Harrodsburg, KY
Army	Moffatt, Fred Vincent	Pvt	Moline, IL
Army	Moore, Roger Garland	Sgt	Monroe, LA
USMC	Morris, "E" "C"	Pfc	Jacksboro, TX
USMC	Morris, Orland Otis	Cpl	Warren, ID
AAF	Mullins, Raymond Vincent	S/Sgt	Punta Gorda, FL
Army	Newell, Frank Robert	Pvt	North Tonawanda, NY
Army	Noel, Harry	Pvt	Chicago, IL
Army	Novak, Ernest Julian	Pvt	Watsonville, CA
Army	Otero, Trinidad Fidel	Pvt	Willard, NM
Army	Pitts, James "A"	Pfc	Winter Garden, FL
USMC	Price, Dillard	Pfc	Magnolia, AK
Army	Rankin, Homer Franklin	Cpl	Freeport, KS
USMC	Ray, Daniel Woodrow	Pfc	Austin, TX
Army	Rea, Chester Bentley	Pfc	Ithaca, NY
Army	Rector, Vernon William	Pfc	Phoenix, AZ
Army	Rhoades, Arthur Wayne	Pvt	Fort Wayne, IN
USMC	Rigas, Peter Tom	Pfc	Chicago, IL
Navy	Roe, James Howard	S2c	Stroud, OK
Army	Rudd, James Rollie	Pvt	Cutuno, KY
Army	Saiz, Santiago Sannedra	Pvt	Peralta, NM
Army	Sanchez, John	Pfc	Kansas City, MO
Army	Scally, Henry Fredrick	1Sgt	Silver City, NM
Army	Schubert, Charles Augustus	T/Sgt	Albuquerque, NM
USMC	Schultz, Edward Joseph	Cpl	Pittsville, WI
USMC	Seagraves, Raymond Lewis	Pfc	Lewisville, TX
USMC	Shalley, Charles Earl	Sgt	Glendale, AZ
Army	Sierra, Gabriel Jr.	Pvt	Randsburg, CA
USMC	Simpson, Jesse Herschel	Pfc	Fayetteville, AK
Army	Sirfus, Charlie	Pvt	Des Moines, IA
USMC	Skaggs, Owen Neil	Pfc	Gilroy, CA
USMC	Skidmore, William Burleigh	Pfc	Bloomfield, NJ
Navy	Smith, Charles Carlyle Jr.	SM2c	Guntersville, AL
Navy	Smith, Julio Forest	MM2c	Indianapolis, IN
Army	Smith, Kenneth Otto	Pfc	Hoisington, KS
AAC	Snyder, Cecil James	Pfc	Coalport, PA

BRANCH	NAME	RANK	HOMETOWN/NEXT OF KIN HOME
Army	Spindler, Carroll Frank	Sgt	Edwardsville, IL
Army	Stanley, Dervert Eugene	Pvt	Dallas, TX
Army	Stanley, John Marvin	Pvt	Lakeview, TX
Army	Stevenson, Robert Louis	Pvt	Muskegon, MI
Army	Stidham, James Houston	Sgt	Hardshell, KY
Army	Street, Charles Hiram	Cpl	Santa Cruz, CA
Army	Stutts, Harding Elwood	Pfc	Pinetta, FL
Army	Sweany, Leslie Irwin	Pfc	Hamilton, MO
Army	Swinney, Homer Everett	Pfc	St. Louis, MO
Army	Teel, Glen Eugene	Pfc	Columbia Junction, IA
Army	Terry, Jolly "E"	Pvt	Cache, OK
Army	Thomas, Delbert Raymond	Pfc	Canadian, TX
Army	Turner, Glenn "C"	WO	San Antonio, TX
Army	Uballe, Joseph John	Cpl	Boone, IA
Army	Vitatoe, Ted Edgar	Pvt	Rockwood, TN
USMC	Waddell, George McClelland	Pfc	Kansas City, MO
Army	Walker, Carl "M"	S/Sgt	Elizabeth City, NC
USMC	Walker, George Murray	Cpl	Columbia, SC
USMC	Warren, John Otis	Pfc	De Kalb, MS
Army	Whitecotton, Horace	Pfc	Mesa, AZ
USMC	Williams, John Grant	Pfc	Wichita, KS
USMC	Williams, Maurice Scott Jr.	Sgt	Kansas City, MO
Army	Yeast, Willard Rue	Pvt	Harrodsburg, KY

Key source: A number of lists are presented in various Palawan war crimes documents, but most are incomplete. This list is based on the final Palawan Prison Clothing Issue Memoranda (National Archives Record Group 407, Entry 1063, Box 46, File 650-2-3), typed up sometime after mid-September 1944 and found in the Puerto Princesa camp in 1945. It contains exactly 150 names, with penciled notations beside the eleven survivors. Hometowns given indicate those of prisoner's next of kin. Quotation marks indicate initials given versus a full formal name.

APPENDIX B

SURVIVORS OF THE PALAWAN MASSACRE, DECEMBER 14, 1944

BRANCH	NAME	RANK	HOMETOWN	UNIT AT TIME OF CAPTURE
Army	Balchus, William Joseph	Cpl	Mahoney City, PA	Coast Artillery Corps; 60th Coast Artillery Regiment (AA); I Battery
Navy	Barta, Fern Joseph	RM1c	San Diego, CA	U.S. Navy
USMC	Bogue, Douglas William	Sgt	Los Angeles, CA	4th Marine Regiment; A Company, 1st Battalion
Army AC	Daniels, Thomas Tinsley	Pvt	Talco, TX	20th Air Base Group, 28th Material Squadron
Army	Deal, Elmo Verl	Cpl	Yuba City, CA	Coast Artillery Corps, 59th Coast Artillery Regiment, A Battery
Army	Koblos, Ernest John	Pfc	Chicago, IL	Coast Artillery Corps, 59th Coast Artillery Regiment, C Battery
USMC	McDole, Glenn Weddell	Cpl	Des Moines, IA	4th Marine Regiment, M Company, 3rd Battalion
Army	Nielsen, Eugene Peter	Pfc	South Logan, UT	Coast Artillery Corps, 59th Coast Artillery Regiment, B Battery
Army	Pacheco, Alberto Duran	Pfc	Deming, NM	Coast Artillery Corps, 200th Coast Artillery Regiment (AA), Headquarters Battery
Army AC	Petry, Edwin Avren	Pfc	Venice, CA	Air Corps, 19th Bomb Group (H), 7th Material Squadron
USMC	Smith, Rufus William	Cpl	Hughes Springs, TX	4th Marine Regiment, L Company, 3rd Battalion

APPENDIX C

AMERICAN POWS OF PALAWAN CAMP 10-A HELD BETWEEN AUGUST 1, 1942 AND SEPTEMBER 14, 1944

Sources: Captain Fred T. Bruni diary and roster, Record Group 331 Entry 1364, Box 2028, Folder 6; Roster of men sent to Manila and Escapees, Palawan Prison, 1942–1945, RG 407, Entry 1064, Box 97, Folder 1; Roster of Men Received and Transferred, Palawan Prison, RG 307, Entry 1064, Box 97, Folder 2.

* Indicates man who died on *Arisan Maru* on October 24, 1944.

** Indicates man who died on hellship *Oryoku Maru* or on ship subsequently transferred to. Deaths of these men occurred between December 14, 1944, and February 1, 1945.

BRANCH	NAME	RANK
Army	Adami, Grant "E"	Cpl
Navy	Adams, Joseph John	BM2c
Army	Adleman, Max	Pfc
Army	Allen, Arthur Milton	Pvt
Army	Amato, Salvatore Joseph	Pfc
Marines	Anderson, Arthur William	Cpl
Navy	Anderson, Gerald L.	S1c
Marines	Anderson, Ralph Wilmer	Pfc
Marines	Anderson, Victor Samuel	Cpl
Army	Angert, Alfred Andrew	Pfc
Army	Atkinson, John "C"	Pvt
Army	Atkinson, Morris L.	Sgt
Army	Aubuchon, Alvin James	Pfc
Marines	Babler, Edmond J.	Cpl
Marines	Bacon, Bobby Terrell	Pfc
Navy	Bailen, Louis	SF3c
Navy	Bajorek, Aloysius Stanley	F1c
Army	Baker, John Lacy	Pvt
Navy	Balen, Louis B.	SF3c
Army	Bales, Ernest Jr.	Pfc
Army	Ballou, Billy Eugene	Sgt
Army	Bardine, Anthony	Cpl

BRANCH	NAME	RANK
Navy	Barger, Herman Boris	BM2c
Marines	Barna, James George	Pfc
Army	Barnett, Robert Eddie	Pvt
Army	Beach, Amos	Pvt
Army	Bell, James Edward	Pfc
Marines	Bennett, James Oscar	Sgt
Army	Bernard, Lawrence Patrick	Pvt
Army	Berthiaume, Marshall Joseph	Pvt
Army	Betts, Edwin Caughy	Sgt
Marines	Bigelow, Elwin Earl	Sgt
Navy	Bingham, Cordell	Bmkr1c
Army	Blau, Sanford Jack	T/5
Marines	Boswell, John Ray	Cpl
Navy	Bostian, Lester Aran	S1c
Army	Boyd, Donald Lawrence*	Cpl
Army	Bragg, William Isaac	Pvt
Army	Brewer, Norman	Cpl
Army	Brodginski, Henry*	Pvt
Army	Brodsky, Philip	Sgt
Army	Brooks, Delbert Henry	M/Sgt
Army	Bruns, Howard Albert	Pvt
Navy	Bryan, Alton B.	GM2c
Navy	Buchenau, LaVerne Andrew	S1c
Navy	Budzaj, Zygmond	CGM
Navy	Bullard, Delmar Albert	Cox
Marines	Bunn, Evan Frank	Pfc
Army	Burchell, Etheyl Edman	Sgt
Army	Burk, Lloyd Steven	Pvt
Marines	Burlage, George Edward	Cpl
Army	Burson, Alton Conrad (Died 12/20/43)	Pvt
Marines	Carrington, James W.	Cpl
Army	Cashman, Russell G.*	Pvt
Navy	Carson, Elbert Earl	S1c
Army	Castle, James E.	Pvt
Army	Chaney, William M.	Pvt
Army	Chavez, Ernest Arthur	Sgt
Navy	Cheek, John Marvin	CTM
Navy	Chipman, Marvin Lee	F1c
Navy	Christensen, Arthur	CMS
Army	Cichocki, Henry Anthony	Pfc
Army	Clark, Jeppie	Pvt
Army	Clarke, Richard S.	Sgt
Army	Clegg, Clifford Eugene	Sgt

BRANCH	NAME	RANK
Marines	Cleere, Neal Clark	Cpl
Marines	Clemons, Aaron Lee	Pvt
Marines	Clough, Clarence Sylvester	Pfc
Army	Coleman, Floyd Sylvester	Sgt
Navy	Cook, Alonzo Edgar Jr.	BM1c
Navy	Cook, Thomas Jefferson Jr.	GM3c
Army	Cooper, Francis James	Pvt
Army	Corder, Eugene Stuart	Pfc
Marines	Coulson, Dale Duwane	Pfc
Marines	Craft, George Arnold	Cpl
Navy	Craig, Charles Frank	BM2c
Army	Crandall, Orrin Edwin	Sgt
Marines	Crocker, Harry Delmore	Pfc
Army	Crossman, Donald Wayne	Pfc
Army	Crowe, Malcolm Palmer	Sgt
Army	Crowley, Daniel William	Pvt
Marines	Curtis, Louis Newton	Pfc
Army	Damm, Richard	Sgt
Army	Darnell, James Harold	Pvt
Army	Daugherty, Coy Elmo	Sgt
Marines	Davis, George Dorrell (Escaped 8/10/42)	Pfc
Navy	Day, Robert M.	F2c
Marines	DeBlasio, John Joseph	Cpl
Navy	Deisinger, George Michael*	Cox
Army	De Mello, Ernest Correia	Pfc
Marines	Demouth, Lester Jacob*	Pfc
Marines	Densmore, Raymond Albert	Sgt
Army	Dertz, Frank Joseph Jr.	Pvt
Marines	DeSerio, John Donald	Pfc
Marines	Dimeo, Carmen Mario	Pfc
Navy	Dingess, Naaman	AMM1c
Marines	Ditto, Walter Albert	Pvt
Navy	Dobbs, Francis Eugene	AMM2c
Navy	Donohue, John Thomas**	BM2c
Navy	Dorsey, James Lovell	F2c
Marines	Dupont, Joseph Emile	Pfc
Army	Durham, Jesse W.	Pvt
Marines	Edwards, Joe T.	T/Sgt
Navy	Eichers, Joseph Armund	S1c
Army	Elkes, Frederick William*	Pfc
Navy	Elliott, Bruce Gordon (Escaped 8/10/42)	Cox
Navy	Elliott, Jesse "E"	Ptr2c
Army	Ellman, Julius Eugene	Pvt

BRANCH	NAME	RANK
Army	Enebrad, Eddie Fuller	Pfc
Navy	Epping, Kenneth Joseph	S1c
Army	Etzel, Elwood J.	Pvt
Marines	Farmer, Robert P.	Cpl
Marines	Ferriss, James Furr	Pfc
Marines	Flippen, Milton Cook Jr.	Pfc
Navy	Flynn, Jack Burton (Died 9/1/43)	BM1c
Army	Foster, Wade Thomas	Pvt
Navy	Fournet, George Joseph Sr.	S2c
Navy	Fox, William Earl	CWT
Navy	Freeman, Clarence Anderson	S2c
Marines	Gabler, Albert Jr.	Pfc
Army	Galligan, Francis Albert	Pfc
Army	Gann, Ivan Paul	Pfc
Army	Garr, Carl Edward	Pvt
Army	Gervais, Joseph F.	S/Sgt
Marines	Gibson, Donald Clay	P/Sgt
Army	Gilliam, Hubert Cleo	Pfc
Navy	Girard, William	F2c
Army	Glowacki, Peter Anthony	Pvt
Navy	Golden, Francis Xavier**	Lieut (j.g.)
Navy	Golightly, Robert Lee	F1c
Army	Gorcett, Clifford	Pfc
Army	Grady, Jerome Peter	Pfc
Navy	Graham, George	BM2c
Navy	Gray, John Douglas	MM1c
Marines	Green, Cecil	Pfc
Army	Green, Joseph Clinton	Pfc
Navy	Griffin, Mark James	BM2c
Marines	Griffiths, William Edward	Sgt
Marines	Guaren, Joseph	Pfc
Marines	Guiraud, Jean Auguste	Pfc
Army	Hagnes, S. S.	Pfc
Navy	Hambley, Louis Clark	SM1c
Army	Hammond, James Fleming	Pvt
Army	Hampton, Velton Curry	Pfc
Army	Hange, Donald Warren	Pvt
Navy	Hanson, Jess Willard	AMM3c
Army	Hanson, Richard Charles (Escaped 2/2/43, recaptured)	Pvt
Navy	Harper, Raymond Junior	Y1c
Army	Harris, Malvern Palmer**	Pfc
Army	Harvison, Ernie Carrol	Pfc
Navy	Hausman, Edwin John	CBM

BRANCH	NAME	RANK
Army	Hawkins, "B" "M"*	Pvt
Army	Hawkins, J. B.	Pfc
Army	Head, Herbert H. Jr.	Pfc
Marines	Heard, James Monroe	Cpl
Marines	Heatley, Charles Davis Jr.	Pfc
Marines	Henderson, Buddy (Escaped 8/10/42, killed)	Pvt
Army	Henderson, Francis Marion	Cpl
Navy	Henderson, Henry Clay Jr.	CMM
Marines	Henderson, Roy Laverne	Pfc
Army	Heuer, John	Pvt
Army	Hickman, Harry Samuel*	Capt
Army	Hinkle, Virgil L.**	Pvt
Army	Hite, James McDonald*	Sgt
Navy	Hodge, Allen Jones	Cox
Marines	Hodge, Robert Roland	Pfc
Navy	Hodges, Robert Morris (Escaped 8/10/42)	M1c
Navy	Hoefling, Delbert Leon	CM3c
Army	Hoffman, Edward Ingutz	Pfc
Army	Hogg, Harold Wendell	Pfc
Army	Holladay, Otha Leonard*	S/Sgt
Army	Holm, Holger Larsen	Pfc
Army	Hols, Gilbert Oscar	Pvt
Army	Holup, Gene John	Pvt
Marines	Hoop, James Leonard	Pfc
Army	Hoskins, Thomas Jefferson	Sgt
Navy	Hough, Hubert Dwight	Y1c
Navy	House, Jay Albert	BM2c
Army	Houston, Thomas Virgile	Pvt
Army	Howard, Olvin J.	Pvt
Army	Howard, Walter	S/Sgt
Army	Humes, Donald Thomas	Pfc
Navy	Hummell, William Allen	SF1c
Army	Hurelle, Walter Elmer	Pfc
Navy	Hutchinson, A. C.	WT1c
Navy	Ingrams, Osburn Furr	S1c
Army	Ison, Raymond	Pvt
Army	Jackson, Charlie Jr.	Sgt
Marines	Jackson, Frederick Lafayette	Cpl
Navy	Jacobs, Abe Jr.	S1c
Navy	Janson, John Ragner Jr.	Lt (j.g.)
Navy	Jaquin, Howard Frank**	MM1c
Army	Jenkins, Hugh William	Cpl
Marines	Jones, Douglas Charles	Pfc

BRANCH	NAME	RANK
Army	Jones, Jack	Pvt
Army	Jones, Robert David*	Pvt
Army	Kamendat, Charles	Pvt
Army	Kampf, Theodore	Pvt
Navy	Kellam, Robert William (Escaped 8/10/42)	Cox
Army	Keenan, Ralph William	Sgt
Navy	Kerr, John Charles	S2c
Marines	Kerr, William Andrew	Cpl
Army	Killion, Loyd Richard	Pvt
Army	Kimball, Coy Allen	Cpl
Navy	Kimball, Murry Bryan	MM1c
Army	Kinard, John	Pfc
Army	Kinard, Dorris Lavelle*	Pvt
AAC	Kincaid, Hoke Henderson	Sp3/c
Navy	King, Frank	Cox
Army	King, Joe Raymond	Pfc
Army	Kinnard, John	Pfc
Army	Kisner, Lloyd Chester	Pfc
Navy	Kneeland, Harold William	SM3c
Army	Kolekofski, Don Clair	Pfc
Army	Korczyk, Joseph John	Pfc
Army	Kroll, Leroy Henry	Pfc
Navy	Laidlaw, Robert John	MM2c
Army	LaCourse, Howard Edward	Pvt
Army	Lane, Jesse Palmer	Pvt
Army	Langbecker, Norbert Earl	Pvt
Army	Lash, Russell LeRoy*	Cpl
Army	Lawrence, Joe Billy	Pvt
Army	Leath, Roy	T/Sgt
Army	LeDeau, Edward	Pfc
Navy	Lee, John Wilson	S1c
Army	Leehan, Edwin Daniel	Pvt
Army	Lelito, Florek Philip	Pvt
Army	Leroy, Frank Harry	Sgt
Army	Lewellen, Walter Dee	Pfc
Navy	Little, JoPaul (Escaped 8/28/42)	AOM3c
Army	Lowe, Harold Seldon*	Pvt
Navy	Lowman, Ralph Seaton*	SC3c
Army	Ludwig, Fred Allen	Pvt
Army	Luper, Chester Evans	Pfc
Marines	Lutz, Frederick Clair*	Pfc
Army	MacAdoff, John	Sgt
Navy	Macknicki, Stanley Walter	MM2c

BRANCH	NAME	RANK
Navy	Malone, Luther Harry	BM1c
Army	Mann, James S.	Pvt
Army	Mansgill, Guy Sanderford	Pvt
Army	Marangiello, Anthony Joseph	S/Sgt
Army	Marashio, Vito Salvatore	S/Sgt
Army	Martinez, Clifford Andres	Pvt
Army	Martinsen, Frank Harold	Pfc
Navy	Mason, George Frank	RM3c
Marines	Mates, Arthur Franklin	Cpl
Marines	May, Robert Carl	Pfc
Navy	McAfoos, Charles Basil	SM2c
Army	McCann, John Joseph	Pvt
Army	McClellan, Richard Clair	Pvt
Navy	McDougall, Donald Bruce	SC1c
Marines	McFarlane, Jack Durwood	Pfc
Army	McFarley, Albert Eli	Pfc
Marines	McGuire, Albert Cockrill	Pfc
Army	McGuire, Francis Ignatious	Pvt
Army	McGuire, Omar Lee	Pvt
Navy	McKee, Harold Rex (Died January 2, 1944)	MM2c
Army	McKnight, Noble Edgar	Pvt
Army	McLouth, Estie Melvin	Pfc
Army	McNew, Earl Cecil	Pfc
Marines	McVay, William Arthur	Pfc
Navy	Menna, William Albert	Aerog3c
Army	Mickelson, Stephen Laverne	Pfc
Army	Middleton, E.	Pfc
Army	Miller, Donald Scott	T/Sgt
Marines	Minnick, Ray Jackson	Pfc
Army	Montgomery, Cloyd Weldon	Pfc
Marines	Moore, James W.*	Pfc
Army	Moore, Lee Wayne	Cpl
Army	Moore, Neuvell Puckett	Pfc
Marines	Morrill, George Judson	Pfc
Marines	Morris, Charles Douglas	Pfc
Army	Morrow, Melvin Louis	Pvt
Army	Mote, Robert Vergil	Pfc
Army	Motzko, Stephen Mickel	Pvt
Marines	Mount, Alfred Wheeler	Cpl
Army	Munson, Charles Edward	Pfc
Army	Murray, James William	Pvt
Marines	Musick, Lawson Arnold	Pfc
Marines	Myers, Keith Tibbetts	Pfc

BRANCH	NAME	RANK
Army	Nabor, Oscar Lee	Pvt
Marines	Negro, John	Cpl
Navy	Nelson, Clarence Hampton	EM3c
Navy	Nelson, Harold Roy	PhM2c
Army	Nelson, Roland Eugene	Pvt
Army	Nelson, Wayne Arthur	Cpl
Marines	Norris, Charles Douglas	Pfc
Navy	Oleska, John Jr.	SC2c
Navy	O'Malley, James Marcellus	CM1c
Army	Osborne, David Lyle	Pvt
Army	Overley, George R.	Pvt
Army	Owens, Alvin Louis	Pvt
Navy	Owens, Samuel Robert	TM1c
Marines	Packer, Richard Stanley**	Pfc
Army	Paddock, Thomas Eligha	Sgt
Navy	Parrish, Francis Marion	BM2c
Marines	Parsons, Franklin Randolph	Pfc
Marines	Paulson, Frederick Gustave	Cpl
Navy	Pawloski, Louis Stanley	BM2c
Navy	Payne, Harold Keysar*	Aerog3c
Navy	Pearman, Charles George	GM1c
Marines	Perri, Albert	Sgt
Navy	Peters, James Orval	S1c
Marines	Pike, Donovan Sanky	Cpl
Marines	Pine, Edward C.	Cpl
Marines	Pitts, Bernie Byron	Cpl
Marines	Pountain, James Edward	Pfc
Army	Powell, Harlan E.	Pfc
Navy	Powers, Theodore Howard	MM2c
Marines	Preslar, Lyndal Buford	Pfc
Navy	Pryor, Ray Sherman (Escaped 2/2/43)	MM1c
Army	Pulaski, Bernard Leroy	Pfc
Marines	Pulos, Ted Ernest	Cpt
Army	Ramos, Andres G.	Pvt
Army	Rash, Robert Louis	Pfc
Marines	Rawls, James Conley	Pfc
Army	Ray, Harry Francis	Pvt
Navy	Ray, John Patrick	WT1c
Army	Reed, Thomas C.*	Pvt
Army	Rankin, Homer Franklin	Corp
Army	Reaves, Fred "H"	Pvt
Army	Rector, Vernon William	Pfc
Army	Reynolds, John Bud**	Cpl

BRANCH	NAME	RANK
Navy	Reynolds, Victor Corey	Cox
Navy	Rhine, Lloyd Raymond	Aerog3c
Army	Rinehart, Willard Carlton ·	Pfc
Navy	Richards, Elmer Lee	S1c
Army	Richards, James Franklin	Pvt
Army	Richards, James P.	Pvt
Army	Richards, Thomas Franklin	Pvt
Army	Rogers, John Edwin Jr.	Pvt
Navy	Roach, Homer Eugene	Cox
Navy	Robinson, David Mason Jr.	TM1c
Army	Robinson, Jack W.	Sgt
Army	Rogers, John Edwin	Pvt
Army	Roszkowski, Joseph Walter	S/Sgt
Navy	Russell, Robert Enson	Ens
Army	Ryan, Mike	Pvt
Army	Sabbath, Jack Sylvester	Pvt
Marines	Sautter, Albert George	Pfc
Army	Savini, Frank James	Pvt
Army	Scaife, James William	Pfc
Army	Schloat, Don Thomson (Escaped 2/2/43, recaptured)	Pfc
Navy	Schrout, Sanford	WT1c
Army	Scranton, Jerry Robert	Sgt
Army	Sealy, Jerome Brian	Pvt
Navy	Seashols, Bob Stuart	SC1c
Army	Seward, Charles Morris*	Cpl
Army	Shaw, Donald Tervolis	Pfc
Army	Shellenbarger, Roy	Pfc
Army	Shirkey, Orville Richard	Pvt
Army	Siegel, Samuel Howard	Pfc
Marines	Skidmore, William Burleigh	Pfc
Marines	Skripsky, Gerald Lee	Sgt
Army	Skubinna, Norman Johnny	Pvt
Army	Slonecker, Gerald Clarence	Pvt
Army	Smith, George Joseph	Pvt
Navy	Smith, Norval Giles	CSM
Army	Smith, William Henry	Pfc
Army	Snare, Vernon Harry	Pfc
Marines	Snyder, Charles Francis	Pfc
Navy	Sosvielle, Clarence Henry	CQM
Army	Sporer, George	Sgt
Army	Stafford, Thomas Edward	Pvt
Marines	Stanley, Abram Francis Jr.	Pfc
Navy	Steigerwald, Warren Gerald	F1c

BRANCH	NAME	RANK
Marines	Stephenson, David Milton	Pfc
Army	Stephenson, Sam	Pvt
Army	Sterner, Owen Allen	Pvt
Army	Straubel, Erich Roy	Pvt
Army	Stroh, Anthony J.	Cpl
Army	Stowell, Gerald Dick	Pvt
Marines	Swift, William Dewey (Escaped 2/2/43)	Cpl
Army	Szwabo, Earl Martin	Pfc
Army	Tamulevich, Anthony Raymond	Pfc
Navy	Taylor, Henry Otto	CEM
Army	Taylor, James Sidney	Sgt
Marines	Taylor, John Flowers	Cpl
Marines	Taylor, Ray F.	Cpl
Army	Telendo, Mitchell John	Sgt
Navy	Teem, Linzie Coy**	CTM
Navy	Tennant, Walter Raymond	CWT
Army	Terry, Jolly "E"	Pvt
Marines	Tervolis, Donald Samuel	Cpl
Marines	Thomas, Donald Hampton	Pfc
Army	Thompson, James Clarence	Pvt
Army	Thompson, Trevold Adolph	Pfc
Marines	Treskon, Stephen J.	Pfc
Army	Truly, George Frederick Jr.	Pfc
Army	Tucker, Merle Eldon	Pfc
Army	Tuley, John A.	Cpl
Army	Turnipseed, John Lincoln*	Pvt
Army	Turrentine, Howard Franklin	Cpl
Navy	Turvey, Thomas	S1c
Army	Tyler, Lawrence Cox	Pvt
Army	Tytko, Zigmund Joseph	Pvt
Army	Urban, Elmer James	Pvt
Navy	Vaitkus, Bennedict Anthony	CM2c
Army	Valencia, Bernard Garcia	Cpl
Army	Van Hoenaker, Jerome Arthur*	Pfc
Army	Vann, Bennie Wesley	Cpl
Army	Van Wie, George Irvin	M/Sgt
Navy	Vaughan, Churchill Edison	SK1c
Army	Vigil, Eliseo Garcia	Pvt
Marines	Vinson, Benjamin Harris	Cpl
Army	Viterna, Joseph	Pfc
Navy	Waggoner, Doyle Winslow	AOM1c
Army	Wakefield, Gerald Lee	Sgt
Navy	Walaszek, Edward Thadeus	S1c

BRANCH	NAME	RANK
Army	Walker, Charles Richard	Sgt
Navy	Wallace, Albert Victor	WT2c
Army	Wannebo, Peter Ellsworth	Pvt
Navy	Ward, Jack Charles	Cox
Navy	Watkins, Charles Oscar (Escaped 8/28/42)	AMM3c
Army	Watson, William Jennings	Pfc
Marines	Webber, Harry Williams Jr.	Pfc
Army	Werner, Melven Vincent**	Pfc
Navy	Westcott, Paul Levern	BM2c
Navy	Weston, Charles H.	BM2c
Marines	White, Seldon T. (Escaped 6/23/43, killed)	Pfc
Army	Wilcox, Wilfred Henry	Pvt
Navy	Willard, Louis Arthur	F1c
Army	Williams, Floyd	Pvt
Navy	Williams, George Rudd	CQM
Army	Williams, Harold M.*	SSG
Army	Williams, L. H.	Pfc
Army	Willoughby, Morton Laverne	Pvt
Army	Wills, Alexander	Pfc
Navy	Wilson, Earl Vance (Escaped 6/23/43, killed)	MM1c
Army	Wilson, William Jr.*	Pfc
Army	Winfrey, Lowell Dever	Pvt
Navy	Winkler, James William	CMM
Army	Wood, Everett Lee	Pfc
Army	Woodall, Andrew Oscar	Pvt
Army	Woodson, James*	Pfc
Army	Wooley, Forrest Edward	Sgt
Marines	Working, Nelson Alois	Pfc
Marines	Wright, Sidney Thomas (Escaped 8/10/42)	Cpl
Navy	Yoder, John Edward	S1c
Army	Young, Jack Cleve*	S/Sgt
Army	Zidar, Joseph Fred	Pfc
Army	Zumar, William Anthony	Pvt

BIBLIOGRAPHY

ORAL HISTORIES AND VIDEOTAPED INTERVIEWS

University of Kentucky, Colonel Arthur L. Kelly American Veterans Oral History Collection:
Rufus W. Smith: 1983 interview with Col. Arthur Kelly.

University of North Texas Oral History Collection:
George W. Burlage: November 18, 1970, interview with Dr. Ronald Marcello.
Glenn W. McDole: October 10, 1996, interview with William J. Alexander, transcript (shared property of Admiral Nimitz Museum, Fredericksburg, Texas).
Eugene Nielsen: December 11, 1989, interview with George W. Burlage, Number 802, transcript.
Rufus W. Smith: June 13, 1989, interview with George W. Burlage, Number 788, transcript.

T. Harry Williams Center for Oral History Collection, Louisiana State University, Hill Memorial Library:
Dupont, Joseph Emile Jr. Collection 4700.1409, transcription of audiotaped interview. Interview dates February 14, 2001, through January 29, 2002.

Veterans History Project, Library of Congress, Washington, DC:
Crowley, Daniel William. Interviewed January 28, 2011, by Bob Weisel, transcript.
Galligan, Francis A. Videotaped interview with James McCarthy, date unspecified.
Kerr, William Andrew. Videotaped interview with Gary Gift, December 12, 2005.

Russell, Robert Enson. Collection No. AFC/2001/001/39431. Video compilation of Russell narrating selections from his memoirs.

Interviews and Correspondence Conducted by the Author:

Alexander, Nita Smith. Daughter of Rufus Smith. Telephone interviews on July 22 and December 27, 2015, and subsequent conversations, correspondence.

Ancheta, Jennifer. Daughter of Mary Anne Ancheta. Telephone conversations beginning June 13, 2015, and subsequent e-mail and social media exchanges.

Ancheta, Mary Anne Mayor. Telephone interview of June 13, 2015, and subsequent telephone conversations.

Balchus, Joseph R. Son of Palawan Massacre survivor William J. Balchus. Telephone interview of May 23, 2015.

Barta, Joseph P. Grandson of Palawan Massacre survivor Fern Joseph Barta. E-mail correspondence commencing November 2015.

Barta, Maureen. Daughter-in-law of Palawan Massacre survivor Joseph Barta. Telephone interviews of June 9 and August 20, 2015, and subsequent e-mails, correspondence, and telephone calls.

Bell, Milton A. Nephew of Thomas T. Daniels. Telephone interview of February 13, 2016, and subsequent follow-up.

Burlage, Georgianne. Personal interview of May 24, 2015.

Duff, Bart. E-mail correspondence commencing June 14, 2015. Bart is a retired American living in Palawan who shared documents related to the massacre and Palawan's seventy-year liberation ceremonies and helped connect author with Dr. Higinio Mendoza's son.

Cevering, Janet. Daughter of Palawan Massacre survivor Eugene Nielsen. Telephone interview of May 29, 2015.

Dorman, Janet L. Daughter of Palawan Massacre survivor Elmo Deal. Telephone interview of September 2, 2015. Subsequent e-mail and telephone correspondence.

Elliott, Jacqueline. Daughter-in-law of Palawan escapee Bruce G. Elliott. Telephone interview of September 22, 2015.

Hill, Pam. Telephone interview of February 11, 2016, and subsequent e-mail correspondence.

Hooker, Etta. Daughter of Palawan POW Roy L. Henderson. Telephone interview of October 24, 2015, and subsequent correspondence, e-mail.

Johnson, Glenda McDole. Daughter of Palawan Massacre survivor Glenn McDole. Telephone interview of June 14, 2015.

Koblos, John E. Son of Palawan Massacre survivor Ernest J. Koblos. Telephone interviews of May 24 and May 26, 2015, with "Jack" and his wife, Felice. Subsequent correspondence via mail and e-mail.

Mango, Albert L. Nephew of Palawan Massacre victim Carl Mango. Telephone interview of October 23, 2015, and subsequent correspondence.

Martinez, David. Son-in-law of Palawan Massacre survivor Alberto Pacheco. Telephone interview of January 26, 2016.

Martinez, Kathy Pacheco. Daughter of Palawan Massacre survivor Alberto Pacheco. Telephone interviews of December 15, 2015, and January 26, 2016, and subsequent e-mail correspondence.

Mayor, Robert. Telephone interview of July 18, 2015.

McCoy, Jeanette Johnson. Telephone interview of February 17, 2016.

Meixner, Jennifer. Granddaughter of Palawan escapee Bruce G. Elliott. E-mail correspondence of September 24, 2015, and additional materials and photos.

Mendoza, Higinio Clark "Buddy." Son of Dr. Higinio Mendoza. Photos provided via Bart Duff.

Merritt, Joe D. Telephone interview of August 22, 2015.

Murray, Lorna. Daughter of Palawan Massacre survivor Eugene Nielsen. Telephone interview of May 29, 2015, and subsequent correspondence.

Pacheco, Florentino and Juanita. Brother and sister-in-law of Palawan Massacre survivor Alberto Pacheco. Telephone interview of September 1, 2015, and subsequent correspondence.

Parkins, Kathy McDole. Daughter of Palawan Massacre survivor Glenn McDole. Telephone interview of June 14, 2015, and subsequent e-mail correspondence and follow-up phone calls.

Ramirez, Joanne Rae M. Granddaughter of Palawan guerrilla leader Nazario Mayor. E-mail correspondence of June 1, 2015.

Schandelmeier, Wayne. Telephone interview of May 27, 2015.

Spears, Sharon Deal. Daughter of Palawan Massacre survivor Elmo V. Deal. Telephone interview of September 7, 2015, and subsequent e-mail correspondence.

Stillwell, Raymond. Grandson of Palawan Massacre survivor Edwin A. Petry. Telephone interview of March 5, 2016, and subsequent e-mail correspondence.

Stout, Lynhon Hough. Daughter of Palawan POW Hubert D. Hough. Telephone interview of September 23, 2015, and subsequent correspondence and e-mails.

Wright, David S. Son of Palawan escapee Sydney T. Wright. Telephone interview of December 19, 2015, and subsequent e-mail correspondence.

Yale, Linda J. Daughter of Palawan Massacre survivor Joe Barta. Telephone interview of July 19, 2015, and subsequent correspondence.

OFFICIAL DOCUMENTS, REPORTS, STATEMENTS

MacArthur Memorial Archives, Norfolk, Virginia:

Deal, Elmo V., Cpl., USA. Signal Corps messages from Sergeant Cabais to General MacArthur regarding Deal, February 8–18, 1945. Record Group 16, Box 26, Folder 8.

Elliott, Bruce Gordon, Coxswain, USN. Philippine Evacuee Report No. 211, August 21, 1944.

Little, Jopaul, AOM3c, USN. Philippine Evacuee Report No. 169, July 5, 1944.

Swift, William Dewey, Cpl., USMC. Philippine Evacuee Report No. 214, August 21, 1944.

Vicouroux, McVea J., Cpl. Philippine Evacuee Report No. 200, August 21, 1944.

National Archives:

Adams, Hoyett, CWO, USA. July 27, 1945, affidavit concerning the escape of Tommie T. Daniels. Record Group 153, Box 1353.

"Affidavits of Kempei Tai Members, Palawan Case," RG 331, 1214UD, Box 1112, Folder 1. Statements made by Yoshio Yamazaki, Sempachi Abe, Kenkichi Iwaoka, Takeo Kawamura, Munekazu Miyahara, Shiro Isoi, Tatsuo Nakamura, and Taichi Deguchi.

"Affidavits by Kinoshita Unit's Members. Palawan Case, Vol. I." Record Group 331, 1212UD, Box 1112, Folder 4. Statements made by Benji Kubota, Masumi Minamoto, Keitaro Tada, Toshihiro Arima, Tamotsu Kamei, Tadashi Fujitani, Isure Takahashi, Shingo Nakagawa, Gon Oye, Kanji Hichihyo, Yoshimasa Dojo, Takeyoshi Nagao, Masaki Maruyama, Yoshio Honda, Kinsaku Kawajiri, Arira Inuzuka, Mitsuhori Fujimoto, Teruo Saito, Tatsuo Hara, Sadaaki Katsuki, and Ushitaro Hamano.

"Affidavits by Kinoshita Unit's Members. Palawan Case, Vol. II." Record Group 331, Folder 5. Statements made by Isamu Oba, Genichiro Kawaguchi, Tadao Deguchi, Hiroshi Uchiyama, Takeo Goda, Ichiji Mitani, Minoru Terumoto, Kameo Hamamoto, and Masaharu Okubo.

"American POWs." Production transcripts of 6th AAF Combat Camera Unit documentary filmed on Morotai Island on January 19, 1945, with Palawan Massacre survivors William J. Balchus, Ernest J. Koblos, Eugene Nielsen, Alberto D. Pacheco, Edwin A. Petry, and Rufus W. Smith. This document includes testimony given by Petry, Koblos, Balchus, and Nielsen. National Archives, Record Group 153, Box 1353.

Barta, Fern Joseph, RM1c, USN. Transcript of video of his experiences, February 14, 1945. Record Group 38.

Bondad, Rufino G. "American War Prisoners Who Escaped the Massacre at Pto. Princesa on Dec. 14, 1944, and [Were] Rescued by Colony Officials and Some Prisoners from the Japanese." Record of American escapees who were aided by members of the Iwahig Penal Colony. Record Group 331, Box 1112, Folder 2.

Cobb, Alfred Ervin (civilian). Report of evasion from Philippine Islands, June 21, 1944, Record Group 319, Entry 85.

"Death and Wound Reports Compiled and Maintained at Palawan, P.I." Record Group 407, Entry 1072, Box 184.

"Interrogation of Escapees from Bataan and Corregidor." Report of 449th Counter Intelligence Corps (Detachment) APO 926, USAFFE, dated 7 January 1945. Summary of information derived from interrogations of escapees William J. Balchus, Ernest John Koblos, Eugene Nielsen, Albert D. Pacheco, Rufus W. Smith, and Edwin A. Petry. National Archives, RG 331, Box 1111, Folder 7-1.

Interrogation of Tomisaburo Sawa, July 31, 1947, from Sugamo Prison, Japan. National Archives Record Group 331, Box 1276.

"Investigation of the Allied Atrocities Committed at Camp 10 A, Puerto Princesa, Palawan, Philippine Islands, Against American Prisoners of War Between 1 August 1942 and 14 December 1944." Report No. 49. War Crimes Branch, Judge Advocate Section, General Headquarters, AFPAC. National Archives, courtesy of James Scott.

Escape and Evasion (E&E) Report No. 23, United States Pacific Fleet and Pacific Ocean Areas, 15 February 1945. Statements of D. W. Bogue, Sgt., USMC, F. J. Barta, RM1c, USN, and G. W. McDole, Pfc., USMC. National Archives Record Group 331, Box 1276.

"Mistreatment of Crew of U.S. Sub *Robalo*, Palawan." Record Group 331, 1211UD, Box 1265.

"Palawan Massacre." Report of Investigation Division, Legal Section, GHQ, SCAP, March 15, 1948. National Archives Record Group 331, Box 1276.

"The Palawan Massacre." Research report of the General Headquarters Supreme Commander for the Allied Powers, May 15, 1946. National Archives Record Group 331, Box 1112, Folder 7.

"Palawan Military Police Report No. 55, 18 August 1944. Examination of POWs from American Submarine." National Archives, courtesy of Douglas Campbell.

"Palawan Military Police Report No. 56, 28 August 1944. Report on the Movements of Lt. Comdr. Kimmel, Captain of the American Submarine *Robalo*." National Archives, courtesy of Douglas Campbell.

"Record of Proceedings of an Investigation conducted at the headquarters of the Commander Submarines Seventh Fleet by order of the Commander in Chief,

United States Fleet and the Chief of Naval Operations to investigate the circumstances connected with the loss of the U.S.S. *Robalo* and the loss of the U.S.S. *Flier*," 14 September 1944. National Archives and Records Authority, College Park, MD.

Terada, Seeichi et al. (14 others). Record of Trial by Military Commission, August 2–October 8, 1948. National Archives, College Park, MD, Record Group 153, Boxes 1353 and 1354. Trial testimony referenced includes that of Gaudencia M. Manlavi, Pedro S. Paje, Edwin A. Petry, and Fern Joseph Barta.

United States vs. Manichi Nishitani. Record of Trial and Exhibits, Court Docket No. 354, August 5–9, 1948. National Archives, College Park, MD, Record Group 153, Entry 143, Box 1358, transcript.

Wartime Videotaped Interview of Palawan Massacre Survivors Eugene Nielsen, Edwin Petry, Alberto Pacheco, Rufus Smith, Ernest Koblos, and William Balchus, January 1945, National Archives.

National Personnel Records Center, St. Louis, Missouri:

Daniels, Thomas Tinsley, Sergeant, USAAF (Ret.). Military records.

Statements/Affidavits by Former American POWs and Filipinos from the National Archives, Record Group 331, Manila Report No. 49, Entry No. 1214-UD, Box 1111:

Adams, Joseph John, BM1c, USN. January 15, 1946, Folder 5.

Anderson, Gerald Lee, Coxswain, USN. March 19, 1946, Folder 6.

Anderson, Ralph Wilmer, Cpl, U.S. Marines. December 19, 1945, and January 3, 1946, Folder 6.

Aukay, Pedro C., Filipino. June 22, 1948, Folder 2.

Bacon, Bobby Terrell, Pfc, U.S. Marines. December 20, 1945, Folder 6.

Bajorek, Aloysius Stanley, F1c, USN. January 2, 1946, Folder 6.

Balchus, William J. Group affidavit with Edwin A. Petry, Eugene Nielsen, and Alberto D. Pacheco of March 16, 1945, Folder 6.

Ballou, Billy E., Sgt, USA. Affidavit of August 19, 1946, Folder 4.

Barta, Fern Joseph, RM1c, USN. February 13, 1945, and August 28, 1946, Folder 6.

Blau, Sanford Jack, T/5, USN. April 20, 1945, Folder 6.

Bogue, Douglas W., Sgt, USMC. January 23, 1945, and February 17, 1945, Folder 6.

Bogue, Douglas W. and Glenn W. McDole, joint statement of February 17, 1945, Folder 6.

Bragg, William Isaac, Pvt. September 18, 1945, Folder 6.

Bryan, Alton B., CGM, USN. September 10, 1946, Folder 5.

Budzaj, Zygmond, CGM, USN. January 7, 1946, Folder 6.

Carrington, James W., Cpl, USMC. August 21, 1946, Folder 4.

Cheek, John Marvin. CTM, USN. December 20, 1945, Folder 6.

Cleere, Neal C., U.S. Marines. May 3, 1946, Folder 6.

Clemons, Aaron Lee, Pfc, U.S. Marines. October 3, 1945, and December 27, 1945, Folders 4 and 6.

Clough, Clarence Sylvester, Cpl, U.S. Marines. January 31, 1946, Folder 6.

Craig, Charles Frank, BM2c, USN. February 4, 1946, Folder 6.

Daugherty, Coy Elmo, Sgt, USA. August 10, 1946, Folder 4.

Dimeo, Carmen M., Sgt, USMC. August 26, 1946, Folder 4.

DiSerio, John Donald, Sgt, USMC. July 22, 1946, Folder 2.

Ditto, Walter A., Cpl, USMC. Undated, Folder 2.

E&E (Evasion and Escape) Report No. 23, January 26, 1945. Joint statements of Douglas W. Bogue, Fern Joseph Barta, and Glen W. McDole, Folder 7-1.

Galligan, Francis A., S/Sgt, USA. October 2, 1946, Folder 6.

Gibson, Donald C., P/Sgt, U.S. Marines. August 30, 1946, Folder 6.

Glowacki, Peter Anthony, Pfc, USA. November 15, 1945, Folder 5.

Green, Joseph Clinton, Pfc, USA. August 19, 1946, Folder 4.

Harrell, Thomas Eugene. September 19, 1945, Folder 6.

Heard, James M., P/Sgt, USMC. September 19, 1946, Folder 4.

Henderson, Francis Marion, Pfc, USA. August 7, 1946, Folder 4.

Holm, Holger Larsen, Cpl, USA. August 26, 1946, Folder 6.

Johnston, Robert T. Jr., Cpl, USAA. January 16, 1945, Folder 6.

Kerr, William Andrew, Cpl, USMC. October 4, 1945, Folder 6.

King, Frank, Cox, USN. August 23, 1946, Folder 5.

King, Joe R., Pvt, USA. September 12 and September 13, 1945, Folders 5 and 6.

Kincaid, Hoke Henderson, Sp3/c, AAC. August 13, 1946, Folder 4.

Kisner, Loyd C., Sgt, USA. August 23, 1946, Folder 4.

Kneeland, Harold William, CSM, USN. September 17, 1946, Folder 5.

Koblos, Ernest John, Cpl, USA. May 11, 1945, Folder 6.

Lawrence, Joe Billy, Pvt, USA. September 16, 1945, Folder 5.

Macaset, Valentin, Filipino resident. March 4, 1945, Folder 4.

Macknicki, Stanley Walter, F1c, USN. October 3, 1945, and August 23, 1946, Folders 4 and 6.

Malone, Luther H., CBM, USN. October 15, 1946, Folder 6.

Marangiello, Anthony Daniel, S/Sgt, USA. December 27, 1945, Folder 6.

Martinez, Clifford A., Pvt, USA. September 9, 1946, Folder 5.

May, Robert Carl, Pfc, USMC. September 10, 1946, Folder 4.

McAfoos, Charles B. September 14, 1946, Folder 2.

McClellan, Richard C., Cpl. May 8, 1945, Folder 6.

McDole, Glenn W. Pfc, USMC. February 17, 1945, Folder 6.

McDougall, Donald Bruce, CSM, USN. August 28, 1946, Folder 6.

Moore, Lee Wayne, Cpl, USA. May 15, 1945, Folder 6.

Nelson, Clarence H. Jr., Coxswain, USN. August 29, 1946, Folder 4.

Nelson, Wayne Arthur, Sgt, USA. August 22, 1946, Folder 6.

Norris, Charles Douglas, Pfc, USMC. August 26, 1946, Folder 6.

Parrish, Francis Marion, BM2c, USN. October 4, 1945, Folder 6.

Perri, Albert, Sgt, USMC. September 5, 1946, Folder 6.

Pitts, Bernie Byron, Cpl, U.S. Marines. September 4, 1945, Folder 6.

Preslar, Lyndal B. Affidavit of September 7, 1945, Folder 6.

Richards, James P., Pvt, USA. October 22, 1946, Folder 6.

Robinson, David Mason, CTM, USN. September 16, 1946, and March 31, 1947,
    Folders 2 and 6.

Robinson, Lawrence, Cpl. January 20, 1946, Folder 6.

Russell, Robert Enson, Ensign, USN. 1945 (date unspecified), Folder 6.

Schloat, Don T., Pfc, USA. April 27, 1945, Folder 5.

Skripsky, Gerald L., Cpl, USMC. September 11, 1946, Folder 5.

Smith, Norval Giles, CTM, USN. August 27, 1946, Folder 6.

Snare, Vernon H. January 14, 1950, Folder 4.

Spencer, Aldon L., Cpl. November 30, 1945, Folder 6.

Stafford, Thomas Edward, Pvt, USA. September 16, 1946, Folder 6.

Stanley, Abram Francis Jr., Sgt, USMC. September 26, 1946, Folder 6.

Stephenson, Sam, Pvt. September 17, 1945, Folder 6.

Taylor, Fernie William (Baptist ministry). June 20, 1945, Folder 6.

Taylor, John Flowers, Cpl, U.S. Marines. October 8, 1946, Folder 6.

Vaughan, Churchill E., CSK, USN. October 7, 1946, Folder 5.

Wakefield, Gerald L., Sgt, USA. October 2, 1946, Folder 5.

Wannebo, Peter Elsworth, U.S. Army. July 8, 1948, Folder 1.

Weston, Charles H., Cpl, U.S. Marines. March 6, 1945, Folder 6.

Williams, George Rudd, CQM, USN. September 25, 1946, Folder 5.

Woodall, Andrew Oscar, Cpl, USA. September 7, 1946, Folder 6.

Working, Nelson Alois, Pfc, USMC. October 6, 1945, Folder 6.

ARTICLES / MEMOIRS / DIARIES

Beck, Mary. "Dreams Come True. $4000 Back Pay Given Liberated Sergeant." *El
    Paso Herald Post*, April 10, 1945, 5, 14.

Bogue, Douglas W. "Survivor Tells How Japanese Murdered Yanks." *Fresno* (CA)
    Bee, March 5, 1945, 10.

Burlage, George W. "The Palawan Massacre." Unpublished manuscript, courtesy of Georgianne Burlage.

Coons, Hannibal. "Massacre at Palawan." *Liberty*, August 18, 1945, 26–27, 83–84. Courtesy of Nita Smith Alexander.

"Dramatic Story of Local Sailor, Who Escaped Japs, Lived Two Years with Filipino Guerrillas, Finally Revealed." *St. Petersburg* (FL) *Times*, Sunday, January 14, 1945.

"Groesbeck Soldier Escapes from Jap Prison Camp after Corregidor's Fall." *Mexia* (TX) *Weekly Tribune*, May 5, 1944, 4.

Henderson, Henry Clay. "The Diary of Henry Clay Henderson." Accessed http://www.tendertale.com/ttii/ttii-2.html on June 4, 2015.

Hough, Hubert Dwight. Personal diary, correspondence, and various documents regarding Palawan.

Lieberman, Bruce. "Veteran Won't Let Massacre Be Forgotten." *San Diego Union-Tribune*, December 13, 2009.

Mango, Albert L. "Carl Louis Mango, 1907–1944." Unpublished tribute compilation, courtesy of Al Mango.

Moore, Stephen L. "New Light on the Last Days of the USS *Robalo*." *Journal of the Australian Association for Maritime History*, Vol. 34, No. 1, 65–79.

Ogden, Col. Bruce, USMC (Ret.). "An Extraordinary Marine." Tribute to Major Douglas W. Bogue, accessed www.keepingapace.com/blogarchives/marines/lest_we_forget_real_heroes.php on August 15, 2015.

"Outwitted Enemy for Years after Escaping in Philippines," *Milwaukee Journal*, January 14, 1945, 2.

Placido, Carlos S. Guerrilla diary, May 23, 1944–April 18, 1945. Courtesy of Douglas A. Campbell.

Poyatos, Celerino O. Statement made for war crimes trials in 1947. Record Group 331, Box 1112, Folder 2.

Ramirez, Joanne Rae M. "A Hero We Call 'Grandpa.'" *Philippine Star*, April 28, 2015.

Russell, Lieutenant Commander Robert Enson. "A Kind of Personal History." Unpublished memoirs.

Tillman, Barrett. "Two Coconuts and a Navy Cross." *Naval History Magazine*, February 2010 (Vol. 24, No. 1), 34–39.

"Wedding Bells Will Ring Joyously in Unusual War Romance." *El Paso* (TX) *Herald-Post*, April 6, 1945.

"Wife Escapes in Sub," *Mason City* (IA) *Globe Gazette*, July 7, 1943, 8.

Wright, Sidney T. "Wartime Experiences." Unpublished narrative, courtesy of David S. Wright.

BOOKS

Campbell, Douglas A. *Eight Survived*. Guilford, CT: Lyons Press, 2010.

Cave, Dorothy. *Beyond Courage: One Regiment Against Japan, 1941–1945*. Santa Fe, NM: Sunstone Press, 2006.

Galdorisi, George and Tom Phillips. *Leave No Man Behind: The Saga of Combat Search and Rescue*. Minneapolis, MN: Zenith Press, 2009.

Forsyth, John F. *Hell Divers: U.S. Navy Dive-Bombers at War*. Osceola, WI: Motorbooks International, 1991.

Gandt, Robert, and Bill White. *Intrepid: The Epic Story of America's Most Legendary Warship*. New York: Broadway Books, 2009.

Henderson, Bruce. *Rescue at Los Baños*. New York: William Morrow, 2015.

LaForte, Robert S., Ronald E. Marcello, and Richard L. Himmel (editors). *With Only the Will to Live: Accounts of Americans in Japanese Prison Camps, 1941–1945*. Wilmington, DE: SR Books, 1994.

Levine, Alan J. *Captivity, Flight, and Survival in World War II*. Westport, CT: Praeger Publishers, 2000.

Manlavi, Diokno. *Palawan's Fighting One Thousand*. Privately published, February 1976.

Michno, Gregory F. *Death on the Hellships: Prisoners at Sea in the Pacific War*. Barnsley, South Yorkshire, UK: Pen & Sword Books, 2001.

Ponce de Leon, Dr. Walfrido R. *The Puerto Princesa Story*. Puerto Princesa, Palawan: City Government of Puerto Princesa, 2004.

Poweleit, Alvin C., M.D., Major, U.S. Army Medical Corps. (Ret.) *USAFFE. The Loyal Americans and Faithful Filipinos. A Saga of Atrocities Perpetrated During the Fall of the Philippines, the Bataan Death March, and Japanese Imprisonment and Survival*. Privately published, 1975.

Russell, Lord. *The Knights of Bushido: A History of Japanese War Crimes During World War II*. New York: E. P. Dutton, 1958.

San Juan, Carolina F., ed. *Puerto Princesa During the Second World War: A Narrative History, 1941–1945*. Puerto Princesa City, Philippines: Natural Historical Foundation, 1998.

Sides, Hampton. *Ghost Soldiers: The Forgotten Epic Story of World War II's Most Dramatic Mission*. New York: Doubleday, 2001.

Sloan, Bill. *Undefeated: America's Heroic Fight for Bataan and Corregidor*. New York: Simon & Schuster, 2012.

Summers, Stan. *The Japanese Story*. Tampa, FL: American Ex-POW, Inc. National Medical Research Commission, 1979.

Tomblin, Barbara Brooks. *G.I. Nightingales: The Army Nurse Corps in World War II*. Lexington, KY: University Press of Kentucky, 1996.

Villarin, Mariano. *We Remember Bataan and Corregidor: The Story of the American & Filipino Defenders of Bataan and Corregidor and Their Captivity*. Baltimore, MD: Gateway Press, 1990.

Wilbanks, Bob. *Last Man Out: Glenn McDole, USMC, Survivor of the Palawan Massacre in World War II*. Jefferson, NC: McFarland & Co. Inc., 2004.

Wright, John M. Jr. *Captured on Corregidor: Diary of an American P.O.W. in World War II*. Jefferson, NC: McFarland & Company, 2009.

ENDNOTES

1. THE DEATH MARCH

1 Cave, *Beyond Courage,* 146.

2 Ibid., 53. Pacheco was sworn into federal service in Luna County, New Mexico, on January 6, 1941.

3 Ibid., 4–5, 14–15. The men of the 200th referred to themselves as the "Old Two Hon'erd."

4 Ibid., 28, 37.

5 Wartime interview video of Alberto Pacheco, January 1945.

6 Bruce Elliott biographical information from Jennifer Meixner e-mail of September 24, 2015; Bruce Elliott interview with Roger Mansell, 2001; Mansell archives. Elliott, born in Kansas, had moved with his family to Alameda, California, to escape the Dust Bowl. He joined the U.S. Navy in 1940 at age seventeen, but since December 1941, two of the apprentice yeoman's assigned ships had been destroyed.

7 Villarin, *We Remember Bataan and Corregidor,* 118–119; Daniel William Crowley Oral History transcription.

8 Cave, *Beyond Courage,* 160.

9 Sloan, *Undefeated,* 109.

10 Edwin Petry was born July 15, 1920, to Edgar Avren and Helen Wallace Petry, who had been married in Temple, Texas, in 1912. They had two daughters and then son Edwin, who had been working as an attendant on a used-car lot in San Antonio when he enlisted in the Army on May 20, 1941.

  Thomas Daniels, having only a fourth-grade education, signed all of his military papers as "Tommie," and that name would remain on all of his records. Tommie's mother, Louisa Indiana Saxon Daniels, had eight children born to several different fathers, and Tommie was thus raised without a real father figure. His mother died in 1929.

11 "Interrogation of Escapees from Bataan and Corregidor," 2.

12 Philip Brodsky Oral History, UNT Collection No. 815; interviewed by George Burlage on December 11, 1989, pp. 1–2, 11–12.

13 "Interrogation of Escapees from Bataan and Corregidor," 3.

2. PRISONERS OF THE ROCK

1   Ibid., 3.
2   Fern Joseph Barta testimony of February 14, 1945, transcript, 1.
3   "Wife Escapes in Sub," *Mason City Globe-Gazette*, July 7, 1943, 8; Tomblin, Barbara Brooks. *G.I. Nightingales: The Army Nurse Corps in World War II.* Lexington: University Press of Kentucky, 1996, 30–31.
4   Eugene Nielsen Oral History, UNT No. 802 transcription, 4.
5   Bruce Elliott interview with Roger Mansell, 2001, Mansell archives.
6   Nielsen Oral History, 6.
7   Fern Joseph Barta testimony of February 14, 1945, transcript, 2.
8   Sloan, *Undefeated*, 218–219.
9   Ibid., 220–221.
10 Rufus W. Smith, 1983 University of Kentucky Oral History; Lukacs, *Escape from Davao*, 86.
11 Sloan, *Undefeated*, 224–225.
12 Ibid., 225–227.
13 Videotaped memoirs of Lieutenant Commander Robert Enson Russell, USN (Ret.), Veterans Oral History Project.
14 Fern Joseph Barta testimony of February 14, 1945, transcript, 2.
15 Glenn McDole Oral History, 3, 19.
16 Wilbanks, *Last Man Out*, 25.
17 Eugene Nielsen Oral History, UNT No. 802 transcription, 7.
18 Eugene Nielsen Oral History, UNT No. 802 transcription, 10.
19 E&E (Evasion and Escape) Report No. 23, January 26, 1945. Joint statements of Douglas W. Bogue, Fern Joseph Barta, and Glen W. McDole. RG 331, Box 1111, Folder 7-1, 1.

    Douglas William Bogue was born in 1918 in Omaha, Nebraska. He left his job as a railway switchman to fulfill a boyhood dream by enlisting in the U.S. Marines on February 10, 1935. Bogue arrived in Shanghai, China, on April 27, 1941, with the 4th Marines, and was moved to Olongapo in the Philippines in November. Following the Japanese attacks on December 8, he was ordered to evacuate through Bataan to Mariveles. Bogue was then transferred to Corregidor, where he celebrated his twenty-fourth birthday and seven-year anniversary in the Marines while serving on beach defense.
20 "Interrogation of Escapees from Bataan and Corregidor," 1.
21 E&E Report No. 23, 4.

3. PASSAGE TO PALAWAN

1   E&E Report No. 23, 4; Wright, John M. Jr. *Captured on Corregidor: Diary of an American P.O.W. in World War II.* Jefferson, NC: McFarland & Company, 2009, 10.
2   Francis Galligan, Veterans Oral History, videotaped interview.

3 Eugene Nielsen Oral History, UNT No. 802 transcription, 8; McDole Oral History, 23.
4 Wright, *Captured on Corregidor*, 10; Galligan videotaped Veterans Oral History.
5 Daniel Crowley Oral History transcript; Russell, Robert Enson, "A Kind of Personal History," 26–27.
6 Wilbanks, *Last Man Out*, 32.
7 Ibid., 33.
8 Ibid., 34; Eugene Nielsen Oral History, UNT No. 802 transcription, 9.
9 Daniel Crowley Oral History; Wilbanks, *Last Man Out*, 35.
10 Francis Galligan, Veterans Oral History, videotaped interview.
11 Wilbanks, *Last Man Out*, 36–37.
12 Eugene Nielsen Oral History, UNT No. 802 transcription, 13.
13 Escape and Evasion Report No. 23, 4.
14 Wilbanks, *Last Man Out*, 39–40; E&E Report No. 23, 4.
15 E&E Report No. 23, 5; Joseph Dupont Oral History, Tape 2039 transcription, 6–7.
16 Sloan, *Undefeated*, 250.
17 Joseph Dupont Oral History, 8–9.
18 Wilbanks, *Last Man Out*, 42.
19 Eugene Nielsen Oral History, UNT No. 802 transcription, 15–16.
20 Rufus Smith Oral History, 7; Joseph Dupont Oral History, Tape 2039 transcription, 11.
21 Robert Russell, "A Kind of Personal History," 28.
22 William J. Balchus statement of March 16, 1945, from Manila Report No. 49, RG 331, E 1214, Box 1111, Folder 6; Wilbanks, *Last Man Out*, 42–43; Hubert D. Hough wartime diary.
23 Philip Brodsky Oral History transcription, 13, 17.
24 Burlage, "The Palawan Massacre," 22; Henry Clay Henderson diary; Bruce Elliott interview with Mansell, 2001.
25 Wilbanks, *Last Man Out*, 43; Joseph Dupont Oral History transcription, 12.
26 Russell, "A Kind of Personal History," 28.
27 Hubert D. Hough wartime diary; Elliott interview with Mansell, 2001.
28 Hough diary; Wilbanks, *Last Man Out*, 43–44.

4. CAMP 10-A

1 Philip Brodsky Oral History transcription, 13.
2 Hubert D. Hough wartime diary.
3 Ponce de Leon, *The Puerto Princesa Story*, 3.
4 Ibid., 26.
5 Ibid., 30, 42, 96, 84–85.
6 Ibid., 99–100, 116–118.
7 Russell, "A Kind of Personal History," 29.
8 Francis Galligan, Veterans Oral History, videotaped interview.

9   Pitts, Corporal Bernie Byron. Affidavit of September 7, 1945. Record Group 331, Manila Report No. 49, Entry No. 1214-UD, Box 1111, Folder 6; Philip Brodsky Oral History transcription, 13.

10   Elliott interview with Mansell, 2001.

11   Wilbanks, *Last Man Out*, 48; George Burlage Oral History transcription, 57–67.

12   Wilbanks, *Last Man Out*, 49.

13   Ibid., 49–50.

14   Ibid., 50–51.

15   Norval Giles Smith affidavit of August 27, 1946. Record Group 331, Manila Report No. 49, Entry No. 1214-UD, Box 1111, Folder 6.

16   Ballou, Billy E., Sgt, USA. Affidavit of August 19, 1946. RG 331, Manila Report No. 49, Entry No. 1214-UD, Box 1111, Folder 4.

17   Wilbanks, *Last Man Out*, 51; Philip Brodsky Oral History transcription, 15; Fern Joseph Barta testimony of February 14, 1945, transcript, 3.

18   Wilbanks, *Last Man Out*, 52.

19   Mango, Albert L. "Carl Louis Mango, 1907–1944," 2–4. Unpublished family tribute compilation, courtesy of Al Mango.

20   Wilbanks, *Last Man Out*, 52.

21   Rufus Smith Oral History, 7–8.

22   Joseph Dupont Oral History, transcription, 14.

23   Richard C. McClellan affidavit, May 8, 1945, from Manila Report No. 49, RG 331, E 1214, Box 1111, Folder 6; Francis Galligan, Veterans Oral History, videotaped interview.

24   Joseph Dupont Oral History, transcription, 15–17.

25   Wilbanks, *Last Man Out*, 54.

26   Clarence Clough Memoirs.

27   Bruce Elliott interview with Roger Mansell, 2001.

28   Burlage, "The Palawan Massacre," 23; Bruce Elliott Philippine Evacuee Report No. 211, August 21, 1944; Sidney T. Wright, "War Experiences" compilation, courtesy of David S. Wright. Another who contemplated escape, Chief Water Tender William Earl Fox, finally decided he was too old to try it.

29   Elliott interview with Mansell; Wright, "Wartime Experiences."

30   Campbell, *Eight Survived*, 98, 138–139.

31   Cobb, Alfred Ervin (civilian). Report of evasion from Philippine Islands, June 21, 1944, Record Group 319, Entry 85.

5. PALAWAN'S "FIGHTING ONE THOUSAND"

1   Russell, "A Kind of Personal History," 30; Burlage Oral History, 64–65.

2   Wilbanks, *Last Man Out*, 54.

3   Hubert D. Hough to Glenn McDole, January 16, 1971.

4   Hubert D. Hough diary transcription, 3.

5   Burlage Oral History, 64–65.

6   Henry Henderson diary.

7   William Andrew Kerr interview, December 12, 2005, Veterans History Project.

8   Wilbanks, *Last Man Out*, 56.

9   "Dramatic Story of Local Sailor," *St. Petersburg* (FL) *Times*, Sunday, January 14, 1945. Joe Little had been a newspaper delivery boy and then a paint salesman for Montgomery Ward before joining the Navy in August 1940. All of his personal possessions were removed from him by Japanese soldiers at Corregidor, where he watched as a fellow sailor was killed near him just for eating a can of food. At Cabanatuan, he had witnessed the execution of four American prisoners who had attempted to escape. Little, Charlie Watkins, and his brother, Dodd Wayne Watkins, had served together in VP-102 before the fall of the Philippines.

10 Little, Jopaul, AOM3c, USN. Philippine Evacuee Report No. 169, July 5, 1944.

11 Ibid.

12 "Outwitted Enemy for Years after Escaping in Philippines," *Milwaukee Journal*, January 14, 1945, 2.

13 Cobb, Alfred Ervin (civilian). Report of evasion from Philippine Islands, June 21, 1944, Record Group 319, Entry 85.

14 Ponce de Leon, *The Puerto Princesa Story*, 153–154. Higinio Mendoza was the fifth of six children of Agustin B. and Juana Acosta Mendoza. His beautiful wife, Trinidad, was the daughter of John Tompson Clark, who had moved to the Philippines from Pike County, Illinois, settled in Puerto Princesa, married local girl Miraflores Palanca, and was blessed with nine children. Higinio and "Triny" Mendoza became parents of four children: John, Higinio Jr., David, and Julie Mendoza.

15 Ibid., 117–121; Manlavi, *Palawan's Fighting One Thousand*, 1.

16 Ponce de Leon, *The Puerto Princesa Story*, 115–117, 127; "Interrogation of Escapees from Bataan and Corregidor," 9. The Mendoza company started with twenty-two members but grew in time to number 299 men, armed with only fifty firearms of various calibers.

17 United States vs. the Moros Ipil, et al., August 21, 1914, Supreme Court, Republic of the Philippines, Manila. Courtesy of Mary Ann Ancheta.

18 Thomas F. Loudon to sister Nell, August 10, 1913. Although the mob was brought to justice, Loudon was left a broken man. He moved away from Balabac, first to resume his lumber business on Bakalon Island, another island off the coast of Palawan. His murdered daughter, Nellie, was one day short of being fourteen months old.

19 Manlavi, *Palawan's Fighting One Thousand*, 15. Mayor was originally under the command of Major Guillermo Maramba and served a former PC soldier, First Sergeant Emilio Tumbaga.

6. "WE GOT THE THIRD AND FOURTH DEGREE"

1   Hubert Hough diary transcription, 3.

2   Ibid., 4.

3   Ibid., 57.

4   Wilbanks, *Last Man Out*, 7–9, 17–19.

5   Russell, "A Kind of Personal History," 33.

6   Ernest J. Koblos to John Koblos, March 31, 1940, and March 28, 1941. Courtesy of Jack and Felice Koblos.

7   Ernest John Koblos affidavit, May 11, 1945, from Manila Report No. 49, RG 331, E 1214, Box 1111, Folder 6.

8   Eugene Nielsen Oral History, UNT No. 802 transcription, 17–18.

9   Ibid., 19–20.

10 Richard C. McClelland affidavit of May 8, 1945. Record Group 331, Manila Report No. 49, Entry No. 1214-UD, Box 1111, Folder 6; Hubert D. Hough diary transcription, 4.

11 Skripsky, Gerald L., Cpl, USMC. Affidavit of September 11, 1946. RG 331, Manila Report No. 49, Entry No. 1214-UD, Box 1111, Folder 5.

12 Burlage, "The Palawan Massacre," 24; Wilbanks, *Last Man Out*, 57–58.

13 Wilbanks, *Last Man Out*, 60–61.

14 Ibid., 64.

15 Eugene Nielsen, "World War II Stories," 2006 interview transcription, 5–6.

16 Wilbanks, *Last Man Out*, 60.

17 Mango, "Carl Louis Mango" tribute, 4–6.

18 Wilbanks, *Last Man Out*, 60.

19 Ibid., 80.

20 Ibid., 62–63.

21 Burlage Oral History, 70.

22 Munekazu Miyahara deposition, "Affidavits of Kempei Tai Members, Palawan Case," RG 331, 1214UD, Box 1112, Folder 2.

23 Shiro Isono deposition, "Affidavits of Kempei Tai Members, Palawan Case," RG 331, 1214UD, Box 1112, Folder 2.

24 Hough to Glenn McDole and Donald Thomas, June 16, 1971; Hubert Hough diary transcription, 4.

25 Dimeo, Carmen M., Sgt, USMC. August 10, 1946. RG 331, Manila Report No. 49, Entry No. 1214-UD, Box 1111, Folder 4.

26 Cleere, Neal C., U.S. Marines. May 3, 1946. RG 331, Manila Report No. 49, Entry No. 1214-UD, Box 1111, Folder 6; Richards, James P., Pvt, USA. October 22, 1946. RG 331, Manila Report No. 49, Entry No. 1214-UD, Box 1111, Folder 6. Some prisoners would later offer the name of Boatswain's Mate 2c George Graham as being involved in the punishment for this offense.

27 Wilbanks, *Last Man Out*, 64.

28 Charles H. Weston affidavit, March 6, 1945, RG 331, Box 1111, Folder 6.

29 Wilbanks, *Last Man Out*, 65.

30 Russell, "A Kind of Personal History," 37; Norris, Charles Douglas, Pfc, USMC. August 26, 1946. RG 331, Manila Report No. 49, Entry No. 1214-UD, Box 1111, Folder 6; Weston affidavit; "Report of Atrocities at Camp 10A, Puerto Princesa."

31 Francis Galligan affidavit, October 2, 1946, from Manila Report No. 49, RG 331, E 1214, Box 1111, Folder 6.

32 John Flowers Taylor affidavit of October 8, 1946, and CTM John Marvin Cheek affidavit of December 20, 1945. Record Group 331, Manila Report No. 49, Entry No. 1214-UD, Box 1111, Folder 6.

33 Donald H. Thomas to Hubert D. Hough, June 28, 1971; Wilbanks, *Last Man Out*, 66.

7. ESCAPE AND EVASION

1 Rufus W. Smith Oral History, University of North Texas Oral History Collection, No. 788. Interview date: June 13, 1989, with George Burlage. Transcription, 1–2.

Rufus Smith was born on November 12, 1918, in the farming community of Nashville, Arkansas. He had two half brothers, born to another mother who passed away before Taylor Brooks Smith married his second wife, Elizabeth, and had five more children. When Rufus was eight years old, his family relocated to East Texas and settled in Cornett, a community near the town of Hughes Springs.

2 Bajorek, Fic Aloysius Stanley. Affidavit of September 7, 1945. Record Group 331, Manila Report No. 49, Entry No. 1214-UD, Box 1111, Folder 6.

3 Hubert D. Hough diary transcription, 5.

4 Ibid., 5; Fern Joseph Barta affidavit of August 28, 1946. Record Group 331, Manila Report No. 49, Entry No. 1214-UD, Box 1111, Folder 6; Preslar, Lyndal B. Affidavit of September 7, 1945. RG 331, Manila Report No. 49, Entry No. 1214-UD, Box 1111, Folder 6.

5 Wilbanks, *Last Man Out*, 66–68.

6 Russell, "A Kind of Personal History," 32.

7 Philip Brodsky Oral History transcription, 16.

8 Levine, *Captivity, Flight, and Survival in World War II*, 65–67; Sidney Wright, "Wartime Experiences."

9 Manlavi, *Palawan's Fighting One Thousand*, 29. The guides, named Hamja and Lahoud, had teeth filed flat and stained black with beetle juice. "I'm sure they thought our white teeth were ugly," thought Elliott.

10 Sidney Wright, "Wartime Experiences."

11 Manlavi, *Palawan's Fighting One Thousand*, 13–19, 24–27.

12 Ibid., 29.

13 "Interrogation of Escapees from Bataan and Corregidor," 8.

14 Macaset, Valentin, Filipino resident. March 4, 1945. RG 331, Manila Report No. 49, Entry No. 1214-UD, Box 1111, Folder 4.

15 Johnston, Robert T. Jr., Cpl, USAA. January 16, 1945. RG 331, Manila Report No. 49, Entry No. 1214-UD, Box 1111, Folder 6. Johnston learned of Palawan's Camp 10-A from Watkins and Little but remained behind when the pair moved toward Palawan's northern tip after Christmas. Johnston moved to Cuyo Island in June 1943.

16 "Dramatic Story of Local Sailor," *St. Petersburg* (FL) *Times*, Sunday, January 14, 1945.

17 Elliott interview with Mansell.

18   Swift, William Dewey, Cpl, USMC. Philippine Evacuee Report No. 214, August 21, 1944.

19   Schloat, Don T., Pfc, USA. Affidavit of April 27, 1945. RG 331, Manila Report No. 49, Entry No. 1214-UD, Box 1111, Folder 5.

20   Hubert D. Hough diary transcription, 5; Burlage, "The Palawan Massacre," 25.

21   Johnston, Robert T. Jr., Cpl, USAA. January 16, 1945. RG 331, Manila Report No. 49, Entry No. 1214-UD, Box 1111, Folder 6; Vicouroux, McVea J., Cpl. Philippine Evacuee Report No. 200, August 21, 1944.

22   Manlavi, *Palawan's Fighting One Thousand*, 83–87; Levine, Alan J. *Captivity, Flight, and Survival in World War II*, 74–75. The two servicemen were Army Air Force Corporal McVea J. Vigouroux and Private Calvin R. Hogg. The Filipino was Reynalda Abandiene. Hogg dropped out of the sailing party on northern Palawan at Bacuit after developing malaria.

8. CHANGING OF THE GUARD

1   Wilbanks, *Last Man Out*, 69.

2   Ibid., 81.

3   Clarence Clough Memoirs.

4   Joseph Dupont Oral History, Tape 2039 transcription, 26–27; Joseph E. Dupont Jr. Veterans Administration Statement in Support of Claim, November 4, 1982, Hubert D. Hough Papers.

5   Wilbanks, *Last Man Out*, 70.

6   Russell, "A Kind of Personal History," 30.

7   Wilbanks, *Last Man Out*, 72–73.

8   Ibid., 73–74.

9   Ibid., 75–76.

10   Mango, "Carl Louis Mango" tribute, 8.

11   Wilbanks, *Last Man Out*, 78.

12   Francis Galligan, Veterans Oral History, videotaped interview.

13   William J. Balchus statement of March 16, 1945, from Manila Report No. 49, RG 331, E 1214, Box 1111, Folder 6.

14   Rufus Smith OH, 9.

15   Wilbanks, *Last Man Out*, 77.

16   Burlage Oral History, 74–75.

17   Francis Galligan, Veterans Oral History, videotaped interview.

18   "Interrogation of Escapees from Bataan and Corregidor," 6.

19   Hubert D. Hough diary transcription, 6.

20   Wilbanks, *Last Man Out*, 80.

21   Munekazu Miyahara, Taichi Deguchi, and Shiro Isono depositions, "Affidavits of Kempei Tai Members, Palawan Case," RG 331, 1214UD, Box 1112, Folders 1–2.

22   Edwin A. Petry statement of March 16, 1945, from Manila Report No. 49, RG 331, E 1214, Box 1111, Folder 6.

23 Clough, Pfc Clarence Sylvester. Affidavit of January 15, 1946. Record Group 331, Manila Report No. 49, Entry No. 1214-UD, Box 1111, Folder 6.

24 Aaron Lee Clemons affidavit, December 27, 1945, and Edwin A. Petry statement of March 16, 1945, from Manila Report No. 49, RG 331, E 1214, Box 1111, Folder 6.

25 Sadaaki Katsuki affidavit, "Affidavits by Kinoshita Unit's Members, Palawan Case, Volume I," RG 331, 1214UD, Box 1112, Folder 4; Burlage, "The Palawan Massacre," 25; Anthony Daniel Marangiello affidavit, December 27, 1945, from Manila Report No. 49, RG 331, E 1214, Box 1111, Folder 6; Kneeland, Harold William, CSM, USN, September 17, 1946 affidavit, RG 331, Box 1111, Folder 5.

26 Wilbanks, *Last Man Out*, 86–87.

27 King, Frank, Cox, USN. Affidavit of August 23, 1946. RG 331, Manila Report No. 49, Entry No. 1214-UD, Box 1111, Folder 5.

28 Wilbanks, *Last Man Out*, 87; William Andrew Kerr interview, December 12, 2005, Veterans History Project.

29 Ibid., 88; Frank King affidavit of August 23, 1946; Douglas Bogue testimony in trial of Manichi, RG 153, Entry 143, Box 1358, transcript, 20–21. Earl Szwabo and Sanford Schrout assisted Bogue and Bingham with the tea. Schrout assisted Bogue once Bingham was burned.

30 "Interrogation of Escapees from Bataan and Corregidor," 3.

31 Wilbanks, *Last Man Out*, 89–90.

32 "Death and Wound Reports Compiled and Maintained at Palawan, P.I." RG 407, Entry 1072, Box 184; Jack Burton Flynn death report, September 2, 1945, typed by Hubert D. Hough. Prisoners Phil Brodsky, Alonzo Cook, and Russell Lash narrowly escaped death when the dive-bomber crashed into the shack.

33 Burlage, "The Palawan Massacre," 26; Wilbanks, *Last Man Out*, 89–90.

34 Wilbanks, *Last Man Out*, 88.

35 Burlage Oral History, 72; Kerr interview, December 12, 2005, Veterans History Project. Camp barber John Warren suggested the plan to steal the truck.

9. CODE NAME "RED HANKIE"

1 Lee Wayne Moore affidavit of May 15, 1945, and Clifford A. Martinez affidavit of September 9, 1946, Record Group 331, Manila Report No. 49, Entry No. 1214-UD, Box 1111, Folders 6 and 5. Martinez was paralyzed by the beating.

2 Holm, Holger Larsen, Cpl, USA. August 26, 1946. RG 331, Manila Report No. 49, Entry No. 1214-UD, Box 1111, Folder 6; Burlage Oral History, 75. Holm was the POW badly beaten by Oguri.

3 Wilbanks, *Last Man Out*, 90–91; Walter A. Ditto affidavit, RG 331, Entry 1364UD, Folder 2.

4 "The Palawan Massacre." Research report of the General Headquarters Supreme Commander for the Allied Powers, May 15, 1946. National Archives Record Group 331, Box 1112, Folder 7, 5. Demitrio Otero and Urubano Tabinga assisted Pipori with the escape plans.

5 May, Robert Carl, Pfc, USMC. September 10, 1946. RG 331, Manila Report No. 49, Entry No. 1214-UD, Box 1111, Folder 4.

6 Affidavit of Walter Ditto, RG 331, Entry 1364UD, Folder 2.

7 William J. Balchus statement of March 16, 1945, from Manila Report No. 49, RG 331, E 1214, Box 1111, Folder 6; "Death and Wound Reports Compiled and Maintained at Palawan, P.I." RG 407, Entry 1072, Box 184; statement of Moore, Pfc Neuvell Puckett, December 10, 1943. Driver Moore was ordered to make a sharp turn, whereupon Willie Balchus saw Burson fall, strike the post, and be crushed by the truck. Captain Harry Hickman determined that the victim had suffered an internal pulmonary hemorrhage.

8 Budzaj, CGM Zygmond. Affidavit of September 7, 1945. Record Group 331, Manila Report No. 49, Entry No. 1214-UD, Box 1111, Folder 6; Ponce de Leon, *The Puerto Princesa Story*, 141. On December 21, Budzaj was beaten with a shovel by a guard named Takaytada and suffered a broken forearm. Doctors Mango and Hickman put his arm in a splint and left Budzaj on light duty for thirty-nine days. Joe "J. D." Merritt was among the stevedores who helped smuggle notes to his Palawan comrades.

9 Wilbanks, *Last Man Out*, 92–94.

10 Russell, "A Kind of Personal History," 38–39. The American cigarette brands favored by the Japanese guards included Lucky Strike, Chesterfield, and Camel.

11 Wilbanks, *Last Man Out*, 94–95. McDole also learned that his sister was dating a young man named Johnny Sirfus, the son of fellow Palawan POW Charlie "Pop" Sirfus, who was separated from his wife and had lost contact with his son.

12 Ponce de Leon, *The Puerto Princesa Story*, 127; Manlavi, *Palawan's Fighting One Thousand*, 4, 142.

13 George Davis was declared dead by the military in 1946. The two Australians sailing with Bruce Elliott and Sid Wright were Walter Wallace and Charles Wagner. Wagner was killed in January 1944 while fleeing from Japanese patrols.

14 Sidney Wright, "Wartime Experiences."

15 Ponce de Leon, *The Puerto Princesa Story*, 122.

16 Manlavi, *Palawan's Fighting One Thousand*, 60.

17 Ibid., 60–61; de Leon, *The Puerto Princesa Story*, 150.

18 Manlavi, *Palawan's Fighting One Thousand*, 62; Taichi Deguchi statement, RG 331, Entry 1364, Box 2028, Folder 2.

19 Ponce de Leon, *The Puerto Princesa Story*, 151.

20 Taichi Deguchi statement, RG 331, Entry 1364, Box 2028, Folder 2.

21 Ponce de Leon, *The Puerto Princesa Story*, 123.

22 "Palawan Massacre" report, RG 331, 105; de Leon, *The Puerto Princesa Story*, 152; Manlavi, *Palawan's Fighting One Thousand*, 63.

23 Ponce de Leon, *The Puerto Princesa Story*, 128; Manlavi, *Palawan's Fighting One Thousand*, 5-10, 65, 31–32. General MacArthur had appointed Colonel Macario Peralta as a regional corps commander of the guerrilla units on several islands, all charged with gathering intelligence for the Allies based in Australia. On August

13, he appointed Major Pablo P. Muyco to go to Palawan Island and formally organize the Palawan Special Battalion as a unit of the 6th Military District. Muyco divided Palawan into four sectors on October 4. Captain Mendoza's Sector A covered the areas from Puerto Princesa to Caramay, with its headquarters at Tinitian. Sector B was under Lieutenant Felipe Batul, with his headquarters in Danlig, while Sector C under Captain Carlos Amores operated from Sibaltan.

24 Elliott/ Mansell interview.

25 "Dramatic Story of Local Sailor," *St. Petersburg* (FL) *Times*, Sunday, January 14, 1945.

26 "Death and Wound Reports Compiled and Maintained at Palawan, P.I." RG 407, Entry 1072, Box 184; Sergeant Douglas William Bogue Affidavit of Witness to Accident, Hubert D. Hough collection, courtesy of Lynhon Stout; Hubert D. Hough to Mrs. Burson, November 7, 1945.

27 Wilbanks, *Last Man Out*, 92.

28 Hubert D. Hough diary transcription, 7; Norris, Charles Douglas, Pfc, USMC. August 26, 1946. RG 331, Manila Report No. 49, Entry No. 1214-UD, Box 1111, Folder 6.

29 Hubert D. Hough diary transcription, 7.

30 Ponce de Leon, *The Puerto Princesa Story*, 123.

31 Hubert D. Hough diary transcription, 7; Hough to Rear Admiral John D. Bulkeley, November 28, 1971; Villarin, *We Remember Bataan and Corregidor*, 179–180.

32 Hubert Hough/Trinidad Mendoza correspondence, July 1946.

33 Wilbanks, *Last Man Out*, 98; Eugene Nielsen Oral History, UNT No. 802 transcription, 22–23.

34 Hubert D. Hough diary transcription, 7–8; Russell, "A Kind of Personal History," 33–34.

35 Hubert D. Hough diary transcription, 8.

36 Pedro S. Paje trial testimony, September 7, 1948, Seeichi Terada et al. trial, Record Group 153, Box 1354, 424.

37 Mrs. Triny C. Mendoza to Hubert D. Hough, January 7, 1946.

10. SUB SURVIVORS AND COASTWATCHERS

1 Campbell, *Eight Survived*, 87–89; Ponce de Leon, *The Puerto Princesa Story*, 157. The other members of the Corpus unit were Sergeant Raymon F. Cortez, Corporal Teodoro J. "Butch" Rallojay, Sergeant J. "Slug" Reynoso, and Technician 5 R. D. "Dac" Dacquel.

2 Carlos Placido guerrilla diary, May 28–July 24, 1944.

3 Moore, *War of the Wolf*, 382–384.

4 Escape and Evasion Report No. 23, 16; Edwin A. Petry August 13, 1948, testimony from Seeichi Terada et al. trial, Record Group 153, Box 1354, 185–186; Williams, George Rudd CQM, USN. Affidavit of September 25, 1946. RG 331, Manila Report No. 49, Entry No. 1214-UD, Box 1111, Folder 5.

5 Statements of Poston and Martin made to Palawan guards, Palawan Military Police Report No. 56, August 28, 1944. Traditional accounts of USS *Robalo* list its date of loss as July 26, 1944. For the lesser-known true story of its survivors, see Moore, "New Light on the Last Days of the USS *Robalo,*" *Journal of the Australian Association for Military History,* 65–79.

      Three men on the bridge drowned soon after *Robalo*'s sinking. They were Lieutenant Reginald Proseus, the officer of the deck; and two lookouts, Fire Controlman Second Class Edward Joseph Paw and Seaman First Class Marvin Clifford. The executive officer, Lieutenant Commander Charlie Fell, and *Robalo*'s senior radar man, Radar Technician Second Class Holley Berry Ivey, were seen swimming toward Comrian Island, but the other four survivors did not see them again.

6 "Palawan Massacre" document, RG 331, 104; Affidavit of Pedro C. Aukay, RG 331, Entry 1364UD, Folder 2; Takeo Kawamura statement of December 12, 1949, from "Affidavits of Kempei Tai Members, Palawan Case," RG 331, 1214UD, Box 1112, Folder 1; "Palawan Military Police Report No. 55, 18 August 1944. Examination of POWs from American Submarine." National Archives, courtesy of Douglas Campbell.

7 Kawamura statement; Statement of Charles B. McAfoos, Office of Naval Records and History, USS *Robalo* file; Michno, *Death on the Hellships,* 225, 333.

8 "Mistreatment of Crew of U.S. Sub *Robalo,* Palawan." RG 331, 1211UD, Box 1265.

9 Campbell, *Eight Survived,* 162–180.

10 Campbell, *Eight Survived,* 188–211; Manlavi, *Palawan's Fighting One Thousand,* 43; "Record of Proceedings of an Investigation conducted at the headquarters of the Commander Submarines Seventh Fleet by order of the Commander in Chief, United States Fleet and the Chief of Naval Operations to investigate the circumstances connected with the loss of the U.S.S. *Robalo* and the loss of the U.S.S. *Flier,*" 14 September 1944. National Archives, College Park, MD.

11 Campbell, *Eight Survived,* 216–218.

12 Ibid., 220, 227.

13 Carlos Placido guerrilla diary, August 19–26, 1944.

14 Campbell, *Eight Survived,* 150, 234–239.

15 Ibid., 240–248; Manlavi, *Palawan's Fighting One Thousand,* 30; Carlos Placido diary, August 30–31, 1944.

16 "Dramatic Story of Local Sailor," *St. Petersburg* (FL) *Times,* Sunday, January 14, 1945.

11. THE WEASEL AND THE BUZZARD

1 Mango, "Carl Louis Mango" tribute, 7.

2 Philip Brodsky Oral History, 17.

3 Hubert D. Hough to Ben Guyton, circa November 1977; Hough to Guyton, January 18, 1978.

4 Francis Galligan, Veterans Oral History, videotaped interview.

5 Michno, *Death on the Hellships*, 241; Peter Elsworth Wannebo affidavit, July 8, 1948. Record Group 331, Manila Report No. 49, "Palawan Massacre," Entry 1364UD, Folder 1.

6 Hubert D. Hough to Mrs. Frances Lipe, November 11, 1979. Hough collection courtesy of Lynhon Stout.

7 Russell, "A Kind of Personal History," 42.

8 Coons, Hannibal, "Massacre at Palawan," *Liberty*, August 18, 1945, 26; Wilbanks, *Last Man Out*, 128.

9 "The Palawan Massacre," May 15, 1946, RG 331, Entry 1214UD, Box 1112, Folder 7, National Archives, 7.

10 "The Palawan Massacre," May 15, 1946, RG 331, Entry 1214UD, Box 1112, Folder 7, National Archives, 11; Kojima biographical information from RG 125, Box 2. Kojima is also listed as Chokichi Kojima in some war crimes documents.

11 Interrogation of Tomisaburo Sawa, July 31, 1947, pp. 2–3, Sugamo Prison. National Archives, Record Group 331, Box 1276. Some accounts list Yoshikazu Sato as Masahiko Sato.

12 Wilbanks, *Last Man Out*, 100.

13 Ponce de Leon, *The Puerto Princesa Story*, 129.

14 Eugene Nielsen Oral History, UNT No. 802 transcription, 21.

15 McDole Oral History, 43.

16 Tillman, Barrett. "Two Coconuts and a Navy Cross," *Naval History Magazine*, February 2010 (Vol. 24, No. 1), 36–37.

17 Ibid., 37.

18 Edwin A. Petry statement of March 16, 1945, from Manila Report No. 49, RG 331, E 1214, Box 1111, Folder 6.

19 Tillman, "Two Coconuts and a Navy Cross," 38.

20 Villarin, *We Remember Bataan and Corregidor*, 187; Mrs. Triny C. Mendoza to Hubert D. Hough, January 7, 1946.

21 Wilbanks, *Last Man Out*, 105.

22 de Leon, *The Puerto Princesa Story*, 142.

23 Edwin A. Petry August 12, 1948, testimony from Seeichi Terada et al. trial, Record Group 153, Box 1354, 167.

24 Fern Joseph Barta testimony of February 14, 1945, transcript, 3; Fern Joseph Barta affidavit of August 28, 1946. Record Group 331, Manila Report No. 49, Entry No. 1214-UD, Box 1111, Folder 6.

25 Rufus Smith Oral History, 11.

26 "Death and Wound Reports Compiled and Maintained at Palawan, P.I." RG 407, Entry 1072, Box 184.

27 Interrogation of Tomisaburo Sawa, July 31, 1947, pp. 1–8, Sugamo Prison. National Archives, Record Group 331, Box 1276.

28 Edwin A. Petry August 12, 1948, testimony from Seeichi Terada et al. trial, Record Group 153, Box 1354, 168.

29 Wilbanks, *Last Man Out*, 104.

12. "ANNIHILATE THEM ALL"

1   Tillman, "Two Coconuts and a Navy Cross," 38.
2   Mrs. Triny C. Mendoza to Hubert D. Hough, January 7, 1946.
3   The four aviators were from Bombing Eighteen. (VB-18: Ensign Ralph Beatle, radioman Ralph "Bud" Johnson, Ensign Everett Bunch Jr., and his radioman, Edwin Cunningham. They were assisted by Filipinos and spent weeks being shepherded toward safety on Palawan Island.)
4   Tillman, "Two Coconuts and a Navy Cross," 38; Forsyth, *Hell-Divers*, 120.
5   Wilbanks, *Last Man Out*, 106.
6   Ibid., 105.
7   Ibid., 107–108.
8   Michno, *Death on the Hellships*, 244–249.
9   Ibid., 249–250.
10   Ibid., 251–258.
11   Henderson, *Rescue at Los Baños*, 170.
12   "The Palawan Massacre," May 15, 1946, RG 331, Entry 1214UD, Box 1112, Folder 7, National Archives, 13.
13   Wilbanks, *Last Man Out*, 109.
14   Ibid., 110.
15   William J. Balchus statement of March 16, 1945, from Manila Report No. 49, RG 331, E 1214, Box 1111, Folder 6.

13. THE GAUNTLET

1   Wilbanks, *Last Man Out*, 111.
2   Eugene Nielsen Oral History, UNT No. 802 transcription, 23–24; Nielsen, "World War II Stories," transcription, 8.
3   Wilbanks, *Last Man Out*, 111.
4   Coons, "Massacre at Palawan," *Liberty*, August 18, 1945, 27; Summers, *The Japanese Story*, 22; Edwin A. Petry August 13, 1948 testimony from Seeichi Terada et al. trial, Record Group 153, Box 1354, 186–187.
5   Eugene Nielsen statement of March 16, 1945, from Manila Report No. 49, RG 331, E 1214, Box 1111, Folder 6.
6   Edwin A. Petry statement of March 16, 1945, from Manila Report No. 49, RG 331, E 1214, Box 1111, Folder 6.
7   Eugene Nielsen statement of March 16, 1945, from Manila Report No. 49, RG 331, E 1214, Box 1111, Folder 6.
8   Edwin A. Petry August 13, 1948 testimony from Seeichi Terada et al. trial, Record Group 153, Box 1354, 187–188.
9   Interrogation of Tomisaburo Sawa, July 31, 1947, pp. 8–10, Sugamo Prison. National Archives, Record Group 331, Box 1276.
10   Ibid., 10–12.

11 Ibid., 12.

12 Ibid., 20.

13 Nielsen Oral History, 25.

14 Edwin A. Petry statement of March 16, 1945, from Manila Report No. 49, RG 331, E 1214, Box 1111, Folder 6.

15 Rufus Smith, UNT Oral History No. 788, transcription, 12.

16 Interrogation of Tomisaburo Sawa, July 31, 1947, p. 13.

17 Edwin A. Petry statement of March 16, 1945, from Manila Report No. 49, RG 331, E 1214, Box 1111, Folder 6.

18 Rufus Smith, UNT Oral History No. 788, transcription, 14.

19 Balchus, William J., May 28, 1945 affidavit, RG 331, Manila Report No. 49, Entry No. 1213-UD, Box 1098.

20 Interrogation of Tomisaburo Sawa, July 31, 1947, p. 13.

21 Ibid., 14–15.

22 Edwin A. Petry statement of March 16, 1945, from Manila Report No. 49, RG 331, E 1214, Box 1111, Folder 6.

23 Edwin A. Petry August 13, 1948 testimony from Seeichi Terada et al. trial, Record Group 153, Box 1354, 190–191.

24 Fern Joseph Barta testimony of February 14, 1945, transcript, 3.

25 Wilbanks, *Last Man Out*, 115.

26 Bogue testimony from E&E Report No. 23.

27 Douglas Bogue statement of January 23, 1945, RG 331, Box 1111.

28 William J. Balchus statement of March 16, 1945, from Manila Report No. 49, RG 331, E 1214, Box 1111, Folder 6.

29 *Puerto Princesa During the Second World War*, 91; Villarin, *We Remember Bataan and Corregidor*, 179–182; Manlavi, *Palawan's Fighting One Thousand*, 99; "Interrogation of Escapees from Bataan and Corregidor," January 7, 1945, RG 331, Box 1111, Folder 7-1, 5.

30 Rufus Smith, UNT Oral History No. 788, transcription, 14.

31 Fern Joseph Barta testimony of February 14, 1945, transcript, 3.

32 Eugene Nielsen Oral History, UNT No. 802 transcription, 26–27; Nielsen, "World War II Stories," transcription, 9–10.

33 Eugene Nielsen statement of March 16, 1945, from Manila Report No. 49, RG 331, E 1214, Box 1111, Folder 6.

34 Wilbanks, *Last Man Out*, 117.

35 Summers, *The Japanese Story*, 23.

14. HUNTED

1 Fern Joseph Barta affidavit of August 28, 1946. Record Group 331, Manila Report No. 49, Entry No. 1214-UD, Box 1111, Folder 6.

2 "Survivor Tells How Japanese Murdered Yanks." *The Fresno* (CA) *Bee Republican*, Monday, March 5, 1945, 10.

3 Barta statement from E&E Report No. 23.

4 Fern Joseph Barta, August 12, 1948 testimony from Seeichi Terada et al. trial, Record Group 153, Box 1354, 147, 150. Barta's account says age twenty-one, but Hamric was born on December 14, 1920.

5 Ibid., 148.

6 Eugene Nielsen Oral History, UNT No. 802 transcription, 27–28; Eugene Nielsen statement of March 16, 1945, from Manila Report No. 49, RG 331, E 1214, Box 1111, Folder 6.

7 Eugene Nielsen Oral History, UNT No. 802 transcription, 29.

8 Wilbanks, *Last Man Out*, 117–118.

9 Rufus Smith, UNT Oral History No. 788, transcription, 15.

10 Rufus W. Smith Oral History, 1983 Interview with Colonel Arthur Kelly, University of Kentucky.

11 Sommers, *The Japanese Story*, 23.

12 Glenn McDole Oral History, Admiral Nimitz Museum and University of North Texas Oral History Collection, No. 1317, October 10, 1996, 56.

13 Eugene Nielsen Oral History, UNT No. 802 transcription, 29; Eugene Nielsen statement of March 16, 1945, from Manila Report No. 49, RG 331, E 1214, Box 1111, Folder 6.

14 Wilbanks, *Last Man Out*, 118.

15 Ibid., 119.

16 Eugene Nielsen Oral History, UNT No. 802 transcription, 29–30.

17 Ibid., 29–30; Eugene Nielsen statement of March 16, 1945, from Manila Report No. 49, RG 331, E 1214, Box 1111, Folder 6.

18 Wilbanks, *Last Man Out*, 119.

19 Eugene Nielsen Oral History, UNT No. 802 transcription, 30.

20 Ibid., 30–31; Nielsen, "World War II Stories," transcription, 14.

21 Interrogation of Tomisaburo Sawa, July 31, 1947, 15.

22 Ibid., 14, 17.

15. FIGHTS AND FLIGHT

1 Sommers, *The Japanese Story*, 23.

2 Rufus Smith, UNT Oral History No. 788, transcription, 17.

3 Ibid., 18.

4 Sommers, *The Japanese Story*, 23.

5 Eugene Nielsen Oral History, UNT No. 802 transcription, 31.

6 Eugene Nielsen statement of March 16, 1945, from Manila Report No. 49, RG 331, E 1214, Box 1111, Folder 6.

7 Nielsen, "World War II Stories," transcription, 11; Eugene Nielsen statement of March 16, 1945, from Manila Report No. 49, RG 331, E 1214, Box 1111, Folder 6.

8 Eugene Nielsen Oral History, UNT No. 802 transcription, 31–32.

9 Koblos narrative of January 17, 1945, from Terada trial documents, RG 153, Box 1353.

10 Nielsen, "World War II Stories," transcription, 14.

11 Eugene Nielsen Oral History, UNT No. 802 transcription, 32–33.

12 Nielsen, "World War II Stories," transcription, 15.

13 Wilbanks, *Last Man Out*, 122.

14 Edwin A. Petry statement of March 16, 1945, from Manila Report No. 49, RG 331, E 1214, Box 1111, Folder 6.

15 Fern Joseph Barta, August 12, 1948 testimony from Seeichi Terada et al. trial, Record Group 153, Box 1354, 148.

16 Edwin A. Petry statement of March 16, 1945, from Manila Report No. 49, RG 331, E 1214, Box 1111, Folder 6.

17 Rufus W. Smith, 1983 University of Kentucky Oral History; Rufus Smith, UNT Oral History No. 788, transcription, 19.

18 Rufus W. Smith, 1983 University of Kentucky Oral History.

19 Sommers, *The Japanese Story*, 24.

20 Rufus Smith, UNT Oral History No. 788, transcription, 20.

21 Elmo Deal was the son of Floyd Joseph Edward Deal, who moved his family to California in the 1930s. Mo was working at the Mayers Brothers automotive shop in Modesto when he enlisted in the Army, where he became an expert marksman with both a .30-caliber rifle and a .45-caliber pistol.

22 William J. Balchus statement of March 16, 1945, from Manila Report No. 49, RG 331, E 1214, Box 1111, Folder 6.

23 Ibid.; "Interrogation of Escapees from Bataan and Corregidor," January 7, 1945, RG 331, Box 1111, Folder 7-1, 5.

24 Several sources report that Deal was both shot again and bayoneted before being left for dead by his assailants: Manlavi, *Palawan's Fighting One Thousand*, 99; Villarin, *We Remember Bataan and Corregidor*, 182; Poweleit, *USAFFE*, 139. Colonel J. K. Evans of the War Department reported on January 13, 1945, that he had information from Palawan guerrillas that Elmo Deal had suffered "24 wounds from a blunt instrument and third degree burns." See Evans to Major C. B. Warren Jr., January 13, 1945, in Terada trial documents, Record Group 153, Box 1353.

25 Eugene Nielsen statement of March 16, 1945, from Manila Report No. 49, RG 331, E 1214, Box 1111, Folder 6.

26 Eugene Nielsen Oral History, UNT No. 802 transcription, 34.

27 Nielsen, "World War II Stories," transcription, 15–16.

28 Edwin A. Petry statement of March 16, 1945, from Manila Report No. 49, RG 331, E 1214, Box 1111, Folder 6.

29 Alberto D. Pacheco statement of March 16, 1945, from Manila Report No. 49, RG 331, E 1214, Box 1111, Folder 6.

30 Summers, *The Japanese Story*, 22.

31 Edwin A. Petry statement of March 16, 1945, from Manila Report No. 49, RG 331, E 1214, Box 1111, Folder 6.

32 Ernest J. Koblos testimony of January 19, 1945, from "American POWs" transcript, 6th AAF Combat Camera Unit documentary film. National Archives, Record Group 153, Box 1353.

16. SWIMMERS AND SURVIVORS

1 Fern Joseph Barta testimony of February 14, 1945, transcript, 5.

2 Bondad, Rufino G. "American War Prisoners Who Escaped the Massacre at Pto. Princesa on Dec. 14, 1944, and Rescued by Colony Officials and Some Prisoners from the Japanese." Record of American escapees aided by members of the Iwahig Penal Colony. Record Group 331, Box 1112, Folder 2.

3 Edwin A. Petry statement of March 16, 1945, from Manila Report No. 49, RG 331, E 1214, Box 1111, Folder 6. Petry testimony of January 19, 1945, from Terada trial documents, Record Group 153, Box 1353.

4 Beck, Mary. "Dreams Come True. $4000 Back Pay Given Liberated Sergeant." *El Paso* (TX) *Herald Post*, April 10, 1945, 5, 14; Summers, *The Japanese Story*, 22.

5 Rufus Smith, UNT Oral History No. 788, transcription, 21.

6 "Palawan Massacre" report of March 14, 1948. RG 331, Box 1276, Folder 3. Kojima invited members of Captain Tsuneji Shoji's Kempei Tai military police unit to join in the celebration, as well as First Lieutenant Rokumi Obayashi's 4th Company, 174th Independent Infantry Battalion.

7 Pedro S. Paje, September 1948 testimony from Seeichi Terada et al. trial, Record Group 153, Box 1354, 403–406, 426, 441.

8 Ibid., 408–416.

9 Manlavi, *Palawan's Fighting One Thousand*, 99–100; Villarin, *We Remember Bataan and Corregidor*, 182.

10 Ponce de Leon, *The Puerto Princesa Story*, 126.

11 Nielsen, "World War II Stories," transcription, 16–17.

12 Eugene Nielsen Oral History, UNT No. 802 transcription, 35.

13 Ibid., 36; Nielsen, "World War II Stories," transcription, 18.

14 Eugene Nielsen statement of March 16, 1945, from Manila Report No. 49, RG 331, E 1214, Box 1111, Folder 6; Eugene Nielsen Oral History, UNT No. 802 transcription, 38.

15 Eugene Nielsen Oral History, UNT No. 802 transcription, 39.

16 Ibid., 40; Nielsen, "World War II Stories," transcription, 21.

17 Ibid., 39–40; Eugene Nielsen statement of March 16, 1945, from Manila Report No. 49, RG 331, E 1214, Box 1111, Folder 6.

18 Eugene Nielsen Oral History, UNT No. 802 transcription, 39. Nielsen says it was Petry and Koblos in his 1989 recollections, but Filipino records show that the other American was Pacheco at this time. Nielsen, in "World War II Stories," transcription, 21, says Petry and Pacheco.

19 Bondad, "American War Prisoners Who Escaped the Massacre at Pto. Princesa on Dec. 14, 1944," Record Group 331, Box 1112, Folder 2.

20 Fern Joseph Barta testimony of February 14, 1945, transcript, 5; Fern Joseph Barta, August 12, 1948 testimony from Seeichi Terada et al. trial, Record Group 153, Box 1354, 151.

21 Bondad, "American War Prisoners Who Escaped the Massacre at Pto. Princesa on Dec. 14, 1944," Record Group 331, Box 1112, Folder 2. The colonists Smith spotted

were Inteng Moro, Rogelio Martino, Dayato Moro, Francisco Ulina, Gregorio Sato, Tumanbud Moro, and Pedro Sacoso.

22 Rufus Smith, UNT Oral History No. 788, transcription, 22.

23 Ibid., 23.

24 Bondad, "American War Prisoners Who Escaped the Massacre at Pto. Princesa on Dec. 14, 1944," Record Group 331, Box 1112, Folder 2.

25 Rufus Smith Oral History, 23.

26 Wilbanks, *Last Man Out*, 126.

27 Statement of Celerino O. Poyatos, circa 1947, for the war crimes trials, Record Group 331, Box 1112, Folder 2.

28 Rufus Smith, UNT Oral History No. 788, transcription, 26–27.

29 Pedro S. Paje, September 7, 1948 testimony, Seeichi Terada et al. trial, Record Group 153, Box 1354, 439.

30 Bondad, "American War Prisoners Who Escaped the Massacre at Pto. Princesa on Dec. 14, 1944," Record Group 331, Box 1112, Folder 2.

31 Koblos narrative of January 17, 1945, from Terada trial documents, RG 153, Box 1353.

32 Ibid. They were Anacleto Canada, Dioscoro Rivaldo, Dionisio Ando, and Macaraya Moro.

33 Ibid.

34 Eugene Nielsen Oral History, UNT No. 802 transcription, 41–42.

17. MAC'S ODYSSEY

1 Wilbanks, *Last Man Out*, 124.

2 Glenn McDole Oral History No. 1317, 58.

3 Wilbanks, *Last Man Out*, 124–125.

4 Ibid., 125.

5 Ibid., 126.

6 Filipinos later said that the Allies had bombed the Catholic church in Puerto Princesa, exploding ammunition and explosives the Japanese had stored inside.

7 Wilbanks, *Last Man Out*, 127.

18. ELEVEN AGAINST THE ELEMENTS

1 Rufus Smith, UNT Oral History No. 788, transcription, 28.

2 Eugene Nielsen Oral History, UNT No. 802 transcription, 42–43.

3 Ibid., 43.

4 Rufus Smith, UNT Oral History, transcription, 29.

5 Nielsen, "World War II Stories," transcription, 22; Eugene Nielsen Oral History, UNT No. 802 transcription, 43.

6 Eugene Nielsen Oral History, UNT No. 802 transcription, 44.

7 Wilbanks, *Last Man Out*, 128.

8 Glenn McDole Oral History No. 1317, 61.

9 Bogue, "Survivor Tells How Japanese Murdered Yanks," 10.

10 They were Kirin C. Lim, Maximino Liwag, Ponciano Bautista, and Alejandro Bautista.

11 Glenn McDole Oral History No. 1317, 63.

12 Ibid., 129–130; Glenn McDole Oral History No. 1317, 64.

13 Bondad, "American War Prisoners Who Escaped the Massacre at Pto. Princesa on Dec. 14, 1944," Record Group 331, Box 1112, Folder 2. The men were Mayor Kirin Lim, Maximino Liwag, Ponciano Bautista, and Alejandro Bautista.

14 Ibid., 130.

15 Rufus Smith, UNT Oral History No. 788, transcription, 30.

16 Eugene Nielsen Oral History, UNT No. 802 transcription, 44–45.

17 Villarin, *We Remember Bataan and Corregidor*, 183.

18 Poweleit, *USAFFE*, 139.

19 Manlavi, *Palawan's Fighting One Thousand*, 100.

20 Mrs. Triny C. Mendoza to Hubert D. Hough, January 7, 1946.

21 Villarin, *We Remember Bataan and Corregidor*, 188; Elizabeth Clark Alba account in Ponce de Leon, *The Puerto Princesa Story*, 126. "He was very badly cut up," Alba wrote, "having around 23 wounds all over his body."

22 Villarin, *We Remember Bataan and Corregidor*, 182.

23 Fern Joseph Barta interview transcription, 4.

24 Bondad, "American War Prisoners Who Escaped the Massacre at Pto. Princesa on Dec. 14, 1944," Record Group 331, Box 1112, Folder 2; Fern Joseph Barta, testimony of August 12, 1948, from Seeichi Terada et al. trial, Record Group 153, Box 1354, 151–152.

19. EXODUS FROM BROOKE'S POINT

1 Wilbanks, *Last Man Out*, 130.

2 Glenn McDole Oral History No. 1317, 64.

3 Wilbanks, *Last Man Out*, 131.

4 Escape and Evasion Report No. 23, 16.

5 Bondad, "American War Prisoners Who Escaped the Massacre at Pto. Princesa on Dec. 14, 1944," Record Group 331, Box 1112, Folder 2.

6 Pedro S. Paje 1948 testimony from Seeichi Terada et al. trial, Record Group 153, Box 1354, 417.

7 Manlavi, *Palawan's Fighting One Thousand*, 30–31.

8 Rufus W. Smith, 1983 University of Kentucky Oral History.

9 Pedro S. Paje trial testimony of September 7, 1948, Record Group 153, Box 1354, 420. The interpreter was Kintoku Uehara.

10 Wilbanks, *Last Man Out*, 131.

11 Bondad, "American War Prisoners Who Escaped the Massacre at Pto. Princesa on Dec. 14, 1944," Record Group 331, Box 1112, Folder 2.

12 Wilbanks, *Last Man Out*, 132.

13 Rufus Smith, UNT Oral History No. 788, transcription, 31; Carlos Placidos guerrilla diary, December 10–24, 1944. The survivors were particularly interested in the coastwatcher group that had set up a station near Captain Mayor's headquarters. Sergeant Carlos Placido was in charge of the four men who had helped secure safe passage from Palawan for the nine survivors of the lost submarine *Flier* in August. Placido's men had the only working radio in southern Palawan, and they communicated to the U.S. Army that American prisoners of war had been liberated and were in reasonably good health.

Two of Placido's men had been sent farther north to man a remote radio station near Inagawan while Placido remained near the Brooke's Point home of Harry Edwards with his other two men. Placido had long since run out of gasoline, so their radio set was now functioning on coconut oil and battery power from a windmill generator hooked to Edwards's rice mill. Another coastwatcher group under Master Sergeant Eutiquio Cabais was stationed much farther north on Palawan.

Coastwatcher Ray Cortez had been married to a local girl in a simple ceremony on December 21, with Sergeant Placido serving as his best man. On Christmas Eve, Placido made doughnuts, and the entire group enjoyed midnight services conducted by the priest. The second wedding ceremony on December 29 was conducted to solemnize the Cortez couple's union.

14 Eugene Nielsen Oral History, UNT No. 802 transcription, 46.

15 Ibid., 46–47; Nielsen, "World War II Stories," transcription, 25. Captain Solander, from Iron River, Michigan, was twenty-seven, flying with First Lieutenant Wayne Lucas Schandelmeier as his copilot.

16 Nielsen, "World War II Stories," transcription, 26.

17 Rufus Smith, UNT Oral History No. 788, transcription, 31.

18 Sides, *Ghost Soldiers*, 17–19.

19 Ibid., 269–282; Henderson, *Rescue at Los Baños*, 170–171.

20 Glenn McDole Oral History No. 1317, 68.

21 Wilbanks, *Last Man Out*, 133.

22 Patrol Bombing Squadron Fifty-four war diary, January 1945; Carlos Placido guerrilla diary, January 21, 1945. Placido, whose 978th Signal Service Company men who had helped arrange the previous PBY, had asked for more supplies from this PBY when it came to get three more Americans. "It was supposed to bring us about four tons of supplies and equipment," Placido wrote in his diary. "We only got radio equipment and medicines, however. Four tons? Heck no! Just about 1,500 pounds, that was all."

23 Wilbanks, *Last Man Out*, 134–135.

20. THE LONG ROAD HOME

1 Rufus Smith Oral History, 33.

2 Eugene Nielsen statement of March 16, 1945, from Manila Report No. 49, RG 331, E 1214, Box 1111, Folder 6. The 6th AAF Combat Camera Unit filmed a

twenty-one-hundred-foot documentary, narrated by the MIS-X (Military Intelligence Service, Experimental) officer in charge at Morotai, Captain Eykes.

3 Joint survivors statement of March 16, 1945, from Manila Report No. 49, RG 331, E 1214, Box 1111, Folder 6. G-2 officer Perry Nelson accompanied them to Hollandia, where Lieutenant Colonel Joseph H. Steger offered them hope they would be headed home soon.

4 Ibid., Sides, *Ghost Soldiers*, 323–325.

5 Wilbanks, *Last Man Out*, 135. McDole was down to 113 pounds.

6 Glenn McDole Oral History No. 1317, 72.

7 Wilbanks, *Last Man Out*, 137.

8 Villarin, *We Remember Bataan and Corregidor*, 183.

9 Ponce de Leon, *The Puerto Princesa Story*, 126. A large group of Filipino civilians was still there, including Elizabeth Clark, Triny Mendoza's sister. The group included Chief Torpedoman Hugh H. Pippin and Lieutenant Edward J. Pope Jr., a Yale graduate from Rye, New York, who was skipper of *PT-134*—an eighty-foot vessel of Motor Torpedo Boat Squadron 25 stationed in the Philippines.

10 Ibid., 161. Lieutenant Antonio Palanca, Sergeant Vicente Aizo, and Pascual de la Cruz of Mayor's company returned with the PT boats.

11 VPB-17 War Diary, February 1945. Mulford, from Woodbury, New Jersey, and his VPB-17 were temporarily operating from the USS *Orca* (AVP-49) in Lingayen Gulf on Luzon.

12 Deal to parents letter, March 25, 1941; courtesy of Sharon Deal Spears.

13 Poweleit, *USAFFE*, 139; Thomas Tinsley Daniels military records; Hoyett Adams, CWO, U.S. Army, affidavit of July 27, 1945, National Archives Record Group 153, Box 1353. En route home, Daniels shared some of his story with a naval officer and with Warrant Officer Hoyett Adams, who had been a POW in Manila until U.S. forces overran Bilibid Prison. Daniels reached California on May 31, 1945, having spent three years, eleven months, and twenty-five days overseas.

14 Lofgren, Stephen J. *Southern Philippines Campaign.* The U.S. Army Campaigns of World War II. United States Army Center of Military History, CMH Pub 72-40, 10; Interrogation of Tomisaburo Sawa, July 31, 1947, 21.

15 Carlos Placido guerrilla diary, January 1–April 19, 1945. Placido accompanied Captain Mayor's guerrillas to Balabac Island on March 6 to secure boatloads of ammunition, food, and equipment for Brooke's Point.

16 RG 331, Box 1111, F4.

17 "Palawan Massacre," Report of Investigation Division, Legal Section, GHQ, SCAP, March 15, 1948. National Archives Record Group 331, Box 1276, p. 8.

18 Nielsen, "World War II Stories," transcription, 28–29. John Koblos received a telegram in Chicago from his son, Ernie, on March 24. He had received two prior letters from the War Department on January 12 and February 2, stating that his son was slightly injured but had been recovered from a POW camp. Now, the elder Koblos learned that Ernie was at Letterman General Hospital, "convalescing from slight malnutrition, condition good."

19 "Wedding Bells Will Ring Joyously in Unusual War Romance," *El Paso* (TX) *Herald-Post,* April 6, 1945.
20 Rufus Smith, UNT Oral History No. 788, transcription, 35.
21 Wilbanks, *Last Man Out,* 139. Ditto, like McDole, would serve with the highway patrol after the war.

21. TRIALS AND TRIBUTES

1   "Palawan Massacre," RG 331, 28.
2   Ibid., 29.
3   Ibid., 31–32.
4   Ibid., 35–38.
5   Wilbanks, *Last Man Out,* 142.
6   Ibid., 141.
7   Ibid., 142.
8   Ibid., 143.
9   Pedro S. Paje, September 7, 1948 testimony, Seeichi Terada et al. trial, Record Group 153, Box 1354, 430–431, 441.
10 Wilbanks, *Last Man Out,* 144.
11 Ogden, Col. Bruce, "An Extraordinary Marine."
12 Wilbanks, *Last Man Out,* 155. Per his nephew, the horrors of war had taken a toll on Daniels, and he made little contact with former military companions, although he did enjoy squirrel hunting with some of his Blalock relatives. He lived on the sixty-five-acre farm of his stepbrother, Walter Blalock, for a while before establishing his own property west of the little Sugar Hill community.
13 Nielsen, "World War II Stories," transcription, 27; Wilbanks, *Last Man Out,* 155.
14 Wilbanks, *Last Man Out,* 148–152.
15 Smith Oral History, 36–37.
16 Ponce de Leon, *The Puerto Princesa Story,* 152.
17 Ibid., 153.
18 Villarin, *We Remember Bataan and Corregidor,* 188.
19 Lieberman, Bruce. "Veteran Won't Let Massacre Be Forgotten." *San Diego Union-Tribune,* December 13, 2009.

INDEX